THE REAL AMERICA

THE REAL AMERICA

A Surprising Examination of the State of the Union

BY BEN J. WATTENBERG

with an Introduction by

RICHARD M. SCAMMON

Doubleday & Company, Inc.
Garden City, New York
1974

Library of Congress Cataloging in Publication Data

Wattenberg, Ben J
　The real America; a surprising examination of the
state of the Union.

　Includes bibliographical references.
　1. United States—Social conditions—1960–
I. Title.
HN59.W315　　309.1′73′0924
ISBN 0-385-07074-8
Library of Congress Catalog Card Number 73–14422

To:
Ruth Wattenberg
Daniel Wattenberg
Sarah Wattenberg

and tens of millions of other young Americans
who may benefit from knowing more
about America before they change it
to make it still better.

Acknowledgments

This book, like most books, represents a personal vision, a personal statement, and a personal prism through which the author views reality. But, because of the peculiar nature of this volume—keyed on almost every page to hard data —the authoring of such a book represents an *enterprise* as well as a vision and a statement. The data shapes the vision and the statement—and the data comes not full blown from the author's head but from the efforts of an army of hard-working, diligent, careful, usually unsung statisticians, demographers, economists, sociologists, psychologists, pollsters and researchers of many stripes and shades.

Accordingly, it is the remarkable statistics-gathering and statistics-dissemination complex in America that must get first thanks here. And first among first are the steady and astute men and women of the U. S. Bureau of the Census who have helped me for well over a decade now. In this most recent enterprise, these professional people were particularly helpful:

The director of the Census' Public Information Office, Jack Casserly, was invariably helpful and co-operative in this venture, and the work of his assistant, Beulah Land, was nothing short of prodigious. In addition, grateful thanks go to Tobi Bressler, Campbell Gibson, Paul Glick, Stanley Greene, Jean Griffith, Roger Herriot, Charles Johnson, Louis Kincannon, Don Knowles, Renee Miller, Dr. Morris Moore, Robert Rowland, Henry Smith, Emmet Spiers, Larry Suter, Murray Weitzman, Meyer Zitter, Daniel Levine, Richard Forstall, Nampeo McKenny, Jack McNeill, Paula Schneider. Wherever possible Census experts verified the data (but not the opinions) that appear in this book.

Beyond the Census, there was aid and assistance from many other government agencies.

From the Bureau of Labor Statistics, acknowledgments and thanks are extended to John Breger, Joseph Finerty, Joseph Goldberg, Denis Johnston, Hy Kaitz, Donald Landay, Leon Lundun, John Stimpson.

In addition, thanks go to Molly Orshansky and Walter Kolodrubetz of the Social Security Administration; Joseph Laitin and Daniel Tunstall of the Office of Management and Budget; Dr. Vance Grant of the Department of HEW, Office of Education; Leo Bernstein, Ed Coleman, John Gorman and Robert

Graham of the Bureau of Economic Analysis; Elmer Glaser of AID; Robert
Heuser of the National Center for Health Statistics; George Perry of the
Brookings Institution; Burt Seidman of the AFL-CIO.

The second substantive part of this volume deals with American attitudes.
In that field, too, there has grown up a large and variegated complex of data
gatherers. Just as the first half of this volume could not have been written
without the aid of the objective data-gathering sources, so the second half of the
book could not have been written without the services of the polling profession.
And so deep thanks are extended to Paul Perry, Tom Rankin and Ann Pyshon
from the Gallup Organization; Louis Harris from the Louis Harris Company;
Daniel Yankelovich, Arthur White and Sara Horack from the Daniel Yankelovich Co.; Joel Aberbach, Marty Gold, Kent Jennings, Warren Miller and
Howard Schuman from the University of Michigan Survey Research Center;
Philip Hastings from the Roper Center; Peter Hart from the Peter D. Hart
Research, Inc.; and the late Oliver Quayle from Oliver Quayle & Co.

A work of this nature also is derivative of a wide range of contacts and conversations, often not made with a book in mind, but which nonetheless help form
and shape opinions and judgments. This list includes members of the Washington political and press community, from academia, from labor and from friends
and family. They include Eliot Abrams, Rabbi A. Nathan Abromowitz, Joseph
and Stewart Alsop, Al Barkan, Rev. Geno Baroni, Louis Bean, John Bedell, Ar-
nold Beichman, Paul Berger, Elihu Bergman, Howard Bird, Albert Blackburn,
Ken Bode, Congressman Richard Bolling, Daniel Boorstin, Andrew Brimmer,
David Broder, Les Brown, Hal Bruno, Herrington Bryce, Horace Busby, Robert
Campbell, Albert Cantril, Les and Liz Carpenter, Douglass Cater, George
Christian, Wilbur Cohen, Brian Corcoran, Clare Crawford, Tom Cronin, Ray
D'Argenio, Midge Decter, Roy Dexheimer, S. Harrison Dogole, Andrew Dolk-
hart, Fred Dutton, Avush Dworkin, Mel Elfin, the late Susan Eisenberg,
Rowland Evans, Howard Feldman, Dan Fenn, Vic Fingerhut, Jim Flug, Con-
gressman Tom Foley, Dorothy Fosdick, Wyche Fowler, Lloyd Free, David
Freeman, Andrew Frey, Ed Garvey, Andrew Glass, Nat Goldfinger, Stanley
Goldstein, Sandy Greenberg, Mort Grossman, Alyn Gruber, David Gutmann,
Judy Hade, Michael Halberstam, Robert Hartman, Seymour Hersh, Donald
Hertzberg, Stephen Hess, Norman Hill, Stephen Isaacs, Kirby Jones, Vernon
Jordan, Herman Kahn of the Hudson Institute, publishers of a fascinating book,
The Forgotten Americans by Frank Armbruster (with contributions by Doris
Yokelson), Tom Kahn, Max Kampelman, Steve Klaidman, Doris Kearnes,
Robert Keefe, Penn Kemble, Stewart Kessler, Robert Kilmarx, Carrol
Kilpatrick, Lane Kirkland, Evron Kirkpatrick, Neal Kozodoy, Joseph Kraft,
Richard Krikus, Irving Kristol, Scott Lang, D. J. Leary, David Lebedoff,
W. Colston Leigh, Jr., Peter Lisagor, Sol Linowitz, John Lofton, Art McAnally,
Jeb Magruder, Robert Markel, Frank Mankiewicz, Leonard Marks, Carol
Marlantes, Louis Martin, Tom Mathews, Dick and Paula McDonald, Gib
McCabe, John McNulty, Harry McPherson, Herman Miller, George Morrisey,
Dr. Herbert Moskovitz, Bill Moyers, Sterling Munro, Dorothy Newman,
Bernard Norwitch, Robert Novak, James O'Hara, Arthur Okun, Allen Otten,

Fred Panzer, Neil Pierce, Howard Penniman, Richard Perle, John Pfriender, Kevin Philips, Norman Podhoretz, Carl Pope, Richard Ravitch, John Roche, Peter Rosenblatt, Eugene Rostow, Harold Roth, Harold Rothwax, Bayard Rustin, Norman Ryder, William Safire, Richard Schifter, Herb Schmertz, Marty Schramm, David Schuchat, Gene, Rebecca, Elinor and Deborah Schull, Charles Schultze, Milton Shaw, Norman Sherman, Stephen Shulman, Hugh Sidey, Ira Silverman, Donald Slaiman, Jeff Stansbury, Gerald Stern, Rick Stearns, William Steiff, Robert Strauss, Gerald Strober, David Swit, Conrad Teauber, Larry Temple, Fred Thompson, John Tolbert, Jack Valenti, Ted Van Dyk, Milton and Judith Viorst, the late Leon Volkov, Mike Waldman, Judah and Rachel Wattenberg, William Watts, Paul Weaver, Charles Westoff, Hank and Roberta Wexler, Richard Whalen, Jules Witcover, Lee White, James Q. Wilson, Herman Wouk, Sam Yette, Bob Young.

Also John Albertine, Clancy Adamy, Myles Callum, Jeanne Kirkpatrick and Jack Rosenthal.

A number of people were active, at different times, in researching and preparing parts of this manuscript: Conner Wheatly, Natalie Swit, Linda Sutherland, Alice McGillivray, Jonathan Schull, Sarah Mazle, Cynthia Johnston, Marcy Wilkov, Deirdre Lavrakas, S. Amoy Allen.

At Doubleday & Company this book was treated with a sense of great importance, and I am deeply thankful for that. The editor Betty Prashker understood the book from the outset and edited it with skill and remarkable speed under a tight deadline. The publisher at Doubleday, Samuel Vaughan, is an old friend who started me out more than a decade ago and is one of the great people. Diana Matthews, editorial assistant, proves that the next decade at Doubleday will also be peopled by energetic and creative editors.

My family—wife Marna, children Sarah, Daniel and Ruth—were exposed to many of the incredibly astute ideas in this volume as I went along. We all argue a lot—which is good for an author with an argumentative soul.

I teach a seminar at Mary Washington College in Fredericksburg, Virginia. My title is "Eminent Scholar," but I must confess to the sixteen young women and one young man who were my students in early 1974 that I can only hope I taught as much as I learned.

The agent on this book was Peter Matson. Women have babies in only nine months. Mr. Matson sweated this one out for almost two years.

Ervin Duggan, not for a change, was instrumental in titling this volume and was of invaluable editorial assistance.

My research assistant, Brenda Krieger, was of critical importance in getting this book out. She has become the only walking data bank in Washington.

Finally, a word about a remarkable man who has been a great influence on me over the last dozen years—the years that this book deals with. Richard M. Scammon was formerly the director of the U. S. Bureau of the Census, is now director of the Elections Research Center, and is perhaps the most knowledgeable man in the world on the general subject of elections. Mr. Scammon and I were coauthors of the political book *The Real Majority* (and we are already collaborating on a new political book). For a time, we considered doing this volume as a collaboration, but a variety of circumstances—mostly time pressures —made it impossible. Still, in the course of working on this book I spent many hours of conversation with him. And so, there are ideas of his in this book— uncredited.

More important, there is an overview here that Dick Scammon has helped drum into me over the years. "Marinate yourself in the data" is his favorite line.

I have tried to do that. And that, really, is what this book is about—an attempt to go to data as a way of seeing the first dim outlines of reality.

Contents

Introduction

By Richard M. Scammon

This is a book about fact versus perception in American life. Its thesis is that many of our most fashionable *perceptions* about life in the United States—about politics, jobs, money, pollution, population and race, for example, are flatly wrong, or at least badly distorted.

Because it questions so many myths and treads on so many toes, and because it sounds an optimistic note in a time of pessimistic conventional wisdom, THE REAL AMERICA is bound to be controversial.

But because of its method—a rigorous appeal by the author to the *data* and to *facts*—this book deserves to be carefully read and seriously understood.

Much is made these days of novel trends in American letters; we are treated almost daily to books and articles that purport to be something new: the "nonfiction novel"; "fiction as history" and "history as fiction." In journalism the latest fashion is the "new journalism" or "advocacy journalism." Amid this welter of newness, Ben Wattenberg practices a more precise craft, what might be called "data journalism."

Naturally enough, what is one man's precision is another's advocacy, and no one could accuse Mr. Wattenberg of approaching his work without some very specific ideas of his own.

He does not eschew opinion, far from it. But his recourse, first and last, is to data: to numbers, charts, graphs and tables. Mr. Wattenberg is a thorough professional who follows Mark Twain's advice: "Always tell the truth. It will gratify some and astonish the rest."

Ben Wattenberg—my friend, colleague, collaborator on two past books and one future one—has made a career of transforming statistics into lively and readable prose. But the reader should not let the ease of Mr. Wattenberg's style blind him to the real breadth and depth and range of this book.

In THE REAL AMERICA Mr. Wattenberg mines almost every available vein of factual and statistical ore.

First, there is the United States Census, 1970 version. As Director of the U. S. Bureau of the Census in the early 1960s, I know how much digging Mr. Wattenberg did on the first book on which he and I worked—*This U.S.A.* And as the years have passed the wealth of Census data has broadened and deepened, increasing its utility to the data-oriented investigator.

Second, Mr. Wattenberg has assembled facts from the vast and growing statistical efforts of private business and industry, an output of material which has also been developing and expanding over the years. In fact, even a datum or two of my own in the area of electoral statistics can be found in this new review of life in our United States.

Finally, the author has gone, in his quest for the truth about contemporary America, to the opinion pollsters, both national and regional, who are continually probing the public mind. Such continuing attitudinal studies are of relatively recent vintage in America and are of enormous importance. In my own field of political studies, I have long felt that the advent of public opinion polling has been the most important development in our democratic system since the coming of the direct primary election. In any event, if we are indeed in a McLuhanite world, then attitudinal studies may be just as important to our understanding of our country as are the "harder" data of wage rates, years of school completed, median family income and the like.

The result is a vast and fascinating compendium of facts. But it is more: a portrait of America that will be fascinating to every reader—and astonishing to those who have casually absorbed from the popular media an image of America as a society in economic, moral, attitudinal and political decline.

Ben Wattenberg rejects forcefully the powerful contemporary myth of American failure. The facts he has uncovered inspire him to some spirited (though good-natured) jousting with what he calls the Failure and Guilt Complex in America.

The Failure and Guilt Complex, as I understand it, is not a conscious conspiracy, merely a loose confederation of reformers who depend upon lurid recitals of the nation's shortcomings to spur their fellow citizens to reform.

Mr. Wattenberg's rejoinder—one with which I warmly agree—is that lurid recitals can sometimes be a dangerous and counterproductive political weapon. Raised to a pitch of stridency, catalogues of national woe may become, not spurs to positive action, but blows to national morale and self-confidence. Aimed too far off the mark of accuracy, the reformers' well-intentioned jeremiads may be taken only as a form of political wolf crying.

The author takes an almost mischievous delight in hunting down and exposing lurid reciters, fact ignorers, doom sayers, woe spreaders and wolf criers. If his prey occasionally includes some of the nation's most celebrated spokespersons—Women's Liberationists, black militants, environmentalists, New Leftists, Old Rightists, population Explosionists— well, so be it.

Let no one conclude, however, that this is a conservative book or that the author is hostile to change in American life. Quite the contrary: Mr. Wattenberg's story throughout is one of successful transformations in our national life. The American people, as the author describes them, are cautious and deliberate, commonsensical and slow to embrace political or social fads. But they are, most decidedly, progressive and open to favorable change. They refuse to be stampeded—but they never stand still. In all of these qualities, the author is like the citizens he describes.

THE REAL AMERICA is first of all a book of facts about America. But the book's significance, in my judgment, lies beyond its descriptive thoroughness—and even beyond its myth-breaking potential.

I believe this is a book of enormous *political* meaning in its broadest sense—and of great potential impact on our current politics.

So much of our political discourse, after all, takes place with scant appeal—or no appeal—to facts. The so-called Great Society programs of the Johnson era, for example: Were they a partial success, or have they ended in a sad ruin of inflated promises and meager results? Are black Americans, after more than a decade of struggle to share in the American middle-class dream, better off now or worse?

These questions, and others like them, are intensely important political questions. And this book, better than any recent work I have seen, will put citizens who debate these questions in touch with the facts.

Those citizens who once were called liberals and now are called other, less flattering, names will find in these pages vindication for their efforts over the past dozen years—and they may find an agenda for the future. For Mr. Wattenberg assembles impressive evidence that the domestic policies of the New Frontier and the Great Society have, despite some mistakes and false starts, worked pretty well. And Mr. Wattenberg offers some sound advice to progressives who are uncertain what trumpet call to sound: If you wish to achieve success in your future political efforts, resist the temptation to call your past successes failures.

One might hope, then, that the final effect of this book could be one of reconciliation—reconciliation between old liberals and young Turks; between the graybeards and the longhairs in our society. For another theme of THE REAL AMERICA is the common ground on which we all stand.

This book tells the story of the remarkable *accommodations* Americans have made over these last few turbulent years. We are, in Ben Wattenberg's discerning eye, a people of great good sense and enormous flexibility. The "system," so scorned by young militants as unchanging and unresponsive, responded to their attacks—by changing. The "institutions" flayed by critics as hopelessly rigid and inflexible—business and industry, government, the universities, the family—have in the past several years undergone some notable transformations. Perhaps with this understanding, progressives of many stripes can once again wield the lance together.

That is encouraging news.

And that phrase, *encouraging news,* sums up my final point about THE REAL AMERICA.

This book could have, and I hope will have, a deep effect not only on our politics but upon our national morale. We have gone through some trying years, years of immense contentiousness and confusion in America. Swift social changes, a bitter war, assassinations and attempted assassinations, political scandals, the earsplitting wails of a thousand Cassandras—all these have made us, understandably, nervous and confused.

A book like this one—a putting-in-perspective book if you like—based solidly on fact, and finding, in the turmoil of these past few years, so much that is good can help refresh the national spirit, if not exorcise demons.

A warning: Ben Wattenberg is both analyst and advocate. His style is happily pugnacious. He would rather twist the ear of an adversary, any day, than write elegant euphemisms.

Some readers may find Mr. Wattenberg's aggressive optimism difficult to accept. Those who are incorrigibly churlish may wish to dismiss him as a strange blend of Pollyanna, Dr. Pangloss and the late Émile Coué. Many may feel their own definitions and parameters for the facts of life give findings far less positive than those of the author. Some readers, bowing under the weight of Mr. Wattenberg's arguments, may protest that his optimism is perverse—that the cup is half empty, not half full.

Well, that is a question for philosophers, not pollsters or demographers or political analysts.

I would remind the recalcitrant that the author is neither Pollyanna nor Pangloss. He is a careful analyst who has not often been mistaken. And he still believes, after examining the evidence, he still believes what he wrote in our first book: "In American history . . . it is the optimist who has been the realist."

I.

WHEREIN THE QUESTION IS POSED

CHAPTER 1

The Question

Almost every controversy of the current era swings on the hinge of a single, simple question: *What happened in America in the last dozen or so years?*

Thus, if one says that what happend in the 1960s and the first two or three years of the 1970s was American failure, then a series of corollaries immediately comes to mind. So potent are some of these corollaries of American failure that many have already been crowned by the highest of ideological awards: contemporary cliché.

Accordingly, we hear:

- Our institutions have failed.
- America has lost its way.
- None of the programs worked.
- Liberalism doesn't work.
- Integration doesn't work.
- We are moving to two Societies separate and unequal.
- The welfare mess.
- We are destroying our environment.
- Our cities are in crisis.
- Malaise.
- Our schools don't educate.
- Americans are fed up.
- Work has become dehumanized.
- Income is distributed unfairly.
- There is a crime wave.
- Women are oppressed.
- Chicanos are oppressed.
- America is overextended.
- We have to reorder our priorities.

And so on, through an entire litany of woe and crisis. And if indeed those dozen years were a failure, it may well be that these corollaries of gloom are quite correct.

But suppose for a moment—just suppose—that the decade of the 1960s was by and large a *successful* American decade. Suppose that the first third of the new decade of the Seventies continued not all, but much, of the progress of the Sixties. Suppose, instead of saying that we lived through an era of despair with some spots of success, suppose one viewed what happened in America this way: It was a successful era with some spots of despair.

If that is the case, then many—most?—all?—of the clichés listed above would be at least diluted if not wholly invalidated. More substantively, such an invalidation of the catechism of woe would also invalidate many of the premises upon which our contemporary social policy rests. Given such a potential payoff, it would seem that an investigation into the possibility of American success is an investigation clearly worth pursuing.

But the importance of the quest for an answer to the success-failure question goes still deeper. It concerns the nature of our future and how we will respond to it.

As the galleys of this volume are reviewed in mid-May of 1974, America faces some serious problems. Political scandal in the highest places has laid a pall over the land, and the jarring spectacle of an impeachment seems likely. An "energy crisis" of greater or lesser order will be an ongoing part of our lives for many years to come. An international situation that looks euphoric one day and dangerous the next calls for a redefined notion of America's role in the world. Perhaps most critically, the onset of high inflation—in "double digit" magnitude as this is written—has wracked the citizenry and turned many Americans sour. Economists who are not generally alarmists wonder if traditional economic correctives will work, or whether this inflation is of a new and more serious strain.

Whether these problems, and others, will be well solved or not solved depends in some large measure on what Americans, and their leaders, think about themselves and their nation. If they are convinced that nothing works any more and that our society is tottering, then the solutions proposed may be timid, piecemeal, nervously pursued and of dubious outcome. On the other hand, if Americans, and their leaders, feel that this society—having lived through a turbulent dozen years—has *coped* and *progressed,* then we may well pursue our problems with a vigor and vitality more traditionally associated with the American style. In either instance, we deserve to be able to base our judgments on the social facts of our time, not the social fictions.

We mortals have no way of knowing what the future holds. *But if we can assess what we have done we can also gain a sense of what we are able to do.*

* * *

How, then, does one determine whether a society has been "successful" or not? How can the "progress" of a nation be judged? Suppose an intelligent visitor from Mars joined us for a while; how would such a being rationally seek to assess what's been going on here?

Three ways come to mind.

First: Observe the objective indices.

Second: Ask the people.

Third: Consider the pronouncements of those who are supposed to be the particularly smart people.

These, in fact, are the three prisms through which America will be looked at in this volume: rhetoric, objective data, attitudinal data. The difference in what is seen through these three prisms is what makes this exploration so interesting and so puzzling, and ultimately, to this author, so rewarding.

Hard Data

In the first half of this book an effort is made to observe and tally the objective indices of American society.

After examining the data, the conclusion here is that the human condition in America—as measured by the data—has in fact improved rapidly in recent years. Indeed, it may well be that conditions have improved more rapidly than at any time in recent American history, in fact, improving to such a degree as to create a new human situation, a society whose massive majority is "middle class." The emergence of this Massive Majority Middle Class, it is suggested here, is a benchmark of major historical importance, and its ramifications are enormous.

This judgment is based on an enormous corpus of data, the major parts of which come from the U. S. Bureau of the Census, producers and tabulators of the 1970 decennial census.

Thus, in April of 1970, more than 83 million questionnaires went out across America seeking information about somewhat more than 200 million Americans. Some of these questionnaires contained as many as 89 questions. More than 185,000 people were involved in checking, processing and analyzing this treasure trove of demographic and social and economic data. The final published product ran to 200,000 printed tables.

Beyond the decennial Census itself, and in part a by-product of it, are the month-by-month and year-by-year reports produced by the Census Bureau that are derived from the monthly "Current Population Survey" and a host of other special and regular surveys. In all, the Bureau produces three thousand reports a year—and the attempt has been made here to include available data through the end of 1973 and up until May of 1974, which in some instances meant inserting new material in the galley proof phase of the work.

A selection of particularly relevant Census data is presented in the appendix of this volume, under the title "The Short Census."

But even that is not the sum of it by any means. There has grown up in the United States in the last thirty years a most remarkable and most valuable statistics generating complex, unmatched in history. From government agencies on every level, from trade associations, from private industry, from academia, numbers that mean something pour forth in a mighty stream.

These data—flowing from a hundred sources—are critical to an understanding of the condition of America today. And so, they too are dealt with.

The Rhetoric

The argument is made here that the data shows there was great and healthy change in the United States since 1960—on almost every measurable front:

- Social and economic conditions for blacks in America improved sharply, probably more rapidly and more significantly than during any time in American history since the end of the Civil War.
- Economic progress, as measured by the real purchasing power of dollars in the hands of ordinary Americans, was substantial during the last decade—even after any tax bite and after the erosive effects of inflation. In point of fact, economic advancement was probably greater than at any other time in the twentieth century.
- A misperceived threat from a "population explosion" has disappeared, with essentially beneficial results.
- Work in America, far from becoming "dehumanized" is now established in the most "human" and creative pattern in the history of mankind.
- Educational levels in America soared during the 1960s. And we ask this question: How can the same people say "the educational system is a failure," and (when commending student activism) "this

has been the brightest, best-educated, generation in American history?"

- The social and economic independence of women has reached unprecedented levels.
- The incidence of poverty in America has been halved.

But a funny thing happened. A new rhetoric grew up in America with a new name for success. It is called failure. Dedicated to this rhetorical shell game is a nonconspiratorial, hydra-headed, articulate infrastructure that has assumed great power and potency in American life and letters.

In the 1950s Dwight Eisenhower was able to perceive the existence of another hydra-headed infrastructure. He called it the military-industrial complex. In the 1960s an astute observer should have been able to perceive the growth of a failure infrastructure, a loose unorganized organization, apparently uneasy, unhappy and unpleasant about the idea of creeping success. Thus, in the 1960s the Failure and Guilt Complex was born.

Traveling sometimes under the banner of "the movement," sometimes as a wandering tribe of people with a cause,[1] sometimes only as freelance naysayers, it is the contention here that this Failure and Guilt Complex came quite close to dominating the intellectual discourse of our time, spewing forth reams of rhetoric organized around these simple and closely related ideas: crisis, failure, guilt.

Thus,

- From the demographic branch of Failure and Guilt Complex we heard about a horrific "population explosion" that was destroying America.
- From the woman's auxiliary of the Failure and Guilt Complex we heard that women were oppressed, indeed enslaved.
- From the O. Kerner Chapter of the Failure and Guilt Complex we heard that America is a white racist nation "moving toward two societies, separate and unequal."
- From the environmental branch of the Failure and Guilt Complex we heard that the whole world was coming to an end because rich Americans polluted the planet and stole its resources.
- From the economics faculty of the Failure and Guilt Complex we heard that pollution was the real result of economic growth and that henceforward, accordingly, GNP would be redefined as "Gross National Pollution."
- From the sociology faculty of the Failure and Guilt Complex we heard similar tales of woe about jobs, poverty and education— each enunciated by a separate but often interlocking mafia of the F&GC.

[1] Frank Mankiewicz has called them, simply, "the cause people."

- From the internationally minded members of the Failure and Guilt Complex we heard that America was an imperialist, immoral, genocidal superpower intent on repressing freedom around the world.
- From the political clubhouse of the Failure and Guilt Complex, accustomed as politicians are to broad generalities, we heard that America was "a sick society," that our "priorities must be reordered" and that only a new politics or a new left could possibly do that.[2]

Attitudes

And so, conflict.

The dominant rhetoric of our time is a rhetoric of failure, guilt and crisis.

The evidence of the data is the evidence of progress, growth and success.

For some help in resolving the conflict, the reader is invited into the attitudinal arena. Through the tool of the modern public opinion poll, an attempt is made to find out what people think. Do Americans believe the hard data or the harsh rhetoric? Do Americans believe things are getting better or worse in America?

And another set of thoughts: how have opinions generally been *changing* in America? Do *changed* opinions in themselves perhaps give a clue as to how fares America? Can changing opinions yield up a judgment about progress?

So one must look at polls and surveys from national pollsters like Gallup, Harris, Roper, Yankelovich and Opinion Research, from academic institutions like the Institute for Social Research (University of Michigan), and the National Opinion Research Center (University of Chicago), from state polls like the *Minnesota* poll, the Field *California* poll, the Belden *Texas* poll and from assorted private polls as well.

In the area of public opinion, unlike the cool and precise realm of Census data and unlike the harsh rhetoric of our time, the answers come out muddy and imprecise. Attitudes can change quickly, they may be influenced by yesterday's headline and tomorrow's scandal. Yet public opinion polling is the best device available to us, and an examination of the data does bear heavy fruit.

We have no attitudinal counterpart to the Gross National Product, but perhaps we ought to. Perhaps we need an index of the Gross National Spirit, an opinion indicator to tell us where we've been and where we're going, an index to answer one of the haunting questions

[2] While about an authentic explosion of criminality in America, we heard from the Failure and Guilt Complex—next to nothing.

of our time: *If everything is so good, how come everything is so bad?*
For many of our problems today deal as much with what we *think* as
with what *is*. And that is why we hear so much these days—much of
it wrong—about Americans being "fed up" and "alienated." Attempting
to gauge these views—as shall be seen—can give us still another way to
judge whether or not we are making headway.

* * *

In the course of looking at America through these three prisms and
in the course of trying to adjudge whether America and Americans have
been moving ahead, one ultimately butts head on to a key question. It
is a simple one: *What constitutes progress?*

For that simple question, a simple answer is suggested. Progress is a
condition that is better by far than what it replaces after accounting for
any side effects.

Such is the condition that has prevailed recently in America. Such is
the condition from which any intelligent look into the future must now be
made. And looking to the future from such a perspective tends to give
the lie to many of the new pronouncements of doom, many of which echo
the older statement of Aldous Huxley's ". . . as I look into the future,
it won't work."

II.

THE RHETORIC

CHAPTER 2

By Their Words . . .

There is no way to *prove* that the dominant rhetoric of our time has been one of failure, guilt and crisis. The best-programmed computers could not weigh or measure all the political speeches, newspaper columns, television commentaries and magazine articles of the last dozen or so years and come up with a definitive judgment as to whether a certain sort or a certain substance of gloomy and apocalyptic rhetoric was "dominant."

The notion is accepted only as an article of faith. The author *knows* it is so; for all that nonsense still rings in our ears. Examples will be provided in a moment—scores of them—with additional references interspersed or alluded to throughout this volume. Moreover, having pored over mountains of material, it can be categorically stated that there are thousands, and tens of thousands, of additional quotations that could have been presented. But that is not definitive proof either. There is no proof, only evidence.

So too with what is called here the Failure and Guilt Complex. There are no membership cards. There are no cell meetings. It has no chairperson, not even a commanding general. And surely not all the persons quoted in the bizarre compendium that follows would be members even if there were members—not even most of them. For, included among those quoted, after all, are many of the great intellectual and political luminaries of our era.

Just so. Intentionally so. Failure-and-guilt-and-crisis-and-despair has become a state of mind in America. It is espoused and echoed not only by leaders of the Complex, not only by their spear carriers, flacks, hangers-on and media freaks; not only by a fringe of nuts left and right; but also by so much of the Establishment itself, the best and the brightest if you will.

And that is probably a tragedy.
Here is what we've been hearing:

The whole country is one vast insane asylum and they're letting the
worst patients run the place.

ROBERT WELCH
President, John Birch Society

American society is an explosion of insanity . . . the problem is not
"Who are the madmen?" It is the society that is insane.

HERBERT MARCUSE, 1968

America is threatening to become a giant lunatic asylum.

JACK NEWFIELD, 1970

There is a vague anxiety that the machine of the 20th century is
beginning to run out of control.

Time Magazine, 1970

The white race is the cancer of human history; it is the white race
and it alone—its ideologies and inventions—which eradicates auton-
omous civilizations wherever it spreads, which has upset the ecological balance of the planet, which now threatens the very existence of
life itself.

SUSAN SONTAG, 1967

The evidence is strong that human society is in a stage of comprehensive breakdown.

NORMAN COUSINS, 1970

Something basic and dangerous is eating away at the morality, dignity
and respect of our citizens, old as well as young, high as well as low.

BARRY GOLDWATER, 1964

I would suggest that Technologyland tends to create a psychic condition which is the equivalent of plastic. And just as plastic objects work
well and show no sign of age until the moment when they cease to
work—and then they give no warning; they just split—so certain
things in American society are breaking—with no warning at all.

NORMAN MAILER, 1968

I fear the United States has always been a nation of ongoing hustlers
from the prisons and disaster areas of old Europe. . . . I do not think

that the American system in its present state of decadence is worth preserving. The initial success of the United States was largely accidental. A rich almost empty continent was . . . exploited by rapacious Europeans who made slaves of Africans and corpses of Indians in the process.

GORE VIDAL, 1973

Right now the social soul of America is so sick that even the overthrow of a political regime may be insufficient.

SHIRLEY MACLAINE, 1972

And while each of us pursues his selfish interest and comforts himself by blaming others, the nation disintegrates. I use the phrase soberly: The nation disintegrates.

JOHN W. GARDNER, 1969

The Attica tragedy is more stark proof that something is terribly wrong in America. We have reached the point where men would rather die than live another day in America.

SENATOR EDMUND MUSKIE, 1971

We have created in America a culture of drugs. We have produced an environment in which people come naturally to expect that they can take a pill for every problem.

RICHARD NIXON, 1971

We seem to be in one of those long periods when civilization is in decline.

New Republic, 1971

We must realize that today's establishment is the new George III. Whether it will continue to adhere to its tactics we do not know. If it does, the redress, honored in tradition, is also revolution.

JUSTICE WILLIAM O. DOUGLAS, 1971

I think [*The Godfather*] is about the corporate mind. In a way, the Mafia is the best example of capitalists we have. Don Corleone is just an ordinary American business magnate who is trying to do the best he can for the group he represents and for his family. . . . I think the tactics that the Don used aren't much different from those General Motors used against Ralph Nader.

MARLON BRANDO, 1973

The nation is essentially evil and the evil can be exorcised only by turning the system upside down.

JAMES MCGREGOR BURNS, 1972

What has really got us in its grip today . . . is . . . the breakdown of American life, because American life doesn't work any more. You can't get your garbage picked up and you can't get a quick and easy ride to work on the subway. Or if you get on the freeway with your car, the traffic doesn't move. . . . Every time that the publisher of the New York *Times* gives you a handsome raise, well deserved for the work that you've done so beautifully the past year, prices go up faster, and taxes go up, and in the long run your check shows you have less net money at the end of the month.

Because you can't stand to breathe the air, and if you live in Washington the Potomac River will make you sick when you drink it. And because of the lack of quality from top to bottom in American life. Because when you turn on the television you don't see anything but junk. And when you go down to the store and buy something you don't get anything but junk.

TOM WICKER, 1971

When you reach a point where you realize further efforts will be futile, you may as well look after yourself and your friends and enjoy what little time you have left. That point for me is 1972.

PAUL R. EHRLICH, 1970

You have to belong to the intelligentsia to believe things like that: no ordinary man could be such a fool.

GEORGE ORWELL

WORK

Work and living have become more and more pointless and empty. . . . For most Americans, work is mindless, exhausting, boring, servile, and hateful. . . . Our life activities have become plastic, vicarious, and false to our genuine needs, activities fabricated by others and forced upon us.

CHARLES REICH
Greening of America, 1970

. . . the AFL-CIO has lived happily in a society which, more lavishly than any in history, has managed the care and feeding of incompetent white people.

MURRAY KEMPTON, 1971

Unexpected precincts are being heard from in a show of discontent by blue collar and white. Communiques are alarming concerning absenteeism in auto plants. On the evening bus, the tense, pinched faces of young file clerks and elderly secretaries tell us more than we care to know. On the expressway, middle-management men pose without grace behind their wheels, as they flee city and job.

STUDS TERKEL, 1973

Regimentation and repetition may not have nearly so much to do with worker alienation as does the fact that much work just isn't worth doing at all or is basically corrupt. Even the dumbest worker hired to manufacture spray deodorant containers, or plastic plates, or pressed-sawdust furniture, or ersatz packaged food must realize that it wouldn't really matter if his factory closed down forever. So why should he care about his work?

ROBERT SHERRILL, 1973

INCOME

Less visible but far more influential is the fact that the real income of an American majority has virtually stagnated for half a decade. Combined with a decay of other conditions of life, this means that the standard of living has declined. . . . Political explosion is portended in the spreading knowledge that things are not getting easier or better.

RICHARD GOODWIN, 1973

In these past months I have come to understand that a zooming Gross National Product leads not to salvation, but to suicide.

JOHN FISCHER
Harper's Magazine, 1970

The affluent society and a rising standard of living are cruel illusions to most blue collar workers.

Time Magazine, 1970

EDUCATION

Should not every student develop a cultural paranoia in which every professor is viewed as a potential agent or tacit supporter of the murder factory and every academic system is seen as set against the student's mental and social health until he finds out differently?

NAT HENTOFF, 1968

Over the past few years, I have felt increasingly that something is terribly wrong—and this year ever so much more than last. Something has gone sour, in teaching and in learning. It's almost as though there were a widespread feeling that education has become irrelevant.

GEORGE WALD, 1969

In some campus communities, we have reached the point at which anything remotely resembling a student can, in time of crisis, be gunned down, gassed, and bayoneted by the authorities with impunity, indeed with the applause of millions of voters. Black Panthers and hippies have become for cynical opportunists like Governor Reagan, the scapegoat of Hitler's Jews.

THEODORE ROSZAK
Where the Wasteland Ends, 1972

The American school system will be ended in two years. We are going to bring it down. Quit being students. Become criminals. We have to disrupt every institution and break every law.

JERRY RUBIN, 1970

A case in point is American education. In the past ten years, the cost of elementary and secondary education has doubled; the average expenditure per pupil is three or four times what it was when most adult Americans were going to school. And what have Americans received in return for these tens of billions? A public school system in which the quality of education and the level of learning are plunging in city after city.

PATRICK J. BUCHANAN, 1973

MATERIALISM / ENVIRONMENT

Material well-being is only an instrument for the pursuit of more fulfilling, freer lives. Yet wealth has brought not liberation, but increasing confinement.

> RICHARD GOODWIN
> *Newsweek,* 1972

Blessed be the starving blacks of Mississippi with their outdoor privies, for they are ecologically sound, and they shall inherit a nation.

> WAYNE H. DAVIS, 1970

Freedom to breed will bring ruin to all.

> GARRETT HARDIN
> *Science*

We've become a gluttonous, greedy nation acquiring wealth we do not need, and as we do this, we extinguish the hopes of other, poorer nations.

> STUART UDALL, 1973

Most of the people who are going to die in the greatest cataclysm in the history of man have been born.

> PAUL EHRLICH, 1969

RACE

The sickening truth is that this country is rapidly coming to resemble South Africa.

Our native reserves and Bantustans are the inner city. And our apartheid is all the more disgusting for being insidious and unproclaimed.

> SENATOR WALTER F. MONDALE, 1971

They (blacks and Puerto Ricans) are almost a separate people, really a colonial people. But instead of abandoning them in Africa the way the British and the French and Belgians could do, we abandoned them in our own country.

> EUGENE MCCARTHY, 1971

[We are] moving towards two societies separate and unequal.

KERNER COMMISSION REPORT, 1968

A year later we are closer to being two societies, one white, and one black, separate but unequal.

1969 URBAN COALITION REPORT

The truth can no longer be ignored—white America appears to be seriously considering the possibilities of mass extermination.

JAMES BALDWIN, 1968

I have sold more records than Bach, Beethoven and Brahms put together, but because of the racial problem in the United States, nobody emphasizes this.

JAMES BROWN, 1973

All of the civil rights legislation is absolutely meaningless, and it was meant to be meaningless.

JAMES BALDWIN, 1972

While others moved ahead, his income stagnated, his neighborhoods became ghettos, and his access to the mainstream of American life continued to remain an empty promise. . . .

It would be tempting to assign all this to the realm of the past, and to point to the progress that has been made as the final proof of Negro acceptance. But the facts will not bear this out.

SENATOR EDWARD M. KENNEDY, 1968

ATTITUDES

Wherever I travel, I find that average citizens—poor or middle class or rich; white or black or brown; city or farm or suburb—have a profound dissatisfaction with the way they live.

SENATOR EDWARD M. KENNEDY, 1972

It sometimes seems there's not any damn thing you can buy that's worth a damn. And we all know that.

What's bothering the people today is that life has broken down in this country. In the midst of wealth, in the midst of plenty, above all, in the midst of pretensions, life has broken down. We can't hear our-

selves think for the noise in the streets and most of the noise in the
streets comes from where we are tearing down our heritage and everything that's worthwhile in this country, and putting up plastic and
pressed concrete that twenty years from now we'll have to tear down
and put up all over again.

PETER F. DRUCKER, 1971

POLITICS

We are not sure if the values we have lived by for generations have
any meaning left. We are not sure if the national programs developed
in the past can effectively serve the public need today.

INTRODUCTION TO THE 1972 DEMOCRATIC PLATFORM

McGovern is saying some challenging, uplifting, and highly moral things.
That moral challenge . . . will be welcomed by society teetering
somewhere near the brink of moral bankruptcy and collapse.

GARY HART
McGovern campaign manager, 1972

By promising and not delivering to the blacks and by forgetting the
low-income whites, the liberal Democrats managed to anger and polarize
both halves of the other America. Although in power for eight years,
they failed to make any significant improvement in the day-to-day
life of America's 30,000,000 to 40,000,000 poor.

JACK NEWFIELD, 1971

By 1973, enough evidence had been gathered on the Great Society
programs to return an indictment. Those most committed to the costly
social innovations enacted in the sixties were by January 1973 apolo-
getic, defensive and disappointed at their enormous expense and manifest unsuccess. . . . Surely, a wholesale rip-off of American taxpayers
and working people to feather the nest of a new Poverty-Education
Industrial Complex was not what Lyndon Johnson had in mind when
he stood before Congress and declared, "We shall overcome."

PATRICK J. BUCHANAN, 1973

It was joy to be at the Democratic convention this year. The convention
was a triumph for the young and the young of heart. I managed to
wangle a floor pass and wander around among the delegates during

the decisive vote on the California credentials, and I felt I had lived
to see a miracle. Those who had been in the streets of Chicago were
now, only four years and one convention later, in the delegates' seats
in Miami.

I. F. STONE, 1972

But late in the decade everything seemed to come unhinged. The liberal
system just did not appear to work. At home, the great social reforms
seemed to have little impact.

JAMES MCGREGOR BURNS, 1972

Meanwhile, the billions of dollars spent as a result of the reform
legislation of the Truman, Kennedy, and Johnson years—on such items
as urban renewal, Medicare, the $60 billion highway construction
program, the War on Poverty, and aid to education—have made little
difference for the forgotten families living on less than $10,000 a
year. Administrators profited from these programs, politicians and consultants profited, construction firms profited, but the poor and the
nonaffluent did not.

JACK NEWFIELD AND JEFF GREENFIELD
A Populist Manifesto, 1972

[George McGovern] will appeal to the unrich, unpowerful and un-
privileged majority, and, therefore, he will be elected.

JOHN KENNETH GALBRAITH, 1972

III.

WHAT THE DATA SAY

Pity the plain folks. They work at dehumanized and boring jobs from which they bring home paychecks that are eroded by both inflation and heavy taxes to a point where it is harder than ever to make ends meet. Trying to hold on to this scrawny fistful of dollars, they are gulled into buying useless, shoddy goods and ill-performed services rendered by incompetents.

They live in look-alike homes in plastic and polluted communities. (If they are black they live in deteriorating slums.) Their children go to school, but they are neither cultured nor educated; in fact, they really can't even read too well. As a result of these horrendous conditions, it is no wonder that Americans are alienated and fed up.

Is it so? No.

The facts show something else: American workers are engaged in more interesting, more skilled and more productive work than any other workers at any other time or any other place—including America only a decade ago. They earn more real dollars that can buy more and better goods and services than any other people at any other time or in any other place—again including America a decade ago. They spend their money predominantly on useful, important and often creative goods and services. They live in homes that are the envy of men the world over. Their children go to college and if they cannot read, they fake it well enough to have somehow managed, among other things, to design and effectuate a distributive economy that is aped and envied by capitalist, socialist and communist societies around the globe, to send men to the moon, to create an agricultural technology that has averted starvation for billions of earthlings, and to develop and distribute medicines and sanitary procedures that have increased life expectancy by decades here and around the world. When asked what they think about their own lives they answer, typically, "Pretty good."

Here is what has been happening to plain folks in America.

CHAPTER 3

Worker's Lib (Occupation)

Today, more than *half* of working Americans are working at "white-collar jobs."[1] Beyond question, this ratio has never before existed in any society. Beyond question, too, is the fact that this movement toward white collarization has been misunderstood, misinterpreted and generally beaten near to death.

The huge gains in white-collar jobs have taken place because several separate trends, not all necessarily related, have been moving in the same direction at the same time.

The major trends toward the cerebralization and demanualization of American labor are:

1) The incredible decline of farming as an occupation.
2) The decline of women who work in other women's houses.
3) The decline of "common laborer" as major job description.
4) A stunning increase of professional and technical jobs.
5) A massive movement of women into the labor force.

Each of these trends tends to push or pull people from the lower paying forms of manual work toward white-collar or cerebral work. But at the same time, the *higher paying* blue-collar jobs have remained about as widespread, pervasive and powerful as ever, which is quite widespread, pervasive and powerful indeed. Moreover, there is substantial evidence that in many instances these skilled, blue-collar jobs are becoming more skilled, more pleasant and less physically demanding as the years go on —blurring the symbolic distinction between "blue collar" and "white collar" work. *In short, it is good jobs—regardless of collar color—that have increased enormously in recent years.*[2]

[1] The figure was 48.2% in 1970 and 42% in 1960. A rough extrapolation yields the 1974 "more than half" statement.

[2] A complete chart of changes in occupational distribution is presented on page 328 of "The Short Census" at the end of this volume.

* * *

Farmers

The drop in the number of farmers must be discussed first. For the 1970 Census is the last one that will record a major drop in the incidence of American farmers. If many more leave the field—and the fields—by the 1980 Census, there won't be any left at all, an unlikely situation given the generally acknowledged human propensity toward eating.

At the turn of the century, fully *38%* of the American work force were "farmers," "farm managers," "farm laborers," and "farm foremen." By 1940, the percentage had dropped to *17%*. In 1950, the percentage was down to *12%*. In 1960, the percentage was only *8.3%*. And the 1970 census—incredibly—just about halved that percentage of Americans who till fields and raise livestock to just *4.3%* of the labor force!

The Case of the Fading Farmer is not unique to America. But it has happened here earlier and with a speed unheard of elsewhere. For example, the percentage of the labor force employed in agriculture in Russia is 33%; in France, 18%; in Germany, 11%; and in Japan, 24%.

It is in large measure because so few farmers till our soil that our food prices are as relatively low as they are. How's that for deadpan? Granted that to anyone who has recently passed through a supermarket checkout counter, that may sound like the statement of an idiot. It is not. The percentage of family income spent on food in selected countries looks like this:

EXPENDITURE FOR FOOD AS PERCENTAGE OF TOTAL PRIVATE CONSUMPTION EXPENDITURES IN SELECTED COUNTRIES

United States	18%
Canada	19%
Australia	21%
United Kingdom	24%
Sweden	25%
Israel	26%
South Africa	27%
France	28%
Germany, Fed. Rep.	32%
Japan	35%
Italy	37%
China (Taiwan)	42%
Korea	47%
Poland	48%

(Based on United Nations data, 1968)

Moreover, viewed another way, it can also be seen that the percentage of disposable income spent on food in the United States has also *declined* over the years—from *25%* in the late 1940s, to *21%* in the late 1950s, to under 16% in the first three and one-half years of the 1970s. That is so despite much higher supermarket prices in recent years: The percentage of income spent on food *has gone down*.

Although American food feeds not only Americans but ever-growing hundreds of millions of others around the world, the job has been done by fewer and fewer farmers, farming larger and larger farms with bigger and bigger machines and making more money for their efforts.

Back in 1940, each farm worker provided enough food for *11* persons. By 1971, a farm worker was producing enough food for *39* persons! In the year 1900, there were *10.8* million farmers and farm workers. By 1960—with about two and one-half times as many people in America—there were about *4* million farmers and farm workers. In 1970—after the population had climbed to over 200 million—there were only *2.2* million farmers! In the last decade alone the average *size* of a farm has gone *up* by nearly a third—from 297 acres per farm to 394 acres per farm, and net income for a farm-operator family has gone from $5,101 in 1960 to $13,615 in 1972, and an estimated $17,050 (!) in 1973, a far faster percentage rise than the economy as a whole. With 1974 slated to be the first full year without federal acreage controls, the already apparent trend should be reinforced: the people who remain on farms are doing better than ever, thank you.

Maids

The other truly major decrease in a "major occupation" category has occurred among "female private household workers." Again, a long perspective may be useful: At the turn of the century *35%* (!) of all working women were employed as maids, servants, nannies, cooks, housekeepers and laundresses—working in someone else's house. By 1950, that rate had tumbled down to 8.5%. In the decade that followed, the rate seemed to flatten out, a decline to *7.8%* in 1960. But then the bottom fell out. In the decade of the 1960s, the *rate* was more than halved, going down to only *3.6%* of the female labor force in 1970. And while the total number of working women rose by 8 million, the absolute number of female domestic workers plummeted from 1.65 million to 1.05 million[3] over the decade.

Hardly any farmers, hardly any maids.

[3] About half were black, half white.

Unskilled Workers

One other general category of manual work has shown somewhat thinner ranks in recent years: the so-called "unskilled laborers." At the turn of the century *15%* of the male work force was composed of "unskilled" laborers while somewhat smaller percentages were "semiskilled" (10%) and "skilled" (13%). By the time the 1960 census was taken these ratios had turned upside down. The percentages of unskilled laborers had been *halved* (7%) while semiskilled laborers (19%) and skilled craftsmen (20%) had almost *doubled*. By 1970 these curves had all flattened out. The percentage of semiskilled and skilled workers remained roughly the same at 18% and 20% respectively. The percentage of unskilled laborers continued to decline—from 7.2% in 1960 to 6.1% in 1970—but the decline was somewhat slower.

The farmer syndrome is again apparent: if the decline continues, there aren't going to be any left at all, which is dubious considering some of the vital tasks that are performed under the rubric of "unskilled": garbage collectors, fishermen and oystermen, animal caretakers (except farm), longshoremen, stevedores, etc.

Hardly any poor farmers, hardly any maids, very few unskilled laborers: 4%, 3.4%, 6.1%.

Yet, the labor force has expanded monumentally in recent years—from 64.5 million in 1960 to 77.3 million in 1970. If there were fewer poor dirt farmers, fewer servants and fewer unskilled laborers—where did the jobs go?

Professional and Technical

The most striking increase occurred in the "professional, technical and kindred workers" field. This is not to say that the maids became social workers or the dirt farmers became physicians. They didn't. But maids and farmers likely became "operatives" or "service workers," "clerical workers" or "craftsmen," while some of those—or their recently college-graduated children—move into the professional and technical realm, if not as physicists, then perhaps as dental hygienists or landscape architects.

In 1950, there were *4.92 million* professional and technical workers in America. By 1960, the number had gone to *6.98 million.* And the 1970 census showed *10.82 million* such workers.

What do these almost eleven million Americans do?

Some are in brand-new fields. In 1960, there were only 12,363 "computer specialists" in America. By 1970, that number had grown to 258,215. That represents a more-than-2,000% increase in a decade. Others are in more traditional fields, but ones that have grown with particular speed in the last decade. In 1960, there were 27,697 professional "airplane pilots" (including 173 women). By 1970, there were 52,028 pilots (including 733 women)—about a 100% increase. America has also been blessed with a roughly 150% increase in "public relations men and publicity writers" from 31,141 in 1960, soaring to 75,598 in 1970. Run that one up the flagpole.

Beyond these are the staples of the professional-technical community: 1.2 million engineers, 205,000 scientists, just over half a million physicians and dentists, almost a million nurses, 275,000 social workers, almost half a million college and university teachers (up from about 200,000 in 1960!) and the granddaddy field, teaching (exclusive of colleges and universities)—2,774,797, *up by just about a million* over the decade.

In all, 10.82 million professional and technical workers making up 14% of the labor force versus *11%* in 1960 and *4%* in 1900. An enormous gain? Yes. A testament to the fact of massed phalanxes of Americans moving into the "best" jobs? Yes. The cause of America being the first majority white-collar nation? No.

Working Women

The biggest cause of white collarization is due to quite another factor: women.

For women in recent decades have been much more likely to be working in white-collar jobs than men. In 1940, the percentage of women at work in white-collar occupations was 45% while the comparable figure for men was 31%. Twenty years later, in 1960, more than half (54%) of the working women were in white-collar jobs while only 35% of men were comparably employed. And in 1970, the white-collar rates were 58% for women and 38% for men—the largest gap yet recorded.[4]

That women are at increasingly high *rates* engaged in white-collar work is not the only reason for a white-collar America. But when one combines that with a new and major fact—that women in starkly increased *numbers* are seeking and getting jobs—then one has the makings of an authentically new and different situation in America. It is a situation that has enormous economic, social and political implications—mostly salutary—some of which have already become apparent, and some of which will not become apparent for many years.

[4] Back in 1900, when a huge percentage of women were working in private households, the "white collar" rates for the sexes *were identical*—18%.

The raw numbers of women in the American labor force:

1940	13.0 million
1950	16.6 million
1960	22.4 million
1970	30.8 million

Of course the *numbers* should be expected to go up—America's total population went up. But observe the *percentage* of adult women who now work:

1940	26%
1950	29%
1960	35%
1970	40%
1972	44%
1973	45%

Women coming into the labor force have disproportionately gone into these major occupational fields: "professional," "clerical" and "service."

Although one would never guess it from the recent Women's Lib rhetoric, a greater percentage of women than men are actually in the professional, technical and kindred" category: 14.8% vs. 13.5%. There were 4.3 million such women in 1970 compared to 2.7 million in 1960— a 59% increase. The two biggest specific occupations for women were "nurses" (819,000) and teachers (2.1 million in both college and non-college slots).

The greatest preponderance of working women is in the clerical and kindred field, 33%[5] in 1970 versus 29% in 1960, comprising a stunning gain in raw numbers from 6.2 million to 9.6 million. It is mostly this gain of 3.4 million that has accounted for the fact that we are now a 50% white-collar society. These clerical jobs cover a broad range of jobs: bank tellers, billing clerks, enumerators,[6] interviewers, proofreaders and the really big ones: secretaries (2.7 million), bookkeepers (1.3 million), typists (957,000), cashiers (728,000), office machine operators (423,-000), telephone operators (397,000) and file clerks (308,000).

How good—or bad—are these women's clerical jobs? They have become—by chance—the focus of some important recent discussions. For example, by aggregating these clerical white-collar jobs along with professional, technical and managerial jobs, the social commentator Peter Drucker has stated that half of the American labor force is now made

[5] Versus only 7% for men.

[6] Yes, the census counts temporary Census employees employed in the taking of the census—about 180,000 in 1970.

up of something called "knowledge workers"—and that this represents a great "discontinuity" with the past. This is an overstatement; it is hard to make a case that file clerks and typists are "knowledge workers" with the glamorous electronic/cerebral/technological connotation that normally goes with that phrase.

On the other hand many Women's Liberationists tend to view these jobs as little better than the "shit work"[7] they left behind at home. Why, they ask, aren't women corporation presidents, doctors, lawyers, etc.?[8]

Well, the data shows that a clerical job is a long way from shit work, no matter how you measure it. Consider where it stands on the job ladder: The median wage of female private household workers in 1970 was (incredibly) $1,792 for women who worked 50–52 weeks. This obviously reflects the fact that many domestics do not work *full* weeks although they work *every* week. But it also reflects the fact that domestic work is just about at the bottom of the wage scale—in fact, until mid-1974 such work was not even covered by federal minimum wage laws.

A higher level of occupational category than household worker and with sizable numbers of working females is the "operatives" classification. These are women who work as assemblers, checkers, laundry and dry-cleaning operatives, packers and wrappers, punch and stamping press operatives, knitters, loopers, toppers, spinners, twisters, winders (in the textile industry), etc. The jobs are often situated in a factory or plant. These women averaged $4,432 per year in 1970.

By contrast the clerical field median earnings were $5,636 (again, including part-time but every-week earners), not a fortune by any means, but at least a few rungs up the financial ladder. The jobs are frequently situated in office rather than factory surroundings; the labor is usually not physically demanding; and, at least, in the most common single occupation within the category (secretary) not repetitive to a point of sheer boredom.

Finally, there has been a rise in the number and percentage of female service workers. There were almost 3 million in 1960 and almost 4½ million in 1970, making up 15% of the working women. Who are they? A mixed bag ranging from the glamorous to the tedious. They are not regarded officially as "white collar workers" but some are in those sort of jobs: airline stewardesses (32,000, up from 10,000 in a decade), dental assistants (89,000, up from 48,000), hairdressers and cosmetologists

---

[7] In the words of the poet Marge Piercy.

[8] Some of them are, and in increasing numbers and percentages from 1960 to 1970: Physicians, dentists, etc., up from 27.7 thousand to 46.3 thousand in the decade; lawyers up from 5 thousand to 12.5 thousand; accountants up from 81.8 thousand to 186.8 thousand; engineering and science technicians up from 55.8 thousand to 92.1 thousand. Still, in these "Tiffany" fields, although they are far more prominent than before, women remain far behind men in terms of total participation rates.

(434,000, up from 272,000), and cooks (548,000, up from 385,000). Service workers are not usually thought of as heavy-duty manual workers, but there were 628,000 "cleaning service workers" including chambermaids, charwomen, cleaners and janitors, who surely work as hard with their hands and bodies as do many male day laborers.

* * *

Good or Bad?

In all, what have the various trends that have produced the white collarization of the American labor force yielded in the way of net gain or loss to people who work for a living in America? Is it better than what it replaces?

One by one, it looks something like this:

The decline in the number of farmers, despite the heart-wrenching pathos of men driven from the land they and their fathers have tilled, is to some large degree a plus for the society. It is, for the most part, the poorer and smaller farmers who have left farming. Working less fertile, less productive land, laboring without the requisite machinery, straining to make ends meet by working from dawn to late evening, the farmers-who-leave have in a simple, if harsh, word become "diseconomic." The goods they produce can be produced less expensively by others, with a net gain to consumers.

Often, too, the farmers who "leave" are elderly farmers who retire and—in the absence of a son who feels he can make a living off the old farm—sells his acreage to a larger farm nearby. The retired farmer frequently does not physically leave his place; he stays on in the farmhouse, living—like many of the elderly in America—on social security checks and whatever other income or savings he has managed to accumulate over the years plus the pay-out received from selling his land and machinery. He has become, in census language, "rural non-farm."

When the farmers-who-leave are not elderly, they also often stay put, changing their occupation and often commuting to a nearby town or factory for employment. Despite the massive exodus from the *job* of "farmer" the total population of rural America has remained roughly stable at 54 million since 1950.

Three traditionally poor rural areas have lost population: Appalachia, the black belt of the South, and the Mississippi River counties stretching from southern Illinois to mid-Louisiana. One wealthier—but sparsely populated—rural area, the wheat states of the Dakotas, Kansas, Nebraska, Iowa and the Texas Panhandle, has also seen a net population drain. On the other hand, relatively well-to-do rural areas in Ohio, Indiana, Illinois,

Wisconsin and New York have actually experienced modest population growth.

Altogether, although the number of Americans living in the "rural farm" situation has diminished, the number of Americans living in "rural non-farm" circumstances has actually increased.

But what, then, of those who have left both Agraria and Ruralia?—left farming and left the farmhouse? For although *total* rural population has not declined in two decades, neither has it grown during an era when high birth rates and attendant natural increase of the population has increased total *national* population by large amounts. There has been, then, a steady out-migration from rural areas.

It is a difficult statistical feat to track down what happens to Americans ex-farm. Some ex-rural Appalachian whites can be seen in "hillbilly slums" in Cincinnati, Chicago and other American cities. Some ex-rural Black Belt sharecroppers are visible in America's urban slums. But that's about as far as it goes. For the most part the Former Farmers have statistically disappeared. Very rapidly, they are "lost" in cities and suburbs all over America. With mechanical skills gained from farm experience they fit easily into craftsmen and operative jobs; their sons and daughters graduate from high school and many of them go on to college; they graduate and become computer specialists or airline pilots or real estate salesmen, wholly indistinguishable from the rest of America.

Is all this better than what it replaces? Yes. For all its fabled charms, there is this to remember about rural America: It was, and to a lesser extent still is, the disproportionate home of American poverty. In 1960, 30% of all Americans lived in Ruralia, but rural residents comprised 45% of those "in poverty." In 1970, the percentage of Americans living in rural areas had declined to 27%—and rural residents made up 36% of those in poverty (despite the fact that the "poverty line" is lower for Ruralians[9]).

There is a tendency to romanticize rural life: a pollution-free, pressure-free, population-free area of natural beauty, etc.

There is surely some validity to that view—for those in rural areas who can benefit from its inherent qualities without sharing in much of rural misery. But life in a rural area can also be life in a southern tar-paper shack, and in a shanty with no plumbing in an Appalachian hollow. The shake-out in rural America in recent decades has tended unceremoniously—sometimes cruelly—to push out folk who shared rural Agraria's stark poverty as well as its fabled peacefulness. When viewed statistically, the move they make—either to nonfarm jobs in rural areas,

[9] The "poverty line" was $3,195 for a four-person farm family versus $3,743 for a four-person nonfarm family (in 1970).

or to a whole new life in an urban or suburban area—is very much a plus.[10]

No such statistical extrapolations are needed to make the case that the disappearance of hundreds of thousands of maids jobs is a plus for society. These are often rotten jobs: ill paid, hard, dirty, insecure and sometimes demeaning. That about a third of these jobs have disappeared in a decade —a net loss of 600,000 and a halving of the rate down to a minuscule 3.6%—is surely a gain for the former domestics who, statistically speaking have found clerical jobs. They earn more money, work more regular hours, in more pleasant surroundings, with some chance of advancement, with vacation pay, sick leave, pension plans, and so on.

What about the other side of the coin?

The case can be made—with some validity—that domestic work *should not* be regarded as demeaning; that taking care of children, cooking, running a home may be more creative and more meaningful than running a key-punch machine; that domestic workers ought to get pay raises, vacation pay, sick leave, etc.; that the advent of vacuum cleaners, dishwashers, washing machines and dryers has de-physicalized much of the domestic work. This can be—often is—a persuasive case to all but one group of Americans: the domestics themselves. They want out, and out they're going. If one believes that personal options spell freedom and that an increase of freedom among all classes is the hallmark of a successful egalitarian society then the verdict is clear. The wholesale abandonment of private household service as an occupational way of life must be regarded as a wholesale plus for those who take advantage of new options to improve their lot as they themselves perceive it.

But what about the suburban matron? What about *her* options? Haven't they been decreased? Isn't it harder for her to get a job if she can't get a maid to clean the house? Isn't it harder for her to do volunteer community work if she's pinned down to the routine of housework day after day after day?

Probably so, but with some very important qualifiers that must be mentioned.

First, domestic workers, while harder to find, are not usually impossible to find. There are still a million of them, and typically they may be working in anywhere from two to five different dwellings per week.

Second, the revolution in household technology has benefited not only maids, but women who can't afford, or can't get, maids. Vacuum cleaners,

[10] Nor has "the corporate farm" taken over Agraria, farm-lobby rhetoric notwithstanding. The most recent Census of Agriculture (1969) shows less than 9% of the farm acreage owned corporately. Viewed as a percentage of value of farm products sold, corporate sales run 14% and only about one fifth of that represents sales by corporations with ten or more shareholders. In short: The family farm lives.

dishwashers, washing machines and dryers are rapidly becoming a way of life not only for domestics but for non-domestics.

Surely, it is more convenient for a housewife to have a maid or a laundress take care of the dirty clothes, but barring that, a home washing machine and a dryer beat the hell out of clothespins and a scrubbing board, or even a laundromat at the shopping center.

Third, the difficulty and/or expense of getting domestic help unquestionably influences a change in life style that tends to help cope with the problem. Three examples come to mind: American women are having far fewer children today; American mothers are far more likely to be sending their children to nursery schools and kindergarten; American families are far more likely to live in apartments or mobile homes—at least for a few years. There are, of course, many disparate reasons for each of these developments. But smaller dwellings, fewer children and fewer-children-at-home also happen to be a rational response to a situation in which a wife and mother finds it difficult to get household help.

Finally, as Herman Kahn has pointed out, it should be acknowledged that the passing of the inexpensive domestic worker has indeed caused a decline in gracious living among the upper-middle income folk who used to have no trouble hiring household help. That may be one of the reasons the elite feel everything's getting worse, when in reality most things are getting better. But that process was set in motion with the Fourteenth Amendment. Very few of us live in the manner of slaveholder Thomas Jefferson. If that's a loss, so be it.

The decline of jobs in the "unskilled labor" category must also be counted as a plus for society as a whole—and with not even the caveats accorded to the shift away from female domestic labor. The major declines by specific occupation have come among construction laborers, "lumbermen, raftsmen, woodchoppers" and "vehicle washers."[11] But these declines have not come about at the expense of new buildings, lack of wood or the decline of clean cars. Rather, in each instance, many men working by their muscles at relatively low wages have been replaced by fewer men, often more skilled, operating machines based on new technology. Automatic car-washing emporia, power saws and remarkably flexible cranes and bulldozers have to some degree replaced sweating men with hoses and rags, ax wielders, and men with picks, shovels and wheelbarrows. The men "replaced" have not been unemployed or underemployed or dumped on the industrial slag heap. As shall be seen in a moment, the displaced workers have generally gone on to more

[11] Down, respectively 20%, 33%, 20%, from 1960 to 1970; there were 797,000 construction workers recorded at the time the 1960 Census was taken and only 638,000 in 1970, while the total labor force was going up.

highly skilled, better paid work. The ex-pick and shovel man may well
be found today in the air-conditioned cab of a bulldozer. And that is
progress.

*That the percentage of both men and women engaged in "professional,
technical and kindred" occupations has climbed sharply in a steady progression this century must also be regarded as a clear plus.* Ours is a society that highly regards physicians (up in a decade from 233,000 to 282,
000), engineers (up from 871,000 to 1.23 million), social scientists (up
from 42,000 to 110,000), librarians (up from 76,000 to 124,000), teachers, nurses, public relations men and publicity writers (quantified earlier).
These, by and large, are the jobs that most American parents wish that
their children would aspire to. In the course of a single decade the numbers of such jobs have increased from 7.08 million to 11.2 million—an increase of well more than half while the labor force was increasing by a
little bit over a quarter.

A disproportionate share of these new prof-techs are young people—
21% of the 25–29 age group are so employed compared to only 12%
for those aged 50–59. Considering that the rhetoric of the revolutionary
Sixties told us that young people were engaged in a massive greening, a
dropping out, a lurching toward commune-style basket weaving and
sandal making between spasms of organic farming—the numbers of young
college graduates opting into the establishment are positively astonishing.
A great many of these young people are (shudder) working for Big Corporations, Big Law Firms, Big Government, Big etc., although all the rhetoric told us that those days were going forever. Apparently not. The dropout rate is statistically undiscernible: For example, in 1960, among the
male 25–29 age group, 77% were employed full time. In 1970, the figure
was 76%—about the same. In point of fact, because of a tightening job
market caused in part by the harvesting of B.A.s from the Baby Boom, an
interesting social phenomenon can be observed by the discerning. The
same young men and women who were once hounding corporate recruiters
away from college campuses are today often to be seen sitting politely
and well shorn in corporate waiting rooms thinking how to say what the
man who will be conducting the interview wants to hear.

As might have been predicted, young American college graduates have
been socialized and, with some relatively few exceptions, are actively pursuing pelf and prestige—allegedly scorned. They do this for most of the
same reasons the rest of us do: money, status and—as they become
adults and parents—to assure the ongoing ability to acquire for themselves and their progeny those goods and services they had come to appre-
ciate while growing up to be young revolutionaries—good food, travel, a
decent safe home, good schools, orthodontics, a vacation retreat and so
on. No doubt when they reach thirty-five they will look in the mirror and

ask again, "What is the meaning of life?", receive no satisfactory answer, buy a cabin cruiser, chase a chick, or find a lover, have an identity crisis, and plod onward, trapped—as people are—in a web of birth, school, love, work, family, aging and death. Living is a tough racket and it gets tougher, not easier, if you also have to fight disease and malnourishment while making sandals in a commune. So, after all the revolutionary razzmatazz, young elite America has gone to work. Well-schooled, cocksure and ambitious, the chances seem excellent that as they learn that arrogance and ignorance are twins, they will make useful and productive citizens in the years to come. If they are perhaps not "the best generation ever produced," a tribute they were quite fond of for a while, they are still probably pretty good. After all, like the man said, these are our children.

How does one weigh the striking entry of women into the labor force? From the point of view of those who have been complaining loudest about the oppressed role of women in American society it is surely an unmitigated bonanza. The Women's Liberationists have banged the drum loudly proclaiming that meaningful work in the money economy is the ticket to female salvation. By those lights, the progression of the rate of women in the labor force, particularly the extremely sharp rise in rates among women whose children have left home, should be celebrated by all. In 1940, for example, among women aged 35–44, just 27% were in the labor force. By 1970, the figure for that age group had climbed to 50%. Over the same thirty-year time span, among women somewhat older (45–64) the rate in the labor force went up even more sharply: from 20% to 48%!

In Women Liberationist terms, then, the trend is clean, clear and beneficial. But while the Women's Lib ideologues have always laid claim to the mantle of "speaking for women" there is—in the present instance as in many others—clear evidence that they don't. In mid-1970, Gallup interviewers asked women if they wished they had a job outside their home. Of those women who were not working *61% said they did not.* An additional 29% said they'd like only *a part-time job.*

So then, there is at least valid suspicion that as Women's Lib goes so goes not American womanhood. American women—many, many of them —feel that wives at work are not the best of all possible circumstances and can, in fact, cause detrimental side effects, side effects that are particularly harmful to family life.

Is the strong trend toward working women, then, a plus or a minus? Is it better than what it replaces?

It is a plus, we believe. It is better than what it replaces.

What women in America today really have that they did not have a decade or two ago is not *jobs,* but *the option to get a job.* There is a big difference. A situation where women are forced to work, or pushed into working, can surely be of debatable value. In an earlier era, women who had to work could go to work as domestics, seamstresses, sweatshop garment workers, teachers, or hang up a sign saying "Piano Given"—or starve. Today, the great increase in the women's labor force is among women who don't *have* to work, but *opt* to work—and that is another matter entirely. Furthermore, the surest determinant of an American family above the median income level is when that family has *more than one earner*. Women working today at a far wider range of jobs—as secretaries, computer programmers, key-punch operators and social workers—are bringing home money that is buying a camper trailer, a snowmobile, a vacation home, a college education for the children, a trip to Europe, or maybe just better food, clothing and shelter for the family. They are working not necessarily because they have bought the Lib line that a housewife is a woman in chains, but because they have determined that the benefits gained from working outweigh whatever problems a job brings with it. They are typically bringing home "discretionary income," not stave-off-penury money . . . and there is quite a difference.

It is quite true that it is rare to find women holding the top jobs in our society. While there have been some breakthroughs in recent years, few major corporations are headed by females, most of the leading doctors and scientists are men, and there are presently no women in the Senate or on the Supreme Court. However, just beneath that level—and pervading the entire occupational structure—women have come into the labor force and gone up the occupational ladder: out of domestic jobs into clerical jobs, out of college and into professional-technical jobs.

Whether it is "self-worth" or "prestige" or "money for extras" or "money for new needs" that brings them into the labor force is almost irrelevant. The increasing number of women who make the choice to work now feel—for one reason or another—that it's worth it. If it's good enough for them, it's good enough for us. It's good.

* * *

Beyond these changes in occupational distribution as described in decennial Census tables, there is another massive change that has been proceeding over the years, but which is almost impossible to measure. This concerns the *changing nature of work within specific occupations*.

This development can be seen perhaps most clearly within the major blue-collar categories not discussed so far: "craftsmen, foremen and kindred workers" ("skilled") and "operatives" ("semiskilled"). These two groups make up close to 40% of the male labor force in America, and their proportion in the male labor force has remained about constant since 1950. Despite the lack of soaring percentages, the actual *numbers* of skilled and semiskilled male blue-collar workers climbed by 1.5 million over the decade—nothing to sneeze at. The greatest share of this addition, about 840,000, came in the most highly skilled category: "craftsmen, foremen and kindred workers." Also not worth a sneeze is the fact that today—after all the talk of computers, scientists and white-collar knowledge workers—most *men* in the American labor force are *not* white-collar workers and surely not "knowledge workers." In America, in 1970, among males, there were 9.5 million "craftsmen, foremen, etc."—and 6.5 million professional, technical, etc. The majority of American *men* still work with their hands.[12]

What kind of work do they do now with their hands?

Often a different kind of work—as can be seen by running through some of the blue-collar jobs.

The carpenter is cutting boards with a power saw, not a handsaw. Painters are painting with rollers and spray guns, not with brushes. Garage workers are taking the lugs off your flat tire with a power wrench. Miners (many of them) are working above the ground in enormous steam shovels, not below the ground in dangerous dust-filled pits. Truck drivers are driving their loads over new interstate highways in air-conditioned cabs, which is very different from driving on old Route 30, particularly in August. (And farmers milk cows by throwing a switch, while retail clerks at Sears operate the dazzling computers that have replaced cash registers.)

In short, in many instances, the same jobs have become power-assisted, more skilled, easier, safer and/or more pleasant.

There has been a great deal of talk in America about a "new class." Be it Drucker's discontinuous "knowledge workers" or Louis Harris' nouveau elite "constituency of change," such formulations often ignore a central fact of our time. It is this: The "new class" is for the most part the old class with bells and spangles. The people in the professional-technical-knowledge worker categories aren't brand-new discontinuous, change-

---

[12] Which is one reason why the oft-proclaimed swan song of the American labor movement never seems to come about. Labor union membership in America, non-white-collar labor union membership at that, is *up* in America, *not down* as often reported. There were 15.92 million nonwhite-collar union members in 1960, and 17.39 million in 1970. Preliminary data for 1972 has the figure up again slightly, to 17.43 million. Another reason that labor unions aren't going to wither away is that white-collar workers are unionizing. There were 2.19 million unionized white-collar workers in 1960—and about 3.4 million in 1972. That is a 55% increase. What this demonstrates is a simple idea: Workers these days tend to organize. When there are lots of blue-collar workers, they'll organize—as automobile workers and plumbers organized. When there are lots of white-collar workers, they'll organize—as teachers and government workers organized and are gaining new strength now. In short, as Gus Tyler has written, "the future of unions is in the nature of man." Over the decade of the Sixties union membership as a percentage of the total labor force remained about constant (23%) despite the influx of so many women and teen-agers, disproportionately nonunion, into the labor force. As white-collar workers unionize, this percentage may increase in the years to come.

oriented creatures simply because Mr. Jones is now an airline pilot, not a bus driver, and because Mr. Smith is now an engineer, not a mechanic. They've got better jobs, but they still don't like crisscross school busing or college disruptions; as we shall see later in this volume. What such formulations also ignore is that the statistical "old class" also has new bells and spangles, that is, most of the perequisites of the old middle class: more money, good working conditions, less backbreaking work, more interesting work and as we shall now see, leisure time.

* * *

CHAPTER 4

Worker's Lib (Fringe Benefits)

Beyond the changes of who works at what kind of job, there is an entirely separate, yet massive, change that has occurred amid all the rhetoric of blue-collar blues and white-collar woes. America's working men spend less of their time working than ever before: fewer years in a lifetime, fewer weeks in a year, fewer hours in a day. For these glories, Americans can thank Big: thank Big Government (for Social Security) and thank Big Labor (for vacations with pay and shorter hours), and, even, thank Big Business (which goes along with social change when it has to, sometimes even initiates it, but most importantly provides the technical and managerial miracles that provide the revenue and productivity to let government and labor do their thing).

Fewer years in a lifetime: There has been a steady decline in this century in the rate of men at work in the *youngest* and *oldest* age brackets. In most other societies the process of ending child and teen-age labor and extending school years on the one hand and providing for old-age retirement on the other is known by a simple word: progress. In America, as this process has gone on, a lengthier rhetoric has developed: When the elderly retire they are "thrown on the scrap heap." And when youngsters graduate from high school and go on to college, people as disparate as Spiro Agnew and John Gardner alike have wondered why all those millions of new college students don't stick to vocational education and stop cluttering up the cloistered ivy halls.

Not for the first time, we note the uncanny substitution of the thought "failure" for its close cousin, "success." That people over sixty-five—and many under sixty-five—are retiring in America is not scrap-heapism. In 1950, among men over the age of sixty-five, more than four in ten (*41%*) were still in the labor force. By 1960, the rate had fallen to *31%*. And in 1970 it was down to *25%*.

During the last dozen-or-so years for which data is available, the percentage of Americans over sixty-five who lived in poverty was going down sharply: In 1959, more than a third (35%) of the elderly were in poverty, and by 1971, the rate had dropped to 22% and by 1972, down to 19%—still the highest share of any age bracket in poverty, but shrinking rapidly. This would tend to mitigate at least against the economic side of the scrap-heap argument. The retired elderly are increasingly going into retirement, not into poverty. This has happened in large measure due to truly dramatic increases in Social Security payments since 1960. With the passage of a major Social Security increase in 1973[1] the decrease of the number of elderly poor will continue.

What about the psychological side of the scrap-heapism? What about the elderly who don't know what to do with their time after they have been pushed out of the job market by mandatory retirement and by anti-elderly employment policies?

It is a problem, no question about it, and a serious one in many instances. But it should not be compared in magnitude to the problem it replaces, which was called Dying in the Traces.

It is one thing for a restless man to prowl around the house in search of activity in the face of a limited income and limited interests. That is an unfortunate human situation. So too, often, is the situation for the elderly who live in nursing homes. But it is another thing, of course, when retirement works well. There is no way to quantify it, of course, but a stroll through Miami Beach or the California or Arizona retirement communities shows plenty of happy faces. And there are millions of elderly Americans who retire in their home community, indeed in their same house, and lead rewarding and interesting golden years—in fact by far the great majority of Americans stay put when they retire.[2]

But neither bad-retirement nor good-retirement is really comparable to the situation where a sixty-five-year-old man—or a seventy-five-year-old man—a healthy man—or an unhealthy man—*must* work or else not have the wherewithal to survive. Before the advent of Social Security, before the large-scale growth of union and private company pension plans, most Americans, simply put, worked until they died. Before the advent of Medicare in 1966, those whose health failed were likely to be "a burden on

---

[1] Maximum benefits for a retired couple are now $456 (as of July 1974); typical benefits are $310. Back in 1960, the maximum benefit was $180, and the typical benefit was $124. Social Security benefits went up about 150% compared to a rise in the cost of living of about 50%. In addition, the advent of Medicare, valued typically at $575 per person per year by the Social Security Administration, has helped lift a fearful burden from elderly shoulders all over America.

[2] If you look at the numbers it's hard to figure out at first just who is crowding into Arizona and Florida. In 1970, among Americans aged sixty and over, 72% lived in the same house they lived in five years before and 87% lived in the same county—a vast majority. But the missing 13% represented 3.7 million persons, which is still a lot of out-of-county elderly relocators.

their children" or on the community at large. For many senior citizens this was—literally—a fate worse than death. So too was the route of public support, "over the hill to the poor farm" as the saying went. Today the children—everybody's children through federal, state and municipal taxes as well as through the cost of goods and services—are still "supporting" the elderly. But the method of transfer of funds has become largely destigmatized: Social Security, Medicare and pensions are viewed as "earned," even though to some degree financed now from current—not past—revenues. And middle-aged Americans grumble about high taxes, but not about how their own aged parents are draining their earnings just when they need the cash to finance their own kids through college. That's a comparatively benign grumble. Neither aged-on-welfare nor aged-as-a-burden-on-their-children have disappeared, of course, but, clearly, the scope of the problem has been minimized. In its stead have come other problems—what to do with retirement?—how to guarantee private pensions that have sometimes turned out to be cruel hoaxes?—but these are clearly of a lesser magnitude. *Again:* It is better by far than what it replaces. The new problems are the side effects of success, not the fruit of failure.

Weeks Worked: Americans not only work fewer years in a lifetime, but fewer weeks in a year. The increase—yes, explosion—in vacation time has been dramatic in the last three decades. Before that, paid vacations, particularly among blue-collar workers, were rare. The general not-so-generous practice was to provide production workers with "time off without pay." Such was the conclusion of studies made in the mid-1940s by the Bureau of Labor Statistics and the National War Labor Board.

But in 1949, the beginning of the postwar economy, 61% of American workingmen got *two* weeks of paid vacation time, after having achieved maximum seniority on the job.[3]

By 1966–67, less than twenty years later, 72% of workers received more than *four* weeks paid vacation.

And by 1972, fully 87% of American workers received more than *four* weeks vacation. (More than a third—35%—were getting five to five and a half weeks and 6% were getting more than six weeks.)

As an added fillip to the diminished working year, the number of paid holidays has also increased. In 1950, six paid holidays were typical. By the mid-1960s, more than 60% of American workers got either eight or nine of more than nine paid holidays. By 1972, the rate was up again: 83% received eight or more paid holidays. Moreover, because of new federal legislation, many of these holidays were mandated to fall on Mondays or Fridays, creating long weekend possibilities.

[3] Based on Bureau of Labor Statistics data covering virtually all labor agreements dealing with 1,000 workers or more.

In all, about *three weeks* of paid vacation time has been *added* for the American worker over the last two decades.

A worker with *five* weeks off has options available that simply don't exist for workers with *two* weeks off. If hard pressed financially, he can likely get a full or part-time job. If he wants to fix and paint the house, the time is there. And if he wants to travel cross-country with wife, kids and camper trailer—he can do that, gas permitting. Of course, all those extra people on the road and in the national parks are going to make it somewhat more crowded for those in the upper middle-class who used to be able to see the parks in somewhat lonely splendor. Hence: the "things-are-getting-terrible" wing of the ecology movement, a new shorthand for aristocrats and would-be aristocrats to condemn their boorish inferiors for poaching on the lord's hunting preserve.

Hours Worked: Not as dramatic a recent shift as is evidenced in either "years worked" or "weeks worked," but, still, movement. In 1947, according to Bureau of Labor Statistics figures, the average number of hours worked by "production or nonsupervisory workers" was 40.3 hours per week. By 1957, the rate had fallen to 38.8 hours per week. In 1967, the rate was 38.0 hours. And in 1970, it was 37.0 hours.

A slow trend, but a trend. The 8-hour standard day has changed to a 7½-hour standard day.[4] The man who used to get home at 6 P.M. arrives home at 5:30 P.M. Not a massive change, but a change.

Days Worked: Another nonmassive change, this one apparently slightly negative, occurred over the decade. Base unemployment rates went up. Nixon administration economists argued that the 4% unemployment figure—often regarded as a "full employment" standard that accounted for voluntary job switching and other noncatastrophic factors—was no longer a valid guideline. The changing nature of the labor force—specifically more women working and more teen-agers working—was automatically inflating unemployment figures, the Nixoconomists claimed. Teen-agers and women always have had higher unemployment rates, the economists reasoned, and if you add substantial quantities of these groups into the labor force mix, then unemployment rates will rise even though no group has a higher rate than previously. Accordingly, they said, that even in boom years, unemployment couldn't go down to 4%—and it didn't. The 1973 rate was 4.9%, with only one month as low as 4.6%.

There is good data to back up a good portion of the Administration's factual claims. Women aged 25–54 and young people of both sexes (aged 16–24) made up *21%* of the labor force in 1950—and *44%* in 1970. A careful study by the Bureau of Labor Statistics shows that about 0.5% of the current unemployment rate is indeed caused by demographic

---

[4] In 1909, production workers put in an average of fifty-one hours a week—a ten-hour day for five days, or about eight hours on a six-day-a-week basis.

changes, which would account for much (not all) of the somewhat higher rates. But what the Administration argument does not answer is this question: Given the structural reasons for a climb in unemployment rates, why don't they attempt to do something about it other than explain the phenomenon? Where are the expanded youth-training programs; where are the woman-training programs; where, particularly, is the government-employer-of-the-last-resort programs to cope with the neatly measured problem?

In all, in 1973, there were about 4.3 million unemployed workers. Had the unemployment rate been 4% rather than 4.9%, then 801,000 more Americans (out of a labor force of about 89 million) would have been working at any given time. These extra unemployed are disproportionately young people who generally switch jobs often anyway, and women who are disproportionately part-time workers. Unemployment rates for household heads have not generally increased. Moreover, unemployment insurance benefits have increased moderately: from $33 a week on the average in 1960 to $56 in 1972.

That, generally, is the magnitude of the changes in the unemployment picture through 1973: quite important but not monumental.

Beyond these might also be counted the "discouraged workers," i.e., those who aren't even looking for work, because they are convinced they couldn't find work even if they tried. Unemployment data have been periodically attacked for not taking into account these turned-off workers in the calculation of unemployment rates. A Department of Labor survey in 1971 (a recessionary year) showed that 774,000 Americans felt that way —less than 1% of the labor force.

* * *

In the early 1960s—remember those good old days?—a new cliché had its brief run in the sun. In the wake of that curse-blessing "automation," we were told that work would become increasingly irrelevant as the years went on, that unemployment would rise because automated machines would take away jobs and that "we would have to train our children to use leisure creatively," because "leisure" would be replacing "work."

A decade went by, and a new cliché emerged: Work, we were told, was "dehumanized, monotonous, boring." A workers' lib movement was a-borning.[5]

Not for a change, the alarmists were mostly wrong. Unemployment went down from the high 1960 recessionary levels as industry became ever more automated. A greater percentage of women entered the labor

---

[5] Died in stillbirth, because its role is performed quite adequately by an already extant, hard-nose, successful organization: the labor union.

force. And work, insofar as it can be quantitatively gauged, is less routinized, less monotonous, less dehumanized, less boring.

The flaw in the alarmist ointment of the early 1960s was that "needs" could be measured on an absolute scale, that there was just so much food, clothing and housing that was "needed" and that labor-saving automated machinery would provide for those needs with less man hours required. These views were right up to a point. Automation did increase productivity. But, then, families with one car found they needed two cars as they moved into suburbia. Families with one nice home found they needed a little vacation cottage. Families with children who graduated from high school found it was necessary to send them to college. "Needs" expanded.

The doomsayers of the early 1970s were also right to a point. The men who worked, and struck, the highly automated line at the new and controversial Chevrolet Vega plant in Lordstown, Ohio, were indeed doing hard, repetitive work. "Dehumanizing"—the buzz word—may be strong, but anyone who has seen an automobile assembly line work at top speed knows that it is tough work. But the significance of Lordstown is not that some auto workers are working at hard repetitive work. That has been going on at least since 1908 when Henry Ford started banging out Model Ts on something called an assembly line. Nor was the significance of the Lordstown strike that the strikers were apparently younger workers. There have been lots of auto strikes before, lots of strikes about speed-ups on the line (the big issue at Lordstown), and, as Leonard Woodcock of the United Autoworkers has pointed out, there are auto plants with younger work forces than Lordstown.

The significance of Lordstown is in who doesn't work there.

Lordstown, after all, is a new, highly automated assembly line that turns out about 100 new cars each hour, 1,600 each day and, incredibly, about 400,000 cars every year. In all, only 9,000 workers are employed there— each worker is turning out about 44 cars per year!

Lordstown is not typical of the automobile industry, but it is symbolic of it and many other industries dedicated to turning out mass-produced goods with ever more sophisticated machinery. Because of automated equipment, it takes fewer workers to produce a single equivalent unit than it did in previous years. This is true in farming, true in automobiles and true, too, in a service industry like telephone communications where one estimate has been made that if there were still telephone operators placing calls—*every woman in America* would have to be so employed to handle the current volume.

To produce the identical 400,000 Vegas in 1960, in an older style plant, General Motors would have had to employ more than 9,000 men. For the sake of argument, let us suppose the Lordstown plant—had it been around in 1960—would have required 10,500 men, one-sixth more, to produce the equivalent number of equivalent cars.

If that is so, then the key issue about Lordstown becomes *not* the allegedly dehumanizing conditions, *but what happened to the 1,500 men who don't work there?* Statistically speaking, the men who were *not* working at the hard, boring, monotonous, routinized, dehumanized work at Lordstown were doing more interesting work. They—or perhaps their statistical sons—may have moved into the ranks of "professional, technical and kindred" work, if not as physicians then perhaps as physical education teachers. Their statistical wives may have been housewives or domestic maids in 1960; now they are working as secretaries. The statistical man who might have been a pick-and-shovel laborer engaged in building Lordstown if it had been built in the 1950s was replaced by a bulldozer when the plant was actually built in the 1960s and, statistically, the former pick-and-shovel-worker became a data-processing machine repairman.

So much for those missing 1,500 people—and their occupational cousins —who don't work at Lordstown. But if we view the Lordstown workers as typical, what of them? Are they trapped, alienated, brutalized creatures sapped by Blue-Collar Blues?

They *do* have a tough job. But that is not new; assembly line work has always been hard. But what is new is that—statistically speaking—assembly line workers are likely to start at age nineteen after graduating from high school, not at age fifteen or sixteen shortly after graduating from elementary school. They will retire (according to the new "Thirty-and-Out" plan in the auto industry) in their fifties, not at sixty-five. They get five weeks' vacation, not two; (in the steel industry they get a thirteen-week-paid sabbatical leave every seven years). They work seven and a half hours a day on straight time, not eight or nine or ten—earlier standards.

Make no mistake about it, they do suffer from Blue-Collar Blues—but much less often than did their statistical fathers. In short, it's better than what it replaces. The productivity generated from the most recent round of the Industrial Revolution has been translated into more income (as shall be seen in the next chapter), less grueling physical work, and into more free time, as measured by years worked, weeks worked and hours worked.

This leisure time that the early 1960 pundits claimed the working class would have to be taught to use creatively hasn't turned out to be much of a problem. It's turned out to be much like sex—an activity that adolescents get the hang of pretty quickly. So too with workers and leisure; when they got it, they liked it and they used it. By creating—for the first time in history—a middle class and a working class that is also a leisure class, a remarkable lesson has been learned: Ordinary people are just as extraordinary as extraordinary people are if you give them a chance.

In fact, the ordinary people, given some time and money, have generally tended to ape the intelligentsia and the corporate upper class.

While the common mythology often views the typical working-class Americans as a potbellied slob in a tee shirt swilling beer watching television and cursing Blacks—the reality is far different, as much of the rest of this volume will demonstrate. Given some money, ordinary Americans thought it would be nicer to live on a quarter acre in suburbia rather than a tenement in a city—a move made earlier by upper middle-class Americans, the original suburbanites. Given some money, and some fiscal flexibility, ordinary Americans thought that their children should go to college—just like the kids of richer folk. Given some time off, ordinary Americans thought it would be nice to own a boat—just like the swells. Given some time off, ordinary Americans decided to go camping and see their country and its vast beauty.

Now, ordinary Americans are not plaster saints—but neither are their intellectual, professional or corporate models. The new middle class probably drinks too much and pops too many pills—just like the dukes, duchesses, doctors, book publishers and corporate presidents. Given some financial flexibility, the divorce rate is up—not an uncommon phenomenon in earlier suburbia. And some of the new middle class are even voting Republican!

What has happened, in short, is the re-creation of an old life style among a new, broader class.

It should come as no surprise, then, that the new middle class has further demands and deeper demands—demands not dissimilar from those made by the earlier, narrower, middle class. Americans today from all walks of life have, in the phrase of pollster Daniel Yankelovich, "a psychology of entitlement." They feel they are entitled to college educations for their children, and entitled to a meaningful or interesting job and entitled to feel alienated—just like the earlier, more narrowly based middle class. When reality rubs up against this sense of entitlement, when, for example, workers at Lordstown and elsewhere find themselves still glued to hard and boring jobs (albeit for fewer hours, fewer weeks, fewer years and more money than earlier), they feel entitled to bitch about it and seek redress. Bitch they do—blue-collar blues—and redress of grievances they get—flotillas of commissions about job redesign, a few of which may produce amelioration, and tough union demands, most of which will be effectuated.

The mistake is to view this process as a symptom of an American sickness. When tens of millions of Americans are demanding—and getting—more interesting work, more leisure time and the wherewithal to use that leisure time meaningfully and enjoyably—that's health, not sickness. That's not powerlessness; that's power.

CHAPTER 5

The Massive Majority Middle Class
(Income)

People working at better jobs earn more money.

And so, in 1971—albeit in an oddly ironic sort of way—a great American economic milestone was passed. And in 1973, two more milestones were passed whose only irony was the lack of attention they received.

Here, in the language of the Census Bureau, is what happened in the first instance:

"Median income of the Nation's families went above $10,000 in 1971 for the first time in U.S. history."

The irony is that this milestone was passed not because of any real income gains in that gloomy recessionary year of 1971, but because a 5% inflationary rise pushed personal income up without giving to its recipients anything more than the means to keep even with a rapidly rising cost of living.

But that irony should not cloud an otherwise major fact, that "ten thousand dollars a year"—long the standard symbol for economic adequacy—had been breached, and had been breached largely because of earlier *real* income gains that had escalated income levels to a point where some inflation could push the mercury in the economic barometer to a new and higher level.

By the end of 1972—an honestly good year for real income—median family income had climbed to a bit above $11,000 per year. By the end of 1973—another good year for real income, despite very heavy inflationary pressures—the median family income had increased to somewhat over $12,000—*a thousand dollars a month, and a second milestone.*

Now, of course, this $12,000 figure—like the $10,000 figure—is partly the result of a steady inflation that has been going on in the United States through good real-income years and bad real-income years for many decades. The Consumer Price Index shows that what was worth one dollar flat in 1947 took $1.83 to match some twenty-five years later, in 1972. But a large measure of increasing family income—by far the largest share of it over the years—has come about via real gains, not inflationary rises. Thus, an individual needed $1.83 in 1972 to buy $1.00 worth of goods—but his income had gone up from $1.00 to $3.39!

A look at the history of family income in America leads to the third milestone. In *constant 1972 dollars*, after accounting for inflation, the historical comparisons work out to a $5,757 median family income in 1950 and a $11,116 family income in 1972. By the end of 1973, the median family income level had gone up sufficiently to lead this statement:

Real family income, after inflation, has doubled in a generation.

* * *

The coupling of these three milestones—*$10,000 median family income,* growing to *a-thousand-dollars-a-month* median family income, and adding up to a *doubling* of real income in a generation—point to another idea and a critical one at that. Something has happened in the United States in recent years that has never happened before anywhere: The massive majority of the population of a nation is now in the middle class.

We have had a middle-class explosion.

Now, the drawing of class lines by solely economic criteria is always subject to question and also subject to a large degree of arbitrariness. It is particularly difficult to pin-point during a time of rapid inflation, as will be discussed. In the previous chapter and in chapters to follow, criteria other than money will be considered in the attempt to gauge the extent of American middle classness. In some ways these criteria—particularly educational ones—may be more important than money. But there is no denying either that money is a key ingredient in the middle-class mix, and possibly *the* key ingredient. And there is no denying that the numbers are indeed explosive.

If, for example, one says that the very *lowest* level of the middle-class, or the middle-income class, if you prefer, begins when family income reaches, say, $5,000 per year, then the totals in 1972 were well up into the mid-eighty percentiles. At a $7,000 level the percentage was in the mid-seventy percentiles. At $10,000, one would have put almost 60% in the middle class and at $12,000 about half. Consider the following data:

FAMILY INCOME DISTRIBUTION, CONSTANT (1972) DOLLARS

	1950	1960	1970	1972	1973*
More than $ 5,000	59%	73%	83%	83%	84%
More than $ 7,000	36%	59%	72%	73%	74%
More than $10,000	16%	37%	54%	56%	58%
More than $12,000	—	22%	41%	45%	48%

Our own economic judgment would be that the $7,000 income figure is the most appropriate *lowest* limit of middle classness in America.

Reasons for this judgment, and some alternatives, will be discussed in a moment. But, first, a late word about inflation. It is generally acknowledged that in 1973 inflation got "out of hand" as first food and then energy prices soared. The 1973 rate of inflation was 6.2%, the highest annual rate since 1948. Many observers predicted that the inflation rate would climb still higher and they were right. As the galleys of this volume were reviewed in mid-May of 1974, the data for the first quarter of 1974 showed an annual rate of increase of 14.5% in the Consumer Price Index, or 11.5% when calculated via the Gross National Product deflator—"double digit inflation." Most economists predicted this staggeringly high rate would drop somewhat toward the middle and end of the year but still remain high.

If inflation rates stay "very high" and maybe even just "high" over an extended period of time there will clearly be turbulence and despair among Americans in the months and years to come—as will be discussed later in this volume. For now suffice it to say that inflationary pressures surely appear to be the darkest cloud on the domestic horizon.

For the purposes of the rest of this chapter, however, it has much less real bearing than might be guessed. First, of course, all the long-term real income gains that accrued from 1947 remain intact, as written. Secondly, despite high inflation in 1973, and while some groups of wage earners were hit much harder than others even *losing* real purchasing power as the year went on, as an economy-wide whole per capita personal income climbed *faster* than inflation for the calendar year: a 9.4% increase in 1973 versus a 6.2% rise in the consumer price index yielding a net *gain* of 3.2% and not bad as these things go. Census family income estimates in *constant* 1973 dollars showed a gain from $11,727 per family to $12,039. Not until the first quarter of 1974 did inflation outstrip income,

---

* Estimate based on a real income growth of 3.5% calculated in *1972* dollars. A calculation in *1973* dollars would push the "more than $12,000" over the 50% mark.

yielding a 1.3% *decrease* in per capita real purchasing power in that quarter. Moreover, most economists predicted that the numbers would turn positive for most of the rest of the year, leaving 1974 as a small-plus year for real income despite very high inflation.

There is only one problem—and that is in the mind's eye of the reader. Many dollar figures and relationships between dollar figures here are expressed in "constant 1972 dollars." As these galleys are corrected, these 1972 data remain the latest for which full historical time-series exist. Yet costs have gone up. A $7,000 yearly income in *1972* is perceived to be "worth less" than $7,000 in March of *1974,* when it would require $7,994 —almost $1,000 more—to buy the same goods. A $7,000 income in *1970* equates to $8,610 in March of *1974.*

The reader, then, is asked to put a lens on his mind's eye. Do not say, "Harumph, what can a family buy these days for $7,000—or $10,000— or $12,000," as the case may be. Remember these are *1972* dollars used by persons facing *1972* prices. Since then, prices *and incomes* have gone up, and incomes have in fact gone up *more* than prices. In the 1974 mind's eye, the middle class starting point discussed here should be converted from $7,000 to about $8,000 and would then further be corrected *upward* in the manner that the text indicates. The $10,000 income in 1972 would equate to $11,420 in March '74 dollars and the $12,000 in 1972 income would convert to $13,704. Most important, because real income has gone up, at least the same percentages of people would be above the new lines as were above the old ones.

Although inflation does not affect each income group in precisely the same way, and a case can be made that poor and lower middle class families are now being hurt somewhat worse than the wealthy (as will be discussed), the general effect of the recent inflation has been to push *all* the numbers up—and leave the relative gains described here generally valid.

Now, to return: Why is $7,000 in old 1972 dollars a fair starting point for the beginning of the lower middle class in America?

There are several reasons behind this judgment. First, it is at about the $7,000 income level (in '72 dollars) where the first traces of *discretionary* income begin appearing. Thus, for a typical four-person family (in 1972) earning anything less than $6,000 there was *no* discretionary income. But it is at the $6–8,000 interval (with a $7,000 average) that discretionary income begins—with a modest $223, about enough to buy a small color television set. No claim is made here that $7,000 is a lot of money or that $223 discretionary income is a lot of discretionary money. It isn't. We are talking of a *lowest* threshold, the point at which the *lower* middle class *begins.* This point is surely not one where cabin cruisers and vacations in

Europe are to be found, not even very many camper trailers. But discretionary income[2] measures money that can be used for relatively immediate *wants* rather than *needs*.

If one is looking for a philosophy of economics to use as a bedrock beneath the concept of middle class, that would seem to be an appropriate one: the lowest rung of the middle class begins when people can *start* buying what they *want,* above needs, *now.* The ability to achieve wants-above-needs-now is the essence of economic freedom and it is economic freedom that is the root of so many of the experiences that have long been regarded as the hallmarks of the middle class: it takes freedom money to enjoy the cultural experience of an opera or a play or a movie; it takes freedom money to enjoy the aesthetic and recreational experience of a trip to a national wilderness or national forest; it takes freedom money to gain the educational experience of college. In short, the point where "discretionary income" appears in the income distribution seems a good place to mark as the spot where families and individuals can *begin* to pursue the middle-class mode of life. The *Newsweek* study shows that in 1950 only 43% of the people in America lived in households with *any* discretionary income. By 1972 that percentage had climbed to 74%. The total numbers of Americans in households with discretionary income climbed from 64 million to 164 million in that time.

(For a *two*-person $7,000 family, discretionary income is $1,500; for a *four*-person family at $9,000, discretionary income is $1,000, enough for a color television set and a short camping trip.)

That rough $7,000 level for middle-class entry can also be said to be backed up by interesting statistical work of the Bureau of Labor Statistics concerning "urban family budgets." BLS artfully constructs a series of living standards—"low," "intermediate" and "high"—and correlates these stand-

----

[2] The data concerning discretionary income in this chapter is derived from a study done for *Newsweek* by the author and Roger Herriot using detailed tract data from the 1970 Census as well as the latest studies of family budgets and consumer expenditures prepared by the Bureau of Labor Statistics. Here is the full chart:

DISCRETIONARY INCOME FOR FAMILY OF FOUR IN 1972
BY TOTAL MONEY INCOME

Total Money	Mean Discretionary Income
Under $2,000	$0
$2,000– $3,999	$0
$4,000 – $5,999	$0
$6,000 – $7,999	$223
$8,000 – $9,000	$985
$10,000 – $14,999	$2,924
$15,000 – $24,999	$6,567
$25,000+	$16,091

ards by size of family, by age of family and by type of family ("one-parent" or "two-parent"), providing a useful index of what it actually costs to live in urban America.

A decade or so ago, before the government got edgy about making value judgments, the "intermediate" budget was described, officially, as *modest but adequate.*" More recently, the intermediate budget is only labeled "intermediate"—but it is a direct continuation of the "modest but adequate" series. In 1970, BLS calculated what percentages of American families (when crossruffed by age, size and type) fell into the various pigeonholes, with these results:

DISTRIBUTION OF FAMILIES BY FAMILY INCOME 1969

Below lower budget	8%
Between lower & intermediate	19%
Between intermediate & higher	31%
Above higher budgets	43%

Accordingly, by 1969, one can say that 74% of the American families were living at some level *above* "modest but adequate," some of course, way above it, others barely above it. Interestingly, this 74% figure dovetails almost exactly with the 72% figure given earlier for the $7,000-and-over figure for 1970.

Another thought bolsters the idea that a $7,000 income (in '72 not '74 dollars) is where the bottom of the middle class begins. Perhaps because so much attention is given to the "urban family of four" budget in the BLS series, people often tend to equate the notion of "family" and "typical family" with the concept of "urban family of four." As a result, when the argument is made for a $7,000 level, the rebuttal one hears is often "Well, after all, how can a family live on only $7,000 a year," and in the mind's eye of the objector is often the picture of a husband and wife with two children living in New York City. But the BLS series takes note of about *eighty* different family combinations and the "urban family of four," while of great interest, is only one of these.

Nor is it by any means typical.

Thus, in Census parlance, "family" may mean a retired husband and wife, a relatively newly married young couple perhaps still in college, a young married couple with one baby—as well as what we usually think of as a "family," that is, a unit composed of a husband-wife-and-several-children.

That is a very important distinction to make because there happen to be far more two-person "families" in America than four-person families! To be precise: 18.9 million versus 10.5 million in 1971. There are even slightly more three-person families than four-person families (11.3 million versus 10.5 million). In fact, two-person and three-person families make up together *more than half* the total families in America (30.2 million out of a total of 53.3 million). So, when one talks of "family income" of $7,000, the chances are good that the money is going to support a two- or three-person unit.

If one compares income levels of "all families" with "husband-wife-two-children" families there is about a $1,000 differential in favor of the latter category. If one compares "all families" to "urban" families there is another $1,000 differential. And accordingly, because of these kinds of numbers, one will find that in 1971, 70% of "all families" had more than *$7,000* income, but of husband-wife-two-children families, 69% had more than *$9,000*.

So then, if one uses a $7,000 level of Census family income as a lowest level of middle classness (as is suggested here) that level, if extrapolated in the mind's eye to urban family of four, ought to be replaced again in the mind's eye, by some number in the $8,500–9,000 range. Nine thousand dollars a year is about what a policeman made as a starting wage in an American city back in our base year of 1972. And if a cop isn't a symbol of the middle class, who is?[3]

Beyond that are geography and life style. It is hard to sense the concept of "middle class" by the standards of raising a family in the private schools of Boston, Manhattan and Washington, situations where a relatively high income may be needed to make ends meet.

But most Americans don't live there and they don't spend their summers in Martha's Vineyard, the Hamptons or Rehoboth Beach. The family like as not vacations in a camper trailer near a trout stream. Their kids go to public schools. They live in Ashtabula and Austin, not Chevy Chase and Westport. And the difference is enormous. The BLS "intermediate" budget for an urban family of four ranges from $13,576 in Boston to $9,800 in Austin—i.e., the same level of living costs 38% more!—while, in non-metropolitan areas the budget is still lower (autumn of 1972 data). At the *high* budget level the figure in Austin is $14,119—while in Boston it is $20,210—a 43% hike.

[3] Moreover, Census income statistics don't measure "fringe benefits." They have gone up enormously in a dozen years from $23.4 billion in 1960 to $79.7 billion in 1972, according to Department of Commerce data. That works out to about $325 in fringe benefits per worker in 1960 and $895 in 1972! Statistically speaking, if there are two workers in a family the amounts can be doubled in many situations. The fruits of these fringe benefits can be seen clearly when one examines a specific field affected—like hospital care. Hospital costs, of course, have soared in America. But in 1950, only 37% of consumer hospital care expenditures were paid for by private insurance plans. By 1971, fully 79% of hospital costs were paid by private insurance plans. That fraction of the health insurance paid for by the employer—sometimes half, sometimes more—is not counted by Census as "income." Yet, of course, it represents value to the recipient (Social Security Administration data).

The head of the household may not be a doctor, lawyer, accountant or professor, but rather a plasterer, lathe operator, steelworker, routeman or salesman. But—in our judgment—these Americans are very much a part of the middle class. There are economic and geographic reasons for this that have been discussed. But it goes beyond a mere line drawing in the sociological sand. These tens of millions of middle classians are in fact middle class because they think they are middle class, and they think they are middle class because they fit the criteria that they themselves have established for such status. This thought will be explored at greater length at the beginning of the next chapter. For now, note the results of a 1973 survey by the National Opinion Research Center (University of Chicago) which asked respondents to identify the social class they thought they belonged in, with these results:

Lower class:	4%
Working class:	41%
Middle class:	41%
Upper middle class:	11%
Upper class:	2%

Thus, even excluding "working class," 54% of Americans thought themselves "middle class" or higher. And how many $20,000-a-year truck drivers responded "working class"?

For now, reconsider the key economic fact. If one used $7,000 as a valid lower dividing line, then 74% of American families qualify for the middle class—a *doubling* in twenty-three years. If the reader is obstinate and insists that $10,000 is the proper lowest acceptable level for the beginning of the lower middle class, then 58% qualify, more than a *tripling* in twenty-three years. And if one uses $12,000, then 48% qualify, and while precise twenty-three-year figures aren't available this would clearly represent at least a *quadrupling*.[4] *All these figures are in constant dollars.*

The key fact then is that almost no matter how you measure it there has been an extremely sharp growth of the American middle class in recent years. And that fact colors our entire national existence these days.

*   *   *

If the income picture is relatively roseate, as is maintained here, why all the bitching? After all, one does not have to take a poll to know that

---

[4] It is often said that the key reason *family* income is climbing so rapidly is because so many more wives work now. It helps, to be sure, but it is not the major cause of change. *Male* income increased by 83% from 1960 to 1972 (while the cost of living went up by 41%). Moreover, of course, income from wives is still income, and it's spent for what families want: college education, cars, boats, whatever.

plenty of people—critics and men in the street alike—are convinced that the income situation is not only not roseate, but is rotten. Why?

There are several reasons, offered here for whatever solace they may bring.

First, there is a strange statistical reason. One government series, "real spendable weekly earnings" (produced by the Bureau of Labor Statistics), has tended to show a substantially lower rate of real income growth than any other government data—including other data from BLS itself, let alone Census data. Accordingly, the "spendable" series has been used, often recklessly, by those interested in showing how poorly Americans are making out. Candidate Richard Nixon used it in 1968, and candidate George McGovern used it in 1972. It is also used regularly by those who don't know any better. It is not, in fact, a very useful series, as even BLS personnel will admit, in discussing its limitations. In fact it is not really even designed to be comparable to other sorts of income data. Scholar George Perry of the Brookings Institution has likened the series to a "stopped clock," which inadvertently tells the correct time every twelve hours. Perry points out that the "spendable" series does not properly take into account the changes in hours worked, the overtime factor, taxes, Social Security and, most importantly, the changing mix of the labor force, which in recent years has disproportionately grown among teen-agers and women, typically lower paid workers.[5] The "spendable" series shows an annual average income growth of 1.28% per year from 1962–72, about half of what other series show. The "spendable" shows no growth between 1966 and 1969; other series show around 2% per year real growth. Most recently, in 1973, the spendable series has come up with negative numbers, and these have been widely trumpeted. Other series, however, stayed positive until the first quarter of 1974. For example, Census *family* income medians, in *constant dollars,* show solid growth from 1960 through 1969, a plateauing in 1970 and 1971, and growth again in 1972 and 1973. Here is the Census data:

FAMILY INCOME
IN CONSTANT 1972 DOLLARS

1960	$7,941	1967	$ 9,940
1961	8,019	1968	10,375
1962	8,247	1969	10,768
1963	8,543	1970	10,632
1964	8,861	1971	10,625
1965	9,921	1972	11,116
1966	9,667	1973	11,337 (est.)

[5] Moreover, the series deals only with one class of worker—those in non-supervisory manufacturing jobs—ignoring, for example, the entire service work and government work sectors, the fastest growing ones, as it happens.

The same numbers have been estimated in *1973* constant dollars and show this progression:

FAMILY INCOME
IN CONSTANT 1973 DOLLARS

1960	$ 8,436
1970	$11,277
1972	$11,727
1973	$12,039

(If the reader wants to impute political grades to such economic series, then John Kennedy and Lyndon Johnson get "excellent" and Richard Nixon gets a "pass.")

Beyond the statistical problems is a perceptional one. It has been described as "the revolution of rising expectations"—i.e., people expect more than they used to. But that is only part of it. There is something else at work, let us call it "the reality of realized expectations," and much of the remainder of this book will deal with it.

Thus, consider a typical American family. Consider the Jones family. In 1960 (calculated retrospectively in 1972 dollars), the Joneses' income was $7,941. The Jones family owned one car, lived in a row house in the city, did not send their daughter to college and owned neither a washing machine nor a clothes dryer.

A dozen years go by. Real income for the statistical counterpart of the Jones family rises by 40%, up to $11,116 in 1972, *after* counting the effects of inflation. Jones's daughter is enrolled in a junior college, paying almost no tuition because the costs are paid for by taxes deducted from Jones's paycheck. (The "real spendable" series doesn't count the deducted dollars as income, but isn't Jones receiving value for those deducted dollars? Would he necessarily prefer to get the dollars and pay the tuition?) Jones also owns two cars now. He needs them. He lives in a suburban house on a quarter of an acre lot. In the house are a washer and a dryer.

Is Jones financially strapped? Is Jones angry because his dollar doesn't go as far as it used to? You bet he is. He has run smack into "the reality of realized expectations." He is paying (through the nose) for all, or many, of the things he wanted a dozen years ago. He's got them. And he's strapped. And he complains. And it's no laughing matter.

There is, in fact, cause for sympathy and empathy about Jones's economic situation. But neither of those emotions should be confused with lack of progress.

There is an eternal shorthand for all this: People want more than they've got at whatever income level they're at.

Finally, there is another factor at work. Since early 1973, inflation has gone up faster than at any time since 1974. Despite the fact that real

income (in 1973) went up above and beyond inflation, a sharp rise in the
cost of living has a debilitating psychological effect—and a debilitating real
effect on those with fixed or partially fixed incomes. Hamburger at $1.50 a
pound, gasoline at $.65 a gallon, nickel candy bars at $.15 gets people
angrier than hell. So angry in fact that if you tell them that their real income is still up, that rates of inflation have recently been far higher in
other nations, that taxes really do provide services for them—they only get
angrier. If there is any single factor that can plunge Americans back into
life in the fever zone—it's just that anger, of which, more later.[6]

The Poor

If so many more Americans are middle class—what of the fate of those
who haven't even come close to making do in America? What about the
poor?

In the early 1960s, poverty was rediscovered and, in the American style,
exaggerated. Michael Harrington's seminal book *The Other America*
claimed roughly 40% of the people were "in poverty." By the mid-1960s
a Social Security administration economist, Molly Orshansky, designed
a statistical scale to draw a "poverty line" attuned to urban-rural and small-
family, large-family differences. Using this scale, a standard was established
to measure the extent of poverty in America. While the data did not approach Harrington's estimate, the situation was bad enough: retrospective
calculations to 1959 revealed more than a fifth of all Americans—22.4%
—were living in poverty.

[6] And yet, even regarding inflation, there is a bright side that should be understood
even if the balm salves no wounds. The recent inflation, world-wide and in America,
is essentially a function of economic strength, not weakness. Food prices are up not
only because of Russia's great grain robbery, but because Americans—and French-
men, Englishmen, Germans, Luxembourgers, etc.—have the money now to buy beef
instead of grain as a main dish. Energy prices are up not only because sheiks and
shahs are trying to get top dollar but because they are able to get top dollar because
so many people were able to buy cars and air conditioners and freezers and motorboats and *the energy to run them,* sending demand curves skyward. (It is food prices
and energy prices that are the two principal components of the current inflation.)
Prices for housing, as Paul Samuelson has noted, have climbed sharply precisely because there are so many people around who can afford to pay high prices—with the
money they have earned in this burgeoning, productive economy. People worry about
"shortages," but sometimes fail to note that a "shortage" can also be described as
"chronic excess demand," which is a generally healthy symptom, to which a free
economy responds, not instantaneously, but over a period of years, ultimately reducing demand, and damping the fires of inflation. Don't bother explaining this to
Mr. Jones; he's angry, and he's not in a listening mood right now. He is planning a
vacation trip in his camper trailer and at 4 miles per gallon and gasoline at 65¢ a
gallon he can't go as far as he wanted to.

A full decade passes.

Poverty is almost cut in half. By 1969, the percentage in poverty is 12.1%.

The years 1970 and 1971 are slow, recessionary years and the poverty rate stops sinking; it even rises by a fraction of a point. It is 12.5% in 1971. But a healthy economy in 1972 takes the poverty figure down to 11.9%—an all-time low, and hopefully reversing the Nixon-years plateau. A second healthy year for real personal income, as 1973 is expected to be as this is written (despite heavy inflation), will probably drive the poverty figure down even further, possibly below 11%. In all, over the fourteen years for which poverty data are available: a decrease from 22.4% to about 11%.

A very similar sort of decrease occurred in substandard housing in America. The rate was 16% in 1960 and 7.4% just a decade later.

These are very substantial decreases indeed—*halvings*.

It has been argued—erroneously—that the poverty line does not take into account the rising cost of living over the years. The fact is that the federal poverty line is computed every year in a direct linkage to the Consumer Price Index and it has climbed each year—from $2,973 back in 1959, up to $4,275 in 1972 (for a nonfarm family of four persons).

It has also been argued, most credibly by Dr. Herman Miller, formerly of the Census Bureau, that the poverty line reflects only an *absolute* level of poverty and does not take into account a *relative* concept of poverty that should correct for the rise in the perceived needs of poor people in a society where affluence and amplitude are increasing by leaps and bounds— and where poor persons remain near the bottom. Thus, in 1960, a television set might be regarded as a luxury, or surely a discretionary item, but by 1973 perhaps the same television set ought to be regarded as a required item even in a poverty budget.

Dr. Miller is surely correct in noting that the official poverty line is not a relative concept. But the question is: Should it be? Dr. Miller says yes. We would disagree. To say that 20% of the people who earn the least money are "in poverty" (as some relativists maintain) is to make a statement about income distribution, not poverty. Thus if everybody earns at least $50,000 a year, the bottom fifth would be regarded as poverty stricken even though they earned $50,000. And if perceived needs are growing—television sets, cars, bigger housing, etc.—and many formerly poor people are getting what they now perceive they need, that is an index of some mild progress, not of continued poverty. It is a condition better than what it replaces.

That fourteen million people have crossed the poverty line in the last dozen years is better than what it replaces. That those fourteen million are now able to eat better than the "emergency food plan"—which was the keystone "need" of the original poverty budget—and statistically now are able to live in a structurally sounder dwelling and wear warm clothes—is better than what it replaces. It's still not much, Lord knows, but it is what separates the poverty stricken from the nonpoverty stricken. That there are some people who cannot afford a used car or an additional bedroom is surely unfortunate. But it is a condition that ought to be described by something other than the word "poverty."

* * *

Something else has happened to poverty in America: Increasingly it has become a condition that afflicts those who can't work. That may sound like an unexceptional statement, but it is in fact quite exceptional indeed. Back in 1959, about *a third* (32%) of the families in poverty had heads who worked full time. By 1972, that percentage had decreased to 20%—*a fifth*. Today, with the minimum wage slated to go up from $1.60 to $2.30 an hour, the percentage is sure to decrease still further.

At the same time the percentage of the families in poverty that had *female heads* increased sharply from 23% in 1959 to 43% in 1972. In a sense, this is the flip side of the earlier numbers. Because many of these female-headed families consist of mothers of young children, they are unable to work full time or unable to work at all.

The poor in America, then, are increasingly the dependent. Conversely, and perhaps more important, the independent are far less likely to be poor. That situation, we would suggest, is also better by far than what it replaces. It is obviously unfortunate for Americans in families without a full-time breadwinner to be in poverty. But progress judgers must have a cold and beady eye. Is that situation—of a poor dependent class—not better than the earlier one, where not only dependent persons, but people who worked, people who played the economic game by the existing rules, were poor? The welfare situation is clearly a social tragedy in America. But welfare, essentially, goes to people who can't work. What we have accomplished, at least, is that most people who can work no longer live in poverty.

Not only are there fewer poor, not only have their characteristics changed, but the poor that remain aren't quite as poor as they used to be. In 1959, the median poor family was $1,328 away from the poverty exit line. A dozen years later, after the poverty line had climbed by about 39% to reflect the rising cost of living, the median poor family in America was $1,122 away from the poverty exit line—about $200 closer, or about a 16% gain. This apparently modest increase is perhaps somewhat more than meets the eye: Remember, the percentage in poverty declined by half and it is those who are still in poverty who are now 16% closer to Out than were their counterparts a dozen years earlier.

This gain toward Out is accountable in part by the increase in the amounts of money dispensed by the various welfare programs. But beyond these increasing cash payments are increasing "in-kind" payments such as food stamps, rent supplements, health care, education, manpower training, etc. These "in-kind" payments are *not* counted as "income" by the Census Bureau. A Government Accounting Office study (1973) of some typical "poverty areas" showed that about 70% of those households receiving cash also received at least one "in-kind" benefit and from 60–75% of those households received more than one such benefit—while somewhere between 10–25% received *five* or more benefits. The GAO data, a five-year survey, when aggregated and extrapolated shows that the typical value of "in-kind" services runs to about 15% over and above all cash income—private or welfare—received by residents of low-income areas.

The poor, then, are becoming fewer and somewhat better off when measured against the *absolute* standard of the poverty line. But what about the *relative* standing in the society? The claim has been made, after all, that "the rich are getting richer and the poor are getting poorer." This is an argument about how the pie is split, not about the size of the slices, about *income distribution* and not necessarily *poverty* as such.

Is there statistical validity to back up the claims that we have today a less-fair America, a system in which the poor have even less of a break than they did twenty years ago?

No, not according to most recent Census numbers. The numbers, in fact, show that a modest amount of favorable redistribution of income has taken place *to* the poorest and *away* from the very richest Americans. As the table shows, the "lowest fifth" of the income distribution was the only one to make even a minimal gain. And only the "top 5%" showed a substantial decline.

PERCENTAGE SHARE OF INCOME RECEIVED
BY EACH FIFTH OF FAMILIES

	1960	1970	Change
Lowest fifth	4.9%	5.5%	+ .6%
Second fifth	12.0%	12.0%	—
Third fifth	17.6%	17.4%	− .2%
Fourth fifth	23.6%	23.5%	− .1%
Highest fifth	42.0%	41.6%	− .4%
Top 5 per cent	16.8%	14.4%	−2.2%

In truth, the changes are not major, although also in truth it takes massive shifts to significantly change a *relative* ranking. But such minimal shifts as there are have been toward the poor and away from the well-to-do.[7]

The Well-to-Do

Nevertheless, please do not feel sorry for the well-to-do people in America. They have made out more than all right in an expanding economy and the Census shows clearly that their tribe has increased. In 1952—two decades ago—there were *202,000* households with incomes of over $25,000 a year.

By 1962, there were *464,000* households with incomes of more than $25,000 per year.

And by 1972, there were *4,225,000* households with incomes of more than $25,000.

That is about a *twenty-fold increase* in a couple of decades. Now, some of the increase is due to inflation. And some is due to the climb in the total number of households in the United States. But more than four million households (comprising somewhat over *fourteen million* souls) are a long, long way from two hundred thousand households no matter how it's figured.

[7] There *has* been a major shift in who controls what proportions of *discretionary* income in America—a shift away from the highest income groups and toward middle income groups as this chart reveals:

DECILE DISTRIBUTION OF AGGREGATE DISCRETIONARY INCOME (constant '72 dollars)

Deciles, by income of families & unrelated individuals	1950	1972
0– 10%	0.0%	0.0%
10– 20%	0.0%	0.0%
20– 30%	0.06%	1.28%
30– 40%	1%	3%
40– 50%	2%	5%
50– 60%	4%	8%
60– 70%	6%	10%
70– 80%	10%	14%
80– 90%	21%	20%
90–100%	56%	38%

Source: *Newsweek* study of Discretionary Income, based on Census and Bureau of Labor Statistics data.

The big relative losers are the top 10% (although the data show their *absolute* discretionary income is substantially up). The big relative gainers are in the 40%–80% deciles. They accounted for 22% of discretionary income in 1950—and 37% in 1972.

The 1970 Census was the first one to feel the need for a category of "$50,000-plus" households—425,000 were so tabulated. That's already a substantial number—comprising about 1.5 million persons—and surely growing rapidly, although hard to tabulate historically from Census data just yet.

* * *

In short, then, fewer Americans are poor (halved in a decade) and more are well to do (a twenty-fold increase in $25,000 incomes over two decades). Looking at these two ends of the spectrum, it is not implausible to suggest that the 1980 Census data will show that greater numbers of Americans will be living in $25,000-plus households than in poverty, which is an interesting thought indeed.

More middle classians, fewer poor who are less poor and more well-to-do.

A strange story to be telling after a time when the dominant economic headlines were about inflation, devaluations, job exportation, declining productivity, recessions, balance of payments and the miracle economies of France, Germany, Japan, Taiwan, Israel, Brazil—in fact the miracle economies of almost everyone but poor old America.

In reaction to such portents of economic doom and gloom perhaps one point ought to be stated here with some bluntness. *In the dozen years from 1960 to 1972 real per capita income in the United States and in Canada went up MORE than any nation in the world except Japan. Furthermore, U.S. per capita income was higher in 1972 than Canada's by 19% and higher than Japan's by 208%![8]*

Now, it is true that the *rate* of economic growth has been faster in other nations but to at least some extent this has been because they started from a far lower base, often due to a war-torn economy. (Thus, back in 1952, Japan's per capita income was only $526, compared to the United States' $3,564.) Without in any way deprecating some very impressive economic performances elsewhere, the fact still remains that in real, uninflated, spendable dollars to buy homes, cars, boats, college educations, food and clothing—Americans as of 1972 had by far more than anyone else and had gained more than anyone except Japan.

But what of the strange year of 1973? Things changed. Early in the year a devaluation, a "floating," and rapid American inflation sharply devalued the American dollar to a point where some of the glowing sorts of comparative fiscal calculations didn't quite work out any more. Some post-devaluation, thumbnail figuring showed that by the earlier standards of strict dollar comparability, Americans were no longer "the richest." As

[8] In 1972, the per capita income figures were: United States, $5,353, Canada, $4,497 and Japan, $1,735.

summer turned to fall and fall to winter, the by-then-undervalued dollar began to climb, and this ascendancy was speeded up when the oil-vulnerable economies of Europe and Japan faced stingy Arab oil taps and vastly increased oil prices. As this is written in early 1974, America is probably back on top of the heap using the rates of dollar comparability.

But even at the bottom of the devaluation spiral, America looked pretty good. The rapid fiscal machinations skewed comparable incomes, but in terms of *the consumer's ability to buy what he wants,* Americans were still way ahead of the rest of the world as this calculation, made in mid-1973 *in terms of hours and weeks worked,* clearly showed:

LIVING STANDARDS, INTERNATIONAL COMPARISONS, TEN SELECTED ITEMS

To buy this —	*A typical factory hand must work this long in —*				
	U. S.	Japan	Britain	France	West Germany
Low priced home	4-5 yrs.	12-14 yrs.	6-7 yrs.	8-10 yrs.	10-12 yrs..
Small car	15 wks.	21½ wks.	32½ wks.	33 wks.	21½ wks.
TV set, B & W	36 hrs.	87½ hrs.	99 hrs.	125 hrs.	69 hrs.
Man's shoes	6½ hrs.	7½ hrs.	9½ hrs.	12½ hrs.	9 hrs.
Whiskey, fifth	80 min.	5½ hrs.	3 hrs.	4 hrs.	2 hrs.
Cigarettes, pack	8 min.	7 min.	23 min.	13 min.	17 min.
Hamburger, lb.	14 min.	62 min.	30 min.	47 min.	29 min.
Eggs, dozen	11 min.	22 min.	23 min.	33 min.	21 min.
Milk, half gal.	10 min.	24 min.	15 min.	17 min.	13 min.
Bread, lb.	4 min.	14 min.	8 min.	7 min.	7 min.

(Department of Labor data; official reports from other nations)

* * *

The striking rise in American real income has been generally used in a sensitive, intelligent and creative fashion, as will be detailed in a later section. And yet, incredibly, this success—this massive growth in personal income—has characteristically been greeted by a large and well-publicized portion of the American intellectual community as further symptoms of their favorite prediagnosed American disease: failure.

It is an astonishing development. Here is a land where remarkable economic growth has provided the personal income to lift tens of millions of poor people from poverty, to allow more of the elderly than ever before to live in dignity, to allow workingmen to have decent homes and time off from work, to provide blacks, Chicanos and other minorities with the first beginnings of a legitimate chance at a middle-class way of life. Here is a situation where in a dozen years the numbers of Americans living in families with more than $10,000 income (in constant dollars) increased from 57 million to 115 million.

And here are some of our leading intellectuals, allegedly educated, and the self-proclaimed champions of the poor, the black, the Chicano, the workingmen, the elderly. And what is their rallying cry? No growth! Steady State Economy! Zero *Production* Growth!

Freeze the pie, they say. We have too much affluence. The age of abundance is over.

Harumph. If 85% of the families in America earn more than $5,000 then 15% still earn less than $5,000. If 75% earn more than $7,000 then 25% still earn less. If 59% earn more than $10,000 then 41% earn less, about 85 million Americans. And if the middle class begins at $7,000, as is maintained here, it is not a very plush middle class at all. It is surely not a middle class that includes a vacation cottage, or a boat or a summer gymnastics camp for the children. Such amenities of life, and many others, can only come about by making the pie grow. Redistributing the proportionate size of the slices, no matter how worthy and fair such a goal is, simply will not give the black auto worker in Detroit a vacation cottage or get his wife an automatic dishwasher.

There is a coincidence or a scandal and surely an irony and a tragedy about the no-growth detour taken by at least one stream of American liberalism. For the basic thrust of social welfare liberalism in this country has always been accurately summed up by Samuel Gomper's one word demand: "More." Liberals wanted more for the workingman, more for blacks, more for poor people—more money, more vacation time, more health care, more education, more of all the goods and services that the swells had.

But a funny thing happened on the way to the land of More. Was it a coincidence that Environmental Liberalism demanded that the brakes be applied to the growth machine at just about the time the environmentalists got *their* vacation home, *their* boat, *their* kids into good colleges? Maybe. And maybe it was a new and subtler form of class privilege that suddenly discovered that affluence for the plain folks meant more traffic jams and crowded camp sites for the people who had the good things all along. But in either event—coincidence or scandal—the net effect—is ironic and tragic. The irony is apparent. The tragedy lies in the fact that elitist economics tend to divert America, as a horsefly diverts a horse, from her noblest goal and her most obvious success: the ability to bring the poor and the working class into the middle class.

Luckily, horses have ways of dealing with horseflies.

CHAPTER 6

The Middle Class as a Duck
(Education)

Consider the duck—short, waddling and loud—and consider the ancient formula for identifying the species: if it looks like a duck, walks like a duck and quacks like a duck—it's likely to be a duck.

Consider now the dilemma that sociologists have wrestled with for generations: *how to define that most amorphous condition, "middle class"?* We propose here a simple, ducklike methodology. If it looks middle class, walks middle class and quacks middle class—the chances are good it's middle class. And that procedure then depends upon another: What do people *think* are the characteristics of the middle class? In short, we propose a perceptional definition: if people think it's a duck—it's a duck.

And what do people think middle class involves? That's easy.

Everyone knows that middle-class people own their own homes, live in the suburbs, don't have large families, send their children to nursery school and kindergarten, don't let their teen-agers drop out of high school, send their kids to college, have good jobs, retire, take vacations, own washers, dryers, air conditioners, television sets, dishwashers, cars and second cars, have good incomes, play tennis and get divorced.

Not so long ago—a decade ago, surely two decades ago—most of such middle-class attributes characterized only a minority of Americans. In the last dozen or so years, say, since the 1960 Census, each of these attributes expanded in America, most of them enormously, many to a point where they are now commonly shared not only by a majority of Americans, but by three fifths, two thirds, three quarters or four fifths of the population—massive majorities of middle-class folk (except tennis and maybe divorce).

These changes have made America the first Massive Majority Middle Class society in history.

What has happened, quite simply, is that given the opportunity for highly productive work with relatively high pay (which has been chronicled here in the preceding two chapters) so-called ordinary Americans have shown that in their choice of living style, they have about as much sense, taste and direction as do so-called extraordinary Americans. The new middle class, in short, has aped and emulated the old middle class, a class which lived what used to be called "the good life."

Now, the results of this aping have sometimes been discomforting to some of that old middle class, as when the national park camp sites are crowded, or when the bay is bobbing with boats of every description or when suburbia seems to stretch on and on to the horizon. When this happens, some of the old middle-class elite, and some of their children, tend to describe today's society as plastic, sterile, hollow, bourgeoise, artificial, impure, polluted and ecologically unsound and "crowded."

What they are talking about, in fact, is a limited form of success, better by far than what it replaces. But at best, those criticisms are chic conceits and petulances. The massive majority middle class sees such attitudes as arrogant intellectual nonsense, and they have learned to live with it.

* * *

As much, and maybe more, than any other criteria, including "income" and "occupation" it is "education" that has been, and is, the hallmark of the American middle class. Going way back into our history the notion of an "educated man" has been almost synonymous with the middle class. This is so at the youngest ages—middle-class boys and girls attend nursery school or kindergarten. It is so well into adolescence—middle-class kids don't drop out of high school. It is so well into young adulthood—middle-class kids go to college.

Education, in America and elsewhere, has always demanded a major financial sacrifice by all concerned: students, their parents and governments.

Students and their parents face a two-fold economic burden when they consider the fiscal fallout of education beyond compulsory age levels, usually age sixteen. First, there is the loss of potential earnings. A high school dropout with a forty-hour job computed at the old $1.60 minimum wage brings in $64 a week, or more than $3,300 in a year. Some, much or all of that income is lost to a family that encourages its children to stay in school. To encourage a young man or young woman to go on to *college* involves a potential loss of, say, a $4,000-a-year wage (a little less than $2.00 an hour). To the loss of these potential revenues, of course, must be added the costs of tuition, books and, often, away-from-home expenses—year after year—which today can run up to the $4–5,000 range.

For governments, the costs are obvious and do not occur just for the postcompulsory years. It costs about $1,000 per year to provide a public-

school education to an elementary or secondary school student in the
United States. And the total *public* cost for *higher* education alone comes
to $20 billion each year.

Education, in short, is an extremely expensive business. Yet, given
some money, the first expenditure that the new American middle class en-
gages in is the further education of their offspring. To those who think, as
John Kenneth Galbraith does, that the American consumer is some kind
of gullible fool who will buy any unnecessary trivia so long as it is artfully
huckstered by Madison Avenue, consider the education phenomenon. Since
1960, *consumer* spending for education has gone up faster than for housing, clothing, medical care, food, beverages and tobacco—faster in fact
than for any other tabulated grouping. In terms of actual dollars, expenditures for education—mostly coming from *self-imposed* taxes levied by
elected local and state governments closest to the people—have soared
from *$9* billion in 1950 to *$25* billion in 1960 to, incredibly, *$86* bil-
lion in 1972, the largest major *governmental* dollar increase, absolute or
relative, of any category of public expenditure.[1]

There has been much written recently about the taxpayers' revolt and
how Americans are voting down school bond proposals. That is an accurate
half a fact. There have been many school bond proposals put before the
voters in recent years—many more than in previous years. Absolutely and
proportionately, many proposals were voted down, *but in 1971, more proposals for more money were voted through than ever before in American
history:* 1,687 separate bond sales worth $3.9 billion, compared to about
a billion dollars less in each of the two previous years. The 1972 data was
only a little lower: 1,547 sales worth $3.4 billion.

A good part of the rise of educational spending, of course, is due to the
simple fact that there is a much larger population of young Americans of
school age than ever before, due in large part to the Baby Boom. (There
were sixty million Americans aged five to twenty-four back in 1960—and
seventy-eight million such Americans in 1972.) A second factor is the increased spending *per pupil* in real dollars. In 1950, the per pupil expenditure in America was *$378;* by 1960, it had risen to *$546;* in 1968, it
was *$828;* and by 1972, gone to *$1,026*—in constant, adjusted-for-
inflation dollars.

The third major factor is that the new American middle class is emulat-
ing the older middle class by putting their children in school earlier and
keeping them there later. This phenomenon now deserves closer scrutiny
because it bears heavy weight toward the thesis that a new and broader
middle class has emerged in America.

[1] Defense spending went from $22 billion in 1950 to $51 billion in 1960 and
leveled off at the $87–89 billion range during the five years 1968 to 1972.

Pre-Grade One

Pre-primary school education (for children aged 3–5) used to be an activity of a comparative handful of Americans. The first solid data is from 1965 and comes from the U. S. Office of Education. In that year pre-primary education involved only a bit more than a quarter of the age 3–5 population—*27%* to be exact. Just a half a dozen years later, in 1971, the rate had climbed sharply to *39%*. By 1972 the rate was 42%—rising toward a majority way of life in America.

For poor people—in large measure due to the Head Start program—the increase of aged three to five enrollment has been even sharper relatively and absolutely. For children from families with incomes less than $3,000, the increase was from 14% in 1965 to 33% in 1971, more than a doubling and an absolute gain of 19% compared to a gain of 8% —from 37% to 45%—for families with incomes over $7,500.

The case has been made that "Head Start hasn't done any good. . . ." Proof for this has come from handsome studies with acetate covers that purport to show that once the Head Start kids get into elementary school their grade levels prove to be no higher than non-Head Start kids. Some later studies, however, have shown that even by the measurable standards of the social scientists the Head Start program is a successful one.

We would argue for the success of Head Start—and indeed for the benefits of the entire trend toward pre-primary schooling—on quite different and simpler grounds. *If it's good for the well-to-do, it's good for the not-so-well-to-do.* It is interesting that there have been no publicized studies of how nursery schools for the well-to-do "don't do any good." Parents in the higher income brackets send their young sons and daughters to nursery schools for many reasons: to help the child learn to get acquainted with other children in a group situation, to give the mother a respite at home, to allow the mother to take a job as well as to help the child learn a few academic rudiments. All these reasons seem to apply as well to the not-so-well-to-do and to the new middle class in America. These reasons have only a minimal relationship to "doing better in elementary school." The well-to-do have never been known for wasting money. They don't when they send their three-to-five-year-olds to school. And neither do the not-so-well-to-do when they, or their governments, direct dollars toward preprimary education. Children do learn to get along, the mother does get a respite, she can go to work, and the kids also learn some rudiments. In short, it's better than what it replaces.

The Vanishing American Dropout

Traditionally in America a high school diploma has been the minimum credential for entrance into the educational middle class. Without such a diploma a young American cannot generally become a bus driver, a policeman or a bookkeeper.

In 1940, a majority of young Americans were high school *dropouts*— *55%*. A decade later, in 1950, the dropout rate had changed, but only by a little: *50%* of young Americans did not graduate from high school. By 1960, the rate began falling in a major way: *38%* of the young people did not get a high school diploma. By 1972, that rate had plummeted down to *25%*, and was apparently holding at that level.

The numbers tell an important, if simple, tale. The vast majority of American youth now graduate from high school. They didn't used to. This situation is better by far than what it replaces. Why? It provides more keys to more doors for more people. One may argue that the young people who would have dropped out and are now staying on in school are students in name only who merely occupy desks and are not learning anything much. Yet even if this is so—a notion with which the author would instinctively disagree—it remains unshakably so that with the *credential alone* doors are opened.

Here, hopefully for the first and last time in this volume, reference will be made to a television commercial (for a high school correspondence course). A young man with a stovepipe hat, looking suspiciously like A. Lincoln, approaches the desk of a hard-bitten interviewer in an employment agency. Young Lincoln is asked if he is a college graduate. Sadly, he shakes his head—no. Is he a high school graduate? No, he's not. Stymied, the interviewer asks Lincoln if he has a chauffeur's license— and as the scene fades out we are left to conjure with the image of a latter-day Abraham Lincoln stuck for life driving a delivery truck for Mrs. Wagner's Pies. Of course, it is also possible that by now Mrs. Wagner's Pies hires only routemen who have a high school diploma, and young Lincoln's options would be further reduced.

The increase of human options represents progress. The sharp increase in the rates of young people with high school diplomas represents a sharp increase in options. Accordingly, the dropoff of the dropout rate in America represents important progress.

College

One of the options that is made available by possession of a high school diploma is the option to continue on into college.

That option is being chosen by absolutely astonishing numbers of young Americans. And that option is the driving force behind the explosive growth of uniquely American institutions that, until recently, played only a small role in the educational system.

Enter the two-year junior and community colleges.

They are omnipresent in America today. Outside of Miami sprawls the campus of South Dade Junior College, alabaster in the brilliant sunshine, an architectural display that would stand favorably alongside of Lincoln Center in New York. In the Blue Ridge country is the small city of Lenoir, North Carolina. And in Lenoir is the Caldwell Community College and Technical Institute with an enrollment of 838 students, many of whom, a generation or two ago, would have been pinned behind a plow on craggy Appalachian fields—for a lifetime. In growing industrial Norwalk, Connecticut, in sleek Montgomery County, Maryland, in Coolidge, Arizona, in Alexander City, Louisiana, in Kalispell, Montana, all over New York and California, indeed, all over America, the two-year colleges have mushroomed. In 1960, there were 521 such institutions. By 1970, there were 827, an increase of over 60% in a decade.

This proliferation of the two-year college helped solve some of the toughest problems that faced higher education in America in the last dozen years.

First, the two-year colleges have helped solve, and will continue to help solve, a staggering problem of numbers. In 1960, there were 3.6 million students in American colleges. A dozen years later—thanks to an earlier Baby Boom and a new lust for advanced education—there were 8.3 million college students. That is an increase of well more than double, 133% to be exact, an incredible absolute increase of 4.7 million students, each of whom needed classroom space, teachers, books, and in many instances living accommodations, footballs, basketballs, draft counseling, contraceptive advice and mimeograph machines to grind out statements explaining that colleges were oppressive and irrelevant.

The two-year colleges took up a large part of the numerical burden. There were 451,000 students enrolled in 1960. Five years later, in 1965, junior college enrollees had almost doubled—841,000. Another five years and the number almost doubled again—1,630,000 students were in junior colleges by 1970. By 1972, the enrollment level had climbed to 1,792,000, a *quadrupling* in a dozen years and an absolute increase of 1,341,000. *Moreover, between the five years of 1966–71, the junior colleges accounted for the ENTIRE INCREASE of freshmen and sophomores in American colleges.*

But the two-year schools did something else for American higher education that is probably more important than the mere absorption of numbers.

The new two-year college system in America seems to be doing for the new middle class what the land-grant colleges were so successful in doing for the older middle class: enabling masses of young men and young women to go to college who would otherwise not have been able to get there. The land-grant colleges, established under the Morrill Act of 1862, were revolutionary in that they essentially guaranteed a place in college to any student—*any* student—regardless of high school grades (just so long as a high school diploma was in hand) and regardless of income status (just so long as the student could, typically, go to an out-of-town residential college for a four-year course of study). The land-grant colleges were thus the pioneers of "open enrollment," a concept just now reaching the trend-setting East Coast. Land-grant colleges de-eliticized the university. And that represented one of the landmark achievements of American education.

Still, state university campuses were often far from population centers and if a student was to attend, he or she typically did so away from home and as a full-time student. These constraints made it economically impossible for many young people to go to college. Some young people couldn't afford to live away from home, some were already married and had family responsibilities, some couldn't attend school full time. But in the last decade, the junior and community colleges—many of them run as part of the state university system—have gone a long way toward further de-eliticization of American higher education.

A Census Bureau survey taken in October of 1971 gives a flavor of the sorts of students drawn to junior colleges compared to their colleagues who are freshmen and sophomores in standard four-year schools.

In junior colleges, *35%* of the students *attend part time*. In four-year schools, among students who are freshmen or sophomores, the comparable rate is only *12%*.

In junior colleges, *25%* of the students are *"married, spouse present."* In four-year schools, among students who are freshmen or sophomores, the comparable rate is *12%*.

In junior colleges, *53%* of the males and *43%* of the females are *over twenty* years of age. In four-year schools, among freshmen and sophomores, the comparable rates are *30%* for males and *18%* for females.

In junior colleges, *17%* of the students come from families where the father was a college graduate. In four-year schools, among freshmen and sophomores, *28%* of the students are from families where the father was a college graduate.

In junior colleges, the median family income of students was $11,989, just $1,704 above the median family income for that year which was $10,285. In four-year schools, among freshmen and sophomores, the median family income was $12,826 or $2,541 above the national median.

The junior college student, then, is more likely to be married, a part-time student, older, from less educated families and poorer. In short, a less elite institution that draws students who would have difficulty attending a regular four-year school.

Ironies:

- At a time when everyone was loudly thumping breast about how "our institutions aren't responsive any more, they're failing us," an old but little recognized institution, the two-year college, has been transformed, enlarged, multiplied, redesigned and come out as a new vehicle to bring young and eager Americans into the educational middle class.

- At a time (now) when so much public rhetoric is expended to show how "the Great Society programs didn't work," we forget that from 1965 to 1970 there were 194 new junior colleges opened up in America, about one every nine days for half a decade! Not very coincidentally, federal expenditures for higher education grew from *$1.0* billion in 1960 to *$2.9* billion in 1966 to *$3.3* billion in 1969 and to *$5.9* billion in 1973.

- At a time when the cherished dreams of tens of millions of Americans in the new middle class have come true—a child in college— the elite of the older middle class has come up with a new line: "Education doesn't really do any good . . . it's luck that counts."[2]

But most Americans are too smart to be gulled by intellectual fads. They know that education is a direct variable that produces, if nothing else, an economic payoff. There is little practical interest in a theory of education that translates into the solemn proclamation that education wouldn't make any difference in a society where education didn't make any difference. For in our society, it is quite obvious to all who have eyes

[2] The theme, or the much-publicized interpretation of the theme, of the Christopher Jenks and associates work, *Inequality: A Reassessment of the Effect of Family and Schooling in America.*

to see that education makes one hell of a difference, as the following table, drawn from 1968 Census data, makes clear:

LIFETIME AND MEAN INCOME OF MALES 25 YEARS AND OVER, BY YEARS OF SCHOOL COMPLETED

	Elementary		High School		College	
	Dropout	Graduate	Dropout	Graduate	1-3 years	4 years or more
Annual income for 1968	$ 3,981	$ 5,467	$ 6,769	$ 8,148	$ 9,397	$ 12,938
Lifetime income	$196,000	$258,000	$294,000	$350,000	$411,000	$585,000

A college graduate makes 59% more in a year than does a high school graduate. A man with some college makes 39% more than a man with some high school and 15% more than a high school graduate with no college. In the course of a lifetime, a man with a college degree will only earn about a quarter of a million dollars more than a man with just a high-school diploma. (Later data—from 1972—show the gap at about $380,000.)

Now, it may be true—although we are dubious—that higher education in general fields of study doesn't really do very much educating, as some of the educational critics maintain. It is possible—although we are doubly dubious—that if these credentials were not required then the young men and women who work as corporate salesmen, junior administrators, elementary school teachers, junior executives and political speechwriters could do their jobs just as well without the credentials.[3] It may be true that college education provides only a meal ticket and a credential. But that credential *is* required. And, accordingly, it *is* valuable. And an educational system that has dramatically demonstrated over the last decade that it can provide college education and college credentials for millions of young people who were previously unable to get that education or that credential is better by far than what it replaces. Surely so for the young person who ends up as an accountant, not a bookkeeper, an engineer, not a draftsman, an independent scientifically oriented farmer, not a hired hand. Such upward mobility—the fruits of college training—is a clear symptom of progress.

So much for the material payoff of a college education. But are we to so easily let go of an earlier belief that (aside from economic gain) a

---

[3] Although such is clearly not the case for engineers, lawyers, doctors or the people who study computer programming in junior college.

college education is good in and of itself, good because it makes young people think, expands their horizons and sharpens their intellectual tools? Hardly. College is a broadening humanistic experience. If that uplifting view of college was seen as valid when college students were most typically the offspring of the older middle-class gentry, why is it no longer valid now that the offspring of bus drivers and telephone operators can finally cross the ivy threshold? Can't such young people benefit from exposure to political science, English, literature, philosophy and psychology? Is it coincidence that college became "irrelevant" to some of the elitist upper middle class just when it became available to the lower middle class? Maybe so, and maybe not. But one thought should be made very clear: Neither college nor education generally is seen as irrelevant to most Americans. Offered here into evidence is the following Gallup Poll, taken for *Look* magazine in 1965:

Q. If you had your life to live over again, what would you do differently? (Asked of adults.)

Get more education	43%
Hold different job, enter a profession	9%
Married differently, earlier, later, different person, wouldn't have married	7%
Saved more money	3%
Been more religious, gone to church more	2%
Lived in a different place	2%
Bought a house or bought earlier	1%
Miscellaneous	10%
Don't know, no answer	5%
Nothing, satisfied now	31%

This poll is not unusual. Surveying the broad range of American public opinion data concerning "hopes, fears and regrets," Hazel Erskine, the "Polls" editor for *Public Opinion Quarterly* wrote in 1973 that for Americans *"regrets are almost entirely that they did not get enough education."*

* * *

The opening up of higher education to the new middle class in America was seen in only fragmentary form in the junior college data just presented. The full flower of it can be observed by looking at the data for total rates of college entrance, computed by the Department of Health, Education and Welfare, which includes not only the young men and women in two-year schools, but those going to four-year schools as well.

Here is the striking picture of the blueing of academia:

PERCENTAGE OF YOUNG AMERICANS WHO ENTER COLLEGE, 1960–73

1960	32%
1962	37%
1964	41%
1968	46%
1971	46%
1972	43%
1973	43% (est., HEW)

For a while in the late 1960s and early 1970s it looked as if some very simple straight-line projections would show that in a matter of a very few years one could say, "Most of our children go to college." In the cosmic order of things that would be a super-monumental statement, for rates of college attendance around the world are far, far lower.[4]

But the matter is not quite so simple and for the moment we may have to settle for only the simply monumental statement that "almost half of our children go to college."

What has happened is quite interesting. There was a sharp rise in college attendance rates up through the late 1960s—for both sexes. Then, as the Vietnam war combat diminished, as the student deferments were eliminated, as the military draft went first to a lottery basis and then into history—male enrollment rates dropped. College was no longer needed as a Viet-haven. The male rates, by 1972, were still higher than a decade earlier, but not as high as they had been at the end of the Sixties, when the all-time highs were recorded. At the same time, female rates of college attendance also went up and pretty well stayed up.

PERCENTAGE OF YOUNG AMERICANS WHO ENTER COLLEGE, BY SEX, 1960–72

	Male	Female
1960	41%	30%
1962	43%	32%
1965	44%	33%
1968	52%	41%
1970	52%	43%
1972	46%	42%

[4] Samples: Germany, 12%; France, 16%; United Kingdom, 10%; Russia, 27%; Israel, 20%; Canada, 25%; Sweden, 18%; India, 3%; Kenya, 0.67%. In short, the United States is way, way ahead.

Exactly what these trends augur for the future is somewhat guessy. One thing seems clear: The long-standing differential between rates of men and women going to college has been sharply narrowed—probably permanently. There is no reason to think that women, in this age of feminism, are suddenly going to stop going to college. They've come a long way and they're not going back to teen-age marriage and three fast kids.[5]

But what about male rates? It is quite apparent that the coming together of the specter of Vietnam and the student draft deferment provisions tended to puff up the male enrollment rates in an unnatural way. The questions, unanswered for the moment, are these: How high is "natural" in this day and age? What will happen to those statistical young men who did not enter college because it was no longer needed as a strategic hamlet to avoid the war in Vietnam? Will they stay out of the school market for good? Or will they, after staying out of school for a year or two or three, come back? After all, there was a strong and steady growth in male enrollment rates up to 1965, before the Vietnam pressure was felt. Will that growth continue as the Seventies progress or will it plateau at about the 1965 rates?

There are other questions as well dealing with other new trends: how many young people will opt now for "non-degree credit" post-high school training—essentially, vocational in nature? How many teen-age graduates of high school in this inflationary time of high tuition will choose to work and save for a few years before starting college? How many will just take a year or two off to "get their heads together?"

Just a couple of years ago, before the post-Victnam male slump was apparent, the U. S. Office of Education issued projections showing that by 1975 more than half of U.S. youth would be going on to college and that by 1980 the rate would be over 60%. Those projections now seem inflated, and certain new 1973 Census numbers would tend to say highly inflated. Still, if one were to guess, the enrollment rates will be going up again in the years to come.

It seems plausible that many of those who had viewed college as only an enclave safe from the draft will learn otherwise when they get a little older. Living at the crest of the huge demographic wave known as the Baby Boom these young people will likely be facing intense competition for good jobs in the years to come. They may well begin to feel that entering such a stiff competition without the requisite credentials is a handicap they do not choose to face. And a college education will be seen again as extremely relevant.

What is not at all guesswork at this point is that the total *number* of

[5] An interesting fact about women in college: Though less likely to go to college they are proportionately more likely to graduate.

college students (as opposed to the *rate* of those who enter college) will continue to rise in the years immediately ahead. Here is what the trend has been until now:

COLLEGE ENROLLMENT, 1960–72

1960	3,570,000
1965	5,526,000
1966	6,085,000
1967	6,401,000
1968	6,801,000
1969	7,435,000
1970	7,413,000
1971	8,087,000
1972	8,313,000
1973	8,600,000 (prel. data, HEW)

And here is what the projection looks like for the immediate years to come, based on the *most moderate* of the enrollment projections put out by the Census Bureau:

1975	9,147,000
1980	10,284,000

The reason that the *numbers* of college students will continue to rise almost regardless of the forthcoming *rate* of enrollment is, of course, the echo effect of the Baby Boom. This phenomenon, and its more recent flip side, the Birth Dearth, are explained in some detail in a later chapter. For now, one date will tend to give an orientation: *The peak of the Baby Boom was 1957 when 4,332,000 births were recorded in the United States.* Those "babies" won't be entering college, typically, until 1975 and won't be graduating from college until 1979. Moreover, the Baby Boom didn't end abruptly in 1957. It wasn't until 1965 that the number of births slipped below 4,000,000, after ten straight 4-million-plus years (1973 total: 3,141,000). And those 1965 "babies" won't enter college until 1983 and won't leave until 1987. In short, there is more than plenty of college fodder around for quite a while.

In 1960, there were 3,570,000 Americans in college. If in that year anyone had stopped to fully realize that between the pressures of demography and rising expectations, the number of people in college would more than *double* in a decade and *triple* in another decade—perhaps the most sensible course to follow would have been surrender. To handle *either* the demographic boom *or* the enrollment boom would surely have seemed to be more than a full plate. But to provide in the dozen years from 1960–72 the plant, money, personnel and equipment for an *additional* 4.8 million students—from an original base of 3.6 million students —would seem impossible.

Yet, it was done. The number of faculty members went up by almost 180,000 in the decade of the Sixties; salaries for faculty members came close to doubling.[6] Income for institutions of higher learning went from $5.8 billion in 1960 to $21.5 billion in 1970. And the total number of *all* Americans who had *graduated* from college climbed from *3.4* million in 1940 to *5.3* million in 1950 to *7.6* million in 1960 to, incredibly, *11.7* million in 1970 and to *13.3* million in 1972, almost a doubling in just a dozen years![7]

What this has done—and will do—to American society can perhaps best be understood by these simple data: *Today, about 60% of college students are from families where the head of the household had not even completed a single year of college.[8] And today, 21% of young people from homes with family incomes of from $3–5,000 are enrolled in college, a larger rate than the TOTAL figure for either France or Germany or England or Italy!*

This de-eliticization of American college life, often unnoticed and unappreciated, accounted for much of the misinterpretation of the "college vote" in the years leading up to the 1972 election. While some of the sons and daughters of the old middle class were dominating Ivy League schools, taking over the dean's office, calling Johnson and Nixon murderers, marching on Washington with Viet Cong flags, postulating the greening of America and denouncing the pigs, they captured the headlines. Meanwhile, a new breed of young Americans were quietly enrolling in state universities, extension campuses of state universities, junior colleges and community colleges, studying business administration, education, forestry, dentistry and engineering at schools like Angelo State University,

---

[6] From $6,711 for *"all ranks"* to $11,745 from 1960–1970 and from $9,107 to $16,799 for *full professors*, increases of 75% and 84% respectively. The cost of living in the decade went up by 36% and family income generally went up by 69%— which tell us something about how the academic poor got richer, and the richer of the academic poor got richer faster than the poorer of the academic poor, and that ironically this upward economic mobility was taking place while the trendy academics apparently decided that, contrary to earlier belief, the faculty ought to be learning from their students because young people were so much wiser and sensitive than their elders. (The salary figures are for a nine months teaching year.)

[7] For an even more explosive explosion, consider the matter of advanced degrees: In 1960, there were 74,000 master's degrees earned. In 1972, the number was 239,000. The rate of increase was even a little sharper for doctorates, literally straining the outer limits of profundity. There were 10,000 doctorates earned in 1960— and 35,000 earned in 1972.

[8] Among blacks, that figure is 80%.

Bemidji State, Buncombe Technical Institute, Catawba Valley and Kent State. They accepted some of the "new life style" of the nouveau radicals, agreed that Vietnam was a bummer, but rejected much else. By the time of the 1972 election the college student vote—after predictions of a near monolithic mandate for McGovern—went about even-Steven (49% for McGovern vs. 47% for Nixon in an October 1972 Gallup Poll). And the phenomenon described by Peter and Brigitte Berger as the "blueing of America" seemed well under way.

*   *   *

The magnitude of the expansion of the college system in America in the last decade is hard to overestimate. In terms of monies spent, it far dwarfs the Manhattan Project, putting a man on the moon and, say, from the years 1965–72, was somewhat larger than the Vietnam war. In an era (now) when cocktail party rhetoric tends toward smug recitals, on the one hand, of governmental impotence and, on the other, condemnation of overgoverning—here is a prime example of a) something Americans wanted desperately, b) something only governments could do effectively, c) success at a truly massive endeavor. Almost the entire increment of new college students in recent years has enrolled in *public* institutions. From 1966 to 1972, the number of students in *private* colleges went up by 68,000 and the number enrolled in *public* colleges went up by 1,159,000. In 1960, the students in private colleges made up *42%* of the total. By 1972, private college enrollees made up only *24%* of the total.

In short, the schools, desks, books, equipment, teachers and administrative salaries of the greatest education boom in history was paid for with *public* dollars, legislated by federal, state and local politicians and transmitted via a massive and often bewildering array of "programs." Accordingly, be prepared the next time someone at a cocktail party tells you that "the programs didn't work." Tell him he's wrong. And if he wants proof tell him to ask the plumber's son who's studying business administration at a community college.

This success story of American education doesn't only apply to higher education, of course. As noted earlier, it applies to nursery schools and kindergartens, and the sharply decreased rate of high school dropouts. It applies as well to elementary schools and to high schools generally, which met the crush of Baby Boom babies with limited warning (elementary and secondary school enrollment numbers soared from 36 million to 47 million from 1960 to 1971). Moreover, over roughly the same period the number of Americans enrolled in "adult education" classes went from 8.3 million in 1957 to 15 million in 1973, studying everything from ceramics, acting, yoga, boat building, black culture, meat buying as well as more academic subjects offered on a no-credit basis. All in all—brace yourself—74 million Americans were in some kind of school in 1973!

CHAPTER 7

What Goods Give (Possessions)

If indeed it works like a duck, earns like a duck and is schooled like a duck, does it also own and use the accouterments and perquisites of a duck? Do Americans, and particularly those Americans who make up the Massive Majority Middle Class, have a good life by the earlier standards of middle-class material well-being?

In truth there are two parts to the question.

Do Americans own the goods and get the services?

And are these goods they own and services they purchase really useful and/or enjoyable?

Let us consider the second question first, for a major body of opinion has grown up in recent years to the effect that Americans are huckstered into buying shoddy goods and gulled into purchasing corner-cutting and disreputable services. And if the goods and services are worthless and misdirected, then it makes little difference if more people indeed share such plastic junk.

Material goods, we are regularly told by persons who are not noticeably ascetic in their own lives, are a snare and a delusion—indeed they not only don't make life better they make life worse. The GNP doesn't really represent the Gross National Product but the Gross National Pollution. Those stunning trillion-dollar GNP numbers include the cost of imperial wars and vaginal sprays; of electric toothbrushes and the anti-pollution equipment deemed necessary to clean up the rivers and air from the pollution generated by producing the power needed to turn the bristles on the electric toothbrush, of unsafe $6,000 automobiles and of gyp mechanics who overcharge the consumer to fix something that wasn't wrong.

It behooves us, then, to look at what Americans are really getting from the much-maligned, much-expanding GNP. If the public is indeed being seduced into purchasing useless goods and services, then perhaps the Failure and Guilt Complex has a point. On the other hand, if the GNP—and specifically that portion of the GNP that comes through to the consumer—represents a trend toward honest utility, pleasure and leisure, then perhaps the present *is* better than what it replaced.

The GNP in 1970 was 976 billion dollars, and in that year $617 billion was spent by persons compared to $325 billion in 1960, an increase of 90% in a decade. Here is how each category *climbed* during the decade, providing an interesting picture of how Americans are spending their new middle-class incomes:

PERSONAL CONSUMPTION EXPENDITURES BY PRODUCT 1960–70 (RANKED BY ORDER OF PERCENTAGE INCREASE)

		1960–70 and increase
1.	Private education	181%
2.	Medical care	148%
3.	Personal business	122%
4.	Foreign travel	118%
5.	Recreation	113%
6.	Housing	97%
7.	Personal care	91%
8.	Clothing, accessories and jewelry	89%
9.	Religious and welfare activities	87%
10.	Household operations	83%
11.	Transportation	81%
12.	Food, beverages and tobacco	63%

(U. S. Bureau of Economics Analysis)

We have just examined the burgeoning educational scene in America as viewed through the lenses of "enrollment" and "attainment." Education viewed that way is largely a *public* expense. Still, the dollar amounts spent by *individuals* on education—for tuition, books, equipment, etc.—are also substantial. And such expenditures do not deal only with rich parents sending their children to private schools; they involve tuition for parochial schools and for state universities as well as money to buy equipment for the mechanical drawing student at a community college. The reader's heartstrings have been touched in the preceding chapter; we assume then that it is now acknowledged that education is good, decent, noble and enlightening. Accordingly, as we begin to talk about what people spend their new money on we should immediately note this first fact: Of the twelve categories of "personal consumption expenditures" in the chart above it is *education* that has *climbed most sharply* in this terrible era of electric toothbrushes and one-way disposable cans. In 1960, personal educational spending ran to $3.7 billion.

Ten years later the figure was $10.4 billion, an increase of nearly triple (181%).

If spending for education is to be considered useful, desired and rewarding, surely when compared to tail fins and hot combs, we may add the following halo category as well: "foreign travel." And so it is interesting to note that while for the decade of the Sixties personal spending for education increased the most rapidly, for the decades of the *Fifties and the Sixties combined* the category of personal spending that soared fastest was "foreign travel," rising from $600,000,000 in 1950 to $2.2 billion in 1960 and to $4.8 billion in 1970. Which is a lot of people in Belgium on Tuesday.

The next two[1] categories of personal spending ranked by rate of climb over the decade of the Sixties are also not associated with the fruits of gadgetry, gluttony or gimmickry.

During the 1960s spending for "medical care expenses" soared 148%, from $19.1 billion to $47.3 billion. Some of that rise, to be sure, was caused by a rampant medical inflation in the latter part of the decade, in part triggered by the enactment of Medicare. But the new $28 billion also paid for a lot of needed heart surgery, leukemia treatments, ulcer care, prosthetic limbs and so on. Given some money, Americans not only educated their children and traveled abroad, but they sought out and received health care.

The category of "recreation" was the next highest climber in the decade, an increase of 113%, from a 1960 figure of $18.3 billion to a 1970 total of $39 billion. Again, this would seem to be a sort of spending that is hard to fault. Americans not only educated their children, traveled and sought health care, but pursued all the leisure-time activities they always wanted to: They went boating and camping, played tennis and golf, bowled and photographed, listened to records and eight-track stereo cassettes, played the piano, the clarinet and the drums, collected postage stamps, painted pictures, read books, went to movies rated G and rated X, grilled shishkebob in their backyard barbecue, visited national parks and national forests, watched Tom Seaver pitch and John Unitas pass, Wilt Chamberlain and Willis Reed joust and Dick Butkus slam—and so on through $39 billion worth of expenditures in the year 1970.

The last of the top six categories is "housing," with a 97% increase. Over the decade, spending for housing rose from $46.3 billion to $91.2 billion as Americans by the tens of millions moved into suburban single-family homes. And a family that has moved from an urban tenement or

---

[1] Not included in this order is the catchall statistical category of "personal business," which includes stock brokerage commissions, bank service charges, safe deposit box charges, classified advertisements, legal services, labor union dues and funerals—which climbed by 122% to $35.5 billion.

row house—or from a failing farm—to a quarter acre of suburbia with a patio, a rec room, a family room and a laundry room isn't necessarily a victim of some suburban subdivider's hucksterism. That quarter of an acre —in the eye of its owner—is nothing less than an *estate*, and it is typically tended with care and even passion.

If education, travel, health, recreation and housing were the fastest rising of the spending categories, which were the slowest rising? Ironically, they include just those items about which Americans have been most severely scolded: cosmetics, alcohol, tobacco, jewelry, cars and clothing.

Of particular interest, it should be noted that under the food, beverages and tobacco category there is a subcategory of "tobacco" with only a 60% gain—about a third that of education—and "alcoholic beverages" at 70%, half that of medical care, each well below the all-products increase of 89%.

The purpose here is not to suggest that Americans don't spend money on junk, gimmicks, weeds of one sort or another, frills and hard liquor while, in fact, there are indeed pressing social concerns that face the nation and its citizenry. The point is that given a vast increase in discretionary income over the last decade, the broad spending trends have been common-sensical and worthwhile.

Abbreviated, here is the message: People aren't fools. So often, in fact, they are so very much wiser than their critics.

Some observers of the American scene take manic glee in scorning "middle Americans" and their twisted economic values. Yet, it would seem Americans really deserve little scorn on this account. Given some money they spend it privately on good things like education, travel, recreation, medicine and housing—things even charter members of the Failure and Guilt Complex would have difficulty attacking. For, indeed, these are much the same priorities they establish for themselves when they spend their own grants. The new middle class has aped the old.

But, of course, the F&GC attack on the American way of life and commerce goes well beyond substantive patterns of "personal consumption expenditures." The attack goes beyond substance and cuts deep into the *form and manner* of how America's goods and services are distributed. When critics say Americans buy "junk" or that they live in "plastic" communities, that is in part an aesthetic judgment.

Example: One of the perennial sitting ducks for the F&GC popguns is Strip City, U.S.A. Garish and neoned, asphalted linear tentacles of commerce do indeed now spread outward from just about every major American community. "Every city looks alike on the drive in from the airport," goes a familiar plaint, and it is so. South of McDonald's is a Pizza Hut, a Qwik car wash, a discount store, a used car lot, eleven gas stations (four closed) that, pre-crisis, gave away stamps and tumblers emblazoned with the mug of the local quarterback, three supermarkets shrieking "sale" as meat prices rise, motels with crystal-blue swimming pools designed to catch the carbon and sulphur particles as they drop gently from the sky, and—inevitably—another McDonald's and still another McDonald's.

These ribbons of glitter are criticized largely on aesthetic and qualitative grounds. They are ugly, we are told. The food is dull, flat and stale if not unprofitable.

How does one answer such criticisms? Architecturally and aesthetically, of course, one could simply say Strip City is gorgeous, not ugly, and let's fight about it. Such a case can be made: A commercial belt should not look like a medieval castle or a Louis Sullivan office building, and Strip City, if garish and noisy, is also vibrant, humming and active—indeed it is an automotive version of an oriental bazaar. We pass on that one; someone else can make the case and, in fact, has.[2] So, too, one could defend the quality of the cuisine at fast food emporia: for every rubber hamburger stand there are also some tasty franchise steak houses that give a decent plateful of beef. Again, however, these are the wrong pages for the reader seeking an argument on the merits of A & W root beer compared to a reluctant white wine that travels well.

The argument here begins with the question: What does it replace? Is it better? Is it much better?

And in order to answer such questions we must leave the aesthetic and qualitative and talk about *function*.

What do the contemporary innovations aimed at the Massive Majority Middle Class *do for*, or *do to*, Americans?

The stunning growth of the franchised fast food chains is a perfect case in point.[3] The deepest measure of their meaning to life in America has little to do with either the quality of their pizza or the prettiness of their shingles. Earlier in this volume we suggested that the impact of Lordstown was to be found in calculating how many people *weren't* working there. Later we will suggest that the meaning of the worst of the black slums ought to be weighed by determining *who no longer lives there*. And so too with McDonald's, strangely enough. It's significance also rests with the absence of someone. The missing person in this instance is Mom, and McDonald's allows her *not* to engage in the following activities: shopping, menu planning, food preparation, cooking, table setting, serving, table clearing, dishwashing, dish putting-awaying.

---

[2] See Robert Venturi's *Learning from Las Vegas* (published 1972) and "Ugly Is Beautiful," an interview in May 1973 *Atlantic*.

[3] One chain, McDonald's, does over a *billion* dollars' worth of business a year, recently has been adding an average of one new outlet per day to its total of 2,500 in the United States, and has passed the U. S. Army to become the nation's biggest purveyor of meals.

The function of the fast food business, then, is quite simple: Women's Liberation.

The liberation may involve a major activity like allowing a woman to hold a for-pay job during the day, secure in the knowledge that her family will get a decent, if unelaborate, meal in the evening. Or the liberation may simply involve the freedom to attend a League of Women Voters meeting, or to take half a day off and go to a museum, or go bowling, or plant an azalea bush, or make a centerpiece for a church supper or go to an encounter group session or see her lover. It may turn out to be Kid Lib as well: the suburban mother who knows she can buy a fast, cheap meal for her family may accordingly find time to drive her daughter to a cross-town gymnastics meet or her son to a basketball game. It may even turn out to be Man Lib—if his wife can work at a part-time job, he may not have to moonlight at a second job.

For McDonald's to perform all these wondrous feats they need not serve haute cuisine or be housed in an elegantly tweedy building. What they must be is accessible and inexpensive, and in fact they are. Because they are, they help give Americans some options they didn't use to have. That is better than what it replaces.

We are prepared, then, to answer "yes" to the general question "Are the new goods and services we buy generally useful and enjoyable?" For when viewed by *function,* by what they do to us or for us, they are indeed useful and enjoyable, from education to medical care to foreign travel and on to fast food.

* * *

As we look now to measure the *growth* in some specific sorts of goods that the Census tells us Massive Majority Middle Class Americans have acquired in recent years, we shall continue to watch *function.* For goods of themselves mean little; what is important is what they do for us.

Let us begin with the elementary proposition that washing clothes is no fun. Indeed, not only is it no fun, but it takes hours and hours of work—time that for most women could surely be put to more creative use. In 1960, there were 22 million automatic clothes washing machines, representing a presence in 41% of the households in America. One decade later, in 1970, there were 38 million clothes washing machines in American households, about 60%. *Roughly figured, about one in three women in 1970 have washing machines who did not have them in 1960.*[4]

It is easy to make sport of these numbers and easy, too, to attribute a sexist mentality to this analysis. But the truth is, that for all the noble

[4] And the figure is now still higher. According to trade sources, about 17 million new washing machines were produced in the four years from 1970 to 1974. Some were replacement machines, but many were first-time purchases.

sentiments about husbands and wives sharing household responsibilities, it is women who still do the wash, and washing machines sharply reduce the time and effort involved in doing that wash. The drudgery of housework has been substantially reduced. If there is an irony that this was happening at precisely the moment when household drudgery, after being with us for millennia, became a flaming political cause, it shall not be dwelt upon here.

What is so for the washing machine is probably more so for the clothes dryer if for no other reason than that it is a machine newer on the American scene and one that has come into common usage with a greater rush. In 1950, the Census did not even count dryers. In 1960, there were 9 million dryers, in *17%* of the households. And in 1970, there were 27 million dryers in *42%* of the households! Moreover, from 1970 to 1974, about 13 million new dryers were sold according to industry statistics. Clearly we are reaching a time—indeed we probably have already reached it—where the house *without* a clothes dryer is the unusual one.

If washing clothes by hand is drudgery, so too is the clothespin caper. Of course, there were those syrupy commercials about smiling neighbor women hanging up the wash on clotheslines and figuring out whose sheets were Rinso white and whose were tattletale gray. But that was hokum. Drying the clothes involved wringing them, hanging them, taking them down, folding stiff clothes on a raw day and so on. Having a machine fluff-dry the wash while a housewife reads a book, or watches television, or plays with her child, or goes to a meeting, or plants a garden—or goes to work—is surely better by far than what it replaces.

Always alert to mischief, we offer in evidence here a dilemma designed to confound the opposition. Consider for a moment two of the component parts of the Failure and Guilt Complex. On the one hand is the Women's Auxiliary. Surely, the women must acknowledge that even in this sexist, unjust and enslaving society the clothes dryer represents a force for liberation. On the other hand, consider the ecological wing of the F&GC. One of the reasons the sky is falling, we are told, is because Americans are profligate in the use of fossil fuels, a nonrenewable resource, which we are running out of, and whose use pollutes the world. And what, pray tell, would be a classic symbol of energy profligacy in this energy-guzzling society of ours? Next to the automobile, surely the clothes dryer. From an ecological point of view, after all, it is essentially a heat machine that turns, rather than a turning machine that heats. As a heating machine it uses considerable amounts of voltage, voltage generated most typically by the burning of considerable amounts of coal or oil in generating plants. The leftovers from these fuels, of course, pollute either the water or the air, usually both.

What to do? Either liberate the lady or foul the environment. Our temptation is to allow these two components of Failure and Guilt Complex to compete with each other in a war of rhetoric, one side claiming in characteristically moderate rhetoric that breaking the bonds of female enslavement is the highest priority, the other, with equally moderate rhetoric, that the world will come to an end in a ball of fire or a sheet of ice if we don't stop driving Buicks and using clothes dryers.

Such a temptation to let civil war rage will be resisted. We vote with the women. We vote with technology. We vote for materialism. We vote for labor-saving devices. And we note the root cause of so many of our problems today; they are the side effects of progress, a thought that will be returned to in these pages. The pollution problem—a serious one—is caused by a machine that allows women not to get sores on their hands from wringing out the wash. Alleviating that sort of drudgery represents a considerable human advance. The problems of pollution that such an advance creates in its wake are manageable problems, and they will be managed. On balance, then, what we have is far better than what it replaces; humanistic progress, not ecological failure.

The liberationists' case can also be made regarding the home food freezer, although the numbers are not quite as dramatic. In 1960, there were 10 million food freezers in America—a freezer owned by 18% of American households. As of Census day in 1970 (April 1), there were 18 million freezers sitting in 28% of American dwellings. In the four years from 1970-74, about another 12 million freezers were produced. Figuring some of these as replacement units, one can assume that today about 35-40% of American households have freezers.

In what way is a freezer a liberationist machine? One shopping trip to the supermarket can be used by a housewife to purchase food for an extended period of time (often at sale prices)—saving a number of separate, time-consuming visits to the supermarket. Food can be prepared in larger quantities and saved; a housewife making her own special spaghetti sauce for a Tuesday night can make enough for the next five Tuesday nights—saving time. Finally—and quite important—the advent of the home food freezer birthed the mass marketability of frozen prepared foods, and more recently and highly liberationist, the prepared *meal* or, if you will, the "TV dinner." From a housewife's point of view the TV dinner is instant McDonald's. Just like the fast food emporia, the TV dinner means little preparation, table setting, or dishes to wash. Number-one son can eat a Chinese dinner, the daughter can have veal cacciatore, Mom can have her favorite Polynesian dinner and Dad, meat loaf—all for about $.75 a meal, available today because food freezers are available.

The Census today gathers data about dishwashers. Significantly, in 1960, there was no Census question for dishwashers because there weren't enough around to make such a survey terribly meaningful. When the Census was taken in 1970 there were a total of 12,000,000 dishwashers representing 19% of the households. Industry sources show that about 10,000,000 dishwashers were produced in the first four years of the Seventies. By mid-1974, one could estimate that around a third of American homes have dishwashers.

A dishwasher is probably not as functionally useful as a clothes washer or dryer—the dishes usually have to be scraped and rinsed by hand prior to insertion. Still, it does eliminate the actual hand washing and drying of dishes (and cleans them better). Like a clothes washer and dryer, like a food freezer, the automatic dishwasher gives a housewife more time and more energy to devote to other things. It too is a liberationist machine. At the current rate of sales it is likely that by the time the 1980 Census is taken the typical American house will have a dishwashing machine, not a dishwashing housewife.

The story of air conditioning in America is somewhat different. It is not sexist in its impact, and it is essentially a comfort, not a liberation. In 1960 there were 6.6 million homes in America with air conditioning, either room units or central systems. These 6.6 million homes represented *12%* of the total. In 1970, there were *24* million homes with air conditioning. These homes represented *36%* of the total—*a tripling in a decade!* Moreover, air-conditioning units are selling at the incredible rate of about 5½–6 million a year—or close to 25 million sold from mid-1970 to mid-1974. Some of these units are replacing older units, some may well be second or third units in already air-conditioned houses. But still it is eminently plausible to think that *today more than half the houses in America have air conditioning.*

Just as one must remember what washing clothes by hand was like in order to understand the meaning of the washing machine, so one ought to remember what pre-air-conditioning life was like in America in order to sense the meaning of the advent of air conditioning on a mass scale.

America is a hot country in the summer. A racy publication called *Local Climatological Data*[5] provides statistics for the "Normal Monthly Maximum Temperature" for selected cities. During a typical July the temperature will go as high as 105 in Phoenix, 95 in El Paso and Dallas, 93 in Sacramento, 91 in Boise, 92 in Wichita, 91 in New Orleans, 93 in Oklahoma City, 88 in Denver, 87 in Washington and Des Moines and Baltimore, 86 in Philadelphia, 85 in New York City, 84 in Chicago and Minneapolis, 83 in Pittsburgh—and so on. Hot![6]

Summers in the city used to involve people sleeping on the roofs, on

[5] Published by U. S. National Oceanic and Atmospheric Administration.
[6] Those are "normal maximums." "Record" maximums include: New York 106, Chicago 104, Washington 106, Phoenix 118, Los Angeles 110 (in September!), 109 in Cincinnati, 107 in Indianapolis.

fire escapes or in the parks—anything to escape the sweltering heat of a brick building. Life in the suburbs or on the farm wasn't much happier. The well-to-do fled to the mountains or the shore and the rest of America sweated it out.

Now—for about half of all Americans—their homes have at least individual rooms that are livable even in unlivable weather. Many offices are air conditioned (indeed overly air conditioned), and work goes coolly, even when the temperature rises. Coolness is now also a characteristic of the nation on wheels. In 1970, more than three fifths (61%) of new automobiles had factory-installed air conditioning—versus 7% in 1960.

In short, America is cooling it, and it's nicer.

The only other household appliance whose presence is recorded by the Census is television. It has become a thoroughly ubiquitous machine. Before World War II there were very few. By 1950, there were 5 million television sets in the United States, representing about 12% of households. In 1960, there were 46 million sets, representing 87% of all households, and 11% had two sets. By 1970, there were 61 million sets, representing 96% of all households, while 29% had two sets or more, and 43% had color sets.

The arguments against television are familiar: violence, commercials, stupidity, wasteland, and we even have our own specific criticism, to be voiced in a few moments. Suffice it to say that television in America is, surely, an imperfect medium, often reflecting the imperfectness of our society. That television programming can and should be improved ought really to go wthout saying. But the judgment here is that despite its flaws life with television is better than what it replaces—which was life without television—which is why 96% of the households in America have decided to spend hard-earned money on television. If that sounds simplistic, so be it. People buy television sets because, obviously, they think they're worth tho money.

Personally, the author likes sports and politics on television.

The crunch of hockey and the ballet of professional basketball are joys to behold and before TV were essentially only an occasional experience for most American sports lovers. Now, along with baseball, football, golf and tennis they are standard fare and fun to watch.

Politics too is a spectator sport, and never so close to so many Americans as now, thanks to television.

There was a time, a few years ago, when politics-by-television became the most chic of overblown stories. After the 1968 election, one silly book purported to document how a President of the United States was elected by an advertising agency in New York (despite the curious fact that when the TV campaign went into high gear the candidate, coincidentally or not, began losing votes by the millions). By the time of the congressional elections of 1970, stories about political television consultants graced the covers of national news magazines and the line was that whichever candidate had the better half-hour "documentary" and the better short commercials that candidate was blessed in political heaven and ought to be odds-on for election. So concerned were the forces of good, that Common Cause felt it necessary to call for the abolition of any paid political broadcast of less than five minutes' duration, on the grounds that short commercials couldn't properly deal with the issues and on the apparent corollary that some of the windiest and most elusive men in America could be prevented from saying nothing in five-minute chunks. In 1972, one of the candidates for the Democratic nomination for the presidency was the mayor of New York City whose claim to national fame was a series of appearances on the Johnny Carson show and the idea that his video charisma hung out even in ten-second segments.

By the time the telegenic mayor had been beaten in the first big primary by a candidate who looked malevolent and in the second by a candidate who was described as milktoast, politics by television had come upon sad days. Suddenly, we were told, television commercials had no impact.

Neither diagnosis was valid. The television commercial is neither meaningless nor the be-all or end-all of a political campaign. It was, and remains, a useful tool that enables a candidate to go directly to his constituents with what he thinks they want to hear—which is often a quite genuine tipoff of how the candidate sees the world—and it enables voters to see what the candidate has to say for himself, with no journalistic intermediary between the voter and the candidate. What is true for the paid commercial is far more true for the television news clip, as has been documented in the book *The Ticket-Splitter* by Walter De Vries and Lance Tarrance. Voters, particularly independently minded swing voters, watch the nightly news and see film clips of the candidates doing their number on the stump. They see and hear and sense more than they were ever able to in the pre-electronic age. And if they can see a politician, they can also see his warts. This, of course, injects a third party into the voter-candidate interaction, and this is why most candidates are distrustful of TV newsmen. Still, there is a balance. TV reporters and editors have the power of selection and commentary, but candidates are usually seen speaking for themselves on news shows and surely on their own paid commercials. In the instance of the presidency, networks will pre-empt shows for any major presidential address, allowing the President to communicate directly with the American public. This practice has been criticized by some media observers, particularly when it has been practiced as regularly as President Nixon did in 1969–71. It is unjustified criticism in our judgment. It is one more mechanism that gives Americans a means of judging their elected officials.

In all, television has helped make politics a major American spectator sport, and this is highly salutary in a democracy, where after all, the spectators are ultimately the participants. The best-attended Lincoln-Douglas debates were viewed by only fifteen to twenty thousand people. The Chautauqua circuit took politics to the people, but the tent only held a few thousand souls at best. Today a candidate for national office has direct contact with tens of millions of Americans every time he appears on the network news. The good ones are as much fun to watch as Phil Esposito or Walt Frazier.

Television has also made Election Eve a national institution. No longer do people go to bed early and wait for the significant returns the next morning, the way Harry Truman did in 1948. Instead, the networks devote one evening every two years to a massive exercise in psephology and, again, the public learns more than it was able to know in the pre-television era.

Finally, election fraud may have been reduced by the fast reporting demanded by Election Night coverage. No longer can the votes of the river precincts be held out for three or four days in order to shave a few votes here and few votes there.

Because a later section of this volume discusses the role of the press in the American dilemma, it may be well to close out this section on television with a large fat caveat.

Television does help the election process. It does show nice pictures of basketball and hockey and Julie Andrews. But, of course, there are some deeper questions to be asked, particularly about the news end of the business: Does television present a fair and balanced portrait of America? And the second question is: Can it?

It doesn't really, and it probably can't. The operative fact in the news business—and the television we are now talking about is part of the news business—is that *good news is no news*. It is news when an environmentalist says the sky is falling and not news, the next day, to note that the sky is still there. Gloria Steinem makes news with the rhetoric of women oppressed and the Census Bureau makes no headlines about the number of homes now replete with clothes dryers. The burning ghetto is news; the silent statistical march of blacks into the middle class is barely noteworthy. Spiro Agnew was news when he said the networks are unfair; it is not news if someone says that, at the least, most days on most issues the network news teams serve up news fair, square, copious and with a remarkable degree of technical competence.

This journalistic Gresham's Law is not new with the advent of television, of course. Complaining, contention, argumentation and scandal have always held disproportionate weight in the dialogues of men. But there have never been sixty-one million television sets in a nation before, bringing the sights and sounds of news into every household every night. The question then is what is the effect of the steady drumbeat of problems, crises, arguments and revolutions that are apparent in one's living room every evening?

There are three possible responses: Either viewers believe the stuff, or they don't believe it, or they're not sure whether or not they believe it—and the net results aren't totally encouraging in any case.

The believer sees the world as one steady crisis and develops a demeanor that makes Jeremiah sound like Babbit.

The disbeliever sees that news doesn't reflect life and develops both a skepticism and a contempt for a media system that he fears is trying to degrade and diminish the everyday feelings of health and optimism that many Americans feel.

The third group is simply confused—and they may well be a majority of the viewers. On the one hand, they know their own lives are decent and somewhat successful. On the other hand, they see on the tube the daily scenes of crisis and disintegration. These Americans are genuinely troubled by the split between perception and reality.

The problems posed by television news and the news business generally are real and cannot be brushed under the rug and dismissed as political paranoia. But something else must be understood as well: The problem spawned by so-much-news is the dilemma of a successful and open society able to beam turbulences of every shape, size and complexity to a viewership hungry to understand. The news problem, like so many of our problems, is a side effect of progress and better than what it replaces, which was less news.

* * *

Comes now the final Census-recorded item in the personal inventory of American middle classniks, saved deliciously for last, the driving force of life in America, the great polluter itself, the much maligned, much purchased automobile.

Like washers, dryers, freezers and air conditioning the presence of automobiles in America has accelerated in the last decade. Unlike these other items, and somewhat like television, automotive data suggest that car ownership is in the process of lapping itself, to keep the image automobilish.

There seems to be a good chance that *by the time the 1980 or 1990 Census is taken, more than half of the car-owning households will own two cars, not one. This is so despite the energy crisis.*

Here are the data, guaranteed to generate noise pollution from ecologists: By 1960, cars were obviously already a substantial majority way of life in America: 79% of the households in America owned at least one. By 1970, the percentage of owners had climbed modestly, to 83%. Indeed, there doesn't seem to be much more room for an increase in that rate; some people (say, a retired elderly woman living in a Miami Beach apartment, or a young secretary living in a downtown high rise in New York City) have no need or desire for a car, regardless of cost. But while the rate of households with at least one car remained roughly the same, the rate of households with *two or more cars* soared—from 22% to 35% of all households.

Projecting that rate not too far in the future yields the estimate that half of the *car-owning* families in America will be two-car-owning families. Depending on how you might want to project the numbers, it is, in fact plausible to assume that soon more than half of *all* households will have two cars, and considering that the number of one-person households is soaring these days, that's quite a trick indeed. Only the specter of a deep and continuing petroleum shortage stands in the way of that latter projection, but the guess here is that that problem will be solved not by fewer cars but, more intelligently, by smaller more economical cars.

In all, there were 61 million cars in use in America in 1960. By 1970, the total had climbed to 96 million. Today it is over 100 million. Moreover, as we face now a great boom in new family formations—as the Baby Boom babies reach age sixteen, age eighteen, age twenty-one, get married, get a house etc.—there will be a continuing boom in car sales in the years to come, despite the energy crisis.

The anti-car position has been well-publicized in recent years. Pollution, highways-tearing-up-city-neighborhoods, mothers-who-are-really-chauffeurs and accident rates have been cited to demonstrate the inherent social malevolence of the automobile. Yet, obviously, people continue to buy them, spending massive billions of dollars, and we can assume that the purchasers feel they get something for their money. It is appropriate then —along the lines of our analysis by function—to ask: what? What does the automobile do for Americans? And does what it does outweigh the problems that cars produce? Are a lot of cars better than a few cars? Are the 1972 data better than what they replace, the 1960 data or the 1950 data?

Because the greatest part of the increase in cars occurred due to persons buying second cars, if we are to assess whether the increased number of cars is beneficial, we are really asking if the advent of the *second* car is salutary.

Our judgment—perhaps not unsurprisingly—is yes, energy crisis notwithstanding. For the second car makes suburbia work.

First some facts: Most American men drive to work. In 1960, the percentage of those using a private car to get to work was 64%. By 1970, the percentage had climbed to 78%. At the same time, as we shall investigate in the next section, the numbers of Americans living in suburbia had climbed from 60 million to 76 million. And the percentage of two-car families in suburbia went from 28% to 45%. As of 1970, of all the two-car families 46% are owned by suburban families.

What, then, does the second car do for suburbia?

At least three things. It is one of several developments that make it more feasible for a woman to take a job. If the husband drives off to the office or plant in the morning and the suburban wife wants to work, she often will need a car to get to her job. Public transportation within suburban areas is usually just plain bad. This is in part because America is generally a primitive country in terms of such transportation, caused in part by the super-abundance of cars but more decisively because of the geography of suburbia. So much of the suburban lure is due to low density living; private homes each on a quarter acre lot lead to relatively few people living per square mile, at least by city standards. This leads to major difficulties in establishing bus lines that can be profitable. Distances are great, potential numbers of passengers are small, scheduling must be thin, which reduces the utility of bus service and further shrinks the number of passengers. In short, in many instances, if a wife in suburbia wants to work, particularly if her schedule calls for part-time work requiring non-rush-hour travel when schedules are even thinner and buses may run only every hour or so, she needs wheels, and they usually will be the second set in the household.

Much the same sort of problems holds true for a nonworking woman who wants to make the suburban scene a more fulfilling one. Without wheels, she is often pinned down to the house, either all alone during school hours or with wailing babies and toddlers. Shopping becomes a major production, a luncheon meeting of a civic organization can become a logistical nightmare, participation in a midmorning bowling league may prove to be an impossibility. Second cars, then, provide added options.

Finally, in this examination of what a second set of wheels does for suburban life, we must consider the well-publicized plight of "the chauffeur syndrome." Suburban wives—wives with access to automobiles—complain bitterly about how they are reduced to nonliveried drivers, tooling about not in a Cadillac but in a station wagon, devoting an incredible number of hours taking Ruth to the dentist, Danny to his drum lesson, Sarah to gymnastics, Ann to a dance that night, Ruth to sleep over at a friend's house, Dan to a birthday party, Sarah's friend back to her parents' house, Ann back from the dance—ugh!

No question about it, the chauffeur-mother has a major and legitimate gripe. It's a maddening and tiring procedure. And, as the second-car phenomenon increases, we can assume that the number of chauffeur-mothers will be increasing proportionately. But, once again, we must ask the question: What does it replace?

It replaces, oftentimes, Danny *not* being able to go to drum lessons, Ruth *not* able to sleep over at a friend's house, Sarah *not* able to go to gymnastics classes, Ann stuck at home *not* able to go to the dance. A second car, then—for all its problems—provides a fuller, richer life for suburban kids, albeit a busier and probably more harassed life for their mothers. On balance—for those who opt for suburban life—a better suburban life.

There are, of course, some ways around the lack of a second car in suburbia. The husband can, and often does, go to work via public transportation when it is available or by car pool when it is not. But the public transportation route may convert a drive to work of twenty minutes to an hour's worth of travel—or a two-hour commute round trip. Car pooling can be tyrannical: George has to leave at 5 P.M., but Howard has a last-minute rush job on his desk and would like to work till 5:15, Sam really would have liked to cut out at 4, take a nap, and do some work at home in the evening. Impossible with a car pool.

In short, an obvious statement: Two cars are more convenient than one.

And what of the chauffeur-mothers who complain about their role? They are complaining from a position of affluence and strength. It is a price paid for what suburbia offers: that nice old feeling of a man's-home-is-his-castle, complete with a moat (or a hedge) and a forest preserve (or a backyard). That feeling is difficult—not impossible, but more difficult—to develop in an apartment. Such an option—an apartment in a city where public transportation is easily available, where shops and schools are often within walking distance—exists in many cities in America. There are problems with that alternative in many neighborhoods of many cities, as will be discussed in the next chapter. In the meanwhile, the two-car family makes suburbia more livable than it was. It is a better, more convenient place than it was.

Without attempting to pursue it terribly far, there is another point to be made about multi-car families. There has been a rise in *three*-car families—from 650,000 in 1960 to 3 million in 1971. The three-car family may sound to some like either unmitigated affluence or ecological obscenity. In many cases it is neither. Take, for example, the suburban family with the "normal" need for two cars, as previously outlined, but with one difference. They have a nineteen-year-old son who is attending junior college seven miles away from home. To save money, he lives at home, not in a dormitory on campus. He has a part-time job four miles in the other direction. To do this he *needs* a car. He gets one, and the statistics dealing with three-car families grow by one.

So much for a family-oriented view of cars—they are becoming as common as children in the American household—almost two of each per family.

But before leaving the automotive world generally we must consider, if briefly, some of the more general criticisms directed at our automotive age.

Four sorts of criticisms come to mind: the pollution case, the concrete America case, the automobile safety case, the energy-crisis case.

The pollution argument can probably be discussed most quickly: Federal laws enacted in the last half decade can reduce automobile pollution to acceptable levels within a matter of a very few years. Some argue, in fact, that there has been overlegislation and that the emission standards called for in the new laws are so severe—and with so little benefit at the upper ranges—that the cost of cars will rise to a point where some low-income Americans who can now afford cars will not be able to in the future.[7]

The ribbon-of-concrete argument is not quite as simple. New highways do cut through cities and sometimes destroy decent neighborhoods. Bulldozers do rip through virgin countryside in the course of building new interstate highways. Masses of billboards and rows of gas stations apparently without end cause what purists like to call "visual pollution."

But a central point is often forgotten in the argument. At root, cars and highways are not the cause of crowded cities, torn-up countryside and the visual hurly-burly of the roadside. They are, rather, one of the *remedies*. A city family without an automobile is pretty well condemned to have its vistas limited by the cityscape. It's true that forty years ago—before massive suburbanization—"the country" was geographically closer to the central city resident than it is today, but even if closer, it was harder to reach unless that family owned an automobile, and most didn't. Today, when almost all American families own cars, access to "the country" is far easier. The trip to the beach, to a favorite picnic resort, to a summer cabin,[8] to a forest to hunt deer, to a national park or to a trout stream may be just an hour or two away for a family with a car.

[7] On the other hand, ecologists and environmentalists will continue to be able to afford cars. The author is against that system of ecologically regressive taxation. If some of the emission control machinery is prohibitively expensive and if some group is to be priced out of the automobile market because of expensive and unneeded pollution devices, the recommendation here would be to begin with the membership list of the Sierra Club.

[8] Second homes are becoming ever more common. In 1967, there were 1.6 million such second dwellings. By 1970, there were 2.9 million, an astonishing jump in only three years.

Moreover, the statement that cars and their highways are eating up the scenic and rural America flies in the face of fact: There is more "forest land not grazed" today—more by far—than there was thirty years ago. In 1940, just 11% of American land fell into that category most indicative of scenic beauty. By 1969, that percentage had risen to 21%, a total of 476 million acres compared to 203 million acres three decades ago. Highways do eat up virgin land, but increasing federal dominion over open spaces and the abandonment of many small and unprofitable farms have more than made up the difference.

We will repeat the obvious one more time: People are not damn fools. They wouldn't spend money—lots of money—on cars if they did not receive value in return. At least as much as the clothes dryer, at least as much as the dishwasher or the washing machine, the automobile in America is primarily an agent of personal liberation, not of national pollution and visual destruction. This is well understood in other nations not wealthy enough to feel incessantly guilty. There is not a democratic government in the world that could stand for a week with a conscious and public policy to make it more difficult for its citizens to obtain automobiles. Instead, all over the world, including the far side of the Iron Curtain, the symbol of success and of personal liberation is car ownership.

The real question, then, is this: Does this machine of private liberation destroy the public surroundings to a point that it outweighs the private gain? Our answer is no. The public costs can be legislatively controlled (air pollution) or are in fact a long way from fatal and usually reversible (visual pollution, destruction of open land). The private gains, with one jarring exception, are immense.

The exception, of course, is the astonishing and inexcusable number of people killed in automobile accidents. During the five years from 1967 to 1971, about 55,000 Americans were killed *each year*—a total of 277,000 people! Accidents are the third most common cause of death in the United States (after cardiovascular diseases and malignancies), and about half the fatal accidents are auto accidents. More Americans were killed in *one* year of car crashes than were killed in combat in *all* the years of the Vietnam war, almost as many were killed in the last five years as were killed in combat in the five years of World War II!

In addition, it is estimated that for every death by vehicle there are four permanently crippling injuries.

In large part, this incredible vehicular carnage is due to proportionately more cars being driven more miles than ever before. While traffic death rates per 100,000 persons in the population are at or near all-time highs, the rates per number of active vehicles and per number of miles driven are down somewhat in the last decade and particularly in the last two or three years.

But that the movement toward automobile and highway safety should have remained on a political back burner for so long is at least scandalous, if not murderous. While the auto industry said for years that "safety doesn't sell" (tut, tut) and "people won't buy tanks," while civil libertarians wondered whether enforced usage of seat belts was constitutional, while the federal government passed strict laws about air pollution coming from cars (which has not demonstrably killed anyone) and did next to nothing about stopping the killing on the highways (a crime of the streets that destroys life every hour), 55,000 Americans were dying each year, *and death by car accident was the number-one killer of young people in America!*

The fact is that both government and industry were derelict for an unconscionable number of years in allowing the carnage to continue. Both government and industry have offered excuses. But apologies are more in order. People died who needn't have.

Finally, consider the case of the car versus the energy crisis. We are very rapidly leaving the Age of Cheap Fuel. Accordingly, the nation is turning its thoughts, appropriately, toward mass transit systems. But mass transit is not by any means a whole substitute for the automobile. Europeans have fine mass transit systems, they live in cities not suburbs, and they have been buying cars to beat the band. And so too will it be in America. We'll build mass transit. We'll use it when convenient. And we'll buy cars too, tens and hundreds of millions of safe, ecological and economical vehicles, just like European-style cars. Given a choice between the status and comfort conferred by a Detroit behemoth, and the function bestowed by a small car in an energy-short era, Americans will choose little vehicles and drive to work, and to the supermarket, and to clarinet lessons, and to the dance and to Sarah's friend's house. Suburbia will live!

* * *

Washers and dishwashers, clothes dryers and freezers, television, air conditioning and cars—these are the goods that are tabulated by the enumerators of the Census Bureau, and it is clear that these goods are owned by proportions of the population that have never before enjoyed such ownership. All of them either clearly are, or seem well on their way to becoming, items that are owned by a *majority* of Americans. Moreover, as we have seen earlier, Americans spend their money wisely beyond the goods just mentioned: The fastest growing categories of consumer expenditures include education, medical care, foreign travel and recreation.

It would seem then, to this author in any event, that Americans—working now at better jobs, earning more money, graduating from high school and going on to college—are moving into the material middle class and behavioral middle class as well as merely crossing some arbitrary and invisible dollar line into an economic middle class. The new Massive Majority Middle Class in America is living life according to the popular perception of how the old middle class used to live: kids in college, interesting jobs, two cars, air conditioning, long vacations, early retirement, dishwashers, clothes dryers, washing machines and a generally suburban life style that we shall be exploring in the next section. It's the real middle class.

* * *

Other items, trends and services deserve quick notice. In some instances they involve a majority of Americans, in some instances data is not easily or accurately available to determine other than yearly sales, which can give only a flavor of degree of usage, and in other instances they are clearly minority activities. But one doesn't have to say that a *majority* of Americans own boats or tents, or snowmobiles for it to be significant. One man's boat is another man's snowmobile, as we shall see in this hasty and impressionistic rundown from the pages of the *Statistical Abstract of the United States.*

Here are some sales figures for home appliances of one sort or another:

- 99.8% of American homes have radios; 8.2 million new ones were produced in 1971.
- 94% of American homes have vacuum cleaners, with 7.9 million new ones sold in 1971.
- 84% of American homes have electric food mixers, 40% have blenders; with 4.9 million mixers sold in 1971 and 4.2 million blenders sold in 1971.
- 91% have electric automatic coffeemakers; 8.5 million were sold in 1971.

In the four years from 1969 through 1972:

- 23 million power lawnmowers were sold.
- 34 million tape recorders were sold.
- 18 million phonographs were sold.
- 18 million hair dryers were sold.

Outboard motors for boats sell at a somewhat slower rate: Only 535,000 were sold in 1972. Altogether, however, there were 7,400,000 outboard motors in use in 1972, not an insignificant number, particularly if one were to figure that, say, an average of four people used a boat; that's getting close to 15% of the population living in households with motorboats. And some people don't live in communities that are easily accessible to water.

Earlier we spoke about the percentage increase in expenditures for foreign travel. Now consider how that translates into individual human experiences.

- In 1950, a total of 676,000 Americans traveled overseas.
- In 1960, a total of 1,634,000 Americans traveled overseas.
- In 1965, a total of 2,623,000 Americans traveled overseas.
- In 1969, a total of 4,623,000 Americans traveled overseas.
- In 1971, a total of 5,667,000 Americans traveled overseas.
- In 1972, a total of 6,790,000 Americans traveled overseas.

That's per year. And it doesn't include travel to Mexico or Canada, Puerto Rico or the Virgin Islands, cruise travelers or military personnel. Meanwhile, back in America:

- 15.3 million Americans bought fishing licenses in 1950, 23.3 million in 1960 and 32.3 million in 1971.
- Hunting licenses sold went in numbers from 12.6 million in 1950 to 18.4 million in 1960 to 22.9 million in 1971.
- Sales of books went from $674,000,000 in 1950 to $1.3 billion in 1960 to $3.7 billion in 1971.
- Attendance at professional basketball games went from 1,986,000 (one league) in 1960 to 9,071,000 in 1972 (two leagues). Professional football attendance went from 3,195,000 in 1960 to 11,096,000 in 1972. Major league baseball attendance went from 20.2 million in 1960 to 27.3 million in 1972.
- Expenditures for admission to "legitimate theater and opera" went from $365,000,000 in 1960 to $735,000,000 in 1970.
- And in 1970, among people over nine years old, 35 million went camping; 16 million went horseback riding; 82 million went picnicking and 77 million managed to find an unpolluted place to swim, perhaps in 4,435 municipal and county outdoor swimming pools (up from 2,513 in 1960 and 1,289 in 1950).

In short, in the last dozen or so years, the Massive Majority Middle Class has managed to muddle through and apparently had a good time while doing it—or at least let us say for now they performed those activities and purchased those items that have heretofore been considered as associated with having a good time.

Whether Americans are really having that good time is another question, which will be discussed later.

CHAPTER 8

Where the Ducks Are (Residence)

For at least the last quarter of a century the idea of "middle class" in America has been associated with the idea of "suburbia."

Since one argument of this book is that a) there are vast new numbers of middle-class Americans and b) that one way to demonstrate that is to show that the life patterns of the new middle class emulate that of the earlier middle class, then it should come as no surprise to see data here showing a massive increase in the rate and numbers of suburban dwellers. Here are the numbers:

PERCENTAGE OF AMERICANS LIVING IN CENTRAL CITY,
SUBURBAN AND NONMETROPOLITAN (INCLUDING RURAL) AREAS,
1950, 1960, 1970[1]

	1950	1960	1970	Change, '50–'70
Suburban	27%	33%	37%	+11%(!)
Central city	36%	33%	31%	−5%
Nonmetropolitan (including rural)	38%	33%	31%	−7%

In 1950, suburbia was the minority locale of residence. By 1960, America was a nation of equal and tripartite residence. By 1970, the suburban place of residence had become the *plurality* locale in America.

In terms of numbers rather than percentages, here is what the data look like:

[1] 1970 boundaries in all instances. Rounding of percentages yields totals that do not add to 100%.

U.S. POPULATION BY TYPE OF RESIDENCE, IN MILLIONS

	1950	1960	1970	Change, '50–'70
Suburban	40.9	59.6	75.6	+34.7 million
Central city	53.7	59.9	63.8	+10.1 million
Nonmetropolitan (including rural)	56.7	59.7	63.8	+ 7.1 million

More than thirty-five million additional suburbanites in twenty years! Moreover, even that's not the total story. Cities in America often *annex* suburban areas as they become built up. These once-suburban-now-city areas are counted as "city" by the Census, but in fact such a counting tends to understate the suburban total and overstate the central city total. In 1970, there were 2,871,000 Americans living in "cities," but in areas that in 1960 were still suburban. By and large, the neighborhood hasn't changed and the people are still typically living in the same one-family houses on a quarter acre on a tree-lined street; only the formal jurisdiction is different.

If these 2.87 million Americans are added to the suburban population and subtracted from the city population, the 1970 data would account for 78.5 million suburbanites versus 60.9 residents of central cities. With that adjustment, the suburbs account for almost 39% of the population and the cities almost 30%—with the *absolute* change in central city population roughly *zero* over a ten-year period while suburbs grew by about *19 million* people.[2]

Moreover, if one should choose to go through the same calculation using the 1950-to-1960 annexation data, the suburban totals and proportions would be even larger, the central city totals even smaller, and

[2] Another way of seeing the change is through voting statistics. Back in 1952, with Eisenhower and Nixon the winning ticket, the big-city vote was often vital in a state's voting pattern. Twenty years later with Nixon and Agnew the winning ticket, the city played a much smaller role:

PERCENTAGE OF STATE VOTE CAST IN SELECTED MAJOR CITIES, 1952 & 1972

City and State	Percentage of Total Vote for President	
	1952	1972
New York, New York	48	36
Chicago, Illinois	41	28
Baltimore, Maryland	39	20
Detroit, Michigan	29	15
New Orleans, Louisiana	27	15
Philadelphia, Pennsylvania	21	17
Milwaukee, Wisconsin	20	14
St. Louis, Missouri	20	10
Los Angeles, California	19	13
Boston, Massachusetts	15	9

one could conceivably be looking ahead to the 1980 Census to see if a *majority* of Americans would be suburbanites. As it stands now—if present residential trends and annexation trends continue—we are probably looking to sometime in the 1990s for an official moment when a President of the United States will stand by the Census Clock in Washington and award a packet of ten polyethylene leaf bags to the person who, having just moved into a suburban townhouse, has made America a nation with a suburban majority.[3]

In any event, what is clear is this: Most of America's recent growth, no matter how one counts annexation, has been suburban. And energy crisis notwithstanding there is no real reason to expect that growth in the immediate future will not also be suburban. (The argument has been made that gasoline shortages will push people from suburb to city in order for them to get to their jobs. But mightn't it be just as logical to move the jobs to the suburb—where the people are?)

There is no other nation in the world where suburbia has become the plurality life style nor where it is moving, apparently inexorably, toward majority status. The case can be made, in fact, that the suburban life style is the first new and major residential life pattern to emerge since the rapid growth of the cities during the early years of the Industrial Revolution.

By this sort of accounting, the previous major changes in life pattern would have been the move from cave to tent to farm and from farm to city.

Is such progression valid? Is the move to the suburb as monumental a human occurrence as the move from cave to farm and village or from the farm to city? Perhaps not. Suburbanization, after all, involves a synthesizing of urban and rural life—the change it offers is not as stark as earlier ones although still pretty stark in itself.

Moreover, it should also be noted here that residence data is pretty sloppy stuff. There are handsome neighborhoods of single-family houses within the jurisdictional limits of most central cities just as there are high-rise apartments and some squalid slums in jurisdictions that are counted "suburban."[4] Indeed, annexation itself is by no means a new phenomenon; it has gone on for almost as long as there have been American cities and if we were to count all annexed real estate as truly "suburban" it would include, for example, all of New York City except the tip of Manhattan.

Yet, most of these errors tend to cancel each other out over the decades, and each new recent census does show a massive movement to

[3] What happens statistically if a trend to "metro government" develops is anyone's guess. No major trend has yet developed and it is the author's guess that no such trend will develop in the immediate or intermediate future.

[4] Although here too the balance comes out clearly on the positive side. There are far more good middle-class-type dwellings in cities than there are bad slum-type dwellings in suburbia.

suburbia. Americans are increasingly moving to locations that are "near, but not in, big cities."[5]

What do Americans get when they get there?

First, typically, they get to own a home. Less than half (48%) of the residents of central cities own their own homes; in the suburbs the rate is 70%. With house ownership, suburbanites normally get some acreage typically lacking in central city digs, and they get more room. The typical central city dwelling in 1970 had 4.7 rooms; the typical suburban dwelling in 1970 has 5.3 rooms. That may not sound like a massive difference, but it works out to a 13% increase. Moreover, the newer the house, the larger it's likely to be. Here is the trend for square footage figures for newly constructed single-family houses, more typically found in suburbia than in central city:

1950	800 sq. feet
1956	900 sq. feet
1968–69	1500 sq. feet
1970s	1400 sq. feet

The slight decline is attributed by experts to the advent of subsidized low-and-middle-income town-house-type dwellings in suburban areas.

The arguments about the larger house and yard space used to be offset by the Sterile Suburbia argument: "They are bedroom communities, with look-alike houses, and it takes so long to commute to work."

That was never as true as the cliché had it, and it is somewhat less true today than it was. In 1960, when 52 million Americans lived in suburbs of the larger metropolitan areas, there were 13 million workers working in suburbs—about 25%. In 1970, with 68 million Americans living in suburbia, there were 18 million jobs there—about 27%. By contrast, in the central city the percentage of workers to total population stayed the same from 1960 to 1970. The "bedroom" gap is closing somewhat.

A nonstatistical way of seeing how much business is now in the suburbs can be gained by getting in a car and driving a little way out from almost any major city in America. The Boston circumferential Route 128 houses some of the most advanced electronic plants in the country. Route 70-S heading northwest out of Washington, D.C., is the home of glittering new government agencies and sleek new corporate headquarters. Suburban Minneapolis around Route 494 is the home of some of the most important milling and data processing companies in the world.

So much has this been the case that the old cliché "Suburbs are dormitory communities," has been replaced with a new one—with some truth

[5] That would be the popular way of expressing the Census Bureau definition which would essentially be: "Within a Standard Metropolitan Statistical Area but outside the jurisdictional limits of that SMSA's Central City."

to it—put forth by civil rights leadership: "All the jobs have gone to the suburbs and it's hard for blacks from the cities to get there."

The growth of suburbia as an independent, even a dominant, form of urban life can be seen through many prisms.

Take the "discount store," a uniquely American postwar invention, and one that is largely suburban in its genesis. Selling goods at less than standard markups, from sprawling stores surrounded with acres of parking spaces, using self-service techniques rather than the conventional bow-and-scrape salesmanship of main-line department stores, the discount stores have racked up an incredible sales record in recent years. In 1955, they accounted for less than $2 billion in sales. By 1973, discount-store volume had climbed to $34 billion.

Of course, figures like that demand a response from department stores and two main ones have been forthcoming. Department stores have set up their own discount chains—the May Company "Venture" stores, Rich's "Rich-Way" stores, Federated Department stores "Gold Circle" stores, etc. Department stores have also accelerated the movement of branches of main-line stores into the wealthier suburbs, and sometimes the branches do far greater dollar volume than the main downtown stores, some of which, in fact, have closed altogether.

To further see the growth of the independent suburb, consider professional sports in America. The Washington Senators were hijacked to a place called Arlington, Texas (suburban Dallas-Fort Worth). The city of Anaheim, once just a gag in a Jack Benny routine, hosts the American League entry in the most populous state in America. Hockey and basketball in the nation's capital are to be played in a place called Largo, Maryland. The National Football League champions in 1969 hailed from Bloomington, Minnesota (suburban Minneapolis-St. Paul), and the Boston franchise is now called "New England" and plays in historic Foxboro, Massachusetts. Foxboro?

If you think that's ridiculous, consider the plight of a latter-day Rip Van Winkle who returned after just a decade and found that one of the great football rivalries might be contested between Hackensack, New Jersey, and Irving, Texas (once known as the New York Giants and the Dallas Cowboys).

And so it goes. First-run movie premières now play in suburban or outer city locations; within a ten-minute car ride of Chevy Chase Circle (on the D.C.-Maryland border) there are seventeen movie theaters! New shopping centers spring up with dazzling arrays of stores, big and small, and replete with civic auditoriums and all-weather enclosed malls with bamboo landscaping.

Something new is happening in America. For two decades and more, population alarmists have been watching the thin red line go up on the population graph—from 151 million in 1950 to 179 million in 1960 to 203 million in 1970 to 213 million in 1974—and have prattled on, about like this: "We're not keeping up, we need more planning, we need more new towns, we need 240 new towns of 100,000 each to keep up and there are only four now and three on the drawing boards—whatever will we do?" Meanwhile, sneakily, not only were new towns being formed, but whole belts of new cities, and a new society, indeed, a new way of life, was being born, 76 million strong by 1970 and more today—about double the 1950 levels—*Suburbacity!*

What do you need to make a suburbacity? All the things mentioned earlier plus:

a) Poverty. You can't have a new "way of life" without gray lining on the silver clouds. Poverty has always existed in suburbia. But recently it has become publicized—"squalor in the midst of affluence" is the phrase. The 1970 Census showed that about 8% of the suburban population is poor, about half the central city rate, an even lower percentage of the rural rate, but still involving 6 million people.

b) Obviously, you can't have a suburbacity without apartment houses. Presto—apartment houses! Garden apartment houses, blocks upon blocks of attached town houses and the crown jewel of the suburban diadem: there, often stuck out in the middle of nowhere, full-scale, high-rise, swimming-pooled, tennis-courted, ten-floor, twenty-floor, thirty-floor arching apartment buildings filled with stewardesses, bachelors, elderly folks, young marrieds without and with children, combining the convenience of apartment living with the attractions of suburban life. The data: Since 1969, more than 43% of the new housing units constructed in the United States have been in multi-family units.[6] In 1972, of the multifamily units built in Standard Metropolitan Statistical Areas (SMSAs), fully 59% were in suburbs.

c) Surely no locale of residence can claim true all-American status if it has no mechanism to handle an emergent lower middle class. That, traditionally, has been a criticism of suburbia: "It's too homogeneous; all you ever meet are people like yourselves." No more. Enter the mobile home. With kitchen, breakfast nook, living room, one bedroom, two bedrooms, three bedrooms, patio awning and barbecue area, America is awash in a wave of mobile home developments, very few of which are in central city areas, many of which are in suburbia. Here is the data:

[6] As high as 48.1% in the early months of 1972.

PRIVATE HOUSING STARTS, MOBILE HOMES, 1965, 1972

	1965	1972
Private housing starts	1,473,000	2,357,000
Mobile homes	216,000	576,000
Mobile homes as % of private housing starts	14.7%	24.4%

In 1960, there were 800,000 mobile homes in America. In 1970, there were 2.1 million. By the end of 1973, the estimate was 3.5 million.

And there's another lament exploded. "The only way to solve the housing problem is the modular housing," the plaint goes. Meanwhile, unnoticed, well more than half a million "modular" houses (called mobile homes) are produced *each year*. And yet the demand for a breakthrough in modular housing still goes on.

As a final fillip to this paean to American suburbia one could list what else Americans get by moving to suburbia: better jobs, more education, more income.

Here is the data:

	Nonmet.	City	Suburb
Income: (med. family income)	$7,832	$9,507	$11,586
Education: (med. school years completed)	11.4	12.0	12.3
Occupation: (percentage prof./tech., managerial)	20%	23%	26%

In truth, however, such an argument would be hard to defend beyond the simple numbers. Suburbanites, it would seem, do not become richer, stay in school longer and hold better jobs *because* they live in suburbia or *because* they have moved there. The converse is likelier. It is people with relatively good jobs and educations who earn enough money to be able to move easily to, and live easily in, suburbia. And the record of recent years shows that by the tens of millions they have done so.

While Americans don't "get" more education, better jobs and more money by going to suburbia they do "get" something else that human beings in social situation want deeply: life in a community with others of equivalent status. That may be no more than jargon for "snob appeal," or no more than a rationalization for "white flight" from turmoil and blacks in the inner city. Whatever it may be, people *do* want their children to mingle with their socio-economic equals, or betters for that matter, and, in fact, what they publicly want for their children, they somewhat more privately want for themselves. They want, deeply, to associate with their "own kind." That is apparent among intellectuals in New York City, among millionaires in Grosse Pointe, among middle-class blacks in St. Albans and among white working-class suburbanites in Parma, Ohio. Wanting to be with your "own kind" is sometimes deeply related to racist feelings and sometimes not. Public opinion polls show that there is far more tolerance for black neighbors today than there was a few years ago— provided, too, that the new blacks in the neighborhood are of socio-economic levels equal to those of the original residents. But *low-income* (often largely black) public housing projects scatter-sited into middle-class neighborhoods are still vigorously rejected by the public, probably mostly on class grounds rather than racial feelings.

In any event, Americans seem to be getting what they want from suburban life. Not only do they live with their own kind, but they live in larger dwellings, with some acreage around it, with one car and often two, often near their jobs, surrounded by a plethora of labor-saving and liberating household machines.

It is interesting to note how close these conditions come to matching at least the physical version of "the American dream" of a few decades ago. What was it? "The little white house with a picket fence around it," of course. That's where June Allyson always wanted to move. She did. She got the house. She got the yard, although split rail seems more popular than picket in fencing styles today. She got her flower garden. She got a car, and so, in fact, did her husband, Fred McMurray. If neither of them quite visualized that the little-white-house caper would also involve crabgrass, chauffeuring kids everywhere via a route that includes the scenic beauty of a mile-long row of pizza parlors and gas stations, no matter. It's not such a large price to pay, particularly if one remembers why June and Fred wanted to go there. The suburbs, it was thought, were cleaner and calmer than in-city tenements on the one hand, and lacking the loneliness and back-breaking dawn-to-dusk work on the farm. Such judgments, in our judgment, have proved to be essentially correct. It was, in short, better than what it replaced, at least for those who were displeased with farm or city.

It wasn't such a bad little dream after all. And not only June and Fred realized it. They share it today with eighty million Americans, give or take ten million.

A society that provides its citizens with what they want is not one to be dismissed lightly, particularly if it is a democratic society dedicated to the idea of the pursuit of happiness via the mechanism of self-government and self-determination. What is so incredible about the whole development is that just when the process can be shown somewhat conclusively to be working pretty well, there arises a chorus of voices, heard in every corner of the land, proclaiming first failure, then guilt. Incredible!

* * *

What about the infamous "central city"? How go things there?

The popular notion provides these images: black, poor, crowded, deteriorating services, slums, bad education, bad jobs and much violent crime.

The last item—crime—is certainly valid. The others are to one degree or another not valid, hardly valid, partially valid, partially valid in some parts of some cities, somewhat valid in special circumstances, or perhaps getting valid.

Central cities, by way of definition, are large urban places of more than 50,000 population that dominate an urban area. And in the 1970 Census year:

- Black? 79% of the residents of central cities in America were *white*.
- Poor? 89% of the families had incomes above the poverty level a poverty rate of 11%, compared to 18% in rural areas.
- Crowded? The central cities were no more crowded than earlier, in fact, they were probably somewhat less crowded. The population dwelling on the 1960 land area of central cities was, in 1970, almost exactly the same (60.95 million in 1970 versus 60.63 million in 1960). There was a gain of 2,870,914 souls in areas annexed by central cities, mostly suburban (and relatively uncrowded) land. In all, then, the population density of central cities has declined slightly over the decade—from 5,336 persons per square mile in 1960 to 4,462 persons per square mile in 1970. Moreover, and more significantly, central city population density in the worst areas of the central cities has declined most sharply. When viewed as "housing" rather than "space," crowdedness has also declined. A dwelling with more than 1.01 persons per room is generally considered overcrowded. In 1960, in central cities, 10.7% of housing units were overcrowded. In 1970, the rate fell to 8.5%.
- Deteriorating services? The number of municipal employees (the people who provide the services) has increased from 1,447,000 in 1960 to 2,014,000 in 1972,[7] an increase of 39% while the population was remaining about the same. Excluding educational personnel the percentage increase was 33%. Payroll expenditures in municipalities went up by 178% from 1960 to 1972 while inflationary pressure pushed costs up by only 43% during the same time. (Total local expenditures [and state expenditures] have gone up relatively faster than federal expenditures.)

[7] Full- *and* part-time employees in both instances, expressed in full-time equivalents (source: U. S. Bureau of Census *Public Employment* and *City Employment*).

- Slums? It's hard to measure what a "slum" is, but it used to be measured as "substandard housing," the key element in whose definition was "a housing unit lacking some or all plumbing facilities." In 1960, of all dwellings in central cities, 9.6% lacked some or all plumbing facilities. In 1970, the comparable rate was 3.5%.

- Bad education? Educational attainment rates have gone up in the central city just as they have nationwide: from 12.3 years in 1960 to 12.7 years in 1972, for the 25–29 age bracket (with a 10.8 years to 12.4 years rise for non-whites). The dropout rate in central cities dropped from 24% in 1960 to 16% in 1970.[8]

- Median family income in central cities went up from $8,524 in 1959 to $10,522 in 1972, an increase of 24% in *constant 1972 dollars.*

- Occupational changes in the central city followed the general upgrading pattern discussed in Chapter 3. For example, the percentages of central city black males in "professional and managerial" work rose from 6% to 11% from 1960 to 1969; for central city white males, the rate climbed from 26% to 30%.

And what of crime and particularly violent crime? *It is going up starkly on a national basis:*

RATE OF VIOLENT CRIME PER 100,000 POPULATION 1960–72[9]

1960	160
1965	198
1966	218
1967	251
1968	295
1969	325
1970	361
1971	393
1972	398

(FBI data)

[8] There have, of course, been a spate of studies about how students in those terrible central city schools "don't learn anything." Data to back up this argument generally takes the form of analyses of standardized test scores showing that central city students are achieving at "less than grade level" and are "behind" other schools in other sorts of locales. So? If there is a relationship between educational achievement and family background (and there is) and over the course of a couple of decades the well-to-do and well-educated families (white and black) move to the suburbs, then it stands to reason that the aggregate scores of those left in the city—disproportionately from less well-to-do families—will be lower than those from suburban schools, schools with children who used to live in the city.

[9] These data are of crimes reported to the police. In April of 1974 a massive study of the populations of five major cities was released by the Law Enforcement Assistance Administration. It revealed that only about *half* of the crimes committed in 1972 were ever reported to the police.

or up by about two and one-half times in a dozen years and up almost double in the seven years from 1966 to 1972! And where is violent crime the worst?

VIOLENT CRIME RATE PER 100,000 POPULATION BY TYPE OF COMMUNITY, 1972

Rural areas	128
Suburbs	222
Cities of less than 10,000	204
Cities of 10–24,999	200
Cities of 25–49,999	267
Cities of 50–99,999	323
Cities of 100–249,999	502
Cities of 250–499,999	721
Cities of 500–999,999	856
Cities of more than 1,000,000	1,262!

(FBI data)

Residents of cities of a million or more face a violent crime rate almost *six* times as great as a resident of the suburbs; the rate in medium-size central cities is almost *four* times that of the suburbs; the rate for small central cities is about *twice* the suburban rate.

So, then, two big facts to consider when viewing what has been called, several million times, "the crisis of the cities."

1) By most conventional indices—housing, income, poverty jobs, education, etc.—life in the cities has been improving, and somewhat substantially.

2) Crime conditions are terrible in the city and getting worse.

What are we to make of this?

First, we must put "the improving conditions" in some sort of perspective. Yes, the non-crime conditions are improving, but they are not improving as rapidly as in the suburban areas. Median family income in central cities may have gone up 24% in *constant* dollars from 1959 to 1972, but median family income in suburbia went up during the same time by 52%—and income in non-metropolitan areas went up by 47%. In short, income conditions in America got better in each of the three types of community—but got better *slowest* in the central city. The same pattern holds true for poverty: lowest in suburbia, highest in nonmetropolitan areas, declining everywhere, but declining slowest in central cities. This general outline holds pretty well for other aspects of socioeconomic progress. Thus, the problems of "black cities" has been overstated; four out of five central city residents are white, but "white flight" is still a real phenomenon. Over the decade of the Sixties the number of whites in central cities actually declined by 606,747 while the number of blacks went up by 3,233,937—a decrease of 1.2% in the first instance and an increase of 32.6% in the second.

There is also the evidence of the senses to consider. There are parts—parts, mind you, not totalities—of most big American cities that have become nothing short of catastrophic, inundated by drug addicts, winos, whores, pimps, racketeers and hapless welfare families. At least one of the reasons for this deterioration of specific neighborhoods is an elementary one: success. Rising incomes have allowed many slum dwellers to leave for better neighborhoods; in leaving they have turned over neighborhoods to thugs and drugged psychological cripples.

A further complication concerns the comparative flight patterns of whites and blacks. Successful whites tend to flee to the suburbs; successful blacks have tended to flee from slums but many still remain within central city limits, in better, formerly white, neighborhoods. Thus, although the numbers and percentages of blacks living in big central cities soared in the Sixties, the percentages and numbers of blacks living in "poverty areas" went down substantially. Because the preponderance of central city residents are still white, it is largely the slower *white* rate of socio-economic success in the city that pulls down central city progress rates, preventing the tax base from rising quickly, and setting in motion many of the problems of the central city. (Successful whites move out, with their dollars.)

Examination of the data, then, leads to this sort of general formulation: While there has been substantial socio-economic progress throughout the United States, the central city (despite major black progress) has become progress' stepchild. There are many good neighborhoods within central cities, many good neighborhoods that are getting better, many, many, neighborhoods that are "suburban" in everything but name. Moreover, Newark's problems shouldn't be confused with those of Dallas, Des Moines or Duluth. Still, the harsh fact remains, the central city *is* a statistical stepchild. Progress has been slower there than elsewhere.

Why?

If one looks at the data in a search for causes, the most apparent ones are crime and success.

This can be seen if one views both out-migration and in-migration as a result of both a "pull" and a "push."

The original "pull" of suburban life—larger houses, land, greenery, as well as the desire for homogeneous socioeconomic grouping—has been documented. But what is the "push" that drives whites from central cities and into the suburbs? One cause of "push" is clearly black success; blacks moving into the economic middle class are successfully moving into the geographic middle class, relatively clean and well-built neighborhoods where whites used to live. This is all the push many whites would need, particularly when their own economic success allows them, in many cases for the first time, to respond to the pull of suburbia. Still many whites don't want to leave. Even if they are not wildly enthusiastic about living in integrated neighborhoods, they would rather stay put than go. But they do leave. And to see why they leave, it is logical to point at the one massive downside indicator that dominates life, and fear of life and limb, in the worst areas of many central cities—violent crime.

Crime is a mighty push in these worst areas. Triple padlocked doors, drug addicts, muggings, rape, shakedown of school children for lunch money are enough to drive many of the best intentioned urbanites into the calmer suburbs. For the elderly, and often defenseless, the tragedy is compounded. Many elderly orthodox Jews in New York no longer go to late-afternoon services because they must return home after dark and fear mugging, beating and humiliation. There are elderly in some inner cities of America who buy large quantities of powdered milk so that they won't have to make as many trips to the store, day or night. Those who can afford it leave. They'd rather switch than fight. And those who can't—stay, walking mockeries of the American dream, living distorted and embittered lives, maybe ultimately voting for a cop for mayor in a usually futile gesture.

Nor is flight to the suburbs exclusively a white phenomenon. The "white noose" is becoming a noose of many colors. Although starting from a much smaller base the rate of blacks living in suburbs has actually gone up slightly more sharply than the rate of whites. Blacks make up only about 5% of the suburban population (vs. about 11% of the total population). But the black 60–70 *rate of increase* in suburbia was 29% versus 27.5% for whites. This rate of fast black growth in suburban areas has continued since the taking of the 1970 Census.

The reason blacks are moving to suburbia is much the same as the reason whites move: the "pull" of suburbia and the "push" of black crime. For there is simply no ducking the harsh and ugly fact that violent crime in American cities is a massively disproportionate black phenomenon.

Consider the fact that Negroes comprise only about *one ninth* of the population in the United States and then look at the "adjusted" rates of arrest for violent crime:

ARRESTS, NUMBER, BY RACE, 1972

	White	Negro	Adjusted X9 Negro Rate	Disproportionality Rate
Murder and nonnegligent manslaughter	5,145	8,347	75,123	14½ : 1
Forcible rape	8,684	8,776	78,984	9 : 1
Robbery	28,236	59,617	536,553	19 : 1
Aggravated assault	72,956	62,890	566,010	8 : 1

These numbers, without question, are the saddest in this book—saddest too for blacks who are, of course, also the disproportionate *victims* of violent crimes.

If one wants to face up to the "crisis of cities," there it is. The "push" of crime is driving blacks from inner city neighborhoods and driving whites from the city altogether.

If that is the root cause of the crisis then the root cure of the crisis is also apparent. Cure crime. Very simple. All the grandiose plans of making the inner cities bloom, of urban renewal, of malls and parks will come to very little if people fear for their life in the city. It has become apparent that "law and order" is no mere code phrase for racism—it is shorthand for civilization itself. If people have a choice of rebuilding civilization in the suburbs, as opposed to fearing for their children's lives in cities, they will move. And when their children are grown, and when they no longer want to live in a single-family house, they will move to an apartment in suburbia, with a swimming pool.

So, unless changes ensue, the future of central cities in America is a little glum. Conditions improve—save the crime condition—population growth is at a relative standstill; actually, a slight white minus and a large black plus, and the action, increasingly, is taking place in the suburban rings.

That is a solution America can live with. There's nothing wrong with suburbacity. It's not going to disappear because of any energy crisis either; there are too many good jobs right out in the rings for commuter woes to stifle growth. After a while people will notice that the County Executive of Prince Georges County, Maryland, is elected by more people than elected the mayor of Pittsburgh and that there are more than twice as many voters in suburban St. Louis County as there are in St. Louis City. Corporate headquarters will continue to blossom in suburban areas, but in an expanding economy the big cities will still have their share. New York City will not dry up, nor will St. Louis or Detroit, but all three are in difficult times. Other cities—newer, wealthier, more spread out—will continue to do fine, suburban style, but under the statistical rubric still of "central city."

Is there, then, a way to revitalize the central city in America?

Cure crime.

Can that be done? Can it be done quickly? Is it worth the effort?

Maybe. No. Yes.

There have been two general strategies propounded to "cure crime" in America. Strategy "A" is the long-term cure-the-causes of crime: poverty, slums, mal-education, prisoner rehabilitation, etc. Strategy "B" is the shorter term get-tough-now school of thought: more cops, take the handcuffs off the police, more judges, stiffer sentences, etc.

If the reader accepts one of the key general premises of this book, namely, that conditions of life have improved dramatically for Americans generally in the last dozen years, and improved specifically for the poor and the black, then Strategy "A" raises a question as a cure-crime plan, although it has great validity on other grounds. If crime went up sharply when conditions-that-cause-crime were getting better, then improving conditions would seem to have failed empirically as a valid strategy. There are so many practical, moral, economic and humanitarian reasons for increasing the level of living of poorer Americans that perhaps we ought to stick to those, and let any cure-crime aspects that may also accrue serve as an unexpected bonus.

Strategy "B," the so-called law-and-order approach, offers somewhat more hope.

There are the beginnings of some faint rays of sunlight regarding the crime data—due, probably to Strategy "B." FBI data for 1972 seem to show at least a *slower rise* in the violent crime rate, and an actual drop in the total crime rate. The total data for 1973 was up again, but violent crime rates in the larger cities—the key to the problem—actually declined absolutely in some instances or rose more slowly than usual in others. These data may augur the beginnings of a minimal turnaround. If they do, the reason for the slow-down in crime, even if slight, would almost surely be that Americans have "thrown money at a problem," notwithstanding President Nixon's nostrum that money doesn't cure problems. Expenditures for the criminal justice system in America—on federal, state and local levels—went from $3.3 billion in 1960 to $8.5 billion in 1970 and are still climbing sharply. Federal expenditures went from $291 million in 1960 to $1.97 billion in 1972, as funds from the Law Enforcement Assistance Agency[10] began to pour into local communities. In the seven calendar years from 1965 to 1972, minimum annual pay scales for police patrolmen in large cities went from $5,763 to $9,454 while maximum scales went from $6,919 to $11,287, increases of 64% and 63% respectively, while the cost of living during the same time period went up by 33%.

Of course, money alone won't do it. Professor James Q. Wilson, the Harvard expert on crime, has outlined some of the other likely causes of increased crime rates in recent years: the do-your-own-thing propaganda of the youth culture, stricter standards of evidence, court backlogs and shortage of personnel, light and uncertain sentencing subject to legal razzmatazz, all of which have passed into street wisdom and led to a condition that has eroded much of the reality behind that fine old adage "crime does not pay."

Beyond these factors, which would seem in some instances to be subject

[10] Signed into law in 1968 by President Lyndon B. Johnson, passed by a Democratic Congress.

to some change via public policy decisions, is another massive one that is massively intractable for a while, but one that ultimately will play a major role in "solving" the crime wave in America and pushing down crime rates.

Violent crime is, to a degree far beyond what most people imagine, an age-sex affliction. The perpetrators are *young men*.

In 1971, about three fifths (59%) of serious crimes were committed by persons between fourteen and twenty-five years of age (the single prime-crime year is age eighteen). If one adds larceny and theft (considered "serious" but not "violent" crime) to the violent crime total, then 76% of such crimes are committed by such young persons. Yet, these persons fourteen to twenty-five constituted, in 1970, only 25% of the adult population. In short, young people commit more than twice the actual proportion of violent crime and three times more property crime than that age group "ought" to commit if age were not a determining variable in the commission of crime.

And males, as opposed to females, commit 90% of the violent crime in America and 81% of the nonviolent serious crime.

Not at all coincidentally, in the years when crimes soared in America, the 1960s, so too did the numbers of young men aged fifteen to twenty-four.

In 1950, there were *11.2* million such young men; they were born in the years from 1926 to 1935, years of low fertility rates in America.

In 1960, were were *12.4* million such young men; they were born from 1936 to 1945, also years of low fertility rates.

But in 1970, there were *18.4* million such young men, a 50% increase while total population was rising only 13.5%; these young men were born from 1946 to 1955, big years in the Baby Boom, and in the echo effect of those fertile times, big years for violent crime. By these lights it can be posited that more than a third—maybe as much as half—of the increase in crime in the Sixties was due solely to demographic causes.

The downturn will not occur right away. In 1970, there were 18 million young men. By 1980, six years from the publication date of this volume, there will be *21* million, children born from 1956 to 1965, the last of the Baby Boom years.

Viewed then as a totality over the whole of the Seventies, the numbers of young men will climb. But the peak year of the Baby Boom was 1957, with a slow and steady decline through the Sixties and a precipitate drop in the early 1970s. The boy child born in 1957 will be age eighteen—the single most prime-crime year—in 1975, *next year*. And every year thereafter, the numbers of those at that single most prime-crime year will be *decreasing,* as we see the instant replay first of the hills of the Baby Boom and then of the valleys of the Birth Dearth.

In the latter half of the decade of the Seventies, the climb in the total numbers of young men will begin to stop. And by 1990, when the children of the Birth Dearth reach the prime-crime age bracket of fifteen to twenty-four, there will only be 17.5 million, substantially *less* than 1980, even about a million less than in 1970. Moreover, of course, the total population will be climbing all along, *further reducing the proportion* of young males.

And, accordingly, it will be in the 1980s that we can logically expect a real and major diminution of the crime rate because of demographic factors.

Here is a year-by-year ratio figure of the relationship of men aged fifteen to twenty-four as compared to the total adult male population:

PERCENTAGE AGED 15–24 AMONG TOTAL ADULT MALE POPULATION

1960	20%
1965	24%
1970	26%
1975	27%
1980	26%
1985	22%
1990	20%

Those changes may not seem like much, but they are quite significant. A rise from 20% to 27% represents a *35%* increase from the base percentage, which happens to be most of the universe of potential violent criminality.

Once the crime wave is reduced to manageable proportions, there is a chance that the older, larger central cities will resume some of their earlier dominance of America's life. People may then be attracted to move back in, and with people comes business, and tax monies and health and vitality. Of course, by then, the suburbacities will have had a head start of many decades and many people will remain content with the new civilizations of Bethesda, Bloomington, Irving, Anaheim, Royal Oak and Bergen County.

What will hopefully emerge is *both:* decent livable conditions in both city and suburb, providing a broad range of *options*—safe cities for city-lovers, green yet lively suburbs for the crabgrass set. It is not an impossible dream.

* * *

How fares the rest of the union?

What's left, in Census terminology, is the "non-metropolitan" population, 64 million strong, almost a third of the population, almost half in rural areas and 34 million in non-suburban cities and towns of less than 50,000 population: Small cities, small towns, crossroad villages, rural areas.

There have been sharp economic gains in rural areas, sharper recently than in any other area, but understanding, however, that rural areas have always contained the most impoverished parts of America, idyllic rhetoric notwithstanding.

The same proportions seem to hold true when all "non-metropolitan" areas are viewed as a group, a rubric that includes not only rural but smaller cities and towns as well. Family income from 1959 to 1972 went up by 47% (constant dollars) in non-metropolitan areas versus 32% in metropolitan areas (which is the product of a split between a 52% increase in the suburbs and 24% in the central city).

As a whole, the non-metropolitan areas gained only small amounts of population in the Sixties—6.8% to be exact, compared with a 6.4% gain for central cities and a 26.8% for suburbia. Within the non-metropolitan areas actual *rural* population has gone down slightly while the population of small towns and cities have gone up slightly.

Statistically speaking, just two decades ago if one were to speak of "mainstream America" one would have been talking about "non-metropolitan areas," comprising 37% of the population in 1950, a higher proportion than either central city and suburb. Today, non-metropolitan areas are only 31%, the same as central cities, and they have lost the relevance-publicity battle as well. Nobody views an isolated town of, say, 10,000 souls as mainstream anything any more. Yet, 64 million Americans still live non-metropolitan lives, and while many towns are losing population many are growing rapidly and have healthy economies. Census studies show that when a town or small city has something special going for it—a college, a university, a military base—it grows and prospers. When it does not, population often tends to wither.

This is important to understand given the data presented earlier about central cities and suburbs. Crime is not much of a problem in non-met areas. The crowding that some people now complain about in suburbia is not present. Income levels are up. Attitudinal polls show that people say they would like to live in small towns where, allegedly, the dear hearts and gentle people live.

And yet—population does not rise. There has been only the bare beginnings of a significant met to non-met migration.

This is the dilemma that faces those who seek to solve America's problems by population redistribution. Some demographers, listening to rhetoric about the cancer of megalopolis, about 70% of the people living on 1% of the land (a relatively meaningless number when you think about it for a while), about sewer moratoria in suburbia because of crowded conditions (by suburban standards), about burgeoning "no-growth" movements, suggest that these problems could be solved if we could encourage people to move from Area "A" to Area "B," areas that are clean, calm, potentially prosperous, often with a glut of good vacant dwellings.

It is true that an intelligent, noncoercive, population policy would make a great deal of sense in America. On a federal level, however, it poses massive political problems—just try to find a city or suburban congressman prepared to vote for extra incentives for non-met areas. (Say, like giving every non-metropolitan dweller a 10% cut in income taxes.)

Such a solution hasn't really been tried—yet. It may well be tried in the future. In any event, non-metropolitan America remains a fantastic potential safety valve should things ever get as bad as some people say they are now.

CHAPTER 9

Black Progress and Liberal Rhetoric (Race)

A. The Good Numbers

Amid all the rhetoric of a split and racist nation, behind the lusty statements of black power, black rage and black identity, co-mingled with all the cries for compensatory action and freedom now—something remarkable has happened since 1960. Blacks are still well behind whites, but there has been a major racial catching-up going on. *And for the first time in the history of the republic, "middle class"*—as measured by criteria of income, occupation and education—*became the adjective to describe the majority of black Americans.*

Acknowledging that the *gap* between white and black is still a national disgrace, acknowledging too that the condition of middle classitude is more prevalent outside of the South than in the South and more prevalent among younger blacks than older blacks, *it is the contention here that the emergence of such a substantial number of blacks into the American middle class is nothing less than a revolutionary development.*

America, it should not be forgotten, is a nation to which blacks came in chains. After a Civil War that did away with slavery, blacks were still subjected to economic servitude and social segregation, most cruelly in the South, where upward of 75% of the blacks lived until 1940. Not until the mid-1960s were blacks in the South (where still more than 50% of the blacks reside today) given a full voting franchise or access to the most elementary of social amenities.

Against that backdrop of chains and servitude we may now consider the new phenomenon—the emerging black middle class—and consider what it means in America today and what it portends for America in the future. In passing, and not surprisingly, it will be noted that the rhetoric of recent years has not conformed to the reality of recent years.

* * *

The bottom line in any real mass ranking of status in American life is *money*. And it is to money that we will look first to show the broad outlines of stark upward mobility.

The 1970 Census reveals that during the 1960s, that infamous decade of "deteriorating" conditions for blacks (how many times did we hear that during the riots?), the following income changes took place:

- Income for white families in America went up by 69%.
- Income for black families in America went up by 99.6%.[1]

Of course, if one rounds the 99.6% figure it can be stated that black family income *doubled* during a single decade![2]

This striking increase in black family income led to this changing *ratio* of black family income compared to white family income:

AVERAGE RATIO: BLACK MEDIAN FAMILY INCOME TO WHITE

1950–54	55%
1955–59	53%
1960–64	54%
1965–69	61%
1970	64%
1971	63%
1972	62%

It is true that 62% is a long way from 100% and still scandalously low. It may be argued that the numbers have plateaued during the early 1970s and have even dipped a point or two. But what is open to little argument is that there was sharp progress—a catching up—for black families during the 1960s, which was not apparent during the 1950s, and, as of now, most of this income gain has been held. Remember, these are *ratios;* incomes for *both* races went *up* sharply, but more sharply for non-whites.[3]

---

[1] Actual figures for that and other numbers in this chapter, unless otherwise specified, are for "Negroes and Other Races" as defined by the Census Bureau. As "Negroes" comprise 90% of the "Negroes and Other Races" category, this is a relatively good index of all Negroes in America.

[2] That, however, would be accurate only if inflation had not eroded *everyone's* income. If one deflates the income statistics to account for inflation white income increased by 34% in the decade and black income by 54%.

[3] An argument has been made that the critical income numbers are not *ratios,* but *absolute dollar* figures. The absolute dollar gap, it is true, *widened* slightly ($3,958 in 1971 versus $3,788 in 1961 in constant 1971 dollars) between black and white families. But in our judgment, the relative rate of closure is far more important than the absolute rate. Suppose, for example, that black income were $5,000 a year and white income were $10,000 a year in a given year. Suppose then that a decade later black income had increased to $40,000 and white income had increased to

If one looks at the rates of black families earning above $10,000, this startling progression emerges:

1950	4%
1960	13%
1970	32%
1971	32%
1972	34%

These numbers, it should be stressed, are in *constant* 1972 dollars—the erosion caused by inflation is already discounted (thus, to qualify as a $10,000-or-more family in 1950 a family then had to earn only about $6,000, the equivalent of $10,000 in 1972).

If one views black family income distribution through the same lens of middle classness that was established here earlier for Americans generally, that is, $7,000 per year, then in 1972, just more than half the black families in America were above that line, *51%* as opposed to *29%* in 1960 (in constant dollars).[4] (The white comparison is 76% for 1972.)

American blacks are in the middle class. They can be seen manicuring lawns of their bungalows in Denver, putting storm windows on small homes in Chicago's South Side and driving in a car pool down 16th Street in Washington to get to work at a federal building.

Again let us ask: What does "middle class" mean? As used here it obviously does not refer exclusively to doctors, lawyers and businessmen with cabin cruisers and expense accounts. It refers instead to Americans who have safely put poverty behind them and are now looking ahead, not back. In the words of Thomas Sowell, a black sociologist with the Urban Institute, we are talking about "black men and women who go to work five days a week, pay their bills, try to find some happiness for themselves,

---

$50,000. Given such data, the absolutists could claim that the absolute dollar gap had doubled. In point of fact, in the decade of the 1960s, white income went up by 69% and black income went up by 100%, and this seems to be a fairly decent rate of closure. Were black income to have fully held the line on the absolute dollar gap, it would have had to go up by 136%; were black income to reach total white-income levels, black income would have had to *triple*, an unlikely occurrence over the course of a single decade.

In short, what we are saying, is: You can't get there without passing through here. Even a substantial rate of catch-up would, for a certain time, have to proceed relatively, not absolutely. That is an unfortunate law of mathematics, not of race, but it is a law nonetheless.

4 This $7,000 figure for 1972, as explained in the earlier chapter on income, should be raised in the mind's eye to account for recent inflation, for family size, for urban-rural differences. As with whites, then, the current cut-off line, in dollars of current purchasing power would be higher than $7,000, but the 51% figure would still obtain. In *1973* current dollars, *54%* of black families earned over $7,000.

and raise their children to be decent people with better prospects than they had. . . ."

To begin then at the bottom, "middle class" means that at the very least individuals have the basic necessities of life: enough to eat, healthy, if not necessarily expensive clothes to wear, housing that is at least safe and sanitary.

But that, of course, is only the very beginning—as has been discussed earlier in dealing with "all Americans" rather than "blacks." Once the necessities of food, shelter and clothing are provided for, a vast flow of secondary criteria must also be met.

Middle-income parents want their children to go to good schools, to stay in high school and graduate, and then hopefully go on to college.

The young adults come out of college and they want jobs as programmers, not porters.

A middle-income family wants not only a housing structure that is safe and sanitary but a safe and sanitary housing structure *in a safe and sanitary neighborhood.*

The middle-class blacks referred to here have made much headway in satisfying these traditional middle-class desires, as shall be demonstrated.

There is, of course, also a political point to make. In the wake of this middle-class movement comes social turbulence. The safe and sanitary neighborhoods are white neighborhoods. The good schools are in white neighborhoods. The good jobs are white jobs. Is it any wonder, then, that scatter-site housing, busing, community control of schools and job quotas have become political problems of a major magnitude in the last decade?

*   *   *

The march of blacks into the middle class can be seen even more clearly if one looks at the data at levels less than for all blacks:

About half (52% in 1972) of the blacks in America now live in the South—a stark change from 1950 when more than two thirds (68%) of the blacks lived in the South.

When we look at black life in the South and outside of the South, there is a sharp difference. Thus, in 1972, black family income in the South was 55% of white family income, but outside of the South, black family income was 68% of white income.

A second variable within black-white income ratios concerns family status. As we shall note later, black families are much more likely to be "female headed." But when they are *not*—when the families are "husband-wife" families—incomes are much more likely to be closer to "equality." Among black husband-wife families all over America in 1971, income was 74% of comparable white husband-wife family income. Outside of the South, it was 87%.

Perhaps that most encouraging and most meaningful cross-tabulation of the income data concerns *young* blacks. As we shall see subsequently, younger blacks have made striking educational gains in recent years and subsequent gains in "occupation"—i.e., the *sorts* of jobs they hold. Accordingly, some fraction of these gains have reached the bottom line—income. Thus, young black males age twenty-five to thirty-four earned 70% of what their white counterparts earned, and young black females earned 96% of their white counterparts—compared to the total ratio of 62%.

When one *combines* all these attributes—youth, non-Southern residence and unbroken family—a striking statistic emerges:

MEDIAN INCOME OF HUSBAND-WIFE FAMILIES, IN THE
NORTH AND WEST, WITH HEAD OF FAMILY UNDER 35
YEARS OF AGE, AS PER CENT OF WHITE INCOME

1959	*1971*
78%	93% (!)
of white income	of white income

There is an equally striking word that comes very close to describing that number: *parity*. Among young, non-Southern, unbroken black families income parity has *almost* been achieved. As a matter of fact, if one adds a fourth variable to the equation—looking at black families and white families where *both* the husband and wife were working—these are the numbers that appear:

MEDIAN INCOME OF HUSBAND-WIFE FAMILIES, WITH HEAD
UNDER 35, IN NORTH AND WEST WHEN HUSBAND AND WIFE
BOTH WORKED, AS A PER CENT OF WHITE INCOME

1959	*1971*
85%	105% (!) (!)

If there is a word "super-parity," the number 105% would probably qualify.[5]

[5] Some, but by no means all, of these remarkable husband-wife family gains are due to the fact that young black wives outside of the South are somewhat more likely to work *year round* than young white wives (51% vs. 39%). However, it is important to note that in those young black families in the North and West where wives worked, the husbands were also progressing mightily. They earned 76% of comparable white husbands in 1959—and 90% of comparable white husbands in 1970. Moreover, regardless of the fact that black wives do contribute somewhat disproportionately to young black non-Southern unbroken families, the money, extra money, *is* getting to the family, and that would seem to be what's most important, despite the harder and longer work involved. The family has the money.

Finally, to conclude this brief view of the black movement into the American middle-income brackets, one more index that reveals both the progress made and the distance left to go:

BLACK FAMILIES IN POVERTY

| 1959 | 48% |
| 1972 | 29% |

In thirteen years, it can be said, an enormous change has occurred. From almost *half* in poverty at the dawn of the 1960s, we now have somewhat between a *quarter* and a *third* in poverty. As statistical changes go, that is a substantial difference. But this tragic fact remains, a fact that spells out one of the key aspects of the still smoldering resentments in the black community: 29% of the black families today are in poverty. The white percentage is only 7%—and that too is a substantial difference.

Employment

For about two decades the reality of the black-white employment situation was summed up this way: Black unemployment rates have been *twice* as high as white rates. That is still the unhappy case.

But there has been a massive shift in *who* the black unemployed are. Thus, a cross-tabulation of black *married men* reveals a far sharper drop than for the population as a whole, as this comparison of two early years of the Sixties with two early years of the Seventies shows:

UNEMPLOYMENT RATE AND RATIO,
BLACK TO WHITE FOR MARRIED MEN,
20 YEARS OLD AND OVER,
WITH SPOUSE PRESENT, 1962 TO 1972

	Negro and Other Races	White	Ratio
1962	7.9%	3.1%	2.5 to 1
1963	6.8%	3.0%	2.3 to 1
1971	5.0%	3.0%	1.7 to 1
1972	4.5%	2.6%	1.7 to 1

The drop in the ratio from 1962 to 1972 is 53% (from 2.5 to 1 to 1.7 to 1—with 1 to 1 representing parity).

Again, then, one can observe a steady and powerful movement into the middle class. Black *family* men are—like white family men—"at work," that is, at least 95 out of a hundred even during recessionary times.

At the same time, however, teen-age unemployment has gone up. Among black teen-agers (sixteen to nineteen), unemployment rates in 1960 were 24%—apparently strikingly high. In 1970, the rate had climbed to 29%—substantially higher, and by 1972 it was 34%. In each case the rate for white teen-agers was between 13% and 15%.

But there is something to be said about black teen-age unemployment that is not generally understood. These numbers, from 1972, tell the story:

- In all there were 2.2 million teen-agers sixteen to nineteen.
- Of these, 1.43 million were "not in the labor force," about two thirds. (About 1.2 million of these are *students;* most of the balance are housewives.) They were neither "at work" nor "looking for work." They are not tabulated in unemployment statistics. They are doing what most teen-agers in America do—going to school or tending house.
- That leaves about 770,000. These are the black teen-agers "in the labor force"—either "at work" or "looking for work." About *two thirds*—about 510,000—are at work.
- That leaves about 260,000 who are actually unemployed, i.e., "looking for work." (The fraction of 260,000 over 770,000 yields the high unemployment rate—the percentage *without* jobs who are actively looking for work. If one were to put the 260,000 over the demominator of the 2.2 million total teen-agers, the resultant percentage would be about 12%, which is a far cry from the 34% "unemployment" figure.)
- But even of the 260,000 unemployed black teen-agers, about 45%—116,000—*are in school* and about 83% of these are looking for *part-time work.*
- That leaves about 144,000 black teen-agers—males and females— who are *out of work, out of school and looking for work,* a condition that would somewhat more closely approach the popular perception of what "teen-age unemployment" actually represents.
- The out-of-school out-of-work component represents 6.6% of the total number of black teen-agers!

That is a far cry from the stereotype of hordes of young blacks hanging around street corners staring vacant-eyed toward a dead-end future, remembering a dead-end past. About 70% of black teen-agers are in school. About another 25% are at work or at home as housewives. The rest—about 6%—may well be perceived as hard-core teen-age unemployed.

Why then the stereotype of massive black teen-age unemployment?

Part of the fault lies in the statistical reportage system. The "unemployment rate" is defined as the percentage of those "in the labor force" who are "looking for work." But among young people almost two thirds are "not in the labor force," although they are usefully occupied, typically as either students or housewives. "Unemployed" also involves students seeking part-time work, surely an important consideration, sometimes a critical consideration for a family, sometimes a neccessity to be able to stay in school, but also surely not generally in tune with the notion of desolated young men hanging around on street corners with no future before them. They are students. They are going someplace.

The second reason for the stereotype is the high visibility—and the dangerous potential—of such young, unemployed, black males as there are. Of particular significance in this connection is the ominous—and terrifying —rise in the crime rate generally and specifically the very high rate of young black criminals, particularly in urban areas.

On balance: Teen-age unemployment rates are up, adult male rates down, particularly so among married males. The teen-agers are mostly in school. The adults are mostly supporting families. The net result would seem to be a social and economic plus despite the continuing "two to one" ratio of black to white unemployment rates.

* * *

Middle classness, of course, concerns itself with more than just "income" and more than just "unemployment." Part of the mosaic of middle-class life concerns what *kind* of jobs people hold.

Looking now at that slice of life we see a major march by blacks into the middle-class occupations. If one uses the grouping "white collar workers," "craftsmen" and "operatives"[6] as the one representing the better (middle class) jobs in America, then we see this progression over the decade:

NUMBERS OF WHITE COLLAR WORKERS, CRAFTSMEN AND OPERATIVES

	Negro	*White*
1960	2.9 million	46.1 million
1970	5.1 million	57.0 million
1972	5.2 million	58.3 million
Percentage Increase 1960–72	79%	26%

[6] A grouping used by the Census Bureau in *The Social and Economic Status of the Black Population in the U.S., 1971.*

Over the same dozen years the numbers of Negroes in "other" work—primarily low paying jobs in private households, as service workers, farm workers and laborers—*decreased from 4.0 million to 3.5 million.*

Compare, then, the *balance* of occupational status for blacks in America in 1960 and in 1970. In 1960, blacks in "good" jobs totaled 2.9 million while blacks in "not good" jobs totaled 4.0 million. Far more blacks had "not good" jobs. But by 1972, the number of blacks with "good" jobs totaled 5.2 million, while those with "not good" jobs totaled 3.5 million.

The 1960 data works out to 42% of the blacks holding the "good" (i.e., middle-class) jobs—less than half. By 1972, the rate had climbed to 60%—about three fifths in middle-class jobs.

In 1970, there were 196,000 black "construction craftsmen" of whom, for some examples, 26,000 were "brickmasons and stonemasons" and 14,000 were electricians (up almost 100% since 1960).[7] There were 183,000 black "truck drivers" and 73,000 black "automobile mechanics and repairmen, including body." And there were 223,000 black "teachers except colleges and universities," 9% of the total in America. Back in 1960, there were 4,378 blacks who were engineers. And in 1970, there were 13,000. Some other changes:

BLACK MALES, SELECTED OCCUPATIONS, 1960–70

	1960	1970
Accountants	5,434	9,177
Foremen	20,944	52,894
Printing craftsmen	3,306	8,049
Police	10,803	22,254
Welders and flame cutters	24,787	46,994

Education

Along with higher incomes and better jobs, the 1960s also saw a great breakthrough in the educational realm. Thus in 1960, a little more than a third—only 38%—of young Negro males (aged twenty to twenty-nine)

---

[7] Many of the new and better jobs held by blacks are union jobs, and many of these are in the much-discussed construction trades. Of particular interest are the apprenticeship figures, for these signal the way of the future. In 1972, 13% of the total number of apprentices in the construction trades, and 20% of those enrolled in the first half of 1972, were nonwhite—rates above the nonwhite proportion of the population as a whole. Curiously, despite all the talk about blacks and unions, one central fact is generally ignored: Blacks are slightly more likely, not less likely, to belong to unions than are whites. In 1970, black workers were 12% of all union members. (Blacks are 11% of the total population.)

had finished at least four years of high school. By 1967, the rate was more than half—*52%*. By 1972, it was almost two thirds—*64%*. Among young women the increase was about as great—from 43% in 1960 to 56% in 1967 and to 66% in 1972.

If one were to set an educational level that would accurately separate the American society into "middle class" and "non-middle class," probably the criteria of "completed high school education" serves best. For young blacks, in a dozen years, the rate of finishing high school went from about 40% to about 65%!

There is an even longer range perspective available. Here is the progression of "median school years completed" for *all* young Americans since 1940:

MEDIAN SCHOOL YEARS COMPLETED, ALL RACES, AGED 25–29

1940	10.3 years
1950	12.1 years
1960	12.3 years
1970	12.6 years
1972	12.7 years

Twelve years of schooling equals a completed high school education. Thus, young Americans (i.e., *white* Americans) moved into the "educational middle class" during the 1940s: In 1940, the typical young American was still a "high school dropout," by 1950, the typical young American was a "high school graduate."

Twenty years later the same sort of great leap forward took place for blacks in America:

MEDIAN SCHOOL YEARS COMPLETED, NEGROES, AGED 25–29

1940	7.0 years
1950	8.6 years
1960	10.8 years
1970	12.2 years (!)
1972	12.4 years

In 1940, the young black was typically an *elementary school dropout*. A decade later he could be described only as an *elementary school graduate*. Not until 1960 did the young American black typically reach even the level of *high school dropout*. And not until 1970 did he typically become a *high school graduate*—a bona fide member of the educational middle class.

And there is a shorter range perspective also available to show that the progress hasn't stopped: The high school dropout rate for blacks aged fourteen to twenty-four in 1967 had come down to 24% for males and 22% for females—from about 36% in 1960. By 1972, the dropout rate was 18% for males and 17% for females. In a dozen years, then, a halving!

To give a flavor of the speed with which a major degree of "catching up" came about, we can note that the gap between young whites and young blacks in 1950 was 3.5 years of completed school years. (The young white in 1950 was already a high school graduate—12.1 years of school completed. The young black—with 8.6 years of school completed was an elementary school graduate.) Twenty years later the gap was .4 of a year—12.6 years vs. 12.2 years.[8]

The leap into the educational middle class can also be seen in the college enrollment statistics. Here are the data showing black-white comparisons over a short seven-year period—from 1965 to 1972.

PER CENT OF PERSONS AGED 18-24 ENROLLED IN COLLEGE 1969-72

	1965	1972
Negro	10%	18%
White	26%	26%
"Gap"	16%	8%
Ratio	2.6 to 1	1.4 to 1

Again the gap remains—but it has narrowed considerably.

Viewed in a somewhat different way: In 1967, there were 370,000 blacks in college; by 1972, the number had gone up by 97% (!) to 727,000. In the same time period, white enrollment in college went up by just 26%. Blacks today comprise about 9% of the total college population, not too far off from their relation to the population as a whole (11%).

Finally, let the notion that "these days education doesn't help blacks get ahead financially" be laid to rest. Looking at averages for those aged twenty-five to thirty-four for the four years (1968–71), Census data shows that black families with heads who were high school dropouts typically had incomes only 62% of the income of whites in a comparable demographic and educational situation. Black family heads with just a high school degree and no more had incomes 73% that of whites. And for blacks with some college education the figure was 90% of comparable white income.

Ours is a materially oriented society. Accordingly, if income is up, if

[8] For Americans of *all ages*, there is still a major disparity, reflecting earlier years of inequity. Median school years completed for *all adult* Negroes was 10.1 years in 1971, compared to 12.2 years for all adult whites.

adult male unemployment is down, if jobs are better, if schooling lasts longer, one should expect to see results in the material world.

The results are there.

Before achieving entry into the amorphous middle class a family must —at least—leave the poverty class. One index of poverty in America has been housing and one index of poverty housing has traditionally been plumbing. When a dwelling unit has a flush toilet and an unshared bathtub or shower and hot piped water it can at least be up for consideration as a middle-class dwelling. Lacking these amenities, it would clearly qualify as substandard housing, and indeed, until bureaucratic language criteria changed, that was the key component of the definition of "substandard" housing.

In 1960, astonishingly, 41% of housing units occupied by Negroes "lacked some or all plumbing facilities." Ten years later, the rate was down to 17%. Now, that rate is still substantially higher than the white rate (which was 5% in 1970). But it also represents a monumental change in housing conditions for blacks. Substantially more than half of the blacks who lived in dwellings that lacked some plumbing no longer live under these conditions. That may seem like either an elementary or a trivial improvement. It is elementary, of course; all the more reason for incredulity that two in five black families lived that way only a decade ago. As for triviality, try imagining your own life without the following: hot water or an unshared bath or shower, or a flush toilet,[9] or all of them.

By one other traditional test of middle classness, a majority of blacks have not quite crossed the 50% line, but are coming close. Here are the rates on non-white families who "owned their own house":

HOME OWNERSHIP FOR NON-WHITES

1940	24%
1950	35%
1960	38%
1970	42%

The white rate was 65% in 1970, up just 1% from the 64% recorded in 1960.

And of life-and-death matters? There, too, one can see a pattern of catching up.

Infant mortality for non-whites plunged by 33% from 1960 to 1972—

[9] And, by the way, this lack of plumbing a decade ago wasn't just a function of blacks living in the rural South. In 1960, in *central cities* 21% of blacks resided in dwellings lacking some plumbing facilities. A decade later, again in central cities, the rate had plummeted to 5%.

from 43 per thousand to 29 per thousand. The white rate during the same time went down 39%—from 23 per thousand to 16 per thousand. Black are still behind, but less so.

The death rate for *all ages* stayed about the same for whites from 1950 to 1960 to 1972—9.5, 9.5 and 9.4 respectively. For non-whites the death rates for the same three years was 11.2, 10.1 and 9.3, down substantially, actually lower today than the white rate on a total population basis. However, blacks are younger than whites and *age-specific* death rates are still higher for blacks. Again, however, when one examines data from 1950 to 1970 it is apparent that the gap has closed, although closure was greater in the Fifties than in the Sixties.

* * *

There it is: By most of the standards by which America has in the past calculated what is middle class, Negroes in the last decade have made mighty strides, both absolutely and relatively to whites. If this sounds as if what is being said here is that the stereotype of the black in America must be changed from an earlier portrait of an uneducated, ill-employed, poverty-stricken slum dweller to a new stereotype—that is correct. If it sounds as if we are saying that the new black stereotype involves an individual earning a living wage at a decent job, with children who stay in school and aspire to still better wages and still better jobs, living out of a slum but still in a ghetto, in a decent but unelaborate dwelling, still far "behind" whites but catching up—that too is correct. This new stereotype, it is suggested, represents a middle-class life style and it can be appropriately applied to about half the black population. That is a striking change in the American scene—better by far than what it replaces.

B.   The Not-So Good Numbers—How Bad Are They?

That a slim majority of blacks in the United States may now be described as "middle class" may indeed be a revolutionary statement, but it does not mean:

- that the data are uniformly good,
- that all blacks are in the middle class,
- that blacks have achieved parity with whites,
- that poverty is largely a thing of the past,
- that there is cause for complacency,

for none of these statements are valid.

FEMALE-HEADEDNESS

All the data are not uniformly good. The high incidence of "broken families" among Negroes—regarded by some as the key to the "pathology" of the black slums—has increased substantially in recent years. Here is the stark data that chronicles the rise of the black female-headed family:

PER CENT FEMALE-HEADED FAMILIES

	White	Black
1950	9%	18%
1960	9%	22%
1970	9%	27%
1971	9%	29%
1972	9%	30%
1973	10%	33%

Today, then, a third of black families are headed by women—twenty-odd years ago it was about a sixth. The white rate has changed only marginally.

These numbers tend to validate Daniel P. Moynihan's perceptions in the mid-1960s that the rising incidence of female-headed black families was, and would be, a major problem. For today, it is clear that the phrase "black families with a female head" can usually be described in a more succinct way: "poor."

What used to be called "poverty" is now called—in GOP speak— "below the low income level." In any event, in 1972, more than half (53%) of the black female-headed families were living "below the low income level," i.e., they were poor. At the same time, only 16% of black male-headed families were poor.

From 1959 to 1971, the *number* of black male-headed families in poverty *decreased* by more than half (*54%*) while the comparable *number* of female-headed families *increased* by 60%.

Of all black families in poverty in 1959, more than two thirds (70%) were male-headed. The balance (30%) were female-headed. But twelve years later, by 1971, there was a reversal: Almost six in ten (59%) of the black families in poverty were *female-headed* and only four in ten (41%) were male-headed.

In short, there was a sexual inversion of the poverty numbers for blacks: There were more female-headed families; the male-headed families were exiting from "poverty"; the female-headed families were entering into "poverty."

WELFARE

"Black female-headed families in poverty" can also usually be expressed more simply: "welfare."

As the numbers and rates of black female-headed families soared so too did the numbers and rates of blacks on welfare.[10]

In 1960, there were 3.1 million total AFDC "welfare" recipients in the United States. At that time, the civil rights lobby demanded that statistics be "color blind." So there is no actual black-white cross-tabulation of those 3.1 million welfare recipients. But even if half were black (a little higher than the present rate) there would have been about 1.5 million blacks on welfare. There were, in 1960, 18.8 million Negroes in America. About *8%* of the Negroes, then, would have been on welfare.

Now observe how the data change as the decade progresses and we enter the Seventies:

RECIPIENTS, AID TO DEPENDENT CHILDREN, 1960–71

1960	3,073,000
1965	4,396,000
1967	5,309,000
1968	6,086,000
1969	7,313,000
1970	9,659,000
1971	10,651,000

In 1971, of the 10.6 million on welfare, *43%* were Negro—4.5 million. The black population in 1971 was 23 million. The percentage of blacks on AFDC, then, was 19%—up from *8%* eleven years earlier. When other welfare programs are added to the AFDC numbers, about 25% of the blacks are now on welfare—one in four! The white rate is 4%.

These rates, it should be noted in passing, are reflective not only of human tragedy, but of political poison. Over this same time frame, the phrases "welfare mother" and "relief chiseler" became political buzzwords that clearly also meant "black."

ARE THE NOT-GOOD NUMBERS BAD?

How bad is the rise in female-headed black poverty?

It is bad for millions of black children who grow up without the influence

---

[10] "Welfare," as the term is generally used, is actually primarily "Aid to Families with Dependent Children"—and numbers for that program are used in this discussion.

of a father in the house. It is bad because America stigmatizes its welfare recipients—black or white—and the psychic scars don't heal easily when a young child has to buy food with food stamps, has to get a free school lunch while classmates pay and has to acknowledge—at least to himself—that his family is "on the welfare." It is bad, too, of course, for all the other reasons that poverty is bad—diet, clothing, housing, medical care, etc.

It is bad for the black mother—torn between the desire to devote time and care to her children, particularly children of pre-school age, and the desire to earn a better living than the often inadequate welfare payments provide. Like her children she too is stigmatized. Furthermore, "welfare mothers" are often trapped in deteriorating neighborhoods that are havens for addicts, criminals, drunks, prostitutes, vandals, rapists and muggers. Existence—indeed mere survival—under such circumstances is perilous.

It is bad for politicians and bad for our politics, particularly bad for liberal politicians and liberal politics. Middle-class voters, including, incidentally, many black middle-class voters, don't want to pay the bill for families they believe are "shiftless," for families who they believe ought to be cared for by the absent man of the house, and particularly they don't want to pay the bill when they perceive that the welfare level of living they are supporting begins to approach their own level of living for which they had toiled long and hard to achieve. Politicians with liberal instincts feel compassion for the poor and needy. They also feel the hot breath of the voters on their necks—voters they hope will be motivated to re-elect them. Whipsawed between compassion and self-interest, liberal politicians also face rhetorical torment from more conservative candidates perfectly willing to make liberals squirm.

ARE THE BAD NUMBERS BETTER?

It is, then, a bad situation. But is it a situation that is getting *better* or a situation that is getting *worse?*

Social science, after all, is a field examined essentially in relative terms. "Good" and "bad" are subjective terms and largely unmeasurable; "better" and "worse" can be objective terms, and can often be measured by plotting and examining social and economic trends.

"Welfare" viewed along subjective lines, particularly viewing *increasing* numbers and *increasing* percentage of blacks on welfare, is clearly a "bad" situation. But what does it mean when there is an increase in the rate of blacks on welfare *during a time when the rate of blacks in poverty has sharply decreased?*

For that is what has happened. The percentage of black families in poverty has gone down sharply from 48% to 29% in the years from 1959 to 1972. At the same time, as estimated here earlier, the percentage of blacks on welfare has gone up sharply.

The closure of these two rates means that by 1973 more than half (55%) of *poor* blacks were receiving welfare.[11] An estimate for a comparable figure in 1960 shows about 15%. A black person in poverty, then, is close to four times as likely to be receiving welfare than at the beginning of the Sixties.

Now, it is to be acknowledged that AFDC is a long way from being a perfect program. Nor are the panoply of other welfare programs perfect, including food stamps, Medicaid, subsidized public housing, etc. The shortcomings of the "welfare mess" are well known and need no further chronicle here. But the question that must be resolved is not whether AFDC or any "welfare" program is good. What needs an answer is this: Is it better now that poor blacks are getting welfare when at an earlier time they were getting nothing at all? Is the situation getting better?

And with full awareness that "work is better than welfare," that the current welfare system is demeaning, and so on, our answer is *"Yes."* It may well be demeaning for a child to go shopping with food stamps— but it is surely better than going hungry. It may be demeaning to be subjected to questions about whether there is a "man in the house"—but it is surely better than not having a house at all.

Moreover, there is evidence to demonstrate that those blacks still in poverty in the 1970s, however bad their situation, are better off than their counterparts were a decade ago.

That the condition of the black poor is better than it was can be demonstrated thusly:

MEDIAN INCOME DEFICIT FOR FAMILIES, BY RACE, BELOW
THE LOW-INCOME LEVEL, 1959, 1972 (IN CONSTANT
1972 DOLLARS)

Year	White	Negro and Other Races
1959	$1246	$1838
1972	1126	1410
Change 1959–72	—$ 120	—$ 428

The median black family in poverty in 1959 was $1,838 away from reaching the "poverty exit line." Twelve years later, the median poor black family was $428 closer to exiting from poverty while the poor white family had advanced only $120 toward the goal, although in absolute terms was

[11] The rate of poor white families receiving welfare is 28%, about half the black rate.

still somewhat closer. The "poverty line," it should be remembered, is adjusted upward to reflect the rising cost of living, so the numbers over time are fully comparable. Moreover, and more important, poverty calculations do not include "in kind" services like Medicaid, housing subsidies and food stamps, which are far more extensive today than a decade ago.

So then, what have we? Fewer blacks in poverty. Those blacks in poverty are more likely to be receiving help. Those blacks in poverty are living at levels closer to being out of poverty than before.

MIXED SIGNALS

Those are all clear pluses within the generally negatively perceived area of black poverty. Are there clear minuses in the equation as well?

Not so clear, but there are some further factors to note: The demographic characteristics of the black poor (and the white poor, too, as has been discussed earlier) have changed. *By and large, people who are engaged in full-time work have left the poverty class in the last decade.* Disproportionately today, the poor are those in *female-headed families,* a category where full-time work is harder to come by.

The question then arises: Is this change in the characteristics of the black poor population "good" or "bad"?

Answer: Probably somewhat better, but it can be debated.

The negatives in the equation concern increased dependency. The black poor of the 1950s and the earlier years of the 1960s were poor but not as dependent on welfare, largely because fewer families were "broken." The case has been made, in fact, that the "welfare mess" has driven men from the house and has *created* some of this dependency.

Two rebuttals, offered with much less than customary vigor:

First, if some are to be poor in a society, a notion that by rights has outlived necessity in America, isn't it better that it more likely afflicts those who are dependent and less likely afflicts the independent? A situation where a husband-wife family with husband fully employed and the family *still* in poverty and on welfare would be intolerable for the recipients and surely for the body politic as well.

That those unable to work and reliant upon welfare are still poor is, of course, still a tragedy, but of a lesser social implication than the earlier situation.

Second, it is not correct to view every instance of female-headed dependency as a net social loss. The existence of "the welfare mess" also means that a woman who faced a drunk and brutal husband has the new option of telling him to pack up and get out. To be sure, it puts the newly female-headed family on welfare, but it may also dissolve a destructive family relationship. Separation and/or divorce, after all, are options that the upper and middle classes have had—and used—for a long time.

There is at least one more factor that must be considered in any attempt to assess "betterness" or "worseness" of the black situation in America, circa 1970s: *crime*.

Violent crime rates are very high among poor blacks. But more important from the point of view of this discussion, the *victims* of crime are also disproportionately black. In 1969, blacks were two and a half times more likely than whites to be victims of rape, robbery or aggravated assault. In 1972, *more* blacks than whites were murdered (8,422 compared to 7,158), indicating at least a 10 to 1 ratio.

Moreover, black violent crime rates have gotten worse faster than white rates.

This data is of particular relevance to our discussion of better or worse in the poor black community. For the rise of crime has not occurred equally through the black community. While local precinct data is not gathered by the FBI, some local data from selected cities gives this general picture: As blacks have progressed up into the middle class they have left their old inner-city slum neighborhoods, choosing to live in better, safer neighborhoods, areas that were once white neighborhoods. The old neighborhoods—neighborhoods like Hough and Watts—have actually lost population. As the upward-mobile, mostly husband-wife families, left the slum, its character changed.

Once, the black slum was a generally unsafe and unpleasant neighborhood but with a sizable quotient of stable, hard-working, law-abiding families to provide some sort of social leavening and social stability. These persons, by and large, have left. Those remaining are disproportionately the dependent poor—the female-headed families and the elderly—and the social derelicts: winos, addicts, hustlers, pimps, prostitutes, criminals and bums. And a "generally unsafe and unpleasant neighborhood" has turned into a rotting jungle, with terror on every street corner and alley, with crime rates that are high beyond imagining.

This, clearly, is a social minus, unmitigated, unqualifiable, unfudgable.

Or is it?

It is surely a minus for the female-headed family trapped in the jungle.

But, for the record, it should be noted that the *de facto* segregation of the violent—which is what in effect has happened—provides somewhat of a bonus for those who have left. Crime rates in middle-class black neighborhoods are high, but not impossible. That, of course, is one big reason those newly middle-class blacks moved there—to escape from violent neighborhoods.

So, then, in our measurement of black progress—or lack of it—we must assess the crime rise, it seems, in this way: The over-all crime rise has been a minus—a major minus—for all Americans, black and white. Within the black community the crime rise has been generally severe but has fallen unevenly—affecting most severely the poor, the aged and the welfare families trapped in slums, from which they have great difficulty escaping.

It is a two-track system. For the blacks who escape the slum—the escape is a relative plus. And for those trapped it is a major minus—with again only one caveat.

ON BALANCE

Ever thus. How, after all, does "a group"—an ethnic group, a religious group, a racial group—make "progress"? Is "progress" defined as a situation when a *whole group* is seen moving up and out of poverty or when only a *substantial fraction* moves up and out? If the whole group must go up and out, then even Jews haven't made it yet. One of the reasons the American Jewish Committee lobbies for high Social Security rates is because such a high proportion of elderly Jews are *still* in poverty—despite the generally acknowledged success story that has described the generally successful story of American Jews. What is true for the Jews, is true as well for the Irish and the WASPs—much success and some failure, each chronicled in our literature, our politics and our industry.

The point, then, is a simple, if harsh one: the fact that some blacks have been "left behind" does not of and in itself deny the fact of massive recent black success. For all group progress leaves some members behind. "Progress judging"—if it is to be honest and clear-eyed—is an objective, trend-oriented and historically linked discipline. It is a discipline that can acknowledge both the tragedy and pathos of poverty—but really only in passing. Rather—harshly and coldly—it must bear down and ask the questions: compared to what? compared to when?

It seems to add up to this: For blacks generally in America in the Sixties a massive amount of progress ensued—although there is still a substantial distance to traverse to reach parity. For some blacks—for those three in ten trapped in poverty—there was also statistical economic progress, although perhaps, on balance, this progress may accurately be considered a wipe-out when co-mingled with the stunning rise of violence in the worst areas of our nation.

Is the situation for blacks, on balance, better than what it replaced?

The answer is an unequivocal "yes." In a nation that prides itself as being a "middle-class" nation—blacks are now in the middle class. As a society that scorns the high school dropout and grants epaulets of a sort to the high school graduate—blacks are now finishing high school and suprising numbers are going on to college. In a culture that divides work into good jobs and not-so-good jobs—blacks are now moving into good jobs. There can be, in short, little doubt that these massive socioeconomic developments are better than what they replaced.

C. A Look Into the Future

What, then, of the future? Is there a message in all the data?

The prognosis—while always hazy in the hazy world of the future—seems quite sound. Two possible scenarios seem plausible; a third—an unpleasant one—seems unlikely.

Scenario One calls for continued progress—not only absolutely as the rest of the nation progresses, but 1960-style progress, a catch-up by blacks relative to whites, a continued march toward parity.

At least two good sets of reasons can be advanced to back up the likelihood of Scenario One taking place.

There are, first, structural reasons:

- Black income levels are lowest in the South, yet rising relatively fastest in the South (up 113% from 1960 to 1970 versus rates of from 70–80% for the other regions).
- A majority of all blacks still live in the South (compared to 31% of all Americans).
- The black out-migration has been substantial and seems to be continuing.
- Blacks outside the South make more money than blacks in the South.

There is no reason to expect that any of these trends or situations will change: Blacks will continue to live disproportionately in the South where black earnings are climbing fastest, and they will continue to leave the South, getting an automatic boost toward income parity. From a broad statistical point of view, then, the "Southern" situation augurs favorable both for blacks in the South and those leaving it.

A second structural reason to back up a continuing optimistic scenario concerns the now-young blacks. As noted earlier, it is black families under thirty-five who have made the sharpest relative gains in the last decade. If this pattern continues—and there is no reason to suggest that it won't—it will of its own structural weight continue to move the total black-white numbers closer to parity. Elderly blacks will leave the labor force and die, and they will be replaced by new young blacks. We may assume, under the conditions of this scenario, that the new, young black families will continue at the present close-to-parity rates now held by young black families *and*—a big "and"—the now-young-soon-to-be-middle-aged blacks will hold some, most or all of their present relatively high standing as they reach their late thirties and forties. This seems a logical proposition. If one assumes that young black families have made income progress in large measure because they have more schooling and because they are holding better jobs than they used to, there is no apparent reason to think that the same jobs and the same educational background will not continue to serve them in good stead as they move into middle age. A black who enters the civil service or gets a union job at age twenty-five will not only not lose ground as he ages, but will gain the normal advantages of seniority. With the advent of disproportionately high numbers of black union apprentices today, a time will come in the not-too-distant future when union seniority rules will help, not hinder, black progress.

What this means, in effect, is that the progress that is now discernible in the data is due not to the sheer youth of young blacks as such, but to the fact that something new happened in America beginning in the 1960s and this something new has opened up paths toward parity for young blacks. *It means that those inoculated by the new serum of Parity have been permanently immunized from the disease of Sub-Parity.* As the proportion of those immunized becomes an ever greater share of the total black population (with the inevitable passage of time), the black-white statistics will look better as the years go on.

Beyond the structural reasons to bolster Scenario One are the political and psychic reasons. Something new indeed happened in the 1960s: the log jam broke— politically, psychically, legally, socially, economically—and there is no going back. Not Richard Nixon, not Barry Goldwater, not even Strom Thurmond or James Eastland or George Wallace wants to return to Little Rock, to Greenville, to Bull Connor or Selma.

Scenario Two—less optimistic—takes into account the broad structural factors just mentioned, minimizes the broad politico-psychic factors just mentioned, but takes note of two other factors.

First, insofar as it can be measured over a short period of time, progress in the Nixon years of 1969, 1970, 1971 and 1972 was less dramatic than in the Kennedy-Johnson years. True, this progress slowdown did not single out blacks—it seems keyed to a national economic recession in 1970 and 1971. The sinking rate of blacks in poverty ground to a halt, but so, roughly, did the rate for whites. The rates of black families earning $10,000 a year or more continued to climb, but at a slower rate than earlier. Black income viewed as a function of white income plateaued, even sank a point or two. Unemployment rates climbed for both blacks and whites. On some other fronts progress continued strong—very strong— despite the recession: High school dropout rates dropped and college enrollment rates climbed.

In all, a mixed bag for the first four Nixon years. The key question, of course, is this: Do these four years signal a general slowdown in the trend of black progress that will continue in the future? The answer to this question will have to wait for a couple of better economic years, but Scenario Two maintains that the 1970s will resemble the plateau of the 1950s rather than the sharp ascent of the 1960s.

For beyond the recent slow numbers, the Nixon budget for fiscal year 1974 and his originally stated plans beyond fiscal year 1974 had been described as the "death knell of the Great Society." While that is over-dramatizing things, it is clear that if President Nixon has his way, at least some of "the Johnson programs" that he continued in term one will be cut back or cut out.

The question then arises: Were "the programs" responsible for the great progress among blacks in the 1960s? If "the programs" were responsible for at least some of the progress, then it can be posited that "progress" will be diminished if the programs are diminished. Scenario Two says, in effect, the mutilation of "the programs" will rub out some to all of the likely relative gains due from the structural factors.

Now, no one really knows how much good (or bad, for that matter) "the programs" accomplished in the Sixties. It is a proposition that can authentically be debated by liberals and conservatives. The author's view—in part a political one, in part a statistical one—is that the programs accomplished a good deal, probably not enough to make Scenario Two valid, but probably enough to prevent the full flowering of Scenario One if sharply curtailed.

Scenario Three, a final one, takes advantages of the fact that no one really knows the impact of "the programs." The Scenario Three-ists maintain that the programs were so important that their partial demise will not only wash out the projected structural gains, but more than wash them out to a point of absolute retrogression. Things for blacks will get relatively worse in the Seventies says Scenario Three.

This is plausible, but in our judgment not very probable. President Nixon neither wants to, nor could, undo all the progress of the Sixties. No one has suggested repealing the Voting Rights Act. No one has suggested repealing the public accommodations law. Nor the higher minimum wages. Nor Medicaid. Nor aid to higher education.

In short, while no one can accurately quantify the impact of the New Frontier and Great Society, it is wrong to suggest that programs *alone* accomplished progress. A strong economy is surely the key anti-poverty remedy. Accordingly, it does not seem valid to say—as Scenario Three has it—that the programs were so important to progress that repeal of *some part* of the programs would actually reverse *all* of the progress.

D.   A New Liberal Rhetoric

The author has on occasion been accused of being an optimist.

Assume, for a moment, that it is so. Statistics, after all, can be fiddled with in many ways. The attempt here has been to show the flip side of the "good" numbers, but let us suppose for a moment we have been either dishonest, naive or plain foolish.

Divide, then, by two. Take all the "progress" we have discussed here—income, occupation, education, unemployment, housing, etc.—and divide it in half. *The results still show substantial progress for blacks in recent years.* Two fast examples: Suppose instead of black family income going from 53% of white income in the 1955–59 period to 63% in the 1970–72 period, it had only gone to 58%. That's still a 10% increase (of the 53%) in a dozen years, following a decade of stasis. Suppose the years of school completed for young blacks (aged twenty-five to twenty-nine) did not go up from 10.8 years to 12.2 years in the course of a decade. Suppose it went up to 11.5 years (half) while the white rate barely inched up at all. That is still a major bit of "progress."

In short, even if one discounts and discounts and discounts—there has been a massive gain for blacks in the last decade.

Why, then, the silence? Why have these successes not been trumpeted? Why hasn't the chronicle of black advancement been as trendy as lettuce, Women's Lib, Presidential Power, Bangladesh, Grapes—or Black Poverty?

See the black bus driver living in a nice bungalow. See the black cement mason earning $9 an hour, a member of a union, and a building trades union at that. See the young black college student, studying business administration; see the black family, wife a telephone operator, husband a government worker, thriving in a suburb. Where are the stories?

The blanket of silence is benevolent, or so perceived, by its perpetrators.

In December of 1972 the Lyndon Baines Johnson Library conducted a Civil Rights Symposium on the occasion of the opening of the collection of papers and documents concerned with civil rights during the LBJ era. It was a major occasion, befitting the notable body of documents that was becoming available in a truly impressive scholarly institution. So many of the great, near great, the famous and near famous of the civil rights movement—black and white—attended and spoke out during the two-day session. Among those on hand were Roy Wilkins, Earl Warren, Vernon Jordan, Burke Marshall, Julian Bond, Richard Hatcher, Barbara Jordan, Yvonne Brathwaite Burke, plus a host of panelists. Each had moments at the microphone in an attempt, collectively and individually, to assay the past, present and future of the black man's struggle for equality.

Two general themes emerged as the conference went on. Lyndon Johnson was a sainted man, second perhaps only to Lincoln, in his effort to help black Americans. This theme, it should be noted, was sounded by some who a few years earlier were on the hustings proclaiming that LBJ was a big white honkey and asking innocently how many kids he killed today.

The homage to LBJ was accorded to him for the Civil Rights Acts of 1957 and 1960 (when he was senate majority leader), for the public accommodations law of 1964, the Voting Rights Act of 1965 and the housing act of 1968 (when he was President). These laws, it was correctly noted, broke the back of legalized discrimination in America during the 1960s. Blacks today can vote, can eat at a lunch counter, can legally buy a house in any neighborhood. This was great formal progress and LBJ, and the civil rights movement were to be awarded accolades for this legislative breakthrough—although more than once the note was sounded that now that blacks could go to the lunch counter, they had no money to buy what they wanted.

The talk, then, was exclusively of new *rights*, not of new *achievements*.

The second theme concerned the great ogre—the *new* President, the new great white honkey, Richard Nixon. It seems as if Richard Nixon sought to roll back progress, undo the gains, reduce blacks again to a status of servitude and poverty—all in the cause of the Southern Strategy.

There were two exceptions to this rhetoric. Senator Hubert Humphrey addressed himself to new legislative strategies, noting wisely and movingly that the next round of liberal laws must be targeted to help not just the poor or the blacks but all middle-class Americans, not a bad strategy for blacks these days.

And President Johnson delivered his last public address, fittingly, a stirring plea to America to let blacks stand "on level ground" in the quest for opportunity. The speech ended with the words "We shall overcome."

Astonishingly, one theme was missing. No one—no one—thought it necessary, wise or advisable to note the remarkable black economic, educational, occupational, housing progress made over the last decade—the progress that has been detailed in this chapter.[12]

Julian Bond alone sought to note the current statistical condition of blacks in America and, incredibly, here is what he said:

> . . . We are no longer slaves. Secondly, we can sit at lunch counters, sit downstairs at movie theaters, ride in the front of buses, register, vote, work and go to school where we once could not. But in a great many

[12] In early 1973, at the annual Civil Rights Leadership Conference dinner in Washington, another galaxy of civil rights stars convened and, again, there was no public mention of black achievements—other than legal—over the decade.

ways we are constantly discovering that things have either not changed at all, or have become much worse. A quick look at all the facts and figures that measure how well, or how poorly, a people are doing—the kinds of statistics that measure infant mortality, unemployment, median family income, life expectancy—demonstrates clearly that the average black American, while better off in comparison than his father was, is actually worse off when his statistics are measured against similar ones for white people. It is as though black Americans are climbing a molasses mountain in snowshoes, while the rest of the country rides a rather leisurely ski lift to the top. It is these depressing figures and the accompanying pathology which results from them that causes so much discontent and depression in black communities today. The realization is that, separately over the years the diverse strategies of Booker T. Washington and Dr. W. E. B. Du Bois and Marcus Garvey and Martin Luther King and Malcolm X have not appreciably improved the material lot of the masses of black folk.

Why did all the civil rights leaders de-emphasize the data of progress?
Didn't they know what had happened? The black man in the street knew. A Potomac Associates/Gallup Poll taken in 1972 showed that while whites said life in America had gotten worse in recent years, blacks said things were getting better (the only group of 24 sub-categories who thought that way).

The leaders, of course, did know what had happened and in private conversations acknowledged it. It is, after all, a monumentally important development in American life and one doesn't have to be a statistical genius to know what up is. But the line was, in effect, we can't stress that, *we've got to keep the pressure on to make further gains.*

What they have done indeed is keep the pressure on—themselves.

* * *

This idea—that liberals do not understand how, when or why to claim success—is at the heart of the argument of this volume. This argument ought to concern not only those working for black progress, but those interested in any or all of the aspects of the liberal agenda of our time. For today, liberalism itself is under attack, and it cannot successfully be defended without reference to American success. The liberals have been in the saddle for two generations. If America has failed, or is failing—as liberals have been saying for half a decade and more—then it is liberalism that has failed. And if America is succeeding—then liberalism can claim a share of the credit and ask for an extension of its writ.

Here, essentially, is the corner that liberals have backed themselves
into:

- It's been forty years since liberals became the driving force of American politics, frequently occupying the White House, always influential in the Congress.
- A remarkable body of liberally oriented legislation has been placed
  on the statute books, first in the Thirties, then in the Sixties.
- Great economic and social progress has been made.
- Which *liberals,* incredibly, now deny, saying that "the programs
  haven't worked."
- In a nutshell, say the liberals, "We have failed; let us continue!"[13]

But, suppose, instead of the institutionalized gloom that pervades liberal
rhetoric today, a different rhetoric—incidentally an *accurate* rhetoric—
were substituted.

Suppose liberals tried this formulation:

- In 1960 and in 1964, we elected Presidents pledged to get America
  moving again, to give a better deal to the poor and the black, to
  break the log jam.
- Thanks to these Presidents, thanks to a liberal impulse in the Congress
  in the mid-1960s, thanks to the tireless effort of liberals all over
  America—we passed the legislation to back up that rhetoric.
- Now a decade later we look back at the rhetoric, we look back at the
  legislation and we see—*results.* The Census and other statistical
  indices of our time show an America on the move, an America that,
  in particular, has given a better deal to the poor and the black—
  just what our rhetoric and legislation said it would do.

The progression, then, has been: rhetoric, legislation, results.

Now, that progression does not *prove* that the legislation dictated the

---

[13] A classic of the genre: "We meet tonight in a time of failure of American
liberalism. You can see the failure everywhere in this city and across the country.
For too long the sound of liberal alarms has been answered by little more than the
echo of our own voices. . . . The blunt truth is that liberals have achieved virtually
no fundamental change in our society since the end of the New Deal. We have
made strong efforts, some of them even inspiring. We have made good speeches,
some of them even great. And we have even made some advances . . . too many of
them half measures. So in 1971, we continue to live with institutions . . . that serve
the few who are comfortable at the expense of the many who truly are in need. How
have we gained so little after so long a time and so much work? It is easy to blame
others. But the fault is not primarily in others . . . it is in ourselves. Too often, we
have assumed that we would win because we should win. Too often, we have equated
a hard fight for progress with the hard fact of progress.

Senator EDMUND MUSKIE,
speech before the Liberal Party dinner
in New York, October 1971

results. But by the rules of the political road, the implication is surely there. Surely, the legislation is not totally responsible for the progress. But just as surely, it was contributory toward the progress. Liberalism worked, and liberals should say it has worked, should say we are moving toward valid goals and now give us the money and the statutes to finish the job. Normally, given such a situation, the political burden of proof would be on the President. It would be he and his party forced to show that life in America has deteriorated, or at least that programs haven't worked.

Instead—at a moment when history and data show victory for their ideas —liberals loudly compete with each other to proclaim defeat. America doesn't work, the programs don't work, things are as bad as they ever were. Perhaps they are worse.

Liberals, in short, have shown their characteristic failing, the inability to cope with their own success.

* * *

Unfortunately, the problem is more than just political in the narrow sense. As blacks have moved in massive numbers into the middle class, they are moving (with resistance) into white neighborhoods, moving (with resistance) into white schools, moving (with resistance) into white jobs. Given these facts, is it still useful (let alone valid) to incant again the old stereotype of black poverty? Is it useful to portray blacks in America as living in pathological slums, in rat-infested dwellings, in a self-perpetuating welfare culture, dropouts from school, working as janitors, uneducated and so on?

How easy it is for a white middle-class parent to say, I've got nothing against blacks, I just don't want my kids (my neighborhood, my place of work) contaminated with uneducated, shiftless, ill-employed, slummy people—of any race.

And how much harder it is, too, to resist this line of reasoning: Blacks have earned their way into the middle class, they have gone to school, they have moved from slums, they are well employed—now be fair and give them the same chance as whites. A movement for middle-class whites to be fair to middle-class blacks has a chance; the appeal for middle-class whites to play Lord and Lady Bountiful to lower class blacks is neither a happy nor a productive relationship for either group.

In short, integration—still the only rational solution to the race problem —will only occur as *class* gaps narrow, *and are publicly acknowledged to be narrowing,* which also happens to be a true assessment of what has been happening.

Trumpeting failure, the best deal liberals can hope to get is patronization. Announcing success, liberals might even convince people and get—with luck—more action leading to more progress.

CHAPTER 10

The Birth Dearth and What it Means
(Population)

A book dealing in large measure with Census data must deal with head counts. Simple enumeration was the original function of the Census and it remains today as the key, if no longer the only function, of Census statistical activity.

But beyond simple historical obeisance, an examination of population is critical to both the premise and the promise of this volume. For today, a keystone in the arch of American Failure and Guilt is the notion of the Population Explosion—and its corollaries of overcrowding, pollution, ugliness, ecological catastrophe and resource shortages.

Accordingly, perhaps the single most important new fact of recent statistical vintage is that, *in America, the Population Explosion has ended —if indeed it ever existed. And there is every indication that having ended it will stay ended. The Baby Boom has been replaced by a Birth Dearth. Although the Dearth will not cure all the ills that were wrongly attributed to the Explosion, its effect will be quite salutary. In the years to come, it may well prove to be the single greatest agent of an ever-increasing, ever-wealthier middle class in America.*

If It Ever Existed, It's Ended

In the decade of the 1950s—the decade of Korea, Ike, the cold war, the Silent Generation *and the Baby Boom*—the Census showed that the population of the United States increased by *18.5%*.

In the decade of the 1960s—the decade of JFK and LBJ, Vietnam, the Moon and riots—the Census showed that the population of the United States went up by *13.3%*.

In the decade of the 1970s—the decade of Richard Nixon, Spiro Agnew, Watergate, the energy crisis and Lord knows who and what else—the U.S.

population will grow by about *8%*, assuming that fertility and immigration rates continue at roughly the same levels as now exist.

If current fertility rates continue on through to the year 2000, American population will reach a level of somewhere between 249[1] and 264 million, depending largely on immigration and emigration levels. At these current levels, exclusive of immigration, American population will grow to a maximum of about 273 million in the middle of the *twenty-first* century. Soon thereafter population will *decrease* unless kept up by continued immigration.

This projection of population stability in the twenty-first century—or of "Zero Population Growth" if you prefer—is now a plausible one because for the first time since the Depression the U.S. fertility rate went down first to the "replacement level"[2] and then during the year 1973 actually dipped substantially *beneath* that level.

The concept of "replacement" is an important one to understand. In demographic parlance, "replacement level fertility" is that level of fertility required for 1,000 women to replace themselves in the following generation with 1,000 women of childbearing age. In America in the mid-twentieth century, that level of births is 2,100 per 1,000 women—or 2.1 children per one woman. Somewhat more than half of those children will be boys— who don't bear children (*sic*)—and of the remaining roughly 1.033 female children about .033 will not survive to childbearing age, leaving each woman "replacing" herself with one woman.

Until April of 1972 the American total fertility rate had *never* reached the magic 2.1 number, although in the Depression year of 1936 the rate hovered in that neighborhood. In April of 1972, the seasonally adjusted rate dipped to *2.04,* just *under* replacement![3]

Of course, a one-month drop in the birth rate in itself proves nothing. Month-to-month fluctuations in the fertility rate can vary extensively.

But the entire rest of the year of 1972 continued at a remarkably low level. The yearly rate was 2.025—a little *below* replacement. And

---

[1] A rather far cry from the prediction, made by President Nixon in 1970, echoing then-common estimates of a 300-million population by the year 2000.

[2] "Replacement," as we shall see later, does *not* mean Zero Population Growth, at least not right away. "Replacement" would only equal ZPG if it were in effect for several generations, and there were no immigration into the United States. A replacement rate today would still lead to some population increase because there happen now to be disproportionate numbers of "women of childbearing age" around right now. They are the daughters born during the Baby Boom grown up and now in their fecund years.

[3] Because so much of recent demographic scaremongering has dealt in absurd projections, we offer herewith our own absurd projection: If the April 1972 rate were projected into the future, then sometime between the year 3000 and year 4000 the total population of the United States would increase to none, yielding not Zero Population Growth, but zero population, and a nation composed presumably of little but empty camper trailers.

the data for the first half of 1973 was still lower—down to 1.940, and the second half of 1973 was still lower, 1.860.

But even that longer term data is not in itself wildly significant—even though it was the lowest by far in American history. Even the fact that the prior year, 1971, was also a very low year is not necessarily indicative of a major long-term development. Demography looks to generations for significance, not single calendar years. And that is just why the recent drop is so profound—it represents the continuation and acceleration of a trend that has been apparent for more than fifteen full years! The great Baby Boom actually crested in *1957,* just about eleven years after its beginning in 1946.

We can see the progression clearly by starting in the Depression. The total fertility rates run this pattern:

TOTAL FERTILITY RATE[4]

1936	2,119	all-time low
1937	2,147	)
1938	2,200	) still-low Depression rates
1939	2,154	)

Then, as the war economy took hold, fertility rates rose slowly:

1940	2,214
1941	2,314
1942	2,532
1943	2,616

And they dipped again slightly with so many potential fathers overseas:

1944	2,466
1945	2,392

[4] Number of children 1,000 women would bear if they had children over their fecund years at the yearly rate per age group. When misused, as it sometimes is, this number can provide a distorted picture. By its very definition, it attempts to give an instantaneous (one year) photograph of a process that goes on for a generation. When one erroneously uses the snapshot in place of the movie, in recent years it has tended to slightly over-state the lifetime fertility of women who were in the childbearing age cohorts in the late 1950s.

And then jumped when the GIs returned home:

1946	2,829	(!)
1947	3,158	(!!) (more than three children per woman)
1948	3,013	
1949	3,030	
1950	3,030	

At about which time everything should have begun to get back to normal—but didn't:

1951	3,209	(!)
1952	3,307	(!!)
1953	3,378	(!!!)

during which time, theoretically, the Korean war was pulling some potential fathers away.

And the rate kept climbing:

1954	3,501
1955	3,521
1956	3,634
1957	3,724 [5]

But then the rate began sinking, slowly at first:

1958	3,654
1959	3,669
1960	3,665
1961	3,620
1962	3,476
1963	3,331

but still at quite a high level. Then the slide angled down more sharply:

1964	3,197
1965	2,922
1966	2,728
1967	2,562
1968	2,480

[5] The highest level in recent decades.

back to where it was during World War II.

It stayed low for a couple of years,

1969	2,480
1970	2,447

and then went even lower, down to roughly "replacement" and the onset of the Birth Dearth,

1971	2,284	
1972	2,025	
1973	1,940	(first six months)
1973	1,860	(last six months)

Viewing this progressive fifteen year slide—it is pushing the data only a little to describe it as a drop-off from an almost four-child family to an almost two-child family—one haunting question emerges. Why is it that these were precisely the years when the rhetoric about the population explosion escalated so furiously? It is an important question, particularly when an examination of data shows not only that the U.S. birth rate has been declining for fifteen years, but taking a broader perspective, *that it has been declining for a hundred and fifty years*.

To show this we will have to switch from examining "fertility rates" to examining "birth rates," a somewhat less sophisticated index but one for which continuous historical data exists.

The first recorded birth rate in the United States is for the year 1820, the year when James Monroe was elected President.

In that year the birth rate was *55* births per 1,000 population.

Forty years later, in 1860, the birth rate had declined to *44*.

At the turn of the century in 1900, the rate had fallen to *32*.

After World War I, in 1920, the rate was *28*.

By 1929, the rate was down to *21*.

That the birth rate declined during the 1920s is particularly important. It demonstrates that fertility can skid downward even in times of ostensible prosperity. The trend was clearly and sharply down *before* the onset of the Depression. It continued downward during the early years of the Depression and hit a low of *18* in 1936.

Since the 1930s, the *birth* rate then climbed—and sunk—pretty much in tandem with the *total fertility* rates as described here earlier. The birth rate was at *19* in 1940, at *23* in 1943, at *27* in 1947 and remained in the mid-20s through the years of the Baby Boom, not sinking beneath *24* until 1959 and dipping below *20* in 1965.

By the late 1960s, the birth rate hovered around *18—the level of the Depression era.*

And then it went down further. In 1971, it was *17.3.* In 1972, it was *15.6,* the lowest rate in American history—corresponding to the "replacement" level fertility rates discussed earlier. During 1973, it was down to 15.0.

In one hundred and fifty years, then, the birth rate in America went down from 55 to 15! Population explosion indeed![6]

It is entirely possible, then, that the current low rates will one day look like a continuation of a trend that has been progressing for more than 150 years. The aberration in that long-term trend—and two generations from now it may look like a small aberration indeed—was the fifteen or so years of the Baby Boom.

Whether the Baby Boom will come to be seen as a minuscule bump on an otherwise fairly smooth line on a graph depends, of course, on what happens next. If the fertility rates should by some chance now change direction and go *up,* it is then possible that the 1950s Baby Boom may look like the first of the foothills to the Himalayas. On the other hand, if the fertility rates stay low, or go lower, all the hoopla about the Explosion in America may look retrospectively sillier and sillier.

It's Over, and It Won't Come Back

All the available data and independent trends point to the likelihood that the fertility rate will stay relatively low and perhaps go still lower. The Birth Dearth seems here to stay. It is the wave of the future and its ramifications are enormous.

Looking into the future is always a hazardous profession. In the field of demographics it is particularly so. The groves of academe are littered with the bleached bones of demographers who patiently explained, in the 1930s, why America's population would level off at about 130–140 million people. Ambulatory, but barely so, are the demographers who in the late 1940s cogently explained that urbanization and increased education invariably went hand in hand with a decreasing birth rate. Because urbanization and education were clearly on the upgrade, they posited, the 1950s would clearly be an era of low fertility. It wasn't.

But there are times when projections and predictions are more solidly

[6] And that figure of 15 was *before* any impact of the Supreme Court's abortion decision outlawing anti-abortion statutes, a decision which may well depress fertility rates further, as will be shown subsequently.

based and turn out more realistically. This would seem to be one of those times.

For we live at a time of confluence of two driving forces in the population equation. The first concerns *attitude:* In recent years Americans have decided, for various reasons, that they want fewer children. The second concerns *technology:* Americans who don't want children have access to an unparalleled array of contraceptive techniques—and they are using them effectively.

The Technology of the Birth Dearth

ENTER "THE PILL"

The most effective and most widely used method of contraception in America today is "the pill." It was first licensed for use in 1960. By 1963, just *6%* of married women were using the pill. Two years later, in 1965, the rate had climbed to *27%*. By 1970, the rate was *43%*.

It is not statistically valid to say that the pill *caused* the Birth Dearth. The current decline in fertility actually began a few years before the pill came into general use. But it is equally clear that the pill *contributed* mightily to the decline. Birth control of one form or another, of course, was widely practiced in America before the advent of the pill. (Note the low Depression birth rates.) But the pill is generally regarded as the best contraceptive yet discovered and its use continues to grow.

Moreover, other contraceptives—perhaps even more effective and safer —beckon over the horizon. Research proceeds on both the "male pill" and the "morning after" pill. New surgical techniques are being developed to simplify male and female sterilization procedures. And ever greater numbers of Americans are using sterilization as a birth-control device—16% among couples over thirty in 1970, up from 12% in 1965, according to the National Fertility Study. In short, insofar as new contraceptive technology has contributed to the advent of the Birth Dearth, this influence will, if anything, intensify as the years go on.

ABORTION

The trend concerning legalized abortion also would indicate that the Birth Dearth seems here to stay. There were *6,000* legal abortions performed in 1966. Four years later—after some major states like New York and California had liberalized abortion laws—the number of legal abortions had climbed to over *200,000* per year. A year later, mid-1970–71, the number had reached *505,000* per year. For mid-1971–72, the estimate had climbed to *600,000*.

There is a wide range of opinion regarding what the effect of legalized abortion will be on the birth rate. It is a more complicated analysis than one might think. For example, many of the legal abortions are not—demographically speaking—actually "preventing a birth." What they prevent, in fact, is only an *illegal* abortion.

Still, while magnitudes can be argued about, no one is proclaiming that the availability of legalized abortion *increases* birth rates. Abortion, after all—like it or not—is the definitive and final "morning after" procedure.

A short time before the Supreme Court ruled to legalize abortion, Dr. Christopher Tietze of the Population Council estimated that national legalization of abortion would reduce the U.S. birth rate by about 10% per year.

Some fraction of that 10% loss has already occurred—via state legalizations—say, a third for the sake of argument. If one figures the U.S. fertility rate is at a little below replacement (say roughly 1.90 for 1973) and one subtracts two thirds of 10% (6.66%, which yields a .13 reduction), the resultant rate is 1.77, well under replacement, even with immigration at present levels.

SPECULATION

A short digression: Suppose one looks forward a half a century or so and assumes that the low fertility rates remain roughly constant (at about 1.8) and so does the rate of immigration (at about 400,000 per year). At about that time, say in the year 2025, the total population of the United States will peak at about 265 million souls. Let us now assume that fertility rates stay at about 1.8 and immigration remains at 400,000.

In that event, the United States would lose seven million in population in the next twenty-five years (by 2050). By the year 2094, when some of the children of children alive today will still be alive, our total population would be back down to not far from 1974 levels—around 220 million. If fertility rates still stayed low and immigration were reduced somewhat commensurate to a smaller nation, the population of the United States would sink to about 185 million or so by 2160, roughly the population level here at the end of the 1950s. In another hundred or so years, the American population would likely be approaching 100 million—about the numbers we had here before World War I—and still sinking.

The speculative point offered here has little to do with legalized abortion, for there are many other ways that fertility rates can further shrink.

The point is simply this: If the fertility rate stays below replacement for a considerable length of time, then we start losing *population.*[7]

This is a concept—population loss—*that has been almost entirely absent from the Explosionist discourse. There has been a wealth of rhetoric concerning a geometrically expanding population that will ultimately cover the globe like a head-to-toe skin rash. Up, up, up. More, more, more. So goes the dialogue of doom. But that is one-way dialogue that does not conform to reality. The 2.1 rate is neither magical nor immutable. It can be breached. It is now being breached here. If it stays breached for a while it will lead to an interesting abbreviation: NPG—Negative Population Growth.*

LEGISLATION

Better contraceptives and the increased availability of abortions are two factors that would tend to confirm the idea that the Birth Dearth is here to stay. Another factor is a piece of legislation passed with relatively little fanfare several years ago called The Family Planning Services and Population Research Act of 1970. The purpose of this act is a simple one: to provide to five million poor women in America what nonpoor women have had all along, namely, access to contraceptive technology.

The new legislation is now committing about $100 million per year and it is a highly necessary service. The most recent National Fertility Study showed that 15% of all those births occurring to nonpoor women were "unwanted." But among poor women, 37% of the births were "unwanted"—two and a half times as great a percentage!

Accordingly, birth rates in American families earning less than $5,000 a year have been almost 30% higher than in families earning over $10,000 a year. Those ratios now appear to be changing somewhat, and it may well be that the Family Planning Act will play a major role in further reducing this imbalance.

ATTITUDES

Contraceptive technology does not, of course, guarantee a low birth rate and a continuation of the Birth Dearth. For that to happen, potential parents will have to *use* that contraceptive technology more frequently

[7] The only reason that a net population loss wouldn't occur immediately is because the huge cohorts of Baby Boom babies—now in the fecund-age groups—are currently present in the population in disproportionate numbers. Thus, even with our current fertility rate at below-replacement levels, the total population will continue to climb, although in far smaller magnitudes than had been expected.

than their own parents did. And for that to happen, they will, quite simply, have to be motivated by an equally simple goal: to have fewer children.

In 1967, the Census Bureau's Current Population Survey determined that among American wives aged eighteen to twenty-four the average number of "births expected" was *2.9*—almost three children. In 1973, six years later, a similar Census Bureau survey showed that eighteen- to twenty-four-year-old wives expected only *2.3* children.

That is an astonishing drop of 21% in five years. Moreover, do not be deluded by the new number of 2.3. That is for "wives." But some women don't get married.

When the 2.3 rate of birth expectation is extrapolated to include *all young women,* the rate is actually 2.1, according to the Census Bureau— just about the replacement level. And that was in mid-1972—before some of the latest dazzling decreases in fertility.

The Gallup Poll over the years has asked a question that reveals an identical trend: *"What do you think is the ideal number of children for a family to have?"*

Here are the results for those saying, "Four or more is the ideal number":

1936	34%
1941	41%
1945	49%
1947	47%
1953	41%
1957	38%
1960	45%
1963	42%
1966	35%
1967	40%
1971	23% (!)
1973	20% (!)
1974	19% (!!)

In the matter of a few years the venerable goal of the Planned Parenthood movement has in effect been adopted. The slogan "Two Is Enough" is plastered on billboards and buses all over the developing world. If it has not yet been adopted over there, it has over here.

SPECULATION

Not content with the apparent rationality of the two-child family, the Yahoo fringe of the ZPG movement has now moved onto greener pastures. "None Is Fun," a new movement proclaims, which may well

be the case. Ultimately, of course, it also means self-inflicted, pain-
less genocide, a goal that might be in keeping with the view that
America has failed and is the incarnate evil in the world.

To reach this position, the super-Explosionists have had to follow
some convoluted intellectual byways, but they have managed it. And
left a curious trail to follow.

It is, of course, a profoundly conservative *movement.*

Listen to Paul Ehrlich discourse about what a wonderful place
America was in 1910. Echoing the cry of conservatives since time
immemorial, he says: Ah, those were the good old days. They must
have been good, after all, we only had less than 100 million people
and clean air, clean water, and we had Real Values because people
weren't Overcrowded.

Add to this the Explosionist notion that economically Zero Production *Growth is as happy a circumstance as Zero* Production
Growth. After all, if the economy wouldn't expand we would have
less pollution. Moreover, if the economy wouldn't expand, if all
those beer-drinking slobs didn't have all those cars and all that va-
cation time and all that ugly affluence—well, then, they wouldn't
despoil our national parks.

To this must be added the latest cry of the ZPGers: anti-
immigration. Keep the foreigners out, says ZPG; they'll make Amer-
ica even worse than it is.

Now, if George Babbitt or William McKinley or other classic con-
servatives returned from the grave to say, "Where are the good old
days; keep affluence from the lower middle class and watch out for
the foreigners"—that might be a consistent if misguided position.

It seems bizarre to find it expressed by "liberals."

The Explosionists, or some of them, have now gone further. From
conservatism we now move on to hedonism. "None Is Fun" says
the slogan, and the bumper stickers read "Make Love Not Babies."
This, too, makes some small degree of sense if one believes in
American Flunk. If we have failed—by overpopulating and pollut-
ing—why reproduce the failure, let alone multiply it? Wouldn't it be
smarter, indeed more humanitarian, to just have fun, and avoid
all the responsibility and gradually fade away.

THE REASONS FOR THE ATTITUDES

The contraceptive technology needed for the continuation of the Birth
Dearth exists—and it is being used. There is no indication that there will
be regress on this front. The attitudes regarding size of family have

changed—a necessary condition to a continuing Birth Dearth. But will there be regress on this front in the future? Will attitudes change again —toward larger families—as the twentieth century moves along? No one really knows, of course, but in order to explore the possibilities we must probe deeper into the attitudinal question. *Why* are Americans saying that they will have fewer children? What are the reasons? And, most important, will those reasons continue in the years to come, insuring the continuation of the Birth Dearth?

WORKING WOMEN

One apparent reason that American women are having fewer children is that long before the self-proclaimed Women's Liberationists decided that it was good for women to have a job, many American women reached that decision entirely on their own.

To review that dramatic data:

The 1940 Census showed that only *15%* of American wives were in the labor force.

The 1950 Census showed *24%*.

The 1960 Census showed *31%*.

And the 1970 Census showed that *39%* of American wives were in the labor force. By 1972, the percentage was *42%*.

This continuing and astonishingly sharp movement is no doubt one of the three or four most important socioeconomic facts shown in the most recent Census—and, in fact, probably one of the three or four most significant social changes in America in the last third of a century. The data provoke a number of observations. Here are two:

- There seems to be no reason to doubt that the proportions of wives who will work in the future will stay relatively high and, in fact, probably continue to go higher, in part due to the vast liberationist publicity mill, in part due to a new body of laws that effectively reduces sex discrimination in hiring, and mostly because more women simply want to get a job these days.

- Wives who work are less likely to have large families. This is clearly substantiated by Census data. Among married women aged thirty-five to forty-four employed full time in 1969, for example, the fertility rate was 27% *less* than for women *not* in the labor force.

In short, if we assume that wives will continue to work in large or increasing proportions and that working wives will continue to have fewer children than nonworking wives—then it seems fair enough to chalk up one more factor toward a continuation of the Birth Dearth.

DIVORCE

Another factor sometimes associated with Women's Lib—divorce—is also sharply increasing. Actually there has been a staggeringly sharp increase.

In 1960, there were 393,000 divorces granted in the United States. In 1973, there were over 913,000 divorces granted!

In 1960, the *rate* of divorce was 2.2 per 1,000 persons per year, not terribly different from the 1940 rate twenty years earlier. In 1973, the rate was 4.4 per 1,000! And the sharpest increase has come in the most recent years![8]

There have been a number of explanations offered for this sharp increase in divorce, some of which are probably valid. The correlation between the striking increase in the proportion of wives now *working* and the proportion of wives now *divorcing* leads to some particularly plausible reasons: First, the working woman gets to meet other men. But that is probably only a small part of it. Perhaps more important is the availability of a paycheck. It is one thing for a woman to consider divorce when the alternatives—as in days of yore—are to become a seamstress or put up a sign in the window of the house reading "Boarders" or "Piano Given." It is entirely another proposition when the divorcee can—and does—hold a job as an executive secretary, a computer programmer or a lawyer.

There is also the "marriage squeeze." That is a demographic, not a sexual, phenomenon. Grooms tend to be about two years older than brides. If, roughly twenty years earlier, there was a baby boom, which there was, then today there are disproportionately more females "ready" for marriage than there are males "ready" for marriage.

As Dr. Paul Glick of the Census Bureau points out, this can lead to several sorts of activity. Girls may be inordinately pushing boys into marriage before the boys feel they are ready—increasing the likelihood of a bad marriage and a potential divorce. Or, young girls—sensing the futility of that ploy—may also be inordinately pushing somewhat older, perhaps married, men into marriage. That creates not a potential divorce, but an actual one.

---

[8] Despite this enormous increase, there is a general misconception about divorce rates in America. The standard number in general usage for the last decade or so has been "one out of three marriages end in divorce." The impression this leaves is that one of every three fresh-faced, innocent brides and grooms will end up divorced. Not quite correct. The divorce rate for *first marriages* has been substantially lower than one in three; the numbers are inflated by the added percentages from divorces from second marriages. Actually, even today, after increases, the rate of divorce among first marriages is only in the 25–29% range, according to Dr. Paul Glick of the Census Bureau.

In any event, the divorce rate is high, there is no immediate reason to think that it will decrease, and a high divorce rate is believed to have a small, but distinct, downward pull on the fertility rate. This is so because the typical divorce occurs among women still in the childbearing age group—a seven-year marriage span is average, so the typical divorced woman would be about twenty-eight years old. The average time elapsed between divorce and remarriage is 3.4 years—years when the divorcee is fairly effectively removed from the category of "potential mother." In all, one more reason—a small one—to think that the Birth Dearth is here to stay.

DELAYED MARRIAGE

A further reason for the expected continuation of the Birth Dearth can be explained in terms of a successful program in China. When Mao decided that the Chinese birth rate was too high, one of the key anti-natalist measures enacted was to raise the legal age of marriage.

Without Maoist fiat, Census data reveals the Americans have done it for themselves. In 1956, American women married at the average age of 20.1 years. By 1973, the average age of marriage was 21.0 years. That's an increase of almost a whole year and fairly significant as these things run.

Moreover, newly married women are now tending to have their first baby later than they used to. Thus, between 1960–64, among white women only 14.2 months elapsed between "first marriage" and "first birth." Data for 1965–69 show an increase to 16.0 months, and while the figures for 1972 and 1973 are not yet available, the rates are expected to show a somewhat lengthier interval.

When the months of the increased interval are added to the roughly ten months' increase in the age of marriage described earlier, the sum may well reach about a one-and-a-quarter-year delay of the age of the mother at first birth. That is an important point. "Fertility delayed is fertility denied," goes the demographic saying, and upon the degree of the validity of that axiom depends much of the future of the Birth Dearth.

An American woman who marries in her late teens or early twenties might well produce three or four children in the first six or seven or so years of her marriage, and still finish her childbearing well before her thirtieth birthday. By the time she is fed up with diapers and baby-sitters, by the time she feels that she is perhaps too old for another pregnancy, she already has a relatively big family, and there is very little she can do about it.

But suppose her younger sister doesn't get married until, say, age twenty-four, and then continues working for, say, three years. The couple think they might well like to have a large family—three or four kids. But, by age twenty-seven she's likely got a fairly well-paying job, and possibly an interesting one. She and her husband have been able to sock away a little money on their two-earner income, they've bought a nice sofa and some nice chairs, they've taken a vacation in the Scandinavian countries and have gone out in the evenings to see the good movies.

They decide that now is the time to have a family. She gets pregnant. At age twenty-eight, she has a baby. A year later she is pregnant again. She has another baby. She's now thirty. The oldest baby is chewing on the leg of the beautiful couch. There are two sets of diapers now. The couple hasn't seen a movie in a half a year. The last vacation was a weekend drive to the beach, with diaper bags, car seats, high chairs and bottle warmers. There is only one paycheck.

Another year passes. She's thirty-one. The one-year-old is chewing the leg of the sofa. The three-year-old has found a dead bird in the yard. The bird is now on the living-room rug. Does she have another baby? Another pregnancy? More diapers? No paycheck?

The decision is made: no. Two is enough. Fertility delayed is fertility denied.

So goes the theory, and it seems valid enough. The data is clear that the peak years of fertility are in the twenty to twenty-nine age range, with a sharp drop-off thereafter.

It is a critical question right now. All the current data, as has been demonstrated, shows that actual fertility rates have fallen sharply. We know that, *at the least,* fertility has been "delayed." It seems extremely likely that much of this delayed fertility will prove to be denied fertility. But that will not be known for sure for several more years. If in 1976 or 1977, you start seeing thirty-one-year-old pregnant women with two small children tagging along behind—then it will only have been "fertility delayed." If not, as is likely, it will prove to be "fertility denied" and the Birth Dearth will be rolling along.

THE ECONOMY

There are those who feel that, in large measure due to the energy crisis, America faces an extended time of economic recession, some even say, depression. That is dubious. But if they are correct it might well augur still further drops in fertility. Of even more interest is the fact that the most recent sharp drop in fertility occurred during an economic boom. Accordingly, boom or bust, there is no economic reason to expect an end to the Birth Dearth.

THE CATASTROPHE FACTOR

There is at least one more—important—reason behind the shift in attitude concerning fertility.

Many Americans—particularly young Americans—believe the Explosionist case. In the demographic world it is young people who count. Census data shows that three out of four babies are born to women under age thirty. Nine out of ten babies are born to women under thirty-five.

And while the American public as a whole has bought much of the population-pollution equation, it has been a particularly popular notion among the young.

Here is the data:

"*Think present U. S. population is a major problem now.*"

21–29 years old	30–49 years old	50 and over
53%	38%	37%

(Gallup, 1971)

Accordingly, the demographic future of America rests on decisions that will be made by a nineteen-year-old garage mechanic with pimples on his face, by a buxom seventeen-year-old clerk in a Woolworth's store, by a mechanical-drawing student at Hawkeye Institute of Technology in Waterloo, Iowa, by an Air Force staff sergeant stationed in Spain, by an ecology major at the University of Colorado, by a young engineer in Los Angeles and so on.

So, insofar as we might speculate that the demographic branch of the Failure and Guilt Complex will continue to function, and insofar as we might speculate that young people will continue to believe the Explosionist notion that people are poisoning the planet, and insofar as we can believe that these young people will act upon what they believe—then we must assume yet another reason for the likely continuation of the Birth Dearth.

* * *

In review: If there was a population explosion in America, it has ended. Having ended, it will stay ended.

CHAPTER 11

What the Birth Dearth Will Do —
Income
What the Birth Dearth Won't Do —
Environment

Will the cessation of rapid population growth be beneficial in America?
Probably so, but not for the reasons most commonly believed.

There seem to be two basic and *valid* reasons for believing that the
advent of the Birth Dearth will be beneficial.

The first—and most important by far—concerns the individual families
involved, particularly poorer and lower middle-income families. The relatively small family has always been seen as a *characteristic* of the
middle-class families—they have fewer babies than do poor families.
But in this era of plunging fertility, small family size must be viewed
not only as a *characteristic* of the middle-class family—but as an *initiator*
of a middle-class family. *The Birth Dearth may well prove to be the single
most important agent of a massive expansion and a massive economic upgrading of the already Massive Majority Middle Class.*

A few simple calculations can give a flavor of what is involved as
prospective American parents decide that two, not three or four, children
are best.

Suppose there is a family in America with earnings of $12,000 (roughly
typical in 1972). Suppose further that the family is composed of a husband, a wife and *four* children—not so very far from the rate of 3.724
children per woman recorded in 1957. In that 1950's-style family the per
capita income would be *$2,000*—$12,000 divided by six people.

Now suppose that instead of *four* children in that almost typical family,
we change the model to a 1970's-style family with *two* children. (Remember, the total fertility rate for the last six months of 1973 was 1.86
children per woman.) *Now, suppose income stays the same—$12,000.*

What happens to per capita income? *It goes up 50%!* ($12,000 divided by a four-person-family yields *$3,000* per capita income versus the *$2,000* per capita income in the six-person family.)

So then, *demographics alone plays a powerful role in the changes in per capita income within a family.*

But it goes even beyond that. As family size decreases, *discretionary income* rises even faster than *per capita* income. There was a 50% gain in per capita income as a $12,000 family dropped from six persons to four persons, but there is a 189% gain in per capita discretionary income in that same family. In the six-person family, *each* family member has $253 of discretionary income. In the four-person family, *each* family member has $731 in discretionary income.[1] The four-person family may decide to take a short packaged tour to Europe; the six-person family will be lucky to be able to send the kids to a "Y" summer camp for two weeks.

Perhaps we are overstating or oversimplifying the fertility drop: the data concerning "four child" and "two child" families are minimally distorted due to technical factors, and, besides, the total fertility rate was "only" 3.7 not 4.0 in 1957. Suppose we calculate the differential for the change from a *three*-child family to a *two*-child family at the $12,000 level. Just a change of *one* child. Per capita income goes up from $2,400 (five persons into $12,000) to *$3,000*—an increase of 25%, while per capita discretionary income goes up by a mere 53% from $478 to $731. Thus, again, a major change in family fortune keyed only to one simple demographic change—one less child. The five-person family will have difficulty getting to Europe, the four-person family may be able to do it.

The same sort of economic changes occur all up and down the economic scale—more discretionary income as family size decreases.

For a $20,000 family the extra money might be used to pay for a basketball camp for the boy child, or a car for the teen-age girl, or a family winter vacation to Aruba. Very nice. And "beneficial" too, insofar as camps, cars and travel are generally beneficial, a notion which the author accepts. The only minus on the ledger is the absence of the "joy of a large family." But, then again, the parents have that option if they so desire.

And the changes are particularly dramatic at the lower end of the spectrum. A five-person family at $7,000 has *zero* discretionary income (and is not in the middle class?); a four-person family at the same income level has $223 in discretionary income, not much, but about enough for a television set.

At the $9,000 level, discretionary income rises from $516 to $985 per family or from $103 to $246 (more than a doubling) *per capita,* as family size goes from five to four.

[1] Discretionary income estimates drawn from *Newsweek* study described on page 64.

In short, more spending money for Americans, more spending money for the middle class.

For that $9,000 four-person family, the Birth Dearth bonus money may be used for a down payment on a camper truck, which will be used to take a three-week vacation touring national parks.

Consider, moreover, the plight of the $5,000 per year family. There is no discretionary income.

In a five-person family per capita income is $1,000 per person and living conditions are strained. The dwelling is small, the clothes sometimes thin, the food less nutritious than it should be. If that $5,000-per-year five-person family is suddenly transformed into a four-person family, the diet probably improves, the dwelling will be less overcrowded, the clothing sturdier. Moreover, the absence of the third child may accelerate by perhaps three or four years the ability of the wife to get a job—say, when her youngest child goes into first grade. That job—perhaps it is only a part-time job—may provide an additional $2,000–$3,000 for the family coffers and open up entirely new vistas. For example, a smaller family—with a working wife—may be able to send the oldest son to college. By going to college, the son has delayed entry into the labor force by several years. Had he been a member of a larger family, with a non-working wife, the oldest son may have had to get a full-time job as soon as he graduated from high school in order to help his family make ends meet.

Consider, finally, the dilemma of another type of family—"the welfare family." Suppose a "welfare mother" has three children, aged one, three and five, a welfare check amounting to $2,500 per year, and no husband. If she cannot work until the youngest child is in school—at age six—she will be "on the welfare" for *five* more years. When she is able to work full time, suppose she earns $4,000 a year, that is a per capita income of $1,000, following five years of poverty and, probably, debt accrual. But, if because of the advent of the Birth Dearth—and particularly the advent of contraceptive devices in poor neighborhoods and the availability of legalized abortions—the welfare mother has *two* children, then her situation has changed starkly. She can go off welfare in *three* years, not *five*, and the family will have a per capita income of $1,333, an increase of a third. The additional money may well mean a livable diet, shoes that are not lined with paper in the winter, and the wherewithal to hire an exterminator to deal with rats.

Should the welfare mother have only *one* child—the five-year-old one —plausible enough, considering the data that shows the incidence of "unwanted" birth much higher among poor women, then the welfare mother is off welfare in *one* year not *five* and she and her child have a $2,000 per capita income, the same as the five-person, $10,000-a-year family. The child of *that* welfare mother now off welfare could conceivably end up going to college.

Such, then, is the stark economic leverage that is provided by shrinking fertility rates. Simply put and generally put, it allows families to spend more money on what they *want* rather than on what they absolutely *need*. And that is the hallmark of American middle classness.

SPECULATION

If the Birth Dearth has a major impact on families, so too will it have a major impact on American business. Common mythology says businessmen are always for population growth because it means "good business." The converse is also propounded: Businessmen are against low fertility because it's "bad for business."

In point of fact, it depends very much on what business you're in. If you call the supermarket industry home, then the Birth Dearth is not particularly good news. Essentially, supermarkets make their money by selling necessities. The more people, the greater the need for more food, the more supermarkets sell. Fewer people—less business.

Moreover, as per capita income goes up (because of the Birth Dearth) greater percentages of family income goes to wants not needs, wants like vacations, vacation houses, hi-fi sets, second cars, third cars, Ph.D. educations and so on—things and services not usually sold in supermarkets. If you're in the supermarket business that means a lesser share of the consumer dollar runs through your cash registers for needs like food. Long term, that is not considered a generally desirable state of affairs in corporate board rooms, or among the Wall Street wizards who determine which industries are "growth industries."

On the other hand, if your business is foreign travel, vacations, vacation houses, sports cars, hi-fi and so on, the Birth Dearth may be the equivalent of what the Baby Boom was to Gerber's Baby Foods. Any business dependent upon increasing amounts of middle-income spending power is on the right side of the numbers. The class market is becoming a mass market.

Moreover, if supermarketing is your trade it isn't all that bad either, if you know what to expect. Supermarkets may be selling fewer pounds of hamburger in 1980 than they thought they would before the onset of the Birth Dearth. But as per capita income sky-rockets they will be selling more shrimps, more steaks and more frozen gourmet dinners (convenient for the working wife). But it goes beyond that. Supermarkets, in search of the high-growth sectors, grow into "superstores" and sell tennis racquets, hi-fi sets, etc. As a sign of the times and as a sign that American business is responsive if nothing else, it should be noted that in 1971 the first supermarket opened a booth having a travel agent. That game is called "diversification" and what it means is "responsiveness."

Business that is responsive is not endangered by the Birth Dearth.

And finally, despite the Birth Dearth and because of the Baby Boom, the total population of the United States will continue to go up in the next few decades. *These Baby Boom babies who reach the age of parenthood in the 1970s and 1980s may decide to have only two-child families—but there will be lots of two-child families. So, while supermarket chains likely won't need stores to serve 300 million Americans in the year 2000, they will need stores for at least 250 million Americans in the year 2000, and that's still about 40 million more Americans than there are now, a considerable number indeed.*

Moreover, as the Baby Boom babies reach full maturity in the 1970s and 1980s they will be setting up households, *even if they don't have very many children in those households. Thus, in 1970, before the real onslaught on Baby Boomers coming-of-age, there were 63 million* households *in America. By 1980, the projection is for 77 million* households—*an increase of 22% this decade regardless of size of family.*

That's 14 million new households! That's 14 million new households in the 1970s, a decade of relatively low *population growth. That compares to* 9 million *new households in the 1950s and* 10 million *new households in the 1960s—both decades of relatively* high *absolute population growth. And when one considers that household formation is typically the spark in the tinder of modern commerce, a moment of the most intense sort of consumer activity, then things look pretty good for business. Consider in this regard all the goods and services that go into the setting up of a new household: a dwelling place, sinks, showers, pots, pans, garbage cans, and probably dishwashers, television sets, rugs, paintings, johnny brushes and so on.*

To give a sense of the magnitude of the impact of the demographics involved in the wave of family-forming we are about to see, consider this one datum: From 1972 to 1985 about half of the incremental income of persons will come from people aged twenty to thirty-four! (That involves about $250 billion new dollars.)

For the long-term future, the situation changes somewhat (in the 1990s, household formation will drop as Birth Dearth babies who will be coming of age will be relatively few). But the advantage of dealing with the long-term future is that it is long term and these sorts of long-term demographics telegraph their punch in plenty of time for business to adjust. By the year 2020, American conglomerates will be buying chains of funeral homes—the new growth industry.

In a capsule, what business faces is an equation based on the following situation: We live in an unprecedented demographic era —a Birth Dearth following a Baby Boom. When you couple that notion with another—a time of prosperity—you get these historical guidelines: We have had small *families with* low *incomes (the Depression). We have had* large *families with* rising *incomes (the Baby Boom). Now we face—barring major recessionary occurrences —an era of* small *families and* rising *incomes. In short, unprecedented individual affluence, more people in the massive majority middle, more people with more spending money in the massive majority middle. And good times for most industries.*

* * *

There is at least one more good thing that ought to be acknowledged about the advent of the Birth Dearth. *It had to come sooner or later— and it may as well be sooner.* Ultimately both American and world fertility rates have to reach a ZPG level—or less. The geometric horror projections about American growth going to 400 million and 800 million to a billion and two billion and ten billion—to a point where we will live like sardines in a can—are, and were, preposterous. The data now shows that conclusively.

What It Won't Do—the Environment

There is another interesting aspect of the Birth Dearth: what it will *not* do for America.

It is the contention here that most of the problems that have been attributable to the Explosion by the Explosionists will remain with us long after the Explosion has ended.

For example:

The Claim: Overcrowding in America causes crime.[2]

Rebuttal: There has been a sharp increase in crime in America in recent years. Interestingly, the highest jump in crime rates by far oc-

[2] For example, a full-page newspaper ad with a headline screaming "Have You Ever Been Mugged? Well, You May Be!" The ad was part of a series published by an organization called *Campaign to Check the Population Explosion,* whose membership list reads like the all-star team of the American Establishment (Lessing Rosenwald, Elmo Roper, William H. Draper). The text of the ad makes it clear that excess population is largely responsible for crime, slums and riots.

curred in the low-income areas of central cities—*areas that are losing population.* For example, in the decade of the 1960s, Hough, Watts, Harlem all had major population decreases. Conversely, the areas with the highest population growth—the suburbs—have relatively low rates of crime.

The Claim: America is overcrowded.

Rebuttal: By what standard? Density? Forget it. In 1970, the Netherlands had 829 persons per square mile. England had 593. India had 426. Mainland China had 205. Spain had 174. Nigeria had 156. Turkey had 117. Mexico had 65. And the crowded, crowded, crowded United States? A sparse 57![3]

The case can be made that density figures don't really mean anything when huge parts of a nation are uninhabitable, as is the case in the United States—mountains, deserts, etc. But two other factors should be noted.

First: even our big, almost thoroughly inhabitable states are not terribly crowded by international standards. New York State had 381 people per square mile in 1970, Pennsylvania, 262, Ohio, 260. Only a handful of tiny, solidly urban Northeastern states are in the higher European ranges: New Jersey, 953, Rhode Island, 902, Massachusetts, 727 and Connecticut, 673.

Second: In the United States there are vast *inhabitable* areas that are underpopulated. We know they are habitable because they have been inhabited very pleasantly until very recently. We refer, of course, to parts of small-town America, and to those swaths of mid-continent U.S.A. that have been losing population over the last few decades.

What people really mean when they say that "America is overcrowded" is—statistically speaking—something else entirely. What they mean is: The population of American suburbs has soared at a time when the population in rural, small-town and big-city areas have remained relatively constant or indeed lost population. That development indicates *not* a Population Explosion, but something else that has been explored earlier in this volume: a Population Redistribution.

That Redistribution does not cause "crowding"; in fact, it frequently causes something quite unlike crowding—namely, Suburban Sprawl, a relatively "uncrowded" way of life compared to life in the central city. Suburbia, after all, is composed essentially of families living on plots of roughly a quarter of an acre—quite a bit of land. If it occurs to the reader that the Explosionists are not consistent to attack cities for being crowded (which causes crime) and then attack suburbs for being sprawling (which causes neon-strip cultures), then the reader is only half right. If one is trying to think intelligently about the problem, it *is* inconsistent.

[3] Russia had 29; Brazil, 8; Taiwan had 1,014.

If, on the other hand, as the Demographic Auxiliary of the Guilt Complex, one is trying to show that *whatever* happens in America is bad, then such views are not only consistent, but a call to arms.

Finally, there happens to be a semiofficial "crowded" index, used by those who chart housing statistics. A dwelling is considered "crowded" if it has more than one person per room. And here are the data over a three-decade span:

PER CENT OF HOUSEHOLDS LIVING IN CROWDED CONDITIONS

1940	20%
1950	16%
1960	12%
1970	8%

The Claim: The population explosion has created Suburban Sprawl.

Rebuttal: To some degree, a true statement. So what? In point of fact, Suburban Sprawl is a pejorative phrase that describes perhaps the most comfortable mass residential living conditions in history.

The Claim: We're not coping with the population growth we've had. We're not building any "new towns."

Rebuttal: Suburbs are the functional equivalent of "new towns."

The Claim: Suburban sprawl, caused by the population explosion, creates ugliness.

Rebuttal: That is an aesthetic judgment. It is correct, in the author's aesthetic judgment, only sometimes in some parts of some suburbs. When suburbs or neon-strip cultures are ugly, however, they are not ugly because they are overcrowded. There is no law of architecture, demography or economics that demands ugliness. The many un-ugly suburbs prove that. The phenomenon of ugly development of the suburbs, then, is not related to the population explosion.

* * *

A second group of Explosionist notions deals with the environment and pollution.

The Claim: All those people are destroying the environment. Yellowstone during the summer looks and sounds like the Bronx.

Rebuttal: Not quite like the Bronx. But the problem isn't just "too many people." The problem—if people visiting national parks can sensibly be regarded as "a problem"—is that there are "many more people than before who are able to, and want to, go to national parks."

Consider the numbers. In 1950, there were 33 million Americans who visited the facilities in the national park system. By 1971, that total had gone up to 201 million—an increase of about 500% (!). Now, during the same time period the total population of the United States was going up from 154 million to 206 million, an increase of 33%. Using the 1971 *proportions,* one sees this: Even if the population had remained constant during those two decades, national park visitations would have gone to about 150 million—from 33 million—and, clearly, the population *growth* is not the cause of overcrowded parks.

Rather, the increase has been caused by the changing *nature* of the population. When in the course of twenty years, a society is created where almost everyone owns an automobile, where almost everyone has a paid vacation, where new Interstate highways can take a family six hundred miles in a single day's drive, where people have enough money to spend on tents, camper trucks, Coleman stoves, sleeping bags and freeze-dry cottage cheese—is it any wonder that they flock to observe the natural grandeur of Yellowstone or the Grand Tetons or the Great Smokies? Such are the results of the creation of a Massive Majority Middle Class. Presented here, then, are only two minor disagreements with the Explosionists: It's good, not bad, that more Americans go to national parks, and the fact that they go is not due to any Explosion except one that might well be called the Explosion of Enlarged Options.

The Claim: Population growth causes the destruction of our national environment, the beasts and the woods. The bald eagle is becoming extinct.

Rebuttal: If the bald eagle becomes extinct it will become extinct not because of too many humans but because of lax and lenient laws for humans. The buffalo was driven into near extinction when the U.S. population was less than 70 million people. Buffalo herds are now *growing,* and we are a nation of 210 million. The same holds with regard to protecting the wilderness. It can be destroyed by 100 million or preserved by 300 million. If you want it preserved, preserve it; but don't look for phony crutches to support a feeling of inevitable despair.

The Claim: Large populations cause pollution.

Rebuttal: Wrong. Ancient Carthage was polluted. The small cities of medieval Europe were polluted. The reason they wore high-buttoned shoes and spats in the 1880s was because the gutters were ankle high in horse manure. Sydney, in sparsely populated Australia, has a pollution problem. In short, you don't have to have large populations to have pollution.

The Claim: (Part Two) Large populations cause pollution. Look at Lake Erie.

Rebuttal: Look at Lake Erie. It is an ecological slum. If the U.S. fertility rate went down to 1.0 or so, establishing ZPG overnight at a population level of 210 million, the condition of Lake Erie would remain that of an ecological slum. On the other hand, tough (and intelligent) pollution laws in an America of 275 million persons can probably resuscitate Lake Erie.

Moreover, the same sort of equation discussed vis-à-vis the national parks obtains regarding water pollution and, for that matter, air pollution. Only a part, and only a relatively small part at that, of the pollution of Lake Erie is due to sheer numbers of people. The pollution, like the crowded parks, is due to the nature of what the people do, like manufacturing steel and glass and rubber, to name a few activities in the Lake Erie basin. If aboriginal American Indians lived in tepees in the Lake Erie area instead of urbanized, industrialized Modernmen—the "pollution" of Lake Erie would be minimal.[4]

The problem, then, is this: If just slowing down (or even reversing) population growth won't halt pollution what will? Technology will. But here, too, the Explosionists see a people problem. To wit—

The Claim: Because of the economic strain of increased population, we can't provide the enormous economic resources necessary to curb pollution—or for that matter to do all the other things we have to do. School budgets, for example, are bloated because of the Explosion; that money can't be used to build tertiary sewage treatment plants. Too many people each need a slice of the pie.

Rebuttal: Empirically invalid; theoretically true only for a limited period of time, which time period is now lapsing.

Thus, during precisely the years of the Population Explosion in the United States, the size of the pie grew far faster than the number of slices into which the pie had to be cut. In other words, the slices got fatter. Much fatter—hence the advent of the Massive Majority Middle Class.

There were, then, *extra* amounts of money to spend on what the society opted to spend it on—guns, butter, roads, schools, trips to the moon, mass transit or tertiary sewage plants. If the choices made were not to the liking of the Explosionists, it was not because the resources were not available. The resources were available.

Of course, the case has been made that those remarkable national gains would have been *even more remarkable* had there been no significant population growth. That is probably correct, on a macrocosmic model of what was described earlier concerning family income. Fewer children in the family, same amount of earnings, larger per capita income. And, too, the converse: more children, same earnings, less per capita income. The same essential formula would hold true for society as a whole.

[4] The author, if the reader hasn't guessed yet, is not an ecologist. But Dr. Barry Commoner is, and the gist of his thinking is that the ecological problem in America is primarily technical (i.e., what people do), rather than how many people there are.

But it is critical to understand that on a national basis the "thinning of economic per capita resources"—which is what the Explosionists claim has happened—*happens only once for demographic reasons. It is not a continuing phenomenon unless population growth spirals ad infinitum, which is not happening here.*

A Baby Boom creates a high dependency ratio *for one generation,* while the children are children. After that it levels out.

The key to it all rests with two simple quotations. Bergen Evans said, "We may be through with the past, but the past is not through with us." And an unidentified, but wise, demographer said, "Every child has not only a mouth—but hands."

Thus, a baby and a child are consumers—mouths. But the past will not forget us: that child grows up and he *produces* for the society as well as *consuming.* He can produce whatever public needs the society decides it wants—including tertiary sewage treatment plants. The society does that through an interesting device called taxes. Adults pay taxes. Children don't. But children become adults. When they do they pay taxes.

A final thrust of the Explosionists concerns the international situation— the broad view of what they like to call "spaceship earth."

The Claim: We're running out of nonrenewable natural resources on this spaceship earth.

Rebuttal: It is a major problem. As one septuagenarian has said, "Resources are a serious problem. We've been running out of oil ever since I've been a boy."

The claim is correct—by definition. Nonrenewable resources are non-renewable. That means if you use them, you are running out of them. But America will run out of oil with 200 million people or 300 million people, or even 100 million people for that matter. America will run out of oil with a fertility rate of 3.1 or of 2.1 or of 1.1. And so will the rest of the world, regardless of fertility rates. Does it make a significant difference if we "run out of oil" five or ten years earlier because the fertility rate was 2.1 in America, not 1.9? Only minimally. In the decades and centuries to come we earthlings will have to come up with effective replacement fuels in any demographic situation. The fuels will probably not be as cheap as we have been accustomed to. We will have to plan replacement schedules better than we've done in Round One of the Energy Crisis. We will have to figure out what energy is wasted and what is needed. But these problems of resource development will have to be faced at whatever population levels we have. It's going to take a lot of manpower to make our resources work for us, to get oil from shale, gas from coal, heat from sun in the winter and refrigeration from the sun in the summer. That manpower will be provided by the Baby Boom babies, educated, ambitious and ready to work with the two hands and one brain granted to God's children.

Which leads to an interesting point. What, actually, is a "resource"? Three hundred years ago coal wasn't a resource, but a rock. A hundred years ago oil was a sticky nuisance, not a resource. Forty years ago uranium wasn't a resource. Coal, oil and uranium became resources because the mind of man figured out a way to use them beneficially. There is only one real resource in the world: The mind of man, and it is not nonrenewable. It is probably unlimited. In this vein, Nobel Laureate Dr. Simon Kuznets of Harvard University has studied the economies of underdeveloped nations in the third world and made this profound statement: "Lack of resources is not the cause of underdevelopment. It is underdevelopment that is the cause of lack of resources."

The United States, it should be pointed out, is not an underdeveloped nation. We may have some difficulty in this country of dealing with problems like race relations, but the energy crisis is our kind of problem. Accordingly, it may well prove to be—within the next few years—economically beneficial.

First, we will solve it. This nation happens to sit on the world's greatest mass of hydrocarbons in the world. And we have the technological competence and the materialist desire to solve it.

Second, it will teach us what waste is and what waste is not. Cars, as indicated in Chapter 7, are not a waste. Big cars are a waste. Pollution abatement devices on cars are not a waste. Pollution abatement devices that are so complicated in dealing with the last few per cent of pollutants that they jack up prices and fuel consumption are a waste.

Third, if politically exploited, the energy crisis could provide Americans with a sense of challenge, which may prove to be more beneficial than one can possibly imagine, a notion that will be explored in the next part of this book.

The Claim: Because America is so affluent, because Americans are so numerous, because we need so many resources, we are exploiting other, poorer nations and we're using "more than our share" of the finite resources of "spaceship earth." (The common figure used is that Americans are only 6% of the world's people, but consume 30% of the world's resources.) This, it is stated, will cause animosity, war, tragedy and catastrophe.

Rebuttal: Try flying that one in Bolivia. Tell the tin miners that America, in order not to "exploit" Bolivian nonrenewable natural resources and in order not to use "more than our share" of resources, will cut tin imports by 90%. Of course, this will mean that Bolivia will lack the dollars to buy certain things America produces, like penicillin—but so be it. Tell a peasant in Zaire that America will cut copper imports by

90% in the years to come in order not to be economic imperialists. Of course, this will deny the government of Zaire the funds to build schools, hospitals and roads, but it will have a great redeeming future: It will lighten the self-inflicted guilt load on the shoulders of some affluent environmentalists in America who slept through their college courses in economics.

In fact, the complaint that "we're using more than our fair share" can be described, more accurately, in fewer words: "international trade." America imports tin, and oil, and cocoa, and copper, and rubber, and bauxite and transistor radios assembled in Taiwan. With the monies received from such items, foreign nations buy penicillin from us, and computers, and airplanes and X-ray machines and wheat and also pay for an agricultural geneticist who can help double rice production. The nations that sell resources to America, in short, get a marvelous commodity in return. It is called "money" and with it they can buy all sorts of wonderful things that have, in the last three decades, revolutionized the underdeveloped world so that health, education, life expectancy and communications standards, to name just a few, are at a level that—while low by American standards—are unprecedented in their own national histories.

America's "use" of resources does not "rob" anyone. The proper analogy might be with the nuclear breeder reactor, which creates more energy than it uses. Tin ore in the Andes are just rocks—unless someone wants to buy them. Once someone buys them, those rocks turn into penicillin, schools and food. That is a healthy process—not an imperialist, unfair or necessarily exploitive one.

* * *

What then, caused the problems that America has faced in recent decades and have been ascribed to the Population Explosion? And how will we deal with these problems if mere population diminishment won't do the trick?

What caused suburban sprawl, environmental degradation, shortages of fuel, crowded national parks and traffic jams?

Success.

The root cause of most American problems, and of most allegedly "harmful situations" in America, is progress.

Does that sound contradictory? If success causes major problems and at least some harm, then is it really progress? Maybe that kind of success is really failure.

Not so. Re-offered here is our simple definition of "progress": social and economic situations that are better by far than what they replace.

By these lights we can look at a "problem" such as "the environment" and look at the tradeoffs.

Is it better to have crowded national parks or better to have only the wealthy able to visit national parks?

Is it better to have Americans living in "suburban sprawl" on a quarter of an acre in a private home or in a three-room walk-up apartment or row house in a central city?

Is it better to have some traffic jams or a society where people don't have the personal mobility offered by automobiles?

The answers to these questions are not quite as simple as they might appear, but if the choice must be made, the answer offered here is "yes," it is better to have plain people in the middle class than it is to preserve a pristine environment so that caribou can frolic all across Alaska, and sea gulls can cavort in the Santa Barbara Channel, and upper middle-class buck passers can hear the haunting trill of a rare bird in a true wilderness.

But, there are, of course, harder questions: What about water and air pollution?

Such pollution is demonstrably caused by industrial activity and personal affluence. But is that "progress" if it yields scummy water and foul air?

Yes, for three reasons.

First: The "success" has created more decent, more humane and more creative lives for the American people.

Second: Scummy water and foul air can be dealt with, will be dealt with, are being dealt with. Moreover, in the interim a case can be made that *so far, the amount of severe harm to people caused by pollution has been quite limited.*

Those are fighting words, and certain phrases need further explanation. *So far,* the amount of *severe harm to people* caused by pollution has been *quite limited.*

"So far" means that of all the cataclysmic ecological disasters that have been promised—none have *yet* occurred. The guess here—and it is a guess—is they will not occur. In truth, this guess is based partly on the fact that environmentalists haven't been able to decide yet whether the earth will melt or freeze because we use electric toothbrushes.

"Severe harm to people" does not mean that you can't swim in the river or that the curtains get sooty. These are major nuisances and they are mitigated by the fact that since 1948 about 1.25 million in-ground swimming pools have been built and there is far more recreational swimming in America than ever before. There will be still more recreational swimming to come as water pollution legislation takes hold. The dirty curtains can be washed in the washing machine and dried in the dryer. "Severe harm to people" means sickness and death. There has been *some* of that sort of severe harm associated with "the environmental problem"—but not much not yet that is really provable. It has been, in fact, "quite limited"—insofar as the health problems must also be weighed against the fact that it is precisely an industrial (and pollutive) society that produces X-ray machines, drugs from petrochemicals, hospitals, ambulances, sewage treatment plants, highways to get the ambulances to the hospitals—all aids to health. Remember, life expectancy rates in this polluted country of ours have gone *up* in recent decades, not down. Moreover, as pollution abatement laws take hold, such harm as now exists will probably diminish. Beyond that, of course, we do not really know. Will a world-wide ecological catastrophe occur, will green plants disappear and oceans die? Who knows? All we know is that so far the credibility of the more extreme environmentalists has been close to zero—and they have tarnished thoroughly admirable ecological goals that the American people, and this author, support wholeheartedly.

Third: The affluence that has created both the "success" and the lesser magnitude of environmental problems is the best guarantee that the problems are solvable. Speaking now in a political sense, the vast amounts of money needed to cope with the actual ecological stresses placed upon the environment can only come—will only come—during an era of affluence. The demogogic appeals to "make the polluters pay" is precisely demagoguery. Neither "the government" nor "big business" ultimately will pay for anything, let alone pollution abatement. The taxpayer pays either via higher taxes or increased prices. There is no free lunch. At a time of continuing affluence, when tax *revenues* can go up without increasing tax *rates*—it is feasible to execute the necessary anti-pollution reforms. Conversely, consider the political situation that would result from the success of an anti-affluence economy. Suppose we get Zero Production Growth, and a steady state economy. By far the largest share of pollution remains (i.e., Lake Erie), money is still needed to pay for it, but the money comes by increasing tax *rates* on taxpayers whose incomes have essentially been frozen. Fat chance!

Accordingly, if one accepts that the environmental degradation *so far has caused only limited amounts of severe harm to people* and one accepts that a society affluent enough to pay for the cost of pollution abatement will act in wisdom and will in fact do so—then, one can weigh the benefits that have accrued to Americans in the last decade against its costs, present and future.

On such a balance—surprise!—Americans are better off by far than they were.

IV.

ATTITUDES

The dominant intellectual rhetoric of our time has been, for the most part, a rhetoric of failure, gloom, guilt, crisis, dismality and failure.

The objective facts of our time show, for the most part, progress, growth, increased options and a standard and quality of living better than what it replaces.

Thus, conflict. Rhetoric points one way, fact the other. There is a third way to assay progress, or its lack. Ask people. Ask them what they think is going on these days. By asking people, we can come several steps closer to coping with the nagging questions we seek to answer: What happened in America in these dozen years? Was it good or bad, better or worse than what it replaced? By "asking people," we can hope to discover if Americans share the views of failure and guilt that have been put forth by the rhetoricians. Secondly, we can find out how Americans' attitudes have *changed* in recent years. For "progress" or "regress" should not be measured solely by income, education, jobs or washing machines—however important they may be. Progress also involves the ability of people to cope intelligently with a changing world. Isn't a liberalizing change in attitudes of whites toward blacks just as much an index of progress as is a change in income ratios?

And so, prepare now to enter the attitudinal area, and consider the following sets of questions: What do the American people *believe* happened? What is the state of American *opinion* after a dozen years of turmoil? Do Americans believe the rhetoric of despair or the indices of progress? Do they think things have gotten better or worse? These are very important questions because they ultimately deal with another question: In what way do *attitudes* impinge on real progress? After all, even if real statistical progress can be measured and be demonstrated, if people feel rotten—worse than they used to—then real progress may be illusory. A man can be cured of a major illness, acknowledge the cure, and then suffer a psychological collapse, be committed to a mental institution—and clearly be generally less well off than he was when he was "sick."

The second set of questions deal not just with "better or worse" but with the *substance* of attitudinal change. How have Americans reacted to the monumental issues of our time? To war, to peace and to America's role in the world? To the environment and the population problem? To the race question? To the counterculture? To women's demands?

Has the public changed its mind? And if it has—how? And if it has, does that mind changing itself reveal progress; does that mind changing itself make life easier or better or less abrasive?

* * *

First, a word about attitudinal data: It is simply not in the same league as "hard" Census-type data. It is intrinsically easier to measure how much money a person makes or whether a family possesses a washing machine than it is to measure whether someone is generally happy, or what his real attitude is about a black family moving in next door.

Moreover, beyond the intrinsic difficulty of attitudinal polling, history and law work for the objective survey and against the opinion poll. The Census is promulgated in the United States Constitution and since 1790 we have had objective statistical activity of one sort or another, growing continually, publicly funded, asking the same sorts of questions again and again, and consequently establishing trend lines. And it is trends that are at the root of valid statistical interpretations. No national statistical project, surely not one performed by sampling techniques, is ever wholly accurate. But if one has comparable data stretching back five, ten, twenty or a hundred years, there are reasonable conclusions that can be drawn.

Attitudinal polling, unlike objective "hard" data-gathering activity, is both a relatively new phenomenon and not usually publicly funded, although it is an expensive procedure. And so, long trend lines don't usually exist, and often short trend lines don't exist either. Questions are asked in different ways by different private pollsters. Some data is published—and some is not. Some pollsters will grind an ax in the way in which questions are phrased—and indeed by selecting which questions will be asked. The pollsters whose syndicated work appears in newspapers around the nation sometimes deal only on the very surface of an issue. Academic pollsters sometimes tell you far more than you need to know, far later than you want to know it.

In short, one can defend almost any position on almost any subject by referring to public opinion polls. In fact—it happens all the time. Did Americans support Johnson and Nixon on Vietnam? Sure. Did Americans want to get out of Vietnam? You bet. Do Americans want equality for blacks? Yes, sir. Are Americans racists? Yes.

And so we acknowledge that the soft data presented in this part of this volume simply are not as valid as the hard data that preceded it. So be it. The author has searched the data that exists and that is available; judgments on conflicting data have been made. The attempt has been made to stick with data produced by professional pollsters and an effort has been made not to imply or infer more than the data leads to—at least not by attributing it to the data. Before all is said and done there will be some implications and inferences set forth, but they will be labeled as such.

CHAPTER 12

Hooray, Everything's Wonderful!

To begin at the beginning: *Americans don't regard themselves as unhappy or as dissatisfied, despite all the rhetoric to the contrary.*

The view that "I'm O.K." is verifiable from many sources. The Gallup Organization has been asking "happiness" questions as long as anyone. Here are the results for 1947 (in the mythology a happy, hooray-the-war's-over, boom year), for 1970 (allegedly an alienated, grim year of crisis and chaos) and for 1973 (also not regarded as a vintage moment in American history):

Q. In general, how happy would you say you are—very happy, fairly happy, or not happy?

	Very happy	Fairly happy	Not happy	Don't know
1947	38%	57%	4%	1%
1970	43%	48%	6%	3%
1973	52%	45%	3%	—
(Gallup)				

More people were "very happy" in 1970, happier than in 1947, and 1973 was best of all. What is of most importance is that more than 90% of the people—then and now—consider themselves "happy," either very or fairly.

A similar question was asked in 1972 by a polling group of the advertising agency Batten, Barton, Durstine and Osborn, Inc. These were the results:

Q. All things considered, how happy would you say you are these days, very happy somewhat happy, or not too happy?

Very happy	32%
Somewhat happy	60%
Not too happy	9%

Pollster Louis Harris rated men and women on a somewhat more sophisticated scale and got these results:

PERSONAL SATISFACTION OF OWN LIFE TODAY

Very satisfied	Somewhat satisfied	Only slightly satisfied	Not at all satisfied	Not sure
54%	32%	9%	4%	1%

(Harris, 1972)

Again confirmation of the basic point that most Americans feel that personally things are O.K. Only about one in eight is dissatisfied to one degree or another—and 86% are very or somewhat satisfied.

Of course, it was *youth* who were really turned off and bitter during the bitter years, right? Wrong. Harris, again in 1971, polling those aged fifteen to twenty-one:

Q. Has your life been happy so far?

A. Yes—90%.

Q. Why do you say that?

A. 1) I've had a good home and family.
    2) I've had and done about everything I wanted.

Q. Do you expect your future to be as happy or even happier?

A. Yes—93%.

And so, the young revolutionaries ride happily off into the sunset, happily complaining about alienation.

So much for the generality of "happy" or "satisfied." People say they are, despite the journo-talk of "fed-up." But it is not only in generalities that Americans express satisfaction. As regards the specifics of jobs, income, housing and education, most Americans also say they are satisfied.

Gallup has run a "satisfaction index" over the years and it serves as sort of a base line measure.

Here are the data for whites only. First "work"—the great blue-collar blues, white-collar woes, American tragedy:

Q. Would you say you are satisfied or dissatisfied with the work you do?

	Satisfied	Dissatisfied	Don't know
1949	69%	19%	12%
1963	90%	7%	3%
1966	87%	8%	5%
1969	88%	6%	6%
1971	85%	9%	8%
1973	82%	10%	8%

A jump occurred somewhere between 1949 and 1963 and then the rate remained fairly constant until 1969, when a modest dip occurred. Interestingly, the "dissatisfied" has not climbed as much as the "satisfied" has dipped in recent years. Still, even with the dip, the overriding fact is that in 1973, by *8 to 1*. Americans were "satisfied" with the work they do.

Buttressing the notion that "Blue Collar Blues" was mostly a Failure and Guilt Complex creation is the work of a team of social scientists from the Survey Research Center at the University of Michigan and the Survey Research Program at the University of Massachusetts.[1] A thorough comparison of two comprehensive surveys taken in 1969–70 and again in 1973 showed that worker attitudes on thirty-three separate indicators of job satisfaction showed—*no basic change.*

In early 1972, the magazine *Better Homes & Gardens* ran a public opinion questionnaire in the February and March issues. They received 340,-000 responses. As it turned out, when similar sorts of questions were asked, the *BH&G* survey results tended to square quite consistently with Gallup and Harris polls taken at roughly the same time, providing reason to believe that the *BH&G* data were generally consistent with views that would have been received from a scientifically drawn national sample (which makes sense, as the *BH&G* readership is quite close to national averages in terms of income and other demographic indices). In any event, the survey asked about jobs:

Q. Do you like your job?

A.	Yes	84%
	No	12%
	Did not answer	4%

[1] Robert P. Quinn and Martha S. Baldi de Mandilovitch from Michigan; Thomas Mangione from Massachusetts.

This is very close to the Gallup data. But the *BH&G* survey asked another question as well:

Q. Do you think you're one of the best in your line of work?

A. Yes   73%
    No   23%
    Did not answer   4%

That is an important follow-up question—and an important answer. The rhetoric of our era tells us that workers are dissatisfied and that they have lost their pride. The data of our era does not confirm that view. Americans are still a proud people.[2]

A pattern quite similar to the work data, albeit at a different level, is seen in Gallup data concerning "family income":

Q. On the whole, would you say you are satisfied or dissatisfied with your family income? (Whites only)

	Satisfied	*Dissatisfied*	*Don't know*
1949	50%	38%	12%
1963	68%	30%	2%
1966	67%	29%	4%
1969	67%	30%	3%
1971	65%	33%	2%
1973	64%	34%	2%

Again, a jump followed by a plateau, perhaps with a tiny slide in the last couple of years, but still *two out of three* Americans indicating general satisfaction with their income, even in the recessionary year of 1971.

In 1973, Gallup asked the income question in a somewhat different manner and got an even higher positive response:

---

[2] And don't be misled by the talk of how workers of other nations are so happy and proud. There are lots of stories around about how Japanese workers sing "Glory to General Widget, Co., Inc." at their work benches, but the Gallup affiliate in Japan reports that "satisfaction" levels concerning work in Japan are actually a little lower there than here (74% in Japan vs. 81% for United States, for men; 71% in Japan vs. 68% in United States for women).

Q. On the whole, would you say you are satisfied or dissatisfied with your standard of living? (Whites only)

Satisfied	Dissatisfied	Don't know
74%	24%	2%

About three to one say they are "satisfied."
The public's opinion on "housing" shows the same pattern:

Q. On the whole, would you say you are satisfied or dissatisfied with your housing situation? (Whites only)

	Satisfied	Dissatisfied	No Opinion
1949	67%	28%	5%
1963	76%	21%	3%
1966	77%	19%	4%
1969	80%	18%	2%
1971	77%	19%	4%
1973	77%	20%	3%

A jump—a plateau—a roughly 4 to 1 ratio of "satisfaction." This view is backed up by data from the University of Michigan's Institute of Social Research showing that 80% of respondents felt "completely satisfied" or "satisfied" with "their neighborhood," while only 20% felt either "neutral" or "dissatisfied."

Views on "education" have not been sampled by Gallup as far back as have other subject areas. And the pattern of what is available is somewhat different:

Q. On the whole, would you say you are satisfied or dissatisfied with your children's education? (Whites only)

	Satisfied	Dissatisfied	Don't know
1963	69%	24%	11%
1966	76%	16%	8%
1971	63%	26%	11%
1973	63%	28%	29%

A decline in satisfaction with education is discernible over the last decade. Whether this is due to worse schools, busing, college disruptions, perceived unresponsiveness of school administrators is hard to determine and, for the moment, will be passed over. The most relevant fact still is this one: In an allegedly fed-up nation, more than two out of three parents are still satisfied with the education received by their children.

The Gallup data for blacks shows that levels of satisfaction are substantially lower, as might be expected in a society where, as we have seen, non-white family income is only 62% of whites. Still, in September of 1971 these were the satisfaction indices for blacks:

SATISFACTION AMONG BLACKS, 1971

	Satisfied	Dissatisfied	Don't know
Work	67%	21%	12%
Income	41%	57%	2%
Housing	51%	46%	3%
Education	53%	33%	14%

In work about 3 to 1 are satisfied, in education about 5 to 3 are satisfied, in housing it's about even, in income, a clear negative, but not a massive one. Not the most dazzling picture of contentment surely, but neither would it seem to be a picture of grim despondency, black rage and black frustration.

Generally speaking, then, it would seem that *from a personal point of view* most Americans—surely white Americans—feel that their lives are working out all right. They profess to be happy, working at satisfying jobs, making a decent living, proud of their abilities, living in acceptable housing, and they feel their children are getting a decent education.

In this personal sense, then, Americans would clearly tend to believe the objective data presented in this volume and not believe the pronouncements of failure and guilt that have issued forth in a mighty stream from the Failure and Guilt Complex.

Further verification of this notion of personal contentment and personal progress comes from two unique and valuable studies published by Potomac Associates in Washington, using specially commissioned data gathered by the Gallup Organization.

The first of these studies was *Hopes and Fears of the American People* by Albert H. Cantril and Charles W. Roll, Jr. Using a fascinating polling technique called the "self-anchoring striving scale"[3] Messrs. A. Cantril and Roll show how Americans view themselves as they pass through the years of their life. Respondents are shown a card depicting a ten-rung "ladder of life," with the top rung representing *the most ideal personal state of affairs the respondent can imagine*. The bottom rung represents *the worst possible state of personal affairs*. The respondents

[3] Originally developed by the late Hadley Cantril and Lloyd A. Free.

are then asked to place themselves on this sort of a "ladder of life"—in other words, are asked to rank themselves by *their own definition* of hopes and aspiration. In effect, the pollsters are quantifying the results of the age-old question "How are things going for you?"

In January of 1971, the average American placed himself 6.6 steps up the ladder. Respondents were then asked what their place on life's ladder would have been *five years previously* and what they imagined it would be *five years hence*. The results looked like this:

PERSONAL LADDER RATINGS

Past	5.8
Present	6.6
Future	7.5

(January 1971)

Quite an optimistic statement: *the present is better than the past, and the future will be better than the present.* Hardly the response one would expect from a fed-up population.

A year and a half later, in mid-1972, the same "ladder" question was asked to a comparable Gallup sample and reported upon in the second of the Potomac Associates studies, *State of the Nation,* edited by William Watts and Lloyd A. Free. In mid-'72 the results looked this way:

PERSONAL LADDER RATINGS

Past	5.5
Present	6.4
Future	7.6

Roughly the same as a year earlier, given the margin for sampling error, but if anything an even more optimistic response—the future particularly looked appealing, 1.2 rungs higher than the present in 1972, versus .9 rungs in early 1971.

This ladder of life index is of particular value because it had been taken by the Gallup Organization in two earlier years as part of studies for the Institute for International Social Research. The four surveys, set side by side, look like this:

PERSONAL LADDER RATINGS

	1959	1964	1971	1972˙
Past	5.9%	6.0%	5.8%	5.5%
Present	6.6%	6.9%	6.6%	6.4%
Future	7.8%	7.9%	7.5%	7.6%

If there was a massive desolation of the American spirit over the thirteen years between the first and last samplings it surely is not apparent in these data. In point of fact, all of the changes between the various years fall well within the margin for sampling error. In each instance Americans were optimistic about their personal situation; the present is rosier than the past, the future rosier than the present.

The Gallup Organization runs polling operations in a number of countries and frequently asks the same questions in many nations in order to be able to show international comparisons. In 1971—when the allegedly glum feeling in America was at its most intense—this question was asked:

Q. If you were free to do so, would you like to go and settle in another country?

Yes

A. Great Britain   41%
   Uruguay   32%
   West Germany   27%
   Greece   22%
   Finland   19%
   Sweden   18%
   Brazil   17%
   Netherlands   16%
   United States   12% (!)

Gallup then went further and asked this of all those who wanted to move:

Q. What country would you like to settle in?

These were the top choices:

A. In Great Britain   In Finland
       Australia   Sweden
       New Zealand   *United States*
    In Uruguay   In Sweden
       United States   Spain
       Germany   *United States*
    In West Germany   In Brazil
       United States   *United States*
       Switzerland   Italy
    In Greece   In Netherlands
       United States   Australia
       Great Britain   New Zealand

So then, Americans were *least likely* to want to leave their own country and at the height of troubles in Vietnam and elsewhere, America made the top-two in choices for emigration in *six* of the eight other nations. No other nation did better than a score of *two*.

* * *

Well then, where are we? In the attitudinal struggle between optimistic hard data and pessimistic glum rhetoric, the American people seem— on the basis of polls presented here so far—to have validated the optimistic data. Asked about their personal lives Americans say things go well, progress is being made, it's better here than elsewhere, they don't want to leave and they're happy.

It must be confessed that this would be a nice place to end this book. Nay-Sayers Rebutted, Author Avers. Hoodwinked America Set Straight.

Alas, it is not to be.

CHAPTER 13

Boo, Everything's Terrible

It is not to be, for into this Panglossian portrait one must deal with responses like this one to a Gallup question in October of 1972:

Q. In general, would you say that you are satisfied or dissatisfied with the direction in which the nation is going?

A. Satisfied   35%
   Dissatisfied   58%
   No opinion   7%

Needless to say that is not an isolated view. The notion *that something is wrong with the COUNTRY is perhaps just as strong as the view that things are going well PERSONALLY.*

The *Hopes and Fears* study shows this counterpoise with some precision. Recall that in 1971 Americans viewed themselves *personally* on a sort of 6–7–8 scale on a ten-rung ladder of life, with the present better than the past and the future seen as better than the present. This pattern, it should also be recalled, has remained roughly constant since 1959.

Now observe the same sort of technique when applied to a *national* ladder rating. Respondents were asked to place *America,* rather than themselves, on a rung of "a ladder of life." How, they were asked in effect, did *America* stack up?

NATIONAL LADDER RATING (JANUARY 1971)

Past   6.2
Present   5.4
Future   6.2

Bang! The present is *worse* than the past, the future will be better, but five years *from now* we'll only be back where we were five years *ago.*

Moreover, the 1971 ratings broke an earlier pattern. Seen arrayed with earlier data it looks this way:

NATIONAL LADDER RATINGS

	1959	1964	1971 (Jan.)
Past	6.5%	6.1%	6.2%
Present	6.7%	6.5%	5.4% (!)
Future	7.4%	7.7%	6.2%

Thus, each of the earlier *national* surveys showed the same pattern as the *personal* surveys: present better than past, future will be better than present. Something between 1964 and 1971 broke that line of thinking. "The present" in 1971 was stark bad news. America was somehow off the track.

That, in fact, was the phrase used by Roper pollsters in July 1971:

Q. Do you feel that things in this country are generally going in the right direction today, or do you feel that things have pretty seriously gotten off on the wrong track?

A. Right track   23%
   Wrong track   64%
   No opinion   13%

This sort of data showing a flawed America—the malaise factor—is demonstrated clearly in many ways in many surveys, each with different nuances and flavors. Here is the *Better Homes & Garden* survey, again with a fascinating pair of questions:

Q. In your opinion, is America a good place to raise children?

A. Yes   92%
   No   7%
   Did not answer 1%

Q. Is America a better or worse place to raise children than it was 10 or 15 years ago?

A. Better   33%
   Worse   64%
   Did not answer 3%

The America's-in-trouble theme is heard from young as well as old. From the polling of the Institute for Social Research at the University of Michigan comes this response elicited from young people aged eleven to eighteen, the poll taken in 1972:

Q. Life of the average person is getting worse not better—
11%   Strongly agree
36%   Somewhat agree
19%   Undecided
23%   Somewhat disagree
11%   Strongly disagree

By 47% to 34%, then, *young* Americans feel life is getting worse in America! Not for *themselves* of course. *Their* happiness ratings and *personal* ladder ratings are as high as any group's—in fact, usually substantially higher. It's *the other guy*, the average person (i.e., conditions in America) whose life is not very good.

This *other guy* feeling is very much at the root of the *personal* versus *national* split in opinions. Reading the polls, it often seems as if the only wise, happy, fulfilled, intelligent man in the neighborhood is—you guessed it—the respondent! This carries over into some very specific areas. Remember the question about jobs?

Q. Do *you* like your job?

A. Yes   84%
No   12%
Did not answer   4%

Here's the same question asked about the other guy:

Q. Do you think *most people* like their jobs?

A. Yes   50%
No   49%
Did not answer   1%
(*BH&G*, 1972)

That poor other fellow, he doesn't even have a good job.

That things aren't going well in America is seen perhaps most clearly when pollsters ask about the state of our "institutions" and the people who run them. Here is the question that pollster Louis Harris asked in 1966 and again toward the end of 1971:

Q. As far as the people running these institutions are concerned, would you say you have a great deal of confidence, only some confidence, or hardly any confidence at all in them?

And here, ranked serially by the highest degree of trust in 1966, are the findings concerning "a great deal of trust"

	1966	1971	Change
Medicine	72%	61%	− 9%
Banks and financial institutions	67%	36%	−31%
The military	62%	27%	−35%
Education	61%	37%	−24%
The scientific community	56%	32%	−24%
Major companies	55%	27%	−22%
Mental health and psychiatry	51%	35%	−16%
U. S. Supreme Court	51%	23%	−28%
Local retail stores	48%	24%	−24%
Congress	42%	19%	−23%
Executive branch of federal government	41%	23%	−18%
Organized religion	55%	27%	−28%
The press	29%	18%	−11%
Television	25%	22%	− 3%
Organized labor	22%	14%	− 8%
Advertising	21%	13%	− 8%

The bigger they are, the harder they fall, with the possible exception of "medicine," the only institution in America in 1971 whose practitioners still elicited a majority opinion in the column "great deal of trust." That might just show how valuable a good bedside manner is—except that data presented later will show that not even that remedy works for long.

The University of Michigan polling effort concentrated on "government in Washington" and got similar sorts of results:

Q. How much of the time do you think you can trust the government in Washington to do what is right—*just about always, most of the time,* or *only some of the time?*

	1964	1966	1968	1970
Always	14%	17%	8%	6%
Most of the time	63%	48%	53%	47%
Only some of the time	22%	31%	37%	44%

The key line is the italicized one, representing a "cynical" response according to the Michigan social scientists. The proportion of cynics shows a steady rise over a six-year period and actually doubles, in fact, approaching a rate that would indicate that almost *half* the Americans are cynical about their government.

Pollster Daniel Yankelovich trained his sights on attitudes toward business and found this trend:

Q. Is business doing a good job of achieving a proper balance between making a profit and providing a service?

	Yes
A. 1965	70%
1969	58%
1970	29%
1971	29%

Finally, there was this devastating question and this devastating response in 1971:

Q. There has been a lot of talk in the news recently about unrest in our country and ill-feeling between groups. In general, how concerned are you about this unrest and ill-feeling? Do you think it is likely to lead to a real breakdown in this country or do you think it is likely to blow over soon?

A. Real breakdown	Blow over soon	Don't know
47% (!)	38%	15%

(Potomac/Gallup)

CHAPTER 14

But How Worse?

Where, then, does all this leave us?

First, consider the notion that Americans are personally fed up, unhappy and morose—a central notion in the theory of Flunk, a keystone in the arch of the Failure and Guilt Complex.

It won't wash. Americans are not a miserable people. Viewing their own personal situation, Americans very definitely sense progress. The score, then, is 2–0 against the Failure and Guilt Complex. The objective data show progress. Score one. The people sense personal progress and are personally pleased by it. Score another.

To go beyond that, as we have seen, is difficult and complicated. For while Americans themselves are generally pleased with their lives, they are deeply concerned about America itself, about the state of their *national* well-being. And some of their concerns seem, on the surface, to be very much in tune with the funereal music of the Failure and Guilt Complex: For example, public confidence in target groups such as the Military, Banks, the Executive Branch, Major Companies, Local Retail Stores—has indeed plummeted.

If American perceptions of National Discontent are really the same as the views of the crisis-mongers and the Failure and Guilt Complex, perhaps those perceptions even eradicate the 2–0 lead. If, after all, Americans accept the notion that this is an evil, stingy, genocidal, imperialist, racist, sexist country, then perhaps that's a three-point play, capable of a total wipe-out. And suppose it is the other way: If Americans do not view the crisis of Discontent in the same manner as the Cause People, how *do* they view it? And what does it mean? Does it still mean Failure or does it mean something else?

Beyond that one must explore the *substance* of opinion change as well. How have Americans changed their minds on specific issues? Do these changes of mind in themselves reveal something about progress?

* * *

Thus far, the attitudinal data presented has been clear-cut. Personally, as we have seen, people say they are satisfied. That is clear. When asked about America generally, people say it is in trouble. That too is clear.

Now it is time to ask *why* people think America is in trouble. We ask whether Americans agree with the specific kind of trouble seen by the Failure and Guilt Complex. We ask what changes have occurred in people's thinking.

And the answers are not at all clear-cut. There is, in fact, only a clear-cut ambivalence in much of the data—*and it is to the heart of just that ambivalence that one must ultimately go to get a fix on what has been happening in America.*

CHAPTER 15

War and Peace and the World

The war and America's role in the world were clearly seminal issues in the last dozen-or-so years and they were issues that surely helped galvanize the Failure and Guilt Complex. The war in Vietnam (said the Peace movement) was not our fight, was wrong, wrongheaded, immoral and, ultimately, genocidal. America—or Amerika to a few—was overextended, arrogant, imperialistic, hooked on Commie-hunting and on being the world's policemen, bad things all, causes clearly of America's failure.

Have the American people bought these notions?

Surely, there have been some major changes in public opinion over recent years about Vietnam and about our role in the world. Some of these opinions seem clearly to point to vindication of the views of the Peace Movement.

Thus, in January of 1973, just prior to the Vietnam peace settlement, Gallup asked:

Q. In view of the developments since we entered the fighting in Vietnam, do you think the United States made a mistake sending troops to fight in Vietnam?

A. Yes   60%
   No   29%
   No opinion   11%

Obviously, a dovish response—2 to 1 say it was a mistake, something doves were saying for a long time. Moreover, there is a quite specific time series on this Gallup question and the trend line is clear:

Q.   (Same as above)

A.

	Yes	No	No opinion
1966	36%	49%	15%
1967	39%	49%	13%
1968	47%	42%	10%
1969	52%	39%	9%
1970	56%	36%	8%
1971	61%	28%	11%
1973	60%	29%	11%

It is not only about Vietnam that opinion has changed. Americans have also apparently changed their views, or the intensity of their views, on how serious the international situation is today. The Potomac Associates/ Gallup/Institute for International Social Research series of polls is quite instructive in this regard. Here, at three points in time, are measurements of Americans' concern with "international threats," ranked on a scale of "degree of concern" with 100 signifying "a great deal" and 0 for "not at all":

CONCERN WITH INTERNATIONAL THREATS

	1964	1968	1972	Change 1964-72
The danger of war	90%	83%	66%	−24%
The threat of communism	86%	79%	69%	−17%
Keeping our military strong	74%	81%	61%	−13%
Soviet Russia	75%	73%	61%	−14%

War, communism, military power and Russia are clearly of lesser concern to Americans in 1972 than they were in 1964. These changes in views are clearly akin to the direction the Peace Movement *wanted* views to change.

An even more striking indicator of change comes from the same polling source, this time looking at it from a somewhat different angle. In 1964— during a time of relative peace—these were the *top five* "concerns":

1. Keeping country out of war.
2. Combating world communism.
3. Keeping our military defense strong.
4. Controlling the use of nuclear weapons.
5. Maintaining respect for the United States in other countries.

The top five concerns were all international.

Eight years later, in June of 1972—with America at war—here were the top four concerns:

1. Rising prices and the cost of living.
2. The amount of violence in American life.
3. The problem of drug addicts and narcotic drugs.
4. Crime in this country.

—all domestic concerns!

In fifth place was:

5. The problem of Vietnam.

Tied for twelfth place, immediately after "solid waste disposal," was:

12. Keeping our military defenses strong.

and in twenty-second place, was:

22. The threat of communism at home and abroad.

Much change, and—so far—all of it in the Peace Movement's direction. What is fascinating is that so much change took place at a time when the preponderant majority of Americans bitterly despised some of the flamboyant advocates of such change: SDS protesters burning the flag, priests breaking into draft boards, students taking over the dean's office. Such activity, and the linkage in the public mind it had with the more responsible part of the Peace Movement, probably slowed down the pace of change a bit. But, in the long run, Americans apparently made up their minds on the merits.

Still this picture of agreement with the Peace Movement is only half of the picture—if that much.

First, of course, there is a major variable that must be considered any time attitudes are looked at over a period of time. It is this: How much did reality change in the same time?

In the instance of international affairs, of course, the answer is: very much, and that answer partially mitigates the responses above. Thus, it would be one thing if international conditions had remained roughly the same, and because of the persuasive arguments of the Peace Movement, Americans decided that we were over-extended, that communism was a bogeyman, that we ought to stop playing God, and so on.

But it is quite another thing for such attitudinal changes to come about after a period of substantive changes—and changes initiated not by the Movement, nor by its friends, nor by its apologists, nor even by neutrals or almost neutrals—but, in fact, by its arch villain. It was not Benjamin Spock who went to Peking and Moscow, signed the SALT agreement, toasted Mao, gave Brezhnev a golf cart and orchestrated the general hearts-and-flowers détente. It wasn't John Kenneth Galbraith. It wasn't George McGovern. It wasn't even Hubert Humphrey or Lyndon Johnson.

It was Richard Nixon, the old Communist hunter himself. And so, if there has been a change in American attitudes about the Communist Menace, it is a little too easy to attribute it to the persuasiveness of the Peace Movement or to a growing isolationist sentiment. It may also be too simple to hand over the garland to Richard Nixon. After all, some attribute the changing world circumstances to Russia's sluggish economy and their need of U.S. help; some attribute détente to the mutual fears engendered by the Russian-Chinese split; and there are those who have an even more intriguing theory: America won the Cold War. Finally, following the 1973 Mid-East conflagration, there are those who feel the Russian problem is still very much for real and it will only be a matter of time until Americans sense this again.

All we know for sure is that for the moment it appears as if international circumstances have changed *in fact,* and these new circumstances may well have had a great deal to do with changing *attitudes*—as much and maybe more to do with such changes as the persuasiveness of Movement rhetoric.

Moreover, all the data is not on the side of F&GC, not even all of the data about Vietnam. It's true that by a wide margin Americans feel we "made a mistake sending troops to fight in Vietnam." But by 1972, Richard Nixon might well have agreed with that statement—Lord knows, by 1972, Curtis LeMay might agree with it. Again, circumstance intervenes. Exactly *who* would have been for sending large numbers of troops over in 1965 if they would have known, *in advance,* that the American involvement would last almost eight years, cost $150 billion dollars and mean death to 50,000 American boys? Exactly who would have done it in the way it was done, with 20–20 hindsight? It is a retrospective question, not really of the real world.

Moreover, of course, President Nixon himself ultimately qualified as a "dove," that is, he was for pulling troops out of Vietnam. And it was Lyndon B. Johnson who "stopped the bombing" and "negotiated"—other, earlier, dove demands.

In terms of real-world questions—what should we do *today?*—the American public never really bought the totality of the Peace Movement's position—and perhaps not even a major share of it. In fact, what they did buy was that quaint notion, *peace with honor.*

In March of 1972, the North Vietnamese launched a major spring offensive into the South, overran the town of Quangtri just north of Hue and quickly threatened Kontum in the Central Highlands and An Loc, only sixty miles from Saigon.

President Nixon responded by mining Haiphong harbor and with severe bombing raids in North Vietnam. The Peace Movement and others, too, generally thought Nixon's policy was madness; it raised the specter of Russian response, of World War III and, at the least, of a cancellation of the long-awaited Moscow summit.

But the public did not see Nixon's move the way the doves saw it. A few days after the mining of the harbor, Louis Harris interviewers in the field asked:

Q. Do you approve or disapprove of President Nixon's order to mine all the harbors of North Vietnam?

A. Approve   59%
   Disapprove   24%
   Not Sure   17%
   (Of those with an opinion, 71% favored Nixon's action.)

This was viewed by some as an instinctive let's all-support-the-President-in-a-movement-of-crisis response, but in fact it stuck—and stuck solidly until American combat participation in the war ended eight months later.

In late August and early September of 1972, the Harris interviewers were again in the field, following a spring and summer of heavy castigation of Nixon by the doves for his immoral handling of the war. And here is what they found:

- By 55%–32% likely voters supported "continued heavy bombings" of North Vietnam by the United States.
- By 64%–22% (almost three to one) there was support of "the mining of North Vietnamese harbors."
- By 51%–26% there was disagreement with Senator McGovern's charge that "Henry Kissinger's travels to Paris and Saigon were no more than a publicity stunt that falsely raised hopes for peace." (Harris' quotation of McGovern).
- By 49%–32% there was disagreement with the claim of former Attorney General Ramsey Clark, after visiting North Vietnam that "the United States was engaged in immoral and inhuman bombings of hospitals, dikes and other nonmilitary targets which should stop," (Harris quotation of Clark).

And, finally, this clincher:

- By 74%–11% (!) there was support of "President Nixon's contention that it is important that South Vietnam not fall into the control of the Communists." (Quoting Harris' syndicated newspaper column's quotation of Nixon.)

And so, although George McGovern came to pre-eminence as an anti-war dove espousing the Peace Movement position, and although he won many primaries at least in part on the basis of those views, by the time the end of September rolled around Gallup got these results:

> Q. Which candidate—McGovern or Nixon—do you think can do a better job of dealing wth the Vietnam situation?
>
> Nixon   58%
> McGovern   26%
> Neither   8%
> No opinion   8%

Not only did the public endorse Nixon on Vietnam, they tended to agree with him generally on questions of national defense. Recall John Connally's television commercials graphically depicting McGovern's (i.e., the Movement's) defense policies—policies of major reductions in defense spending. Swoosh, off go the aircraft carriers, swoosh, off go the airplanes. Swoosh, off goes McGovern. Here is how Nixon and McGovern stood vis-a-vis defense in October of 1972.

> Q. Who best represents your personal views on defense spending?
>
> Nixon   55%
> McGovern   30%
> (Yankelovich, October 1972)

Even after the election Americans emphatically rejected some of the major Movement positions—specifically the condemnation of the "Christmas bombings." On February 1, 1973, Harris released a poll taken "just before the peace settlement terms were announced," that is, mid-January 1973. By 53%–30% Harris reported that Americans *"felt the bombings were pivotal in bringing the North Vietnamese back to the negotiating table."*

Finally, of course, after the peace settlement President Nixon's popularity rose to an all-time high, as the last American troops left and as the POWs came home.

It wasn't until the inflation binge really struck home in the spring of 1973 and until Watergate exploded at about the same time that Richard Nixon became a walking zombie in the opinion polls.

There are those, in fact, who feel that the display of American public opinion from May to September of 1972 was the single most critical factor in establishing the accord to end the war. Three sub-factors can be isolated: a) high support of the mining of the harbors and of the bombing, b) support for the belief that Nixon's policy regarding Vietnam was more palatable to the American people than McGovern's and c) Nixon, for various reasons including Vietnam, established as much as a *40-point* lead in the polls over McGovern by early September.

Facing that—so goes the theory—the North Vietnamese had to get the best deal they could. Hanoi no longer could hope—a hope often enunciated by the Peace Movement—that the American people would ultimately endorse the total abandonment of South Vietnam, to be set adrift with no American military or economic aid (McGovern's position). With that hope vanishing, Hanoi accordingly settled for the available part of the loaf with, at this writing, the ultimate outcome still unclear.[1]

Only ironically, then, was the Peace Movement prescient. They said nominate McGovern and he'll end the war. They said the American people would ultimately force an end to the war. Ironically, he was and they did.

There are some further measurements available to gauge the distance between the attitudes of the Peace Movement and the complex attitudes of the American public.

The Peace Movement, or at least major parts of it, subscribed to the notion that Pax Americana had had its day in the sun and that our role in the world since 1945 had been less than glorious.

Americans would not seem to agree with this idea. Here is a statement shown to respondents by the Roper Organization and the resulting answers:

The United States has seen its best days and will soon begin to decline as a world power.

Agree	26%
Disagree	61%
Don't know	13%

(Roper, October 1971)

And here is another question, asked in the *State of the Nation* survey:

Q. Taking into account the well-being of people throughout the world, do you feel, generally speaking, that in its international actions in recent years the United States has been a force for good in the world, or not?

Has been	69%
Has not been	23%
Don't know	8%

(1972)

---

[1] A section of Louis Harris' book *The Anguish of Change* tends to validate the potency of American public opinion as a negotiating tool. Harris recounts that in the fall of 1972, Henry Kissinger took an advance copy of a Harris poll to Paris and showed the North Vietnamese negotiators that Nixon's lead was holding strong. Harris quotes Kissinger: "When they finally realized President Nixon would indeed be around another four years, they changed their tune and fast."

Americans still think that Americans are a force for good.

And, more specifically, a probing of sentiment on what Richard Nixon insists should be called the Nixon Doctrine:

Q. The United States should continue to play a major role internationally, but cut down on some of its responsibilities abroad.

Agree   87%
Disagree   7%
No opinion   6%

(*State of the Nation*, 1972)

The Peace Movement tended to believe that the war was immoral. Accordingly, many Movement followers also believed that those young Americans who fled rather than fought the war performed a moral act.

The American people have flatly rejected this view. Here are four Harris polls on the subject:

Q. Do you favor or oppose giving amnesty to those men who left the country rather than serve in the armed services during the Vietnam war?

	Oppose	Favor	Not sure
March '73	67%	24%	9%
August '72	60%	27%	13%
June '72	53%	38%	9%
March '74	56%	30%	14%

(Harris)

Opposition is still about two to one, down some from the return-of-the-POW days of 1973, but not much different from the sentiment recorded during the last year of the war.

Yet neither have Americans proved to be vindictive about amnesty. Gallup polled about amnesty in 1973 and found that while sentiment was about as solidly negative as the Harris data above shows, only a comparative handful (one in nine) thought draft avoiders ought to be punished *by jail* if they returned to the United States. By far the greatest share of the public felt that the basic equity of the situation calls for avoiders to be required to serve a period of time in either the military or nonmilitary public service.

* * *

On balance, then, how stands the situation in terms of American attitudes toward the Failure and Guilt Complex position concerning war, peace and America's role in the world? Do Americans generally think things are off the track in this area?

On the one hand, Americans have clearly shifted certain views—i.e., views about the dangers of communism, about whom would we defend, about the high priority of defense spending and about the wisdom of getting involved in Vietnam in the first place. In these respects, public opinion has shifted toward the views espoused by the Movement, although as noted earlier it is hard to say whether this has happened because of advocacy or a legitimate change in the world situation. On balance, probably both advocacy and changing circumstances played a role.

On the other hand, Americans have resisted and rejected many Movement ideas. They went with Nixon, not McGovern, on the war. They are for some defense cuts, but will not buy major slashes seen as irresponsible. They do not think America's sun is setting. They do not think America has been a force of malevolence overseas. They don't buy unconditional amnesty.

What seems to have happened is a certain synthesis—an attitudinal accommodation by the massive majority. Faced with some different ideas and a changing world, Americans chose eclectically what they thought made sense and rejected what they thought didn't. If this be Hegel, make the most of it.

By our lights, and in view of a still muddy world situation, it would appear that Americans have collectively made many decisions that seem logical. The world is changing. We have problems at home. The threats, hopefully, may be less. Even if we were not overextended for the world of the Fifties or the Sixties, those levels of global activity may no longer be necessary.

But, Americans seem to say, neither is the world yet made of cotton candy. There is a sense that comes through from the data that Americans feel that the only foreign policy more dangerous than Hawk is Ostrich. And the notion that America is imperialist, genocidal, evil or arrogant is nonsense, and the American people know it is nonsense.

Such, then, has been the pattern of accommodation, eclecticism and shameless synthesis that the American public has demonstrated in recent years. The public has acted in the attitudinal realm in much the same manner as a housewife, or a househusband, might behave in the economic realm of the supermarket. The shopper comes down the aisle pushing a shopping cart. She has some preconceived notions about what she wants and needs for the next week's menu. As she passes by the shelves she sees some "specials" marked down in price, she sees some "new products" offered for the first time, she sees some new brand names on older products, and, of course, she sees some "old favorite" brands and products. In a relatively short time she must make some important economic decisions. She buys some specials, but rejects some. She buys some new products, but rejects some. She buys some new brand names, but rejects some. She buys some old favorites, but doesn't buy some others.

Roughly the same process seems to have gone on with the public's changing attitudes regarding international affairs—and many other fields —over recent years. Exposed to new doctrines, to old doctrines reformulated, to changing circumstances and to old doctrines, the public made careful choices. In making their choices they remembered their past, considered the present and looked into the future. They put their choice to one essential test: *Did it make common sense?* If it did—fine. If not— back on the shelf.

It is important to understand this process of common-sense shopping-cart eclecticism, of supermarket synthesis and of attitudinal accommodation, because it recurs again and again.

During the hectic decade of the Sixties, Americans were asked to deal with a dazzling array of new ideas. And in field after field they seemed able to smell out what was commonsensical in the valid core ideas and dismiss what was far out, overstated and impractical. They came to accept, quite quickly in some instances, some critically important notions that were highly publicized by the Cause People.

At the same time they saw that the F&GC spokespersons were not all wise and were, in fact, naive and ill informed on some other issues or concerning some fancy extrapolations of some central ideas. In particular, Americans did not accept the notion of American failure, of American guilt, and they resented those who promulgated such notions. In many instances—as we shall see—Americans sometimes came to see the Failure and Guilt Complex not as part of the solution but as a part of the problem.

CHAPTER 16

Women's Liberation

Women's Lib burst upon the American scene in the middle of the Cause Decade. It began in 1963 with the publication of *The Feminine Mystique* by Betty Friedan. By 1972, Gloria Steinem was gracing the cover of *Newsweek* and Sissy Farenthold was being pushed for the Democratic vice-presidential nomination.

What happened during those years of the Women's Lib blitz? Was it all media stuff, or did it take hold in the hearts and minds of the American people?

Again—as with the attitudes regarding the Peace Movement—we see accommodation, eclecticism, synthesis and rejection concerning both the substance and method of the Women's Lib movement.

Observe the Ambivalent Americans as they deal with the precepts of Women's Lib:

Q. If women don't speak up for themselves and confront men on their real problems, nothing will be done about these problems.

	Women	Men
Agree	71%	67%
Disagree	23%	28%

(Harris, 1972)

By more than three to one Americans accept one of the basic Lib premises: *speak up*. Harris had asked the same question a year earlier and got a 66% agreement rate from women and a 64% agreement rate from men —indicating the likelihood of a small but steady climb of agreement on this issue.

Here is another view of the same sort. The question was:

Q. Do you favor or oppose efforts to strengthen or change women's status in society?

In 1971, the responses were:

	Women	*Men*
Favor	40%	44%
Oppose	42% (!)	39%

(Harris, 1971)

Men were in favor of change by a slight margin, women opposed by a slight margin.

A year later, it looked this way:

	Women	*Men*
Favor	48%	49%
Oppose	36%	36%

(Harris, 1972)

A solid increase for men, a major increase for women. Clearly, headway for the Women's Liberationists.

Women in America not only accept some of the tactical notions ("It's time to speak up") and some the substantive notions ("Let's strengthen women's status in society"), but most women also accept at least some of the Liberationists' view of the world they face. Below is a Harris question asking women only, "How often women have certain feelings?" An answer of "Frequently" or "Occasionally" is regarded as some measure of *affirmation*.

HOW OFTEN WOMEN HAVE CERTAIN FEELINGS

Q. To get ahead in this world a woman has to be twice as good at what she does as a man is.

Frequently	27%	)
		) 53%
Occasionally	26%	)
Hardly ever	43%	

(Harris, 1972)

Slightly more than half the women in America accept the notion, at least some of the time, that it's tougher to get ahead in the world for a woman than a man.

A more specific Gallup question asked in 1970 of men and women showed much the same sort of result:

Q. If a woman has the same ability as a man, does she have as good a chance to become the executive of a company or not?

	Men	Women
Yes	39%	39%
No	56%	54%

(Gallup, 1970)

On a number of other issues that are either directly or tangentially related to Women's Lib there is solid public acceptance of the Movement position. Here are a pride of questions asked in 1972:

Q. Should a husband share the responsibility of cooking and cleaning up?

A.

	Men	Women	Total
Yes	64%	52%	55%
No	35%	46%	43%

Q. Do you feel that birth-control methods and information should be available to anyone—including unmarried teen-agers?

A. Yes   78%
   No   22%

Q. Do you approve or disapprove of divorce simply by mutual consent?

A. Approve   59%
   Disapprove   40%

Q. Should sex education be taught in school?

A. Yes   79%
   No   20%

Q. Is there too much emphasis on sex in all aspects of our society today?

A. Yes   82%
   No   17%

And, finally, and rather important,

Q. In general, do you think the new awareness of women's rights has altered the husband-wife relationship significantly?

A. Yes   36%
   No   63%

(BH&G, 1972)

A minority response it's true on that final query but still a potent one it would seem—within a few years of its birth, the Women's Lib movement was apparently changing *more than a third* of the marriages in America.

There is another set of data dealing with women's attitudes that tends to back up the idea that American women are finding some grounds for agreement with the Liberationists. Pollster Daniel Yankelovich offers to American corporations a private service called "Yankelovich Monitor," an ongoing survey that measures social trends, values and changing life styles among consumers. The actual data is embargoed for the use of subscriber clients, but here are some excerpts of what Yankelovich has publicly said about women's attitudes as he has seen them change from 1970 to 1973:

> Women are less fearful of the social stigma or the practical problem of divorce and living alone. On smaller matters, too, social fears have diminished. Housewives aren't as afraid of social disapprobation if they are not great cooks and hostesses or if they don't keep their homes spotlessly neat and clean. . . . People are becoming less uptight. . . . The growth of the fast food business, for example, is linked to the willingness of the housewife to take a more relaxed and casual attitude toward meal preparation. . . .
>
> An amazingly wide swath of products in the past were sold to the American public by arousing the housewife's fear of being found wanting. Advertising blatantly aimed itself at the housewife's anxiety that she would be embarrassed when others found out about her tattletale gray, or ring-around-the-collar, or the dullness of her unwaxed furniture. Some of these appeals continue to be used today because they are directed at more old-fashioned segments of the market. Yet it would be prudent for marketers . . . to be sensitive to the changing mores and consumer habits that *diminished social fear* brings about.
>
> ("Changing Consumer Values," address by Daniel Yankelovich, 1973)

Italics ours. "Diminished social fear" among women is what pollster Yankelovich finds from his surveys.[1]

A solid point, and probably due in some measure to the advent of Women's Lib as well as certain other aspects of the Movement such as the

[1] Some apparent verification of Yankelovich's point:

Q. Do you think many women are overly concerned with household matters, like cleaning and cooking?

A. (Women's responses)
    Yes 51%   No 49%
(*BH&G*, 1972)

Just more than half the women in America accept the notion that women are bothered by things they shouldn't be bothered by.

anti-materialism of the counterculture. "Diminished social fear" is very much of what Liberation is all about and, says Yankelovich, the feeling is growing.

There is, finally, some other evidence of the extent to which the ideas of the Women's Movement have penetrated the national consciousness. The United States Congress, of course, is not a perfect sample of the American population. On the other hand, there is probably no organization in the country whose members attempt so diligently to know what Americans are thinking. Accordingly, it should be noted that on October 12, 1971, the House of Representatives passed the Equal Rights Amendment by a vote of 354–23. The Senate passed the amendment on March 22, 1972, by a vote of 84–8.

It may seem, from the data presented so far, that the precepts of Women's Lib have taken the country by storm.

That would be a very great overstatement. It is accurate to say *some* of its precepts have made great headway. Americans agree that women should speak up, that women's status should be strengthened, that women have to work harder than men to get ahead in the world, that a husband should help with housework, that equal pay for equal work is only fair, that birth control, divorce and sex education should be available. Other data show women becoming more relaxed about social fear and less compulsive about household chores.

That's a lot, but there it ends.

For Americans also take strong issue with the Liberation movement.

We can look first at a series of specific items ranging from the symbolic to the serious.

A Gallup Poll in 1973 asked this question:

Q. Would you, yourself, rather be addressed as "Ms" or as "Miss" or "Mrs."

And these were the results for single women and married women:

SINGLE WOMEN WOULD LIKE TO BE CALLED

Ms	19%
Miss	67%

MARRIED WOMEN WOULD LIKE TO BE CALLED

Ms	6%
Mrs.	89%

(Gallup, 1973)

There was one group that had even less use for the term—married men:

Q. Would you rather have your wife addressed as Ms or Mrs.?

> Ms   2%
> Mrs. 84%

Those opinions deal with a symbolic issue. But this series of questions is anything but symbolic:

Q. Do you think the dominant role of the husband in the American family is declining in importance?

> Yes   79%
> No   21%

And Americans don't like it, either.

Q. Would you consider a decline in the husband's dominance to be:

> Good 28%
> Bad   71%

Nor do Americans like the idea of women with children taking jobs in the money economy:

Q. There are more married women—with families—in the working world than ever before. Do you think this has a detrimental effect on family life?

> Yes   69%
> No   30%

And, in fact, they don't even think that a job is such a be-all or end-all for any woman:

Q. Do you think a job outside the home is necessary to give a woman the fulfillment she needs?

> Yes   18%
> No   81%

(*Series, BH&G*, 1972)

And although the results are closer, there was never a solid majority in favor of legalizing abortion, which, until the landmark Supreme Court decision, was the most actively publicized of Women's Lib legislative goals. The results were sometimes quite close:

Q. Would you favor or oppose a law that would permit a woman to go to a doctor to end pregnancy at any time during the first three months?

	1969	1972
Favor	40%	46%
Oppose	50%	45%
No opinion	10%	9%

(Gallup)

These results were thought by scholars reporting to the President's Population Commission to indicate a liberalizing trend. But when put to the acid test of a referendum, legalized abortion failed by substantial margins in 1972, the most recent year it appeared on any state ballot:

	Michigan	North Dakota
For	39%	23%
Against	61%	77%

And the fact that the Supreme Court ruled favorably on legalized abortion didn't seem to change things attitudinally, at least as of Gallup's March of 1974 poll:

Q. The U. S. Supreme Court has ruled that a woman may go to a doctor to end pregnancy at any time during the first three months of pregnancy. Do you favor or oppose this ruling?

	Favor	Oppose
Men	51%	38%
Women	43%	49%

With women less likely to support abortion than men!

These are some of the specifics of disagreement. It is also true that American women have rejected more than specifics. Far more important, American women simply do not see life the way the Women's Movement sees it.

On some of the truly critical questions raised by Women's Lib—questions that go right to the root of a sexist America's failure and guilt, there is a massive rejection. American women have not accepted the notion that females are the oppressed sex, that they are mere sex objects, that domestic life is demeaning, and so on.

Here are a series of 1972 Harris questions on a "How Often Women Have Certain Feelings" scale:

HOW OFTEN WOMEN HAVE CERTAIN FEELINGS

Q. My education is being wasted, since I never got to use what I learned in school in my everyday life.

Frequently	7%
Occasionally	10%
Hardly ever	80% (!)

Women, then, do not seem to accept the wasted-life thesis. Nor do they buy the notion that they have been robbed of life's promises:

HOW OFTEN WOMEN HAVE CERTAIN FEELINGS

Q. Being a woman has prevented me from doing some of the things I had hoped to do in life.

Frequently	7%
Occasionally	12%
Hardly ever	78% (!)

They disagree, too, with some of the more personal and familial notions that have been popularized by at least some of the Women's Libbers. Here is one:

HOW OFTEN WOMEN HAVE CERTAIN FEELINGS

Q. Having a loving husband who is able to take care of me is much more important to me than making it on my own.

Frequently	56%)	
	)	74%
Occasionally	18%)	
Hardly ever	22%	

And neither are these data exactly a hot seller in Lib-land.[2]

---

[2] These feelings do not seem to be restricted to American women. In Israel, a land where sexual equality has long been a well-established and certainly well-publicized doctrine, a survey team of Hebrew University sociologists found that 75% of married women from Jerusalem and Tel-Aviv responded affirmatively to this statement: "A good mother and a good homemaker is a woman's most noble goal." Which may prove what has long been suspected: American females are nothing but Jewish mothers with station wagons.

HOW OFTEN WOMEN HAVE CERTAIN FEELINGS

Q. Bringing up children properly takes as much intelligence and drive as holding a top position in business or government.

Frequently	64%	
Occasionally	20%	84%
Hardly ever	42%	

Q. My life is much easier than a man's since I don't have to worry about earning a steady income.

Frequently	32%	
Occasionally	25%	55%
Hardly ever	42%	

(Married Women only)
(Harris, 1972)

And perhaps the most critical of all, flying directly in the face of the Lib notion of sexist failure, guilt and crisis, are these results of a Harris survey:

PERSONAL SATISFACTION WITH OWN LIFE TODAY

Very satisfied	Somewhat satisfied	Only slightly	Not at all
	Women		
58%	29%	8%	4%
	Men		
49%	35%	10%	5%

(Harris, 1972)

In short, American women don't believe they are living in a rotten corrupt sexist society that has crushed them. They are, in fact, more satisfied than men. They do not believe that America has failed, or failed them. They see problems and they are prepared to actively seek some specific changes, but they like being women and they even like being women in this kind of society.

American women don't only disagree with some Lib specifics and with many Lib generalities. They say they have major problems with Lib tactics. Here are three statements about activist women's groups that were presented in a survey by Harris interviewers in 1972:

Q. Leaders of women's organizations are trying to turn women into men and that won't work.

Agree   51%
Disagree   43%

Q. Women are right to be unhappy with their role in American society but wrong in the way they're protesting.

Agree   51%
Disagree   34%

Q. Women who picket and participate in protests are setting a bad example for children. Their behavior is undignified and unwomanly.

Agree   60%
Disagree   32%

(Harris, 1972)

These sorts of feelings crystallize as a feeling among many women of being "against Women's Liberation groups." Recall that by 48% to 36% women "favor efforts to strengthen or change women's status in society." But when the question is asked about organizations dedicated to those very ends and when the code-phrase "Women's Liberation" is used, some very different results are obtained:

SYMPATHY WITH EFFORTS OF WOMEN'S LIBERATION GROUPS

	Women	Men
Sympathetic	39%	42%
Unsympathetic	49% (!)	42%

Men are more sympathetic than women to Women's Lib groups and women show markedly less approval of "Women's Liberation groups" than for "efforts to strengthen or change women's status in society."

Why are Americans "against" a movement that advocates changes they favor?

Because Americans are also against other changes that some of the movement favors.

It seems to be a process not unlike the reaction to the Peace Movement described earlier: accommodation, eclecticism, synthesis—and rejection. A vast new body of ideas was served up quickly to the public. Some were accepted. Some were flying in the face of deeply held values—and were profoundly rejected. Because the Women's Lib groups were identified with both the acceptable and the nonacceptable ideas, they were tarnished.

Americans—American women—accept the notion that women should speak up, that there is change necessary, that in some instances the cards are stacked against women. Further, Americans believe in husbands and wives sharing household responsibilities, in birth control, in divorce, in sex education and in relaxing about cooking and cleaning.

But other views—practical and theoretical—they reject. Labels like "Ms" may be only symbolic, but advocacy of family dominance by the husband is not. Nor is the rejection of the idea that a job in the money economy is necessary for fulfillment. Nor is the rejection of abortion.

Beyond such specifics is rejection of some major intellectual underpinnings of the Movement: women don't feel their education is wasted, they don't feel unfulfilled, they feel a husband and children are properly the focus of their lives—and in general they feel satisfied, more satisfied than men. They reject the notion of failure and guilt and crisis—at least they reject that notion as cast by the Feminists.

Because some Liberationists endorse not only shared household duties, but the sense that housework is demeaning, because some Liberationists endorse not only speaking up for women, but also speaking up for a more permissive moral code, because some Liberationists are not only for equal pay for equal work but are for legalized abortion—Americans, or many Americans, reject the "Women's Lib" movement. They also say they reject "the methods" of the Movement—but that is probably because they are methods toward some ends they don't approve. The "methods" didn't stop Americans from agreeing with some aspects of the Women's Lib. No data is available, but our guess is that many of the Americans who disapprove of women carrying placards are not against women carrying placards to protest school busing.

Now, the tactical argument has been made that in this instance, as well as in many others, it's fine to be "in front" of the constituency even if it means temporary unpopularity. The Women's Lib movement, the Peace Movement, the Civil Rights Movement, after all, must be *leadership* forces. If they are unpopular that is all right (so goes the argument): they will get half a loaf of whatever they ask for so they must push hard and still harder.

We would question this line of thought on two grounds—vis-à-vis Women's Lib as well as other aspects of other causes.

First, we would ask, "Are they really up front?" Protest movements always have a remarkable quality of self-righteousness about them. "If we're for it—it *must* be right," and therefore we must do the honorable thing even if it is unpopular. The abortion issue is a case in point. The Libbers demanded, vehemently, that women have the "freedom to control their own bodies." But abortion is not a simple issue.

Abortion kills a fetus and people who are most deeply concerned about that are not necessarily sexists or reactionaries. Neither ought women who feel that home and family are number one priorities be treated as hopeless basket cases drummed insensate by cultural sexism. A persuasive case can be made that "home and family" may well be a damn sight more socially redeeming and personally fulfilling than assembling widgets at a factory, than writing advertising copy for organic foods, or even better than writing articles for the *New York Review*.

There is a second reason why a noble passion for unpopularity and "leadership" is not always productive. There are times in the affairs of men when a frenetic demand for a whole loaf yields not the proverbial half a loaf, but only crumbs.

CHAPTER 17

Environment / Consumerism / Explosionism

Nowhere has protest been more apparently successful than in the realm of the environment, ecology, consumerism and population explosionism. These issues will be discussed here as one basic movement.

None of these movements, sub-movements or causes are brand new, of course. Just as an earlier suffragette and feminist movement preceded the Women's Lib cause, just as earlier pacifism, isolationism, and America First movements preceded the peace movement, so too does the env-ec-oons-pop movement have deep roots in the American past. Upton Sinclair antedates Ralph Nader by half a century. Sinclair never sold socialism to America—which was his goal—but in *The Jungle,* written to show the deplorable working conditions in industrial America, he ignited public sentiment in favor of pure food and drug legislation. And "the environment" was neither birthed by Rachel Carson nor discovered on Earth Day by students who thought burying a brand-new automobile was the way to stop air pollution, and then drove their jalopies back to the dormitory. It was President Theodore Roosevelt and his Chief of Forestry Division Gifford Pinchot who galvanized a massive constituency behind an earlier movement called "conservation." And Margaret Sanger was preaching planned parenthood and contraception long before Paul Ehrlich discovered the population explosion.

The new movement, then, carries within itself the ideological seeds of earlier activity and, indeed, many actual personnel as well. Just as Kingman Brewster was making just about the same peace speech in 1940 and 1970, so too were there dedicated conservationists, consumerists and planned parenthood activists who had been toiling quietly for decades before joining forces with the newer cadre who marched under the flags of environmentalism, ecology, Naderism and ZPG. And beyond that, these ideas—like the central ideas of the peace groups and Women's Lib groups —always had strong grass-roots support among ordinary *nonactivist* Americans.

Every hunter and fisherman in America has a feeling for nature. We're all consumers, and it would be unreal to imagine that only ZPGers know about the costs of children; that is a wisdom that most parents acquire all by themselves.

Still, the startling and passionate re-emergence of these ideas in the 1960s under the catch-all rubric of "the quality of life" was more than just the sum of its component logical and historical parts. Organized by a new breed of activists, fanned to a white head by the press, these older ideas took hold with remarkable speed and with apparent high intensity.

As Hazel Erskine, polls editor of *Public Opinion Quarterly*, wrote in 1972:

A miracle of public opinion has been the unprecedented speed and urgency with which ecological issues have burst into American consciousness. Alarm about the environment sprang from nowhere to major proportions in a few short years. When the first polls on pollution appeared in 1965, only about one in ten considered the problem very serious. Today most people have come to that realization.

By 1970, conservation had even crept into the *volunteered* list of the most important national problems facing the nation today—though usually behind the perennially massive worries about war, the economy, and social unrest, which regularly dominate the list.

These were ideas whose time had come, or so it seemed.

Yet, once again, it's not quite so simple. Beware of the Ambivalent American. Again there was supermarket eclecticism, again there was synthesis, again there was accommodation, and again there was rejection—although not so apparent as in earlier instances.

We can begin by chronicling (quickly) the data to which Hazel Erskine refers.

The Opinion Research Corporation began fishing regularly in the polluted waters as far back as 1965. Here is what their time series show:

Q. Compared to other parts of the country, how serious, in your opinion, do you think the problem of air/water pollution is in this area— very serious, somewhat serious, or not very serious?

A.	Very Serious	or Somewhat Serious
	Air	*Water*
1965	28%	35%
1966	48%	49%
1967	53%	52%
1968	55%	58%
1970	69%	74%

(Opinion Research Corporation)

Well more than a doubling of concern about air and water pollution in just half a decade.[1] Some of this may well be attributable to the fact that the pollution situation actually did get worse. But surely most of the rise was due to a new awareness of old problems.

Not only did Americans come to see pollution as "serious," they saw it as very serious, at least in Minnesota where the highly respected and usually nationally-barometric Minnesota poll showed these results:

Q. Some people say *life itself is in danger* unless something is done about pollution. Others say pollution is not that serious. Do you think *life as we know it today will or will not be in serious trouble* if nothing is done about pollution? (Italics ours.)

A. Will be in serious trouble   87%
   Will not   10%
   (Minnesota poll 1970)

The public also feels that the environment is one of the key areas deserving of high levels of government spending. Successive California polls in 1969 and 1970 show "air and water pollution" as the *number one* suggested recipient of governmental funds, even nosing out "anti-crime, law enforcement" and far, far ahead of aid to cities, defense and the space program. A 1970 Harris poll shows "pollution control" as the number two suggested functional recipient of government funds, slightly behind "aid to education."

And not only are people concerned, not only do they feel the government should respond to environmental problems, but there is some mixed evidence that they are even willing to spend *some of their own money* to accomplish these ends![2]

Q. Would you be willing to pay $15 a year more in taxes to finance a federal program to control air pollution?

	% Willing
1967	44%
1970	54%
1971	59%

(Harris)

[1] Other scattered polls without the same clean time series show a similar pattern of rising concern.

[2] Only when open-ended buzz-phrases like "extra taxes" and "higher prices" are mentioned—with no limit specified—does a negative plurality show up:

Q. How much would you personally be willing to pay this year in extra taxes or higher prices to help clean up pollution?
   Something   22%
   Nothing   40%
   Don't know 38%
(Opinion Research Corporation, 1971)

A Roper poll taken at the end of 1971 asked Americans if they would be willing to pay 10% more for certain products in order to develop methods to prevent pollution. The results were roughly comparable to the earlier Harris data:

	Willing to pay 10% more	Not a Serious Problem
Detergents	69%	17%
Gasoline	68%	16%
Automobile	67%	17%
Electricity	64%	22%
Magazines and newspapers	60%	20%
Airplane tickets	59%	18%

(Roper, 1971)

And when the public speaks, politicians listen and have legislated an astonishing and bewildering array of environmental laws, the full effects of which are still to be unfolded in the years to come. Landmark legislation dealing broadly with national environmental policy, the national wilderness, and land use planning and dealing specifically with clean air, clean water, pesticides, and solid waste disposal, highways, sewage, noise pollution, wildlife, slow growth, no growth, pop-top cans and one-way bottles has tumbled forth from the Congress, the state legislatures and city halls all over the nation.

In all, a remarkable display of consciousness raising—reflected and implemented by statute—in a strikingly short period of time.

* * *

The sharp attitudinal changes in the *environmental* area have probably been matched by attitudinal changes in the field of *population*. It wasn't long ago in America when a burgeoning population was regarded as the hallmark of economic health and manifest destiny. Today, population growth is increasingly viewed as a threat, not only on the other side of the world in places like India, but right here in America.

Q. The population crisis is becoming so severe that people will have to be limited on the number of children they can have.

A. Agree   47%
   Disagree 41%

(Roper, October 1971)

If you think that 47%–41% is a close vote, consider that, in effect, that statement happens to sneakily endorse the use of the coercive force of

government to determine the size of a family that individuals may have!
And a plurality agreed!

Asked in more moderate form the results are far more robust. A 1971
Opinion Research Corporation poll asked simply:

Q. Do you feel that the growth of the U.S. population is a serious
    problem, a problem but not serious, or no problem at all?

A. Serious problem   65%
    Not so serious   26%
    No problem at all   7%
(ORC, 1971)

There is evidence over time as well. The National Fertility Study asked
the "serious problem" question in both 1965 and 1970.

Per cent responding that United States population growth is a serious
problem

                    1965   57%
                    1970   69%
(National Fertility Study)

Not only do Americans agree that the population situation is quite
serious, but they agree with a number of specific propositions that are
generally advanced by the Explosionists.

They believe in government action:

Q. Do you believe that the government should or should not try to do
    anything to slow down population growth in the United States?
    Should   56%
    Should not   35%
(ORC, 1971)

They believe that ZPG, in effect, was O.K. right away:

Q. Do you think the present size of the United States population is
    about right or do you think it should be smaller or larger?
    About right   57%
    Should be smaller 22%
    Should be larger   8%

And they concur with an entire roster of Explosionist views, a few of
which happen to be valid:

Q. Do you agree or disagree with whose who claim

	Agree	Disagree
a. Population growth is causing the country to use up its natural resources too fast?	57%	35%
b. Population growth is the main reason for air and water pollution?	48%	47%
c. Population growth helps keep our economy prosperous?	36%	52%
d. Population growth is producing a lot of social unrest and dissatisfaction?	64%	28%
e. Population growth is important in keeping up our nation's military strength?	36%	56%
f. People should limit the size of their families even though they can afford a large number of children.	57%	32%

That constitutes a good deal of agreement indeed, and across a broad range of subject matters.

* * *

Just as the public has accepted environmentalism and explosionism, so too have they accepted consumerism, or Naderism, to give some credit where some credit is due.

The meteoric rise of Ralph Nader and his continued high standing is probably the best index of the ongoing strength of consumerism in America.

For Nader has managed to stay high, very high, in the public esteem for many years. There is some sign of erosion, but not much and not where it matters much.

In 1971, a Harris poll asked for agreement/disagreement on the statement that "It is good to have critics like Ralph Nader to keep industry on its toes." In 1971, the count was 69%–3% on the "agreement" side. In 1972, the same statement yielded up an 80%–7% affirmative response. Also in 1972, an Opinion Research Corporation survey asked the identical question and got a 71%–4% response. Nader is obviously riding high.

Nor does the public see him as against the American system:

Q. Nader is a troublemaker who is against the free enterprise system.

A. Agree   5%
    Disagree   62%
(ORC, 1972)

Q. Nader's efforts are just part of the way-out and unfair protests of young people against the Establishment.

A. Agree   14%
    Disagree   61%
(Harris, 1972)

The rise and continued high esteem of Ralph Nader is the flip side of some skidding numbers regarding American business generally.

The ORC asked respondents in 1966 and 1971 if they had confidence in "big companies" and got a 55% affirmative in 1966, but only a 27% affirmative in 1971. ORC also polls for specific companies and they chart a "favorability" index over two-year periods. As it happens, both in the 1963-65 and 1969-71 time periods ORC surveyed the public regarding precisely thirty-nine companies. And this is the sheer statistical poetry they came out with:

NUMBER OF COMPANIES

Time period	Evaluated	Gained in Favorability	Declined in Favorability	Stayed same
1963-65	39	13%	0%	26%
1969-71	39	0% (!)	33% (!)	6%

(Exclamation points ours)

To frost the cake, Harris reported in December of 1972 that 56% of the American people agreed with the statement that, compared with standards ten years ago, "The quality of most things I buy has become worse."

And, finally, there is the political cherry on the attitudinal frosting to be found in this survey released in 1973 by Harris:

Q. Do you feel the Nixon administration should be tougher on big business, easier, or no tougher or easier than it was in the first four years?

A. Tougher   77%
    Easier   1%[3]
    About same   13%

[3] Who are these 1 per cent? There are 1,501 households in the Harris survey. There must be 1 per cent (about fifteen) that qualify for that infamous demographic pigeonhole: "corporate fat cats."

In short, required reading for the American businessman is no longer Keynes. The Marquis de Sade will do just fine.

* * *

On the surface, then, the American people seem to have accepted all, or almost all, of the assorted dicta of the environmentalists, the Explosionists and the consumerists. On balance, once again, the public's views seem quite sensible. They want clean air and clean water and they regard the issue, properly so, as quite important. They understand that population cannot grow indefinitely, and that we may as well put the brakes on now as later. By this author's lights, they also buy the mistaken notion that population is the chief culprit of environmental pollution and overcrowding.

Finally, Americans are agreeable to putting the heat on business. The story that puts that feeling in its proper perspective concerns the psychologist who was consulted by some worried parents about their particularly cantankerous eight-year-old son. What should they do to keep him in line? they asked. "Spank the brat every night," the gruff psychologist said. "If you don't know the reason why, don't worry, he does." Americans feel, probably correctly, that a ritual, regular spanking of business is not a bad idea; if they're not exactly sure what it's for, don't worry, business knows.

But there is more to the entire Quality of Life movement than just keeping the big boys honest, cleaning up the air, and having fewer babies. There is a deeper perspective that has a good deal to do with the very nature of our society and the values it holds. And in these aspects the attitudinal sailing has been far from clear.

The Quality-of-Lifers have been deeply concerned about materialism in America and around the world. They feel that we have bartered our souls and our land for a mess of smokestacks, solid wastes, effluents, cars, highways and electric toothbrushes, suburban sprawl and plastic junk. They believe—many of them—that limits must be put on economic growth, either now or soon lest we face ecological catastrophe. They believe— many of them—in a steady-state economy, in Zero *Production* Growth as well as Zero *Population* Growth. They believe—many of them—that "GNP" stands for Gross National *Pollution*. These beliefs come through clearly in the literature of the environmentalists and the Explosionists.

The consumerist literature is on a somewhat different wave length. Part of it, of course, is pro-materialistic: "Let's have good goods rather than let's have less goods." But there is also a sense that the hucksters are on the prowl, selling us products we don't need, products that are "useless," and that Americans are hooked—overly hooked—on *things*. In this sense the consumerists and the environmentalists and Explosionists are marching in concert. In this sense an indictment of failure, of guilt, of crisis, has been handed down on American society.

Do Americans accept these views of the Quality-of-Lifers?

The evidence is mixed, mottled and incomplete, but the judgment here is *"no."*

There are some polls that show that "materialism" is a major concern to the American people, but the flavor that comes through is not the same as one finds from many Quality of Life spokesmen. Instead, the "materialism" that concerns Americans is one that affects "morals" and "values," as in "Materialism is eroding our religious beliefs." There is a sense that material striving must be put in its proper place—behind family solidarity and behind spiritual feeling. *But there is little sentiment afoot that Americans want to, or should, cut down on the production or acquisition of material goods or limit their own share of the fruits of a successful and affluent society.*

The evidence for this is sometimes clear, sometimes disparate and sometimes fuzzy. It is, after all, hard to ask direct questions about abstractions of this sort. But the evidence is there, nonetheless.

First, reconsider all the data presented in Part III of this volume. People so obviously hooked on acquiring cars, suburban homes, washing machines, dryers, air conditioners and lots of money would not seem to be prime candidates for movements that casually condemn materialism.

Consider next this poll, taken by the Opinion Research Corporation at the behest of the Commission on Population Growth and the American Future:

Q.   In your opinion, which of the following factors are important causes of pollution in the United States and which are not so important?

	Important	Not so important	No opinion
a. The kinds of goods produced now and how they are manufactured	80	14	6
b. The total number of people living and working in certain areas	70	25	5
c. The number of automobiles and where they travel	88	9	3
d. How many possessions people have	30	61 (!)	9
. How many people there are	69	25	6

(ORC, 1971)

The one item that smacks most of materialism is the one that Americans are *not* willing to sacrifice: *"possessions."* It's O.K., apparently to be in favor of the generalized forms of pollution-solution, but hold on, Mac, hands off my power mower, my air conditioners, my automatic ice-cube maker, my electric rotisserie, my motorboat, my swimming pool pump, my snowmobile.

Snowmobiles are very interesting. They are a relatively new product and they are immensely popular in northern areas where snow is a climatological constant. In Minnesota, a state of 3.8 million population and 921,-000 families—there are 293,000 snowmobiles! Snowmobile enthusiasts love the machines because they combine some very elemental American passions: machinery, speed, the outdoors—and allow these passions to be exercised all-year round, even during the traditionally hibernative months.

A snowmobiler can tinker with his vehicle, race through the northland woods and fields, and watch the startled deer bounding into the white forest. The trouble is, of course, that snowmobiles are also loud, dangerous, and when a couple of dozen snowmobilers have put away a couple dozen cases of beer they may not only see deer bounding as they zoom across private property and jolt the winter eco-system with the ear-splitting timpany normally associated with the drag strip. They may also see farmers coming after them with shotguns, and ecologists hurling statutes at them.

So how do Americans who are subjected to the problem respond to the situation?

Q. Generally, do you have a favorable or unfavorable impression of snowmobiling?

Northern Minnesota

A. Favorable   60%
   Unfavorable   34%

Q. Do you think there is or is not a need for more restrictions on snowmobile use?

A. More restrictions   69%
   Do not need restrictions   27%
(Minnesota Poll, 1972)

They respond logically. Keep the snowmobiles. They're fun. But keep them in their place.

There is an echo of this sort of attitude in the recent history of the automobile industry in America. The environmentalists have leaned hard on the automobile as the most apparent and most easily identifiable villain in the environmental situation. The consumerists have put their shoulders to the wheel, and to the dashboard and the bumpers and the insurance policies as well. Given the bad press that cars have had—with some merit—

it might be logical to assume that at least some reflection of this would be seen in the yearly sales figures. After all, if such a preponderance of Americans are opposed to the pollutants spewed forth by more than a hundred million automobiles, if a preponderance of Americans are rallying behind Ralph Nader as he shows that automobile manufacturers are unsafe in every deed, and if in addition Americans felt that materialism was a profound evil of our times—it might logically follow to see some, even just a little, consumer resistance in the automobile showrooms. But in 1973, there were 9.7 million new cars sold in America. That was about as many cars as have ever been sold in any single year in American history, despite the slowdown in the last quarter of the year due to the energy crisis.

But there was something very interesting about those 9.7 million new cars. They had extensive pollution abatement devices on their engines, required by federal law. They were smaller in size than previously. They had new safety features, required by law. And although the environmental devices and the safety devices jacked up the cost of the cars, they sold and sold and sold.

The vote in the marketplace, it would seem, was crystal clear. *Yes* to the referendum on environment, *yes* to the referendum on gas economy, *yes* to the referendum on safety, and *yes*, as well, to the referendum on cars.

By our lights, there is much distilled wisdom in being for all of the above. Americans have not abandoned materialism, nor would they be wise to. The idea of freezing-the-size-of-the-pie—which is what many anti-materialist arguments ultimately come down to—is most typically acceptable to those who already own their Swiss villa, or those who have a naive sense of what can be accomplished by changing the size of the slices of the constant-size pie. Median family income in the United States in 1972 was $11,116. If the people with the villas are going to keep the villas, and the economy does not expand, then half the families earning less than the median will continue to earn less than $11,116. Similarly, if it were deemed advisable to raise all the families earning less than $11,116 up to that median figure, then, under the precepts of the steady-state economists, it would also be necessary to *lower* to $11,116 all those families who earn more than that figure. Steady-state economists earning more than $11,116 volunteering to take income cuts have not yet been heard from.

In short, the life style imposed by an economy of Zero Production Growth, or even Zero Per Capita Production Growth, is not a very pleasant thought for either poor, middle class or rich. To be sure, some gains for all could be accrued by directing people not to spend their money on "unnecessary" items like cosmetics, colas, crab-grass killer, funny little hats and the advertising of all these items and others. But the savings would be small, and the price in lost freedom might well be more intolerable than some of the products themselves.

Yet, despite these obvious arguments (and the ones presented earlier in Chapter 7), the notion of a steady-state economy, or something like it, achieved a certain intellectual vogue in recent years.

Now, there seem to be no public opinion polls that detail whether Americans favor a no-growth economy, nor indeed is there any reason to suggest that such a survey would be terribly meaningful. The ideas involved are complex and have far-reaching ramifications. Yet there is a mechanism in our society that takes complex ideas, simplifies them, and then presents them to the public for a judgment. This mechanism is the political system, and it is interesting to see how politics and politicians have handled no-growth and slow-growth.

As the gross-national-pollution argument surfaced, a number of politicians picked up on some of the rhetoric—there are always a number of politicians who will pick up almost any trendy rhetoric. (Some of the quotations can be found in Chapter 2.) But when the full meaning of anti-materialism sunk home, the rhetoric calmed down. Politicians, of course, continued to call for "re-ordered priorities" but without the critical aspect of the economic growth freeze.

Instead, no-growth seemed to undergo a fascinating transformation. It localized; and it no longer came to mean what it once meant.

Once no-growth meant no economic growth nationally—freeze the pie —and either divide the slices differently or not so differently. But the key was to stop the production-pollution-per-capita-income spiral—to pull out the roots of the crab grass of materialism.

Now no-growth means something else. There are geographical constraints advocated. There are demographic constraints advocated. There are industrial constraints advocated. Don't Californicate, Colorado read the signs. Oregon for Oregonians. Keep the oil refinery out. Don't build the nuclear plant.

Wonderful. But is it anti-materialism? No. The one constraint that is *not* present is the personal economic constraint—the constraint upon consumption. The other constraints serve to boost the incomes, the net worth and, ultimately, the consumption of the Oregonians, the Coloradans and so on. Some builders and merchants may be harmed by cutting off new housing subdivisions. Some banks may be hurt. But a building moratorium in a desirable location has one immediate effect: soaring values of homes that are already in place, homes that are owned by people who vote. And when a man's house doubles in value, he can borrow against its appreciated value and suddenly realize that he can afford a lawn mower with a seat on it, he can afford to build a new wing on the house, by

God, he can afford to build a heated swimming pool, and float—wallow
—in the idea that he is being an anti-consumption environmentalist! It's
a great psychic solution. A passion for no-growth has been transformed
into a passion for restrictive zoning and people are pleased—on the
hoary principle that having one's cake and eating it is more desirable
than either of the alternatives.

There is, of course, a certain selfishness involved in the procedure—it
begins to price the lower middle class out of the housing market in some
communities. But, then again, materialism can often be a selfish doctrine
—"I want mine" may well be its guiding force.

The "I want mine" feeling effectively draws the line at the outermost
limits of environmentalism, at which point materialism becomes the
ascendant emotion. Americans want clean air. Accordingly, they will back
legislation to provide clean air via oil low in sulphur content. But when
an energy crisis makes low sulphur oil hard to come by, the standards
are relaxed, air pollution presumably rises, and no one squawks—hardly
even the environmentalists who know a losing cause when they see one.
Clean air is a good cause until it butts up against the ability of people
to heat their homes.

That is an extreme case, it may be argued. Indeed it is; Americans
may well respond to certain other kinds of discomfort or inconvenience
or expense in the attempt to preserve some ecological balance, some environmental purity and some energy usage. They may be persuaded and
legislated to drive their cars at thrifty fifty instead of greedy seventy.
They may work in shirtsleeves or sweaters in office buildings where air
conditioning and heating base temperatures are raised or lowered several
degrees. They may even be convinced that stopping the production of
two experimental SST aircraft will save the environment. They may be
successfully encouraged to drive automobiles with fewer horses under
the hood. They may be trained to turn out the lights and to insulate their
homes. Through these measures—and many others—they may well cut
down on the enormous waste of energy in America.

Well and good. But that is a very different notion from the one that
says energy consumption and materialism are inherently unhealthy, senseless and/or evil. Americans don't accept that for a minute, not in the Sixties in the environmental version and not now in the Seventies in the
energy version of the seven lean years. Americans understand that cars and
air conditioners and washers and dryers and vacuum cleaners and swimming pool pumps and freezers and automatic dishwashers and many of the
other accouterments now owned by the Massive Majority Middle Class
are machines that make life better, not worse, that show success, not
failure, that show an improvement in the quality of life, not a degradation

of it; that they are better by far than what they replace, which was, let us recall, dishwashing by hand, fans, clothespins, brooms, etc.

Should the day come when Americans must choose between washing machines and environmental super-purity it will be no contest.

Materialism triumphant. And if the day should come when the washing machines stop right in the middle of the fluff-dry cycle because of the energy crisis, whoever is seen to be at fault for that occurrence had best start moving his resumé around. If you want to find out how materialist Americans really are—try taking it away from them.

Indeed, by our rhetorical barometer, the advent of the energy crisis in late 1973 proved just how materialistic Americans were. The rhetoric was clear: Use less, don't waste—but preserve function. Get a small car, lower the thermostat—fine. But was there a man in public life who came out against washing machines, dryers, dishwashers, vacations, efficient and accessible transportation or a rising gross national product? No sir. They were, in fact, vehemently against the recessionary push of the energy crisis, a push that might keep the real GNP frozen—just like the steady-state economists would like to have it.

* * *

There is an analogue to the environment-versus-materialism situation regarding Naderism/consumerism. The American people don't want to be ripped off by corporate America. They want products that don't break down and don't give them cancer. They want a product warranty that means something. They want to be able to compare prices of soap flakes or corn flakes even if they don't have a graduate degree in number theory. So they support Nader for keeping business "on its toes" and delivering the requisite ritual spanking.

But that feeling should not be confused with an "anti-business" attitude. Opinion Research Corporation reports that 86% of Americans feel that "large companies are essential for the nation's growth"! Americans understand full well that only business can deliver them the goods and service their wants. And Americans don't regard those goods and services as junk either; they wouldn't buy the products or the services if they didn't find them useful in one way or another. The American consumer cannot be gulled into buying junk—a second time.

Accordingly, when Louis Harris' pollsters go out they also find some negatives on Nader:

Q. Nader gives a one-sided picture of what America does, leaving out many good things industry does.
    Agree   46%
    Disagree   30%
(Harris, December 1972)

A year earlier, incidentally, Americans *rejected* that view by a slender 30–29% margin. So perhaps the wind is shifting a bit, a notion that will be explored at some length a bit later.[4]

Americans also know that the only way that our economic system produces is when people are highly motivated, success oriented, and prepared to work like hell. A Harris survey in 1971 showed that by 77–13% the public felt it was "not healthy for young people to turn their backs on economic gain and success." By 60–28%, the public agreed it was "not healthy for young people to refuse to believe that winning in competition is important." (Interestingly, by counts of 77–13% and 56–37%, young people aged sixteen to twenty also endorsed these views.)

As in the environmental situation, then, Americans reject anti-materialism to whatever degree it exists in the consumerist movement. They want the products that American business produces—and they want honest effort from the businesses that produce and service those products. They see no reason why they can't have their cake and eat it, and neither do we.

The attitudes regarding the population situation are not entirely of the same nature as those concerning the environment and consumerism. Of course, insofar as the Explosionists are anti-materialist and anti-economic growth—and some of them are—the arguments above would apply. But beyond that, on the surface there are few "Yes, but" attitudes to report. Americans apparently not only feel that population growth is a serious problem, but as we have seen in Chapter 10, the birth rates and fertility rates have declined precipitously in recent years.

However, there would, nonetheless, seem to be some mitigation of the Explosionist line.

First is the matter of causation. Lest we give full credit for the Birth Dearth to the Explosionists, one simple fact should be recalled. The recent American fertility rate peaked in the year 1957. The Explosionist rhetoric did not begin to gain deep public recognition until much later. For example, Paul Ehrlich's alarmist fiction *The Population Bomb* wasn't published until 1968, by which time the U.S. general fertility rate had already fallen from 123 in 1957 to 85. And it must also be recalled that birth rates have been falling in America—and throughout the Western world—in a pretty steady pattern for several hundred years.

This is not to deny a role in the Birth Dearth to the Explosionists. Attitudes have changed, and likely the Explosionist publicity helped change attitudes. But it was not a sudden change nor a change with one

---

4 Similarly, in 1972, Americans rejected by 36% to 31% that "Nader and his people make a lot of charges which are not really proven." But in 1971, only 17%—as opposed to 31% in 1972—thought Naderites trigger happy. Again the trend is toward cocking a wary eye at Nader—while still applauding him as business spanker.

simple cause. The Explosionists didn't invent "the Pill." They did not create the burgeoning economy which created the prosperity, which allowed so many single young people to live in their own apartments,[5] which has probably delayed the age of marriage, and which, in turn, has probably played a part in lowering fertility. The Explosionists did not arrange for the rise in the rate of women who work, a trend that has been going on for three decades and a trend that seems to have a depressant effect on the birth rate.

And while Americans have apparently accepted the single major notion of the Explosionists—"more babies are bad"—in another way, there has been an interesting sort of rejection of another Explosionist tenet. The notion of "overcrowding" or "urban sprawl" of a "malignant megalopolis" of people crowded, crowded, crowded, crowded, unhappy, irritable and squeezed by relentless growth is central to Explosionist doctrine. That America is jammed to the gunwales is their notion of failure, guilt and crisis.

Do Americans share that view?

The Opinion Research Corporation poll for the Population Commission probed these attitudes. It asked where the respondent would *prefer* to live, and got this pattern of response:

	Live	Want to live
1. On a farm	9%	14%
2. Open country not a farm	7%	20%
3. In a small town	20%	19%
4. In a small city	13%	11%
5. In a medium-sized city	14%	10%
6. In a large city	16%	7%
7. In the suburb of a medium-sized city	14%	12%
8. In the suburbs of a large city	12%	6%

The variances are not enormous in any instance except that many more people would like to live in "open country not on a farm" than actually do, and the people aren't wild about big city life, either in it or near it.

The pollsters, however, followed up these questions with others to test whether it was crowding and overpopulation that may have spurred their desire to live somewhere else. The results are remarkable:

▪ Of rural residents (items 1 and 2), *93%* said their area's population was either "about right" (85%) or "should be larger" (8%).

[5] From 1970 to 1973 Census data shows that the number of family households increased by 6%, while the number of "primary individuals" increased by 17%. There are now 14 million Americans living outside of a family situation.

- Of small town residents (item 3), *92%* said that the population of their town was either "about right" (75%) or "should be larger" (17%).
- Of small city residents (item 4), *88%* said that population of their city was "about right" (77%) or "should be larger" (11%).
- Of residents in medium and large size cities and their suburbs (items 5 through 8), *71%* said that the population of the "whole metropolitan area" was "about right" (64%) or should be "larger" (7%).

As far as size is concerned then, the vast preponderance of Americans think that where they live is all right, even so for more than seven in ten residents of the most populous communities. They do not apparently accept the squirming, sweating crowd of squeezed humanity that is the Explosionists' own singular vision of hell on earth.

This can be verified in another way. Think for a moment: If people hate the metropoli so much, why don't they up and move to that "open country not on a farm" that polls report so many folk who don't live there claim they like? There is an answer that is often given: "Well they would move, but there are no jobs in rural America."

That answer can be rebutted with another question: What about doctors? Doctors are in great demand in rural areas and in small towns. There are small communities that will offer to build a hospital if they can just get a doctor to move out and settle down to be a leading citizen in a dear town with dear hearts and gentle people, with no crime, no drugs, no noise and a duck blind ten minutes down the road. And yet, the doctors don't go. They remain clustered in and around cities—like most Americans.

Why?

The guess here is that urbo-hate and ruro-love are overstated emotions. It's been at least 2,500 years since men started leaving the calm pastoral surroundings for the corrupt bright lights of the city. In America, this migration has been going on since well before the Constitution was ratified. And all over, the reaction to metropolitan life is similar: Where are the good old days in the country, or, more recently, you can take the boy out of the country but you can't take the country out of the boy.

The cold fact of it is that life in the country and in the little out-of-the-way village is often lonely, boring, gossipy and unstimulating—which is exactly why there has been an urban tropism for so long. How're you going to keep 'em down on the farm after they've seen Paree?

This elemental fact of humanity has even been recognized by planners who, for centuries, have been trying to "redistribute population" back to the healthy open country. Today, the new population schemes for redistribution are mostly based on a sounder idea: People should be encouraged and enticed to move to "growth centers," actually small cities in the 50,-000-population range that are located away from major metropolitan swaths.

In short, Americans are not voting and will not vote with their feet to get back to the country. The Explosionists' apocalyptic vision of asphalt, neon, plastic, circumferentials and pizza parlors is regarded by most Americans today in a simple way: "home," which includes all of the above but also a ranch house on a quarter of an acre, patio furniture, lots of movies nearby, the ability to get to an orthopedic specialist or an NFL football game, and surrounded by neighbors some of whom have swimming pools also. Americans, unlike the claustrophobic Explosionist spokesman, like living near other people.

CHAPTER 18

Civil Rights

The civil rights movement has been regarded, probably correctly, as the antecedent and the model and the moral force behind the Movement of Movements.

In contemporary history, it came first, long before peace, ecology, Women's Lib and the counterculture.

Tactically, it revised and perfected the new techniques needed to get massive publicity and a national consensus behind a major issue.

Substantively, it became—not for the first time in American history— the cutting edge of the fight for decency, fairness and morality.

Retrospectively, it is apparent that the civil rights movement and the legislation it engendered were critical elements in achieving great progress for blacks in America during the 1960s.

Yet, today, there is a heavy gloom hanging over the civil rights movement. The esprit of the early 1960s is gone, and "Where do we go from here?" has not yet rivaled "We shall overcome" as a rallying cry.

One can get a pretty good sense of what's gone wrong, and what's gone right for the civil rights movement by looking carefully at changing American attitudes, which serve, ultimately, as the litmus test of success of any movement seeking change. Change the public mind and the country will change. Set the public mind rigidly against your proposition, and the sledding will be tough.

The first—and surely the most important—point about civil rights in America in the last dozen years is that in terms of those attitudes that used to be thought of under the rubric of "race relations" *there has been a strong and steady liberalization that continues today.*

Here is a fascinating attitudinal situation that was presented to a cross section of white Americans in 1956 and again fifteen years later in 1971:

Q. One day a six-year-old asks her mother if she can bring another girl home to play. The mother knows that the other girl is a Negro, and that her daughter has only played with white children before. What should she do?

1. She should tell her daughter she should never play with Negroes.
2. The daughter should be told that she may play with Negro children in school, but not at home.
3. The Negro child should be permitted to come to the home.

(University of Michigan, Institute of Social Research)

In 1956, the percentage of respondents who answered "The Negro child should be permitted to come to the home" (3) was *40%*.

In 1971, the percentage was *81%*.

Those answers provide a three-pronged sketch of white American attitudes toward black Americans: a) there has been a stark and major change, b) not too many years ago there were a *majority* (60%) of Americans who held deep and essentially racist attitudes, and c) there are still 19% of white Americans—almost one out of five—who still hold those attitudes.

The same sort of pattern is seen in the results of another survey question asked in 1958 and thirteen years later in 1971. This one deals with residential integration.

Q. Would you be at all disturbed or unhappy if a Negro with the *same income and education* as you moved into your neighborhood? (Italics ours)

PER CENT SAYING "YES, DISTURBED"

1958	54%
1971	28%

A roughly similar question commissioned by Potomac Associates from the Gallup Organization one year later (1972) yielded up a roughly similar response, with perhaps one more notch up the liberalization ladder: only 24% said they would be "unhappy" about blacks of *similar status* moving into their neighborhood, as opposed to 28% in the ISR.

But the Potomac Associates Gallup questioning went a little further. They also asked whites what they thought about *lower-class blacks* and *lower-class whites* moving into their neighborhoods. The results were significant. Lower-status *blacks* moving in were most resented (44%); lower-status *whites* were somewhat less resented (37%); but *same-status* blacks were still less resented (24%)! There is a lesson there, and an important one: There is still *racism* left in America, but *classism* is an even tougher hurdle to leap. Americans would far rather have a Massive Majority Middle Class black as a neighbor than a white who hasn't made it yet. Or—economic progress is the shortest, least painful route toward racial integration.

The ISR data on education attitudes also show liberalization:

Q. Personally, do you think white students and Negro students should go to the same schools or to separate schools?

PER CENT SAYING "SEPARATE SCHOOLS"

1958	33%
1971	17%

The rate of segregationist sentiment declined by about half in thirteen years.

Here is another, but imperfect, comparison of changing attitudes over time: In 1959, five years after Brown vs. Board of Education, Gallup asked whether respondents approved of the decision. Nationally, Americans approved 59–35%. In the South, however, the response was 71–22% *against*. Thirteen years later, in the southern state of Florida, the following question appeared on a state primary ballot (following an equally rhetorical question about busing):

Q. Do you favor providing an equal opportunity for quality education for all children regardless of race, creed, color or place of residence and oppose a return to a dual system of public schools?
   Yes   79%
   No   21%

The election data and the Gallup data are keyed to an abstract legal principle—school integration. But look at this change in southern white attitudes when a quite mild *personal* integrationist question is asked:

Q. Would you yourself have any objection to sending your children to a school where a few children are colored?

SOUTHERN WHITES ONLY

A.

	Yes, would object	No, would not
1959	72	25
1965	37	62
1966	24	74
1969	21	78

And so ends the argument that "laws can't change the hearts of men." Laws (Brown vs. Board), and the implementation of those laws, broke up the Southern segregated school systems, and attitudes changed quickly.

Intermarriage is an even touchier subject than residential or school integration. Yet, although there is still massive resistance to the idea, there has been noticeable change.

The questions have been asked in a number of different ways. ISR data show a marked liberalization over only a two-year time span:

Q. If a very close relative married a Negro, would you mind it a lot, a little, or not at all?

PER CENT SAYING "MIND IT A LOT"

1969	68%
1971	51%

That question asked if the respondent would "mind it" if a "very close relative" married a Negro. One Gallup question asked whether respondents *"approved"* of intermarriage, and got a *4%* affirmative response in 1958 and a *25%* in 1972.

Another Gallup query asked for approval/disapproval of state miscegenation laws "making it a *crime* for a white person and a Negro to marry." In 1965, a slight plurality of Americans *approved* of such "criminal" laws (48%–46%). Five years later, in 1970, the count was 56–35% *disapproval* of such laws, still a huge number, but clearly diminishing.

Finally, since 1958 Gallup has been running a series on prejudice in politics dealing with the idea of whether or not race would be a critical variable that would determine whether or not voters would pull the lever for a candidate for President. Here are the results:

Q. If your party nominated a generally well-qualified person for President and he happened to be a Negro, would you vote for him?

	Yes	*No*
1958	38%	53%
1961	50%	41%
1963	47%	43%
1965	59%	34%
1967	54%	40%
1969	67%	23%
1971	70%	23%

There were a few little bumps in an otherwise clear trend line, but the direction is clear and the amount of shifting is massive.

A good catchall sequence of surveys by the Texas poll deals with a wide range of social situations—and shows a sharp change in opinion over an eight-year period. These data *are for white Texans,* and can be considered as reflecting a somewhat more conservative view than for the population as a whole. Still, the change has been enormous.

Situations in which white Texans accept racial contacts:

	1963	1971
Working side by side with you in the same kind of job.	56%	84%
Riding in the same sections of trains and buses.	49%	83%
Eating in the same restaurants.	40%	80%
Staying in the same hotels with you.	36%	76%
Attending your church.	46%	75%
Sending your children to the same schools.	41%	73%
Attending the same social gathering outside your home.	23%	59%
Using the same public swimming pools with you.	19%	50%
Attending a social gathering in your home.	13%	45%
Having as a roommate for your son or daughter in college.	8%	32%

Now, it has been said that some of these responses are only lip-service answers. Some critics say that racism has merely become unfashionable, that people still don't want blacks in their neighborhood, that they still wouldn't vote for a black for President, that they still don't want to send their kids to schools with blacks—but they will no longer tell it to the pollsters because they don't want to be regarded as bigots.

It is possible that this is the case. But there is a second step that is necessary if one accepts such an analysis. The fact that racist sentiment has become so unfashionable that a citizen does not even feel able or willing to tell it to a pollster is in itself very significant. It means, for example, that it will be unlikely and unprofitable for a politician to run a blatantly racist campaign, and even unlikely for him to endorse obviously racist legislation lest he become known as a bigot, an unappealing image for a politician seeking to appeal to voters who won't acknowledge that they themselves are bigots. It means, for another example, that if being a bigot is no longer publicly acceptable (even if privately felt), it is far more difficult to organize a middle-class neighborhood "to keep the niggers out." Progress is achieved in strange ways.

Now, while all this generalized attitudinal liberalization over roughly a decade and a half was going on, there were some other things going on as well. There blossomed in these same years:

- The non-violent demonstrations of the civil rights movement (free-dom rides, sit-ins, marches, etc.).
- A number of major and specific substantive pieces of federal legis-lation (public accommodation, voting rights, open housing).
- A series of violent disruptions that were associated, rightly or wrongly, with civil rights (urban riots, some college takeovers, Black Panthers, etc.).
- A second round of substantive civil rights demands (busing, quotas, scatter-site housing and, by association at least, welfare).

In watching the reaction to, and the interplay of, these developments one can get a sense of the current status of the civil rights movement.

NON-VIOLENT DEMONSTRATIONS

Americans don't like demonstrations or demonstrators. This is so ob-viously true of the latter-era huff-and-puff supermilitants that we tend to forget that it is also true—to a lesser degree—even when the goals of the demonstrators are generally accepted and when the demonstrators are kind, courteous, well-behaved, clean-cut, God-fearing and wholly nonviolent.

The year 1961 was long before "Burn, baby, Burn," before Black Panthers, and before "May Day" and "Days of Rage," to recall some nonracial supermilitancy as well. It was in an era when "demonstrations" involved "sitting in" to get a hamburger at a lunch counter or "freedom riding" to desegregate public transportation. There is no question that the American people endorsed those goals in 1961:

Q. The United States Supreme Court has ruled that racial segregation on trains, buses, and in public waiting rooms must end. Do you ap-prove or disapprove of this ruling?

A. Approve   66%
   Disapprove   28%
   No opinion   6%
(Gallup, 6/2/61)

Considering that those respondents in the South answered 66%–22% *against,* the reaction *outside of the South* was particularly strong.

Yet, at the same time there was this reaction to the "freedom rides," which were, of course, designed to bring about just the desegregation the public said they wanted:

Q. Do you approve or disapprove of what the freedom riders are doing?

A. Approve   24%
    Disapprove   64%
    No opinion   12%

(Gallup, 6/2/61, asked of the 63% of the sample who had heard or read about the "freedom rides."

One of the reasons Americans did not endorse demonstrations was because they did not believe it would help achieve the goals the demonstrators aimed for:

Q. Do you think "sit-ins" at lunch counters, "freedom buses," and other demonstrations by Negroes will hurt or help the Negro's chances of being integrated in the South?

A. Help   27%
    Hurt   57%
    No opinion   16%

(Gallup, 6/2/61)

We would submit that in the instances of early-1960s freedom-riding and sit-in-style demonstrations the public was wrong in their judgment and that the civil rights movement was correct. Observe what happened:

Q. What do you think is the most important problem facing the nation today?

PER CENT SAYING RACIAL PROBLEMS OR CIVIL RIGHTS

rank order

1962 (April)	6%	4
1963 (March)	4%	4
1963 (October)	52% (!)	1
1964 (May)	41%	1 (tie)
1964 (June)	47%	1
1964 (August)	40%	2
1964 (September)	35%	2
1965 (March)	32%	1
1965 (March)	52%	1
1965 (May)	23%	1 (tie)
1965 (September)	27%	1
1965 (October)	17%	2
1965 (November)	19%	2
1966 (May)	9%	3
1966 (August)	24%	2
1967 (October)	21%	2

(Gallup)

Of course, these rankings can fluctuate sharply, keyed to specific events that crop up in the current newspaper headlines. Still, what happened is clear. In the early 1960s, civil rights was on the back burner. Under the pressure of events, typically events such as Selma, Bull Conner's dogs and James Meredith's entry into the University of Mississippi, which were forced by "demonstrations," civil rights became the number-one problem. It should be noted that between March of 1963 and October of 1963 there occurred the granddaddy of all the peaceful protests, the March on Washington, organized by Bayard Rustin and starring Martin Luther King, Jr., who had a dream. More than any single act, that "demonstration" galvanized the nation.

Civil rights remained on the front burner for two full years before "Vietnam" pre-empted the number-one position.

NEW LAWS

Thus forced to rivet their attention to a problem, Americans—even though they disagreed with the methods used to gain their attention—responded favorably to the overwhelming moral force of the argument. It is no accident that the two landmark civil rights bills of the era—voting rights and public accommodations—were enacted during precisely this time. And there is no doubt that President Johnson's vigorous and passionate campaign for these laws was made possible by American public opinion, which supported a public accommodations law by 61–31%[1] in 1964 and which supported a voting rights bill by 76–16% in 1965.[2] (Gallup data)

The progression seems clear. *Unpopular* demonstrations forced public action *in favor* of causes that were *popular*.

VIOLENT DEMONSTRATIONS

The story, of course, does not end at this point. The perception of the civil rights movement changed. The image of lunch-counter seats and seats in the front of the bus as the symbols of civil rights changed suddenly to a blur of burning cities, gun-toting Panthers and invaded colleges. Demands perceived of as reasonable and fair gave way to demands perceived of as idiotic. Civil rights activist James Forman put forth his notion of the next step with a media show demanding that white churches and synagogues fork up $500 million dollars in what he called "reparations." Gallup pollsters were out in the field shortly thereafter and asked

[1] For whites, the percentages were 71–21% outside the South.
[2] Even southern whites favored it by 49–37%.

respondents what they thought of the idea. Five per cent thought it was a good idea. Eighty-nine per cent thought it was not a good idea.

As for the Black Panthers, they fared even worse in the hearts and minds of the American people. In 1970, Gallup asked respondents to rate various organizations along a scale with "highly favorable" on the top and "highly unfavorable" on the bottom:

Q. How would you rate each of the following organizations?

A.

	Highly favorable	Highly unfavorable
Black Panthers	2%	75%
KKK	3%	75%
NAACP	23%	16%

The urban riots were vigorously condemned by Americans. A 1968 Gallup poll found out that about half of the respondents felt that "the police ought to shoot on sight anyone found looting stores."

And in the summer of 1967—the hottest summer of a series of long hot summers—Gallup asked Americans this devastating question:

In the last several months, have your attitudes toward Negroes changed in any way—and if yes—in what way?

Here is Gallup's report on the answer to that chilling query:

"About *one person in three* (32%) says he thinks differently about Negroes today, and *virtually all in this group say they have less regard or respect for Negroes now than before.*
(Gallup, August 1967; italics ours)

The riots clearly struck a raw nerve. They were not perceived of as just a series of tragic and destructive incidents. They were not seen as a change in style, however obnoxious, as perhaps the long hair and obscene language of the peace demonstrators were seen as a change of style. Instead, in a time of increasing violence and criminality, in a time of starkly increasing *black* crime rates—the riots tended to confirm perceived prior knowledge. And this is when an "incident" or a series of incidents takes on deeper meanings, a more lasting impact, and becomes perceived of as a *condition*. The fear of black violence still pervades and corrodes race relations in America. Such fear didn't begin with the riots, but it probably did undergo a quantum jump at that time.

NEW DEMANDS

At roughly the same time that the demonstrations and the disruptions turned ugly, a new set of civil rights demands were placed on the anvil of American public opinion. These included busing, scatter-site housing, quotas and welfare.

Unlike the earlier specific demands—for public accommodations and voting rights—unlike the liberalized attitudes on generalized subjects— children going to school with blacks, voting for a black President, blacks moving into the neighborhood—the American public has emphatically rejected much of "round two" of the substantive program of the civil rights movements:

- In 1970, Gallup began polling on school busing: the question dealt with "busing of Negro and white school children from one school district to another." The response was 86–11% against.[3] In 1971, the same question yielded a 76–18% "against," with blacks also in opposition by 47–45%. In the years since, those ratios have remained roughly constant: massive white opposition, a split black view.

- The housing question is quite complex. People say they are prepared to have equal-status blacks move in next door. Yet some open housing legislation has flopped: the "Rumford Proposition" in California in 1964 went down by a big 65%–35% margin. In 1967, Gallup found that 58% of the public knew what "open housing" meant and by 54–35% rejected the idea of Congress legislating in favor of it. Yet a year later Congress did so legislate—and there was little public outcry.

  But if the view regarding "open housing" is complex, there is no complexity regarding "scatter-site" housing, that is, the concept of placing public housing units for poor people (often predominantly black poor people) in the middle-class neighborhoods. That idea is categorically rejected. There are no available public opinion polls other than the generalized ones cited earlier showing an antagonism toward *class* mixing in neighborhoods. But the specific political evidence is massive. The Forest Hills contretemps in New York City gained national attention, but it was not unusual. Other scatter-site plans generated massive opposition in other communities across the nation.

[3] Interestingly, Gallup reported that persons who described themselves as "liberals" hold views that differ little from those who call themselves "conservatives."

- Because of the disproportionate number of blacks on welfare and probably also because the visible leadership of the Welfare Rights movement has been black, many white Americans have tended to see welfare as primarily a black problem. But black or white, they don't like it. The Potomac/Gallup *State of the Nation* survey shows that among twenty domestic issues, "welfare programs to help low-income families" ranks ninteenth in terms of perceived need for increased government spending ahead only of the space program. The same 1972 survey shows that by 81–19%, Americans are prepared to have the government spend *more* total money for services to get people trained and on a job (even if it demands subsidized child care) than they are to spend *less* money to provide for cash welfare payments. And by 53–36%, Americans believe that welfare mothers with school-aged children should be required to "take any job offered them."
- And, finally, "quotas." There seems to be little attitudinal data available just yet. Turning to our political barometers, however, it is important to note that in 1972 both Nixon and McGovern felt constrained to announce their unwavering opposition to quotas —although it was the Nixon administration guidelines that initiated job quotas (Philadelphia Plan, faculty "goals and timetables") and it was the McGovern's political aides who publicized and advocated what surely seemed like a quota system in the Democratic delegate selection system—until it was decided that "quota" was a bad word, at which point it was decided to keep the plan and deny the word.

There is a fascinating question germinating from all this that begs an answer: *Was it the disruptions, the violence and the demonstrations that poisoned "round two" of the civil rights movement?*

The question is moot, but the guess here is not much. The disruptions obviously didn't help, but the "round two" programs were inherently unacceptable. Consider this data from a series of Harris polls:

Q. Do you feel that blacks in this country have tried to move too fast, too slow, or at about the right pace?

	1966	1968	1969	Late 1972
Too fast	63%	61%	53%	47%
Too slow	8%	9%	15%	13%
About right pace	16%	20%	17%	31%

(Harris)

The data can be read in many ways on many levels. On the one hand, the liberalization of attitudes continued right through the years of rage. On the other hand, the liberalizing trend moved most slowly when disruption was most apparent (1966–68) and that may be said to have slowed it down. Then, as the Panthers turned tame (1969–72), not only did the "too fast" sentiment continue sinking but the "about right pace" sentiments climbed most dramatically.

Looking at the progression it seems likely that at least *no lasting damage had been done either to the civil rights cause in America or to the direction of attitudinal change in America.* As with the Women's Lib and the Peace Movement, Americans were able to sort out substance from style, although they often might attribute their views to certain forms of incivility. In no instance did violent, obnoxious or excessive behavior help the cause of civil rights. It often hurt. But usually the hurt was temporary, and Americans were sophisticated enough to judge issues on their merits.

On balance, in a complex situation, this seems to be about where we are as we move toward the middle of the Seventies: White Americans have changed their views about blacks in the last dozen momentous years. The trend is clearly toward liberalization, and it has progressed *despite* a *distaste* for peaceful round-one demonstrations and an outright *abhorrence* of round-two disruption and violence. Americans, to their credit, have changed their views about blacks in the last dozen momentous years. one hand from the off-the-pigs hoopla on the other.

But just as Americans were able to separate their views on progress from their views on disruption, so are they able to make clear-cut distinctions as to what *kind* of progress they want—and what kind of activity they regard as regress even if the civil rights activists claim it is progress.

White Americans have pretty well bought the proposition that they must be *fair* to blacks. That may not sound like much, but after three hundred years of deep-seated *unfairness* it is an important move forward. Blacks (say whites) deserve every opportunity under law to compete equally in American life. In those instances where special treatment is required to bring disadvantaged blacks *up to the starting line* (i.e., job training), that's fine too.

But there are two major caveats that go with the new Fairness Doctrine, and it is in these caveats that many white Americans part company with at least some of the views of some of the civil rights Cause People. And in a sense, as we shall see, the two caveats are really one.

Caveat one: *Fair yes, unfair no.* The public feels that welfare is not fair if people who don't work seem to earn almost as much as people who do work. Quotas are not regarded as fair if an unqualified man gets a job and a qualified man doesn't, or even if one qualified man doesn't get a job because another qualified man, who is black, gets it because of his race. Scatter-site housing is not regarded as fair because it turns a middle-class neighborhood into a partially lower-class neighborhood when the people in the middle-class neighborhood had moved there or settled there precisely to get away from lower-class neighborhoods. Ditto busing. People moved into middle-class neighborhoods in large part in order to send their kids to middle-class schools; busing the kids back to where and what they moved from is not regarded as fair.

Busing and scatter-site housing also raise a second caveat: *no exposure to violence*. This caveat may well be stronger and even more potent than the Caveat of Unfair. To many Americans a low-income development in the neighborhood or sending a child into a low-income neighborhood means the same thing: *exposure to violence*. If there is one non-negotiable demand that has been set forth by the Massive Majority Middle Class that's it: Thou shalt not mug.

So here we are: As seen by a vast majority of Americans, they will accept reasonable demands or programs designed and promoted to implement *Fair*. But when the Movement goes, even unwittingly, into *unfair* or, even less wittingly, toward *exposure to violence*, an attitudinal stone wall is encountered.

The two ideas are intertwined. They both mean—in different ways— only this: *I'm for it if it doesn't hurt me.*

These attitudinal strictures, when viewed by civil rights activists, lead sometimes to the catchall phrase "white racism." Antibusers, antiwelfare, antiquotas, antiscatter-site equal racism, we are told: ethnic, beer-swigging, pot-bellied, raw, stonewall racism. And if that is the stone wall, we are told, then civil rights progress has been dead-ended.

That is incorrect.

Beneath the broad rubric of Fair there are tools and tactics to both continue the liberalization of racial attitudes and to achieve major substantive gain in the years to come, much the same kind of gain now sought by the civil rights movement.

The doctrine of Fair is broad and deep, deeper than ever before in American history. It includes today, for example, the electability of a black mayor in a predominantly white city even after law-and-order is raised as an issue (Los Angeles, 1973). The doctrine of Fair includes today the policy of open enrollments in public colleges, to a point where in a few short years the percentage of young blacks in college is now very close to the percentage of young whites in college. And the doctrine of Fair includes the truly remarkable changes wrought in the American labor movement in recent years to a point where apprenticeships are now disproportionately going to blacks.

It is to this last item—jobs—that we must look when we look ahead to further progress in America. Jobs, coming well under the doctrine of Fair, ironically, yield up the same sort of *results* that have been rejected under other rubrics. Blacks with decent jobs, middle-class blacks, don't need welfare. They don't need the artificial integration of scatter-sitism—they can buy their way into decent neighborhoods, black or white. Middle-class blacks, living in good neighborhoods black or white, neither need nor want busing—they want good schools and they have the wherewithal to get them. And middle-class blacks don't need quotas—they got decent jobs on merit, and received those jobs with all the psychic pride that goes with it.

Of course, the 1963 March on Washington was called "the March for Jobs and Freedom." Since that time blacks have gained many jobs and much freedom. But instead of pursuing that successful strategy with a single-minded dedication, the civil rights movement diluted it with emphasis on—among other things—busing, scatter-site housing, welfare and quotas.

In short, a successful strategy working smoothly within the now acceptable attitude of Fair was diluted by a strategy that crosses over the line of attitudinal acceptance, a strategy perceived of as unfair and one that often gets hopelessly tangled with fear of violence.

Fortunately, it is not too late. The guess here is that the laws of social gravity will be redirecting the civil rights movement back into the path of least resistance and most progress. There will be a Round Three in the civil rights struggle in America, and it will look more like Round One than Round Two. It will deal with jobs; jobs, gained via education and training; jobs yielding money; jobs and money proving that economic integration leads to almost everything else.

Just when the bell for Round Three will ring no one knows. But herewith some thoughts about it: When the bell rings it will remind us all of the still long way to go. It will be soon. And it will probably ring shortly after a well-publicized effort from the black community to curb black crime. Round Three, in short, will be fair and will not expose anyone to violence.

CHAPTER 19

The New Culture / Youth

Remember the counterculture?

Smoke dope. Take over the campus. Free speech, no censorship. Stop repression. America is hung up. Let it all hang out. Be relevant. Don't conform.

If there are less popular ideas afloat they are hard to find. The root idea of a sick society caused by the distorted values of small-minded traditionalism is overwhelmingly rejected by the overwhelming majority of Americans.

Consider that snappy phrase, "the drug culture," which enjoyed a brief day in the hip sun. Consider even marijuana, the most innocuous and harmless drug. In 1973, a Gallup poll showed that by 78%–16% Americans opposed legalization. For hard drugs, of course, sentiment is far tougher. In 1973, Gallup found that by better than 2 to 1 (67%–29%) Americans approved Governor Rockefeller's plan of *life imprisonment without possibility of parole for sellers of hard drugs*.

Or consider that dazzling idea that students needed a little more freedom on campus. At about the apogee of publicity about that notion (mid-'69) Gallup reported that by 70%–25% the public said *no* to the question "Do you think college students should or should not have a greater say in the running of colleges?" For students who got so relevant that they broke a few antiquated laws, the public was even harsher. The Gallup question was "Do you think college students who break laws while participating in campus demonstations should be expelled?" And the public's response (also in 1969) was 82%–7% "yes." The magazine *Seventeen* asked *young people* in 1971, "Should police or National Guard be called during a demonstration where damage or violence occurs?" And the response was only 95%–5% "yes."

Or consider "repression." That was a handy code word for a while, often hawked along with "underground" newspapers—on public street corners. Gallup in 1971 asked, "Some people say that personal freedom and the right of dissent are curbed in the United States. Do you agree or disagree?" Almost two thirds of the public (64%) disagreed, while only 27% agreed.

How about sex? There's been a sexual revolution, everyone knows that. But of what kind? The evidence is not at all clear.

Gallup asked in 1969 for approval/disapproval for "a man and a woman to have sexual relations before marriage?"—and got a 68% "no" response, indicating a high degree of traditionalism. Astonishingly, in 1937—more than thirty years earlier—a Roper-Fortune poll asked a similar question and got only a 57% "no," 21% "yes" and 7% "all right for men only." In other words, sexual attitudes were somewhat more liberal in the thirties than in 1969! Gallup then polled again in 1973 and found a striking 20% drop from the 1969 data in the "no" percentage, down to 48%. Score one for the "sexual revolution," albeit a little late in the game.[1]

But these are data about "attitudes." Some recent independent studies about sexual *behavior* seem to show that perhaps aspects of the "sexual revolution" have either been oversold, underperformed or not very revolutionary. A term of Johns Hopkins social scientists, John F. Kanter and Melvin Zelnik, found in a 1971 survey that two out of three American girls of age eighteen were still virgins. And while comparable historical trends are inexact, one analyst, sociologist Phillip Cutright of Indiana University, has examined the evidence and written ". . . the extent to which unmarried people are sexually active today may not have increased very much after all . . . the image of an abstinent past and a promiscuous present is highly exaggerated." There is other survey data (particularly a late 1973 study presented in *Playboy*) that tends to point toward a growing liberalization, but, in general, one factor should be remembered: The back seats of automobiles and the farmer's-daughter stories existed long before relaxed campus parietal rules came into being. Such observant chroniclers of the American scene as F. Scott Fitzgerald, John O'Hara, Thomas Wolfe and Ernest Hemingway dealt with themes of sex outside of marriage. So did Grace Metalious. And so did the Bible. And from 1964 to 66, before the onslaught of the sexual revolution, 23% of all *legitimate* first

[1] The strictures against *extramarital* sex as opposed to *premarital* sex remain very strong. Here is what a National Opinion Research Center (University of Chicago) study showed in 1973 about "a married person having sexual relations with someone other than the marriage partner":

Always wrong	70%
Almost always wrong	15%
Wrong only sometimes	12%
Not wrong at all	4%

births occurred to women married less than eight months! In addition, in those years, 17% of the total births in the United States were illegitimate.

Also, central to the notion of a "youth culture" or a "counterculture" is the idea of rejection of authority—parental, societal, academic, etc. In 1972, the University of Michigan pollsters did a survey of *young Americans aged eleven to eighteen*. And here is one of the statements presented to the panel:

Q. The world would be a better place if people had more respect for authority.

Strongly disagree	3%
Somewhat disagree	11%
Undecided	11%
Somewhat agree	35% (!)
Strongly agree	40% (!)

All that the permissive generation really seemed to want is a strong guiding hand!

To give some further flavor to the idea that young people in America aren't so terribly different from the rest of us, consider the data from Harris in 1971, concerning the "most admired" persons. The four persons most frequently mentioned by young Americans were not Bob Dylan, or Paul Goodman or Abby Hoffman, or the Beatles or Mick Jagger or Janis Joplin. They were:

MOST ADMIRED

Robert F. Kennedy	Neil Armstrong (!)
Bill Cosby	John Wayne (!) (!)

The "least admired" list was also very interesting. The four people on the bottom were not Spiro Agnew, Lyndon Johnson, Richard Nixon, Hubert Humphrey—Establishment all. They were:

LEAST ADMIRED

Fidel Castro	George Wallace
Eldridge Cleaver	Ho Chi Minh

And we could go on and on. Americans endorse the "work ethic"; Americans endorse "traditional marriage"—a Minnesota poll in May 1973 puts the affirmative rating at 85%. Americans condemn pornography, permissiveness and homosexual marriage. In fact it would seem that the public doesn't want to have any truck at all with the greening of America. They would apparently prefer to see a squaring of America.

But that, too, is too simple. By far, Americans aren't squares, even if they are not for pot, disorder, casual sex, pornography or Eldridge Cleaver. In fact, Americans have absorbed a good deal of the ethic and the style of the youth culture, hard as that may be to believe after the data just presented.

Thus, for what it's worth, there is some data concerning the changing attitudes toward dress and appearance. A Roper poll taken in late 1971 showed a major degree of acceptance toward a number of new fashions that some years earlier had been frowned upon. In large measure these now-acceptable fashions are the ones that were considered "mod" although a few of the "hippie" styles have crept in as well.

At acceptance levels of 50% or greater were these nice things:

	Like	Don't like
Pants suits for women	76%	11%
More colorful clothes for men	62%	18%
Miniskirts	51%	28%
Wide ties for men	50%	20%

Any society that quickly appreciates the merits of the miniskirt can't be all bad.

On a second level of acceptance, barely in a plurality, Roper found these items:

	Like	Don't like
Hot pants	41%	36%
Sideburns, longer hair on men	40%	34%
Mustaches on men	35%	31%

On a third level, here are items that are still generally disapproved, although the vote is close.

	Like	Don't like
Midiskirts	31%	31%
Steel-rimmed or Granny glasses	27%	39%
Maxiskirts	25%	42%
Faded dungarees	24%	37%
Beards on men	23%	46%

Our guess is that in the couple of years since that survey was taken, the ratings of most of those items have moved toward substantially more favorable ratings—with the possible exception of the midiskirt, which doesn't deserve a favorable rating.

And finally, alas, two style trends were soundly rejected:

	Like	Don't like
The braless look for women	14%	63%
See-through blouses for women	13%	63%

In any event, a considerable degree of change from the days when sideburns and long hair were regarded as the stigmata of a drug addict.

Changing dress and hair styles, of course, represent symbolic more than substantive change, and there is a good deal of symbolic co-optation going on. Is it particularly significant if a forty-five-year-old, white, racist, rural, Alabama sheriff no longer wears a crew cut, if he still *thinks* like a racist Alabama sheriff? If baseball players and hockey players wear their hair to their shoulders but still think about women in what Feminists would view as sexist terms, what's changed other than hair style? What's changed if a businessman with wide lapels and flared trousers votes for Richard Nixon?

But if the new culture is seen as a force for anti-traditionalism, then consider this data, which goes far deeper than simple co-optation and deeply into a change of substance, not style, or symbol.

Q. Did you, yourself, happen to attend church in the last seven days?

	Yes	Change from first year
1958	49%	—
1959	47%	−2%
1960	47%	−2%
1961	47%	−2%
1962	47%	−3%
1963	46%	−3%
1964	45%	−4%
1965	44%	−5%
1966	44%	−5%
1967	43%	−6%
1968	43%	−6%
1970	42%	−7%
1971	40%	−9%
1972	40%	−9%
1973	40%	−9%

(Gallup, December 1973)

This data is particularly solid: the identical question has been asked by the same pollster each year for many years, a rare occurrence in the polling business. Moreover, to gain a year-round average and yet account for seasonal differences Gallup has tacked the question on to several surveys during each year. The recent samples actually totaled 3,997 persons, almost three times as large as a normal sample.

Accordingly, the fluctuations in the percentages can be regarded as more significant than in other instances where the swings are not massive.

What the data shows has happened is this: In the last part of the 1950s churchgoing rates fluctuated just below the 50% mark. A slow decline ensued during the next few years, taking the rate down to the mid-40 percentiles. The slide continued and in fact accelerated in the years of the late Sixties and the early Seventies and has now possibly flattened out.

The actual decrease of 9 percentage points over the thirteen-year 1958–71 period doesn't perhaps seem like much—but it is. What it means, speaking relatively, is this: For every *five* people who went to church in a given week in 1958, only *four* people went a decade later.

If we are looking for a change in traditional values we should also note that the decline of churchgoing has been most sharp among the traditionalist major religious group in America: Catholics. In 1955, just about three in four Catholics went to church in a given week (74%). By 1973, the rate had fallen to 55%—a decline of 19%! Catholics, then, are still more likely to be churchgoers than Protestants, but the rates are far closer than they used to be.

Something else about religious feeling in America also ought to be noted here. Ours has been a very religious nation, by whatever standard, absolute or relative, one chooses to test. In 1964, Gallup asked Americans, "Do you ever pray? About how often: frequently, occasionally or seldom?" The responses showed 63% "frequently" and 25% "occasionally," with only 6% "seldom" and 6% "never."

A series of 1968 international comparisons by Gallup showed that, of the nations surveyed, America had the highest rates of churchgoing, Americans were most likely to believe in God, and Americans were most likely to believe in life after death.

When, in 1968, 43% of Americans reported that they went to church during the previous week, responses from other nations ranged from roughly the same in the Netherlands (42%), to substantially lower in West Germany (27%) and in France (25%), to starkly lower in Norway (14%) and in Finland (5%).

Here are the responses for the belief-in-God and life-after-death questions:

	Do you believe in God?	*Do you believe in life after death?*
United States	98%	73%
Greece	96%	57%
Uruguay (cities)	89%	42%
Austria	85%	38%
Switzerland	84%	50%
Finland	83%	55%
West Germany	81%	41%
Netherlands	79%	50%
Great Britain	77%	38%
France	73%	35%
Norway	73%	54%
Sweden	60%	38%

(Gallup, 1968)

That was 1968. Three years later, the *73%* figure believing in life after death had changed in the Gallup poll to *53%*. And the belief in God looked this way:

Q. Which of the statements comes closest to your religious beliefs? (on card)

A. There is a personal God. 40%

There is some kind of spirit or vital force in the world. 37%

I am not sure there is a God or vital force. 9%

I am sure there is no God or vital force. 11%

No response 3%

(Gallup, 1971)

Still a pretty theistic nation, but at a far lower rate than the 98% recorded in 1968, even if one adds the "personal God" and "vital force" answers to get to 77% or, for that matter, even if one throws in the 9% "not sure."

An even surer index of the changing role of religion in American life can be gleaned from this question asked by Gallup:

Q. At the present time, do you think religion as a whole is increasing its influence on American life, or losing its influence?

To see one of the fastest turnabouts in public opinion polling, consider this astonishing trend line:

	Losing influence	Increasing influence
1957	14%	69%
1962	31%	45%
1965	45%	33%
1967	57%	23%
1968	67%	18%
1969	70%	14%
1970	75%	14%

Toward the end of the Fifties, five out of six Americans thought that religion was gaining influence. By the end of the Sixties, five out of six Americans thought religion was losing influence.

These results are not in any way to be seen as *approval* of the loss of influence of religion.

In fact, as we shall see later, exactly the opposite is the case. Americans, more religiously oriented than most folk, are deeply disturbed about the declining role of religion. By about 3 to 1 they opposed the Supreme Court's ruling against prayer in public schools. But despite their concern about religion's diminishing role, they do indeed recognize that it is diminishing. And it diminished at just about the time when the "new" culture dawned, an aggressively anti-traditional culture, an anti-square culture that even seemed to have a branch office in organized religion itself where clergymen preached on Vietnam and racism, burned draft records, and asked, "Is God dead?" all to the beat of *Jesus Christ Superstar*.[2]

Americans, in short, generally scorned the new culture, scorned the secularization of religion—but acknowledged its impact, as the author, too, acknowledges its impact.

There is another signpost of some headway for the youth culture— the attitudes of youth themselves. We have pointed out in this volume in several places that young people are not a breed apart and that "the generation gap" has been vastly overstated and often confused with class differences. Thus, in some sorts of Vietnam questions youth were more hawkish than their elders. The percentage of youth for Wallace was somewhat *above* the population as a whole. Young people were for McGovern and for amnesty by only about 10% more than their elders. They feel a need for authority and discipline. John Wayne and Neil

[2] Harris found in 1970 that 31% of the public "would like never to deal with clergy- men who keep telling me I have to be for the poor."

Armstrong were two of the four "most admired men" by young Americans. And in April of 1972, Lou Harris began his newspaper column this way: "'The generation gap' has come to be a popular cliché, but recent results from Harris surveys indicate that on many issues the generations are not necessarily apart." Still even if there is no maxi-gap, there is at least a mini-gap, and, in the instance of cultural issues and issues of "morals," perhaps even a midi-gap.

Consider, for example, the marijuana situation. A 1973 Gallup poll showed that 16% of the public thought marijuana should be legalized. But this over-all figure masked some splits by age groups. Only 7% of Americans over fifty wanted legalization. For the age group thirty to forty-nine, the percentage favoring legalization was 11%. But for the youngest age group, eighteen to twenty-nine, the percentage favorable was 34%. Now, that's still only a third of all young people, but it's also much greater than the rates for the older population.

Or consider even more dramatic evidence of generational difference released by the Minnesota poll in 1972. Unlike the Gallup data, the Minnesota data had an age cross-tabulation for the eighteen to twenty-four group, younger still than Gallup's eighteen to twenty-nine breakdown, and this tended to magnify the differentials.

The Minnesota poll asked if "the law should allow any type of sexual act, including homosexual acts, between consenting adults?" By 65%–31%, the general public said "no"—and by 62%–33%, the youngest age group said "yes."

Similarly, by 68%–27%, the public as a whole agrees that "exposure to pornography harms the morals of young people," but by 58%–39%, young Minnesotans *disagree*.

Harris, too, has found some important differentials between young people and their elders. In 1971, a Harris survey showed 75% of the public feeling that it was not "healthy for young people to try to avoid the draft." The corresponding figure for age sixteen to twenty was 60%, a good bit lower.

Harris also found particularly sharp divergences among *college students* during the "radicalization" year of 1970. By a count of 81%–17%, students said that "until the older generation comes to understand the new priorities and life style among the young, serious conflict is going to continue." The same students reported that their parents' attitude to the same statement would be 50%–44% approval, a swing of 31%, which is a healthy swing indeed.

Now, the college community, it must be stressed, is quite different from the universe of "all-youth." In recent years no more than about 25%–

30% of "all-youth" aged eighteen to twenty-four were "in college" at a given moment. As registration experts working for Senator McGovern's campaign found out in 1972, "college youth" tended to be registered and to prefer McGovern; noncollege youth were less likely to be registered and tended to prefer Nixon. One reason for this disparity was apparently the college experience itself. Harris' 1970 poll of college students showed that *31%* considered themselves "liberal" or "far left" when they first entered college, while *52%* rated themselves that way when the survey was taken.

This non-representativeness of college youth ought to be borne in mind as we consider the next, and quite remarkable, batch of data.

Pollster Daniel Yankelovich has been surveying America's college community with regularity since 1965. During the four seminal years of 1968, 1969, 1970 and 1971, his interviewers were out in the field with a series of probing questions designed to shed light on the changes that occurred during those turbulent times.

It is Yankelovich's view that for a period of time there were *two* revolutions going on at the same time on America's campuses—a cultural revolution and a political one. During the most tense years of the Vietnam war, these two movements were linked.

But as the war faded, Yankelovich believes, the two separate strains became "unlinked."

The political revolution has faded, says Yankelovich. Thus, in 1970, the year of Cambodia and Kent, *67%* of college students felt that "campus radicalism" was continuing to grow. Just a year later, in 1971, only 34% thought "campus radicalism" was continuing to grow. (And, today, campus activism is more likely to concern streaking than striking.)

In 1970, more than half (53%) of American college students "strongly agreed" that "basically, we are a racist nation." A year later, in 1971, that percentage had shrunk to 37%. Yankelovich also demonstrates that students were less critical of America's major institutions in 1971 than in 1970. Perhaps most significantly, Yankelovich asked students to contrast their present mood with the way they felt a year ago. Out of twenty items, the one with the greatest gain (+49%) was "involved in your own private life and concerns." And the biggest loser (−32%) was "accepting of violence as a legitimate tactic to achieve desired social change."

But what about cultural indicators? The Yankelovich data seems to indicate that far from returning to normal, things are going the other way on campus.

Thus, Yankelovich asked a series of questions about *"which . . . activities do you feel are morally wrong from your own personal point of view."* Consider the responses dealing with sexual behavior:

ACTIVITIES SEEN AS MORALLY WRONG
(COLLEGE STUDENTS)

	1969	1971
Extramarital sexual relations	77%	57%
Relations between consenting homosexuals	42%	25%
Casual premarital sexual relations	34%	25%

Values changing—liberalizing—before our very eyes. But note that these are not data on *behavior* but on *opinion* about behavior. Thus, the numbers concerning extra-marital and pre-marital sex do not necessarily contradict the earlier data presented here, which suggested that perhaps the degree of sexual *activity* may not have increased as rapidly as prophets of the sexual revolution have preached. What the numbers do say is that pre-marital and extra-marital sex are not as condemned as they once were. Sex is more *open*—and that is, in itself, a very great change and quite in keeping with the counterculture precept to do away with hang-ups, both public and private. Accordingly, college students want:

MORE ACCEPTANCE OF SEXUAL FREEDOM

	1969	1971
Would welcome	43%	56%

And about religion:

Q. Belonging to some organized religion is important in a person's life:

	1969	1971
Believe	42%	35%

—the trend is away from organized religion.
And about marriage itself:

Q. Marriage is obsolete

	1969	1970	1971
Agree	24%	28%	34%

—still only a third, but up from a quarter in two years.
And about work:

Q. Hard work will always pay off:

Percentage Agreeing

1968	69%
1969	56%
1971	39% (!)

—an occupational fatalism.
And about technology:

VALUE CHANGES STUDENTS WOULD WELCOME

Q. More emphasis on technological improvements

	1969	*1971*
Would welcome	56%	39%

—the ogre is technology; it depersonalizes and pollutes.
And about authority:

ACCEPTANCE OF SOCIAL RESTRAINTS

	1968	*1971*	*Change*
Prohibition against marijuana			
"accept easily"	55%	42%	−13%
Power and authority of the boss in a work situation			
"accept easily"	56%	36%	−20%
Outward conformity for the sake of career advancement			
"accept easily"	29%	15%	−14%
Abiding by laws you don't agree with			
"accept easily"	29%	13%	−16%

It appears then, as if American college youth were indeed greening during the late 1960s and early seventies. The Yankelovich data, incidentally, are generally verifiable by some other studies of collegiate attitudes. Moreover, Yankelovich maintains that the relaxation of cultural norms continues today.

So a key question arises as we attempt to assay the direction of cultural change in America: Are college youth the cutting edge of change? Do the students change society? Or, perhaps, does society change the students?

Of course, no one knows the answer. But before anyone automatically assumes that students' views are inexorably the wave of the future—Yankelovich indeed has termed the activist segment of the student body, "the forerunners"—we ought to examine some of the new culture notions more carefully.

Consider extramarital sex. A young man in college today may see nothing wrong with it—43% of college students saw nothing morally wrong with it, as the 1971 Yankelovich data shows. But will that young man feel the same way ten years hence when he considers extramarital sex in the context of *his wife and the men in her life?*

Will he consider marriage obsolete—after he gets married?[3]

Will he maintain that "hard work doesn't pay off," when it becomes patently apparent that in whatever field he enters—including legal aid for the poor or lobbying for environmental protection—hard work *does* pay off.

Will he find no place for organized religion in his life when he has to make a decision about whether to enroll his child in Sunday school?

Will he not easily accept "the power and authority of the boss" when his only real choice is to easily accept it, or reluctantly accept it?

Will he sacrifice a job promotion on the alter of rejection of "outward conformity," if the job promotion means he can afford a vacation trip or afford to send his child to a good college where the child can, in turn, be an activist "forerunner"?

Society is a harsh master. It can be changed over time, but it also changes people as they mature, as they leave home and as they leave the university.

Precisely this thought was raised by a Harris survey question in a 1973 release:

Q. Do you feel that this generation of young people will remain different in their manners, styles and tastes when they are past thirty or will most change and not be much different from other generations of adults?

A. Be like other generations *69%*

Yankelovich sees a different process. He quotes Whitehead: "Great ideas often enter reality in strange guises and with disgusting alliances,"[4] and then asks:

Might the college student movement conceivably harbor an idea of [comparable] importance? *Should its claim to transform our moral sensibilities and national life styles be taken seriously? Are we witness-*

---

[3] American youth are getting married a little older, but there has been no apparent decline in the percentage who marry.

[4] Alfred North Whitehead, *Adventures of Ideas,* MacMillan, 1956.

ing the growth of an authentic and, in the European sense of the word, *serious* movement in American history, or merely a nervous spasm elicited in response to the nervous-making events of our time?[5]

Based on his studies and surveys, Yankelovich concludes that "the movement *does* harbor a great idea and that idea has entered current American reality in many strange and misleading guises . . . the cultural revolution—the new naturalism will continue to grow at an ever-increasing tempo . . . the cultural revolution gathers strength and spreads from the university to the rest of the country."

Which now raises this question: Is there necessarily a conflict between the view of the public (as expressed in the preceding Harris poll) that the kids will change and be like other generations and the view articulated by Yankelovich that the counterculture will change America?

There is a single point that this section about changing student values has been leading to; there is a single point that the larger chapter on the new culture has been leading to; and there is a single point that this entire section about American attitudes toward the entire Cause Era has been leading to. It is this: *There is no necessary conflict between the view that the public is changing and the view that the public is also a changer*. There is a synthesis going on—Americans have adopted some of what the movement has advocated and/or publicized. But at the same time the public has set up a stone wall against other changes advocated by the Cause People. And in the chapter that follows we shall detail that the *general public* has an agenda of its own, about which it demands action. And just as it has changed, so too does it change society in its direction.

Change in America is not a one-way street. When citizens feel that America "is on the wrong track," all the solutions are not going to come from one generalized viewpoint. The public's view of what's wrong in America sometimes coincides with the counterculture and yet often vigorously rejects it. Some of what Yankelovich calls "the new naturalism" makes a good deal of sense—and some of it is pernicious (as Yankelovich acknowledges). People sense both the wisdom and the foolishness. Americans are attempting to separate fad from substance and judge substance on its merits. So far they have done a pretty good job, which is only a shorthand for saying that the author tends to agree with many of their choices.

Some time ago in this volume the score was toted up in the running argument with the Failure and Guilt Complex. It was noted that objective data refuted the notions of failure, and we credited our side with one point. It was then noted subsequently that in the attitudinal arena

---

[5] "The New Naturalism," essay by Daniel Yankelovich, appearing in *The Changing Values on Campus*, a survey for the JDR 3rd Fund by Daniel Yankelovich, Inc.

Americans felt *personally* satisfied and not "fed up," and determined that the score was now 2–0. Now it has been noted that, nationally, Americans are deeply concerned about the *society*. In some ways they agree with the Movement conception of what went wrong. And in some respects there is profound disagreement with the Cause People. The score has changed. Let's split the difference. It is now 2½–½, and the contest continues.

CHAPTER 20

What Bothers the Public

There are three basic issues that have been bothering the Massive Majority Middle Class in recent years. Two are quite specific. One is quite general. And they are related.

INFLATION

Inflation bothers the hell out of Americans. This is so even in years when real income, after counting for inflation, goes way *up* as has been the case in most of the post-war years in America. It is particularly bothersome when real income doesn't go up too much. And it is maddeningly inflammatory when, as in the first quarter of 1974, it actually picks pockets by devaluing dollars by more than the prevalent wage increase patterns.

Inflation bothers wives as they watch pennies and then dimes mount inexorably on the price of hamburgers, lettuce, gasoline, steak, bread and milk. It bothers husbands when wives say they need more money. It bothers wives when husbands say they are spending too much money. It bothers anyone on a fairly fixed income. It bothers businessmen and stock brokers. It gives people a feeling that society isn't working; they labor hard at their jobs, and they seem to have little to show for it. It is, in fact, one of the most corrosive of modern dilemmas. Except for a few low-inflation years, and except for flash-perception problems like "energy," inflation has been almost always near or at the top of the Gallup "number one problem" ratings. If inflation stays as bad as it's been in late 1973 and early 1974, if it becomes an ongoing, high-level, permanent part of our lives, a 10% year-in-year-out affair, it seems to be the one issue visible now that could possibly poison the atmosphere of the mid-1970s.

That's what optimists say about it. Pessimists think it's really severe.

The grim scenario is this: Liberal economists have traditionally felt that some inflation was not such a bad thing. It eroded real income to some extent, but if income gains outstripped inflation, the net result could still be salutary. People in certain sorts of "pockets" got hurt, but they too could be protected; for example, those in the "fixed income" pocket of Social Security could be helped if Social Security payments were raised (and they were, substantially). Studies in the Fifties and Sixties showed that poor people were not hurt proportionately more than rich people by inflation.[1] Moreover, they were helped by the inflation-induced tight labor market which boosted wages. Furthermore, the "tax of inflation" was the trade-off to the "tax of unemployment" which *did* fall disproportionately on the poor.

Now, some liberal economists are having other thoughts as they assess what they see to be a new kind of inflation during a very special situation that might, or might not, prove to be a pattern for the future. The impact of inflation in 1973 fell somewhat heavier on the poor than on the non-poor.[2] Unemployment did not sink much, and then rose a little. In the first quarter of '74, inflation ran ahead of wage increases. New factors were involved. The key price increases this time involved fuel, other imported raw materials and food. As Charles Schultze of the Brookings Institution points out, it was no longer simply a question of juggling money from one pocket to another. Much of the monies for fuel and other imported raw materials headed overseas. The food money went from urban to rural areas. And the non-rural wage earners were being honestly hurt.

The opinion polls seemed to echo these conditions. *In the Watergate year of 1973, it was inflation that Gallup pollsters found to be the Number-One Issue.*

How long this situation would last, no one knew. Most economists thought a general rectification would occur. A healthy economy would shape up, would produce the goods to fulfill demand, which would reduce inflationary levels to reasonable, if still high, levels.

But some doubts remained. If 8% or 10% inflation came to be seen as "normal" it could spiral, with wage demands and price levels keyed to this new "normality," triggering still further inflation, rising up to "Latin America" levels. Very scary.

The fact is, *no one knows for sure*. A generation of economists who thought they could "fine-tune" the economy, and did so admirably for quite a while, now acknowledge that the new complicated equations of resources, environment, international situations and new legislation are, for the moment, too much for anyone to be sure of anything just yet. Conservative economists apparently prepared to accept soaring unemployment

[1] R. G. Hollister and J. L. Palmer, "The Impact of Inflation on the Poor."
[2] Staff study, Joint Economic Committee, Congress of the United States, 1974.

are even less helpful. What both have learned, along with every working politician in America, is an attitudinal if not an economic truth: That the new-style, high-level inflation is wholly unacceptable to almost all Americans.

CRIME

And then there is *crime*. Without question the other specific issue that in the last ten years or so has bugged Americans more deeply than any other is *crime* and its related phenomena: violence, disruption, drugs. Civil rights was the number-one problem for several years. Then Vietnam was the number-one issue for a few years. But crime—since the mid-'60s —rolls on endlessly, bothering, irking, scaring and arousing Americans, hovering always near the top of the scale of issues. Actual numbers vary depending on whether one talks about "the nation's number-one problem" or "the nation's number-one domestic problem" or "your community's number-one problem." But all ways of measuring show one common result—a very high level of concern.

The Gallup analysts have written that,

> Worry over crime and lawlessness came into prominence in early *1965* and by the time of the *1968* presidential election had become the number one domestic concern of voters.

And by April of *1972,* after political pundits had dismissed law-and-order as an over-the-hill problem, Gallup's news release was headlined, "GROWING FEAR OF CRIME COULD BECOME NUMBER ONE ISSUE IN NOVEMBER ELECTION."

In January of *1973,* a Gallup news release began this way, "With crime now far and away the number one concern of residents of the nations cities . . ."

In *March of 1973,* the California poll read like this:

CRIME AND FEAR OF CRIME NUMBER ONE
COMMUNITY PROBLEM IN CALIFORNIA

In the minds of Californians, crime and the fear of crime looms as the number-one community problem, surpassing such other public concerns as taxes, drug abuse, the cost of living, unemployment, education and ecological problems.

That California poll showed that 35% of the respondents listed crime as the number-one problem in 1973—the comparable figure in 1972 was 29%. Furthermore, in 1973, an additional 16% of the respondents cited "drugs, drug abuse" as the number-one problem. An additional 6% cited "juvenile delinquency"—a grand total of 57% viewing criminal activity of one sort or another as the number-one problem.

And by *June of 1973,* the Harris survey reported that America's concern about crime was not just an abstraction but attached itself to specifics as well:

MAJORITY OF AMERICANS NOW
FAVOR CAPITAL PUNISHMENT

Despite recent rulings of the U. S. Supreme Court virtually outlawing the death penalty, a majority of the country believes in capital punishment, 59%–31%. *This marks a sharp increase in sentiment supporting the death penalty,* up from a much closer 47%–42% in 1970.

(This tallies pretty well with a referendum vote in California in 1972: Pro-death penalty, 67.5%, against death penalty, 32.5%.)

And the fear is personal:

Q. Is there any area right around here—that is, within a mile—where you would be afraid to walk alone at night?

	1968	1972
Yes, afraid	31%	41%
Women	44%	58% (!)

(Gallup)

In November of 1973 a Yankelovich poll for the New York *Times* showed that crime was the number-one problem in New York, a city that was once regarded as the most liberal in America.

Cross tabulations show the fear to be particularly high in big cities and particularly high among blacks, as this survey in Louisville, Kentucky, showed:

A REAL PROBLEM IN THIS NEIGHBORHOOD—CRIME
Roper Poll—Louisville, 1970

	Negroes	Whites
Breaking into houses	59%	48%
Drunkenness	54%	21%
Gambling	52%	3%
Drug use among youths	38%	14%
Purse snatchings	36%	14%
Prostitution	33%	4%
Knifings and shootings	32%	4%
Muggings	17%	4%
Loan sharking	6%	2%
None or don't know	14%	34%

Americans are also pro-blue. Talk of "police brutality," "pigs," and "repression" has fallen on almost totally deaf ears. A 1970 Harris survey asked respondents to check words and phrases on a card that accurately expressed their feelings about cops. The *highest* six ratings were:

Dedicated	50%
Hard-working	48%
Interested in helping fellow men	42%
Courageous	38%
Intelligent	29%
Kind	21%

And the *lowest* six words were:

Corrupt	9%
Incompetent	9%
Lazy	8%
Violent	6%
Do-gooder	6%
Sadistic	2%
Creative	—

The public's view of the FBI was also highly positive. A 1971 Harris poll showed that by 81%–13% Americans agreed that "the FBI has done a first rate job of protecting the security of the United States for many years," by 71%–14% agreed that "J. Edgar Hoover has done a good job in catching subversives for many years now," and by 61%–28% agreed that "the FBI has done an effective job in cracking down on organized crime," which was not quite the view of the Cause People—at least not until Watergate showed that Hoover was really a member of the ACLU in wolf's clothing.[3]

Nor does the American public buy the idea that crime is lessening. In 1973, this is what a Gallup poll showed:

Q.   Is there more crime in this area than there was a year ago, or less?

A.	More	51%
	Less	10%
	Same	27%
	No opinion	12%

(Gallup, 1973)

---

[3] Gallup's latest 1973 data on the FBI shows a sharp drop from 84% to 52% in the "highly favorable" category from 1965 to 1973. And should the *new* FBI director decide to burn some more Watergate evidence, it will go even lower. Interestingly, however, the combined "highly favorable" and "mildly favorable" ratings ran to 85% in the 1973 survey.

The American public feels strongly that our courts are too lenient with criminals—"stop coddling criminals" is the popular argot. Here is a mixture of Gallup and Harris polls taken over an eight-year period on the general subject of leniency shown to criminals:

"TOO LENIENT"

1965	(Gallup)	45%
1967	(Harris)	49%
1970	(Harris)	64%
1973	(Gallup)	74%

And there are other reasons that the public gives for the high crime rate—and in order to gauge the gap in attitudes between the Cause People and the common people, the reasons ought to be studied carefully:

PUBLIC'S REASONS FOR HIGH CRIME RATE

Laws are too lenient/penalties not stiff enough	25%
Drugs/drug addiction	21
Lack of supervision by parents	13
Not enough jobs/poverty*	13
Too much permissiveness in society	10
Lack of proper law enforcement	8
Ill feelings between groups/races*	7
Lack of responsibility among younger people/ disrespect for law	6
People have too much money/luxury	4
All other responses	23
No opinion	10

(Gallup, 1972)

107%

Because some persons gave more than one response, the total adds to more than 100%. Those responses that listed specific reasons for crime totaled 107%. And of those 107%, an aggregate total of only *20%* could be said to be reasons generally in keeping with the typical Cause-People response—marked with an asterisk in the list above. Thus, 13% said the cause of high crime rates was "not enough jobs" and "poverty," as in "We have to get at the root cause of crime in America—jobs, poverty, education, health care, etc." An additional 7% responded, "ill feeling between groups/races," as in, "The cause of the riots was white racism," or the crime wave is due to "a history of three hundred years of slavery, oppression and discrimination."

But 87% of the 107% weren't buying that—not at all. They would surely consider the so-called "long-range" reasons and solutions—but only after or in concert with consideration of the "short-range" reasons and solutions.

Americans felt that another Head Start program was not going to allow women to feel safe walking at night within a mile of their homes, and if riots were indeed caused by a history of slavery that did not help stop the riots.

So the American people, whites and blacks, have reacted in a tougher fashion. To quote the Gallup poll of 1973, "Fear of crime has become so widespread that a large number of Americans adopt a 'hard line' attitude on ways to deal with crime."

Indeed they have. "Laws are too lenient, penalties not stiff enough" is in first place. Earlier we saw that 74% of the American public said that courts are too lenient—and that a preponderant ratio of blacks (64%) also felt the same way.

Drugs are in second place. Lack of supervision by parents is in third place—a thought not too much removed from the fifth-place item, "too much permissiveness in society."

The other answers are also from the hard line side of the spectrum: "lack of proper law enforcement," "lack of responsibility among younger people/disrespect for law" and "people have too much money/luxury."

In short, Americans want toughness on a problem they feel has been mishandled.

There may be a temptation by some to scorn the reasons presented by the American public. To some they may sound Neanderthal, vindictive, harsh, simplistic and anti-libertarian.

But, recall the thinking of one of America's leading authorities on crime, Professor James Q. Wilson, chairman of the Department of Government at Harvard, cited earlier. His reasons for the crime wave are quite similar to those the public perceives. It is Wilson's contention that a number of converging factors during the 1960s triggered much of the crime explosion. Laws, and interpretations of laws by court rulings, particularly concerning the rights of the accused, *were* made more lenient—and this development quickly passed into street wisdom. Drugs, of course, *did* come into much wider usage. Lack of parental control, permissiveness, disrespect for law—a new attitude fostered in part by the counter-culture ideas—*did* increase during the Sixties. Wilson also cites another critical factor (discussed in Chapter 8) the accidental, demographic one concerning the coming of age of the Baby-Boom babies.

Professor Wilson tends to reject the argument that increased crime is due to "not enough jobs/poverty" and by "ill feelings between groups/races." He points out—with persuasive logic—that these are not *new* factors in the American equation and, if not new, not logically the *cause* of a new development, i.e., the stunning increase in crime rates.

In fact, in terms of "not enough jobs/poverty" there was an exactly *contrary* trend during the 1960s. The economy was hot and healthy. Unemployment went down. The numbers of persons in poverty declined starkly. Accordingly, it is hard to attribute the crime wave to unemployment/poverty.

It is the judgment here, clearly, that the public was, and is, far wiser in its analysis of the crime problem than were many of the Cause People. The view that court rulings were demoralizing the police was probably correct; the view that disrespect for laws was encouraging crime was probably correct. Moreover, the public has *not* turned thumbs down on governmental economic help to the poverty stricken or for aid to help rebuild the cities. All they have said is that, given the breakdown of law and order in America, the "short-term" solutions must *co-exist* with the "long-term" solutions and because they are *short*-term solutions, one can at least hope for faster relief than from longer range actions.

VALUES

Those are the two specific major complaints of the American public. They touch on and feed off a deeper and broader concern, one so broad and amorphous that it does not show up very high on a "number-one problems list," but yet today pervades our entire culture. That concern deals with the perceived erosion of "values" and "morality" in America.

Let us begin our text with two Gallup polls, one taken in December of 1949 and the second in July of 1968. The basic question asked with only a slight change in wording[4] was this:

Do you think that life is getting better or worse in terms of moral conduct?

And the answers:

	1949	1968	
Worse	52%	79%	(!)
Better	20	6	(!)
Same	22	10	
No opinion	5	2	

Two comments.

People always seem to think their society is in moral trouble. Seneca, Pliny the Elder and Amos all worried about morality, eroding values and rambunctious youth. In 1949, by about 2½ to 1, Americans saw morality on the decline.

[4] Actual phrasing, in 1949, "Do you think the human race is getting better or worse from the standpoint of moral conduct?"; in 1968; "Do you believe life is getting better or worse in terms of morals?"

But today, the morality crisis, such as it is, would seem to be more severe than in the recent past. The ratio of 2½ to 1 is not the same as 13 to 1, which was the ratio in 1968.

Look now at some other data, gathered four years later, in 1972:

Q. Do you feel that family life in America is in trouble?

Yes	71%
No	27%

Q. Are most parents these days too permissive with their children?

Yes	85%
No	14%

Q. Do you agree that parents have been gradually losing—or giving up—authority over their teen-agers?

Yes	90%
No	10%

(BH&G, 1972)

Lest anyone feel that morality and values are the plebeian concern of some gauche Middle Americans, let it be noted here that the Harvard Class of 1948 was polled in 1973 on the occasion of its twenty-fifth reunion. When asked to rank the nation's most serious general problems, the results showed that in first place was *"breakdown of morality."*

If some further demonstration is required to show that morality, values, permissiveness and disruption are extremely worrisome, consider first the reasons set forth in answer to this question:

Q. What do you feel is the single greatest threat to family life in America today?

A.

1. Materialism	37%	
2. Permissive parents	29%	
3. Drugs	18%	61%
4. Permissive attitude about sex	14%	

(BH&G, 1972)

The "materialism" referred to here, as we read it, is not "materialism" as the ecologists might see it, i.e., factories belching smoke, too many cars, clothes dryers. Instead, it is a sense that the quest for things and money has replaced deeper human concerns such as religious values, family solidarity and a sense of community. Now, that may be interpretive. But the threats of permissiveness and drugs (items 2, 3, and 4) are not, and they total *61%*—a *majority* of the sample.

Or look at this intriguing data from the Potomac/Gallup study:

Q. And what about your fears and worries for the future of our country?

NATIONAL FEARS[5]

	1959	1972
War (especially nuclear war)	64%	35%
Lack of law and order	*	*16%*
Economic instability; inflation, recession	18%	13%
National disunity and political instability (unrest, tensions, antagonisms, civil war)	*	*13%*
Drug problem	*	*9%*
Communism	12%	8%
Lack of public morality (ethically, religiously)	*	*6%*

An asterisk (*) indicates a less than 5% response. *All the new items on the list relate to values, morality, instability, breakdown of order,* etc. Added together, these "new" concerns total *44%*. And if one sees "communism" as a value morality issue, the total can be revised to *52%* —compared to 12% in 1959.

Finally, as a capstone to this little discourse on morality and values in America, here is a statement shown to respondents by Yankelovich surveyors in October of 1972:

Q. I'm sick and tired of hearing people attack patriotism, morality and other traditional American values.

A. Agree   78%
    Disagree   20%

Interestingly, that statement is agreed to by every demographic or political group. Cross tabulations show that even respondents who consider themselves "liberals" or "radicals" aggregately agree with the statement by 60%–38%. And if anyone thinks blacks are anti-traditional, anti-patriotic, anti-morality or anti-values, American style—they agreed with the statement by 78%–20%, exactly the same as the national sample.

[5] Listing all items that in 1972 received a score of more than 5%.

In short, while Cause People were concerned with sexism, racism, ecology, peace and the creation of a new value system, the Massive Majority Middle were attuned additionally to some issues that were perceived to be of more immediate concern: inflation, crime and the erosion of the old value system.

CHAPTER 21

The New Politics and Today's Politics

Who or what threatened morality? Who or what threatened values?

We arrive now at a critical point in the argument. There are many causes for the American malaise. It may well be that we will never really understand the phenomenon. But in *the public mind, it is apparent that one of the causes of the erosion of values, one of the causes of the erosion of moral standards, one of the causes of the resulting malaise, has been—call it what you will—the Cause People, the Movement, the Failure and Guilt Complex and their assorted camp followers, sub-species, promoters, drum beaters, faddists, apologists, spear carriers and political types, let alone parents who wanted their kids to think they were hip.*

Further, this perception by the public is not just perception, it carries with it a dose of truth.

The charge is serious and must be documented and explained.

Consider once again the argument.

In the last decade or dozen years, life in America, in most measurable ways, has improved. The American middle class has grown to a massive majority. The life choices and life options available to ordinary citizens have grown inordinately. These changes, on balance, have been better by far than what they have replaced.

With these changes have come problems, which Americans recognize as the side effects of progress. They are major problems indeed, but not so major as to wipe out the progress itself. When asked, Americans feel that their lives, their communities, their jobs, their kids, their homes, their incomes are pretty good, even with the problems that exist.

Now, at roughly the moment that so many Americans are beginning to realize the fruits of their hard labors, they hear the earlier middle class derogate their labors, their values, their morality and their achievements. Consider again the thrust of the rhetoric of our time, as heard through the ears of many in the new middle class:

Want to send your kid to college?

Why bother—college is ossified, bureaucratic, irrelevant and unresponsive, a handmaiden of the death dealers of the military-industrial complex.

Want to move to a suburban home, with some green and some safety? Don't do it—suburbia is plastic and escapist. You're not thinking green, mister, you're thinking black. Suburbia is racist, a white noose constructed of plastic ticky-tack.

You think you've got a good job? Wrong again. You've got a *dehumanizing* job, a brutalized job, a boring, monotonous, meaningless and unfulfilling job. The fact that you're doing it is meaningful to *you*, that it means you can live in a nice house and send your kids to college —that doesn't count. And, remember, people on welfare shouldn't be demeaned, only people on work should be demeaned.

You think it's nice to have a car, a washing machine, a swimming pool, a vacation in the Rockies or in Europe, a second car, air conditioning and power steering? Nope, all that means is that you're a materialist, and worse than that you're a greedy polluter. You Americans are only 6% of humanity and you use up 30%, 40%, 50%, 60% of the world's resources—why aren't you kind to the planet like the Indian peasants or the black sharecroppers in the South? Black sharecroppers don't pollute, but you do!

You think it's important to have religion, to believe in moderation, in sobriety, in sexual responsibility, in abiding by the laws, in cleanliness, in family? That's square. God is dead, a rip-off is cute, pot is good, sex is a hang-up, pornography is chic, abortion is noble, family is a middle-class put-on, cleanliness is next to ugliness. Your values, your traditions, your culture, your law, your morality—are no good.

You think a woman can live a decent and dignified life by raising a family and providing a warm home? Wrong again; that's sexual repression.

You think it's important to worry about your family? Sorry—that's cultural Philistinism, that's apathy, that's me-first, that's wrong also. You have to worry about Vietnam, racism, women and ecology until the signal is given. Then, as soon as you hear the magic words "inward looking," then, and only then, start looking inward.

You think America is a great country? Wrong—America is imperialist, racist, fascist, genocidal, colonial and sexist. Amerika is the cancer of the world, and the white race is the cancer of civilization. And if Vietnam didn't prove it, look at Watergate—rotten, corrupt, fascist, repressive— and so natural in America.

* * *

These views, only mildly exaggerated here, are heard by the men and women of the Massive Majority Middle, and elicit two very different sorts of reaction. One is harsh, crisp and sometimes brutal—and has often resulted in a vote for George Wallace. The second is more in a spirit of sorrow than in bitterness, and is usually in the form of a question: *How can smart people be so stupid?* Here are our best and our brightest, *and they just don't understand,* and sorrowfully, in 1972, these questioners voted for Nixon or just didn't vote.

Americans look at the Cause People, at the Movement, at the Failure and Guilt Complex and they know that so many of the causes they helped publicize had a validity and a vitality that was hard to deny.

At the same time they reject—vehemently—the spirit of exaggeration, of guilt, of smugness, of elitism, of arrogance and of wrongheadedness, too. And that, Americans saw, is very much of a problem in its own right. Most Americans felt that these people, these Cause People, went beyond the pale and were destroying what was held dear. And that problem, the destruction of values, was often seen to be a worse problem than all the other problems that the value destroyers raise.

(1971)

Pity, that. As many Americans saw it, *The Movement had become not the messenger of bad news—but the bad news itself. The Cause People, in their own language, were not part of the solution—they were part of the problem. Again in their language, we have met the enemy, and he is them. They are not a cure for malaise, they are part of malaise. They can't tell us why America's on the wrong track—they helped put her there.*

There is just a little more data that may be presented. Consider a few disparate questions, all from Harris surveys, that give a generalized flavor of the feeling about the Cause People, the new culture, values, demonstrations and disruptions:

ABOUT VICE PRESIDENT AGNEW

	Agree	Disagree
He's right to want to crack down on anti-Vietnam protesters.	69%	19%

(1970)

And a year later,

	Favor	Oppose
Stop being permissive with student protesters.	65%	21%

And,

Q. Do you feel that hippies are a real danger to society, more harmful
to themselves than to society, or do you feel they are not particularly
harmful to anyone?

A. Real danger to society   22%
   More danger to themselves   53%
   Not harmful to anyone   22%
(1971)

A danger to society, and a danger to themselves!

* * *

Which brings us to politics.

Ours is a highly responsive political system—elections mirror life in
America—and anything and everything that concerns Americans usually
ends up sooner or later on the political anvil.

If we are seeking evidence as to what kind of national problems we
have, and what kind of national solutions we seek, we must look to our
national elections as the ultimate national survey.

The 1972 election has been called "a referendum on the cultural revolution" and that's probably sound. Here is how Elizabeth Hardwicke, writing
in the fall of 1972 in the *New York Review,* listed the reasons for Senator
McGovern's low standing:

Revenge for the 1960s, for show-off students, for runaways, for attacks
on the family and the system, for obscenity, for pot, for prisoner pity,
for dropping out, tuning in, for radical chic, for store-front lawyers,
for folk singers, for muggings, for addicts, for well-to-do WASPs grogged
on charity binges.

The Democratic Convention in Miami in July of 1972 turned out to be
a national trade show for the Movement. Just as automobile accessory
manufacturers, or barge line operators, or discount store owners, or book
publishing companies or oil companies have a convention, so too did the
Movement. Just as every self-respecting widget manufacturer has to have
a booth at the auto accessory show, so every self-respecting submovement
of the supermovement came to Miami to display their wares and tout their
candidate.

And the Failure and Guilt Complex did have a candidate, whether he
knew it or not. The first phase of the McGovern candidacy involved
capturing the Movement and its young, hard-working, collegiate shock
troops—young men and women deeply concerned about peace, ecology,
women, welfare, ZPG, racism, the new culture. In order to capture these
dedicated young political workers, McGovern, in the first phase of his

campaign, felt that "my one unique position, with reference to the potential competition, is to be to the left of them all . . ."[1] As his strategist Rick Stearnes put it, "We would have to consolidate the left wing. . . ."[2]

McGovern captured the Movement by being "to the left of them all," by agreeing with some and seeming to be sympathetic to almost all Movement positions and, perhaps most important, by adopting so much of the shrill Movement rhetoric of failure. As late as September of 1972 McGovern told a reporter, "I have this feeling I'm working with a historical trend, history is going for me. This country is going to pieces."[3]

When the election was all over, McGovern's shrewd lieutenant Frank Mankiewicz looked back at the campaign for author Theodore White:

> Mankiewicz reflected on what he considered the basic mistake of the campaign. Mankiewicz did not use the word "blackmail" but he expressed succinctly what he had learned. "We were always subject to this pressure from the cause people," said Mankiewicz. "We reacted to every threat from women or militants, or college groups. If I had to do it all over again, I'd learn when to tell them to go to hell."

And so, in July of 1972, the Movement came to Miami for its trade show in the flush of victory. The Peace Movement was there—"Stop bombing the dikes!" was their new rallying cry. The Welfare Rights group was there lobbying for a $6,500 welfare minimum—and a small army of black women chased Lawrence O'Brien out of one Democratic National Committee meeting. Women's Libbers were there demanding legalization of abortion. Gay libbers were there demanding legalization of homosexual marriage. Busing and amnesty planks were voted into the platform.

Long-haired mustached young men who were delegates denounced Richard J. Daley who was not. Young women who were delegates denounced congressmen, senators and governors who were not. And the rallying cry was: *Re-order priorities.*

It was good, exciting, theater—and the tens of millions of Americans who saw it on television enjoyed it as theater. As politics, however, it was catastrophic. For the Movement convention revealed to the American people with finality that it was George McGovern who was fronting for almost everyone they had come to disapprove of in the last five years. And the polls showed it. A Gallup survey taken immediately after the Democratic Convention revealed that George McGovern was running further behind Richard Nixon after the convention than before it. For the first time since the advent of American public opinion polling, the nominee of a

---

[1] Quoted in *The Making of the President, 1972*, p. 43, from the minutes of a July 1971 staff meeting.
[2] Ibid.
[3] Ibid.

major party had *lost ground* during the week of his greatest glory, his greatest accomplishment and his greatest exposure. Even in 1968, after the most bitter and bloody convention in recent American history, with blood literally flowing in the streets of Chicago, Hubert Humphrey had picked up 4 percentage points on Richard Nixon.

But not in 1972. Cause People had identified their candidate to America and America made clear its feelings about the Cause People—which was negative. Having been tarred as the Movement's boy, McGovern spent four months trying to scrub the tar off, but to no avail:

Q.   McGovern's ideas are impractical and too far out.

A.   Agree completely   47% (!)
     Agree partially   27%
     Disagree   22%
     Not sure   4%
(Yankelovich, October 1972)

Q.   Do you consider McGovern a
     Conservative   8%
     Moderate   12%
     Liberal   31%
     Radical   31% (!)
     Not sure   18%
(Yankelovich, October 1972)

Americans considered the Movement/McGovern view of America and said, in effect, "I see problems in America, too, but not the same ones nor in the same way as these people do." Americans decided that *mea culpa* was not their kind of a campaign slogan. And Senator McGovern became the only presidential candidate to give his acceptance speech at 3:00 A.M. and to concede in prime time.

Senator McGovern did not lose because he was an inept candidate; he was never an inept candidate in his other races nor is likely to be inept in any future ones. He is, in fact, a very able political man. McGovern lost because he became a symbol of a cause whose time had not come.

By election day, Americans understood, finally, the difference between "New Politics" and traditional liberalism, a political movement which rarely loses elections by landslides. Traditional liberals—and many non-liberals too—say, "America is a great nation with great problems and the federal government can act to help solve those great problems." What the New Politics people said—picking up the intrinsic rhetoric of the F&GC, was something else: "America is a corrupt and sick nation teetering on the brink of failure, a nation that needs a domestic shock treatment." On

November 8, 1972, Americans rejected that view. Not for the first time, his enemies helped to make Richard Nixon President of the United States.

* * *

As the 1972 election results were sifted and analyzed, as the 1973 off-year elections came and went, an important but little-noticed pattern of politics emerged. The New Politics disintegrated. And the old politics —economically oriented, hard-nosed, socially tough and programmatically activist—seemed again to be the wave of the future, not only for old politicians but for re-imaged new ones.

This transformation occurred for diverse reasons. To some large degree, as always, events were in the saddle. The American combat role in Vietnam ended. The draft ended, and with those terminations the morality-peace crusade also ended. As the professional peaceniks turned inward, the cutting edge of the New Politics blunted. A runaway food inflation in the mid-months of 1973 reminded politicians of the almighty power of the politics of the dollar. The Yom Kippur war in the Middle East reminded reorder-priorities ideologues that American military might still have a function, and the size of the defense budget no longer was issue number one for many New Politicos. The Arab oil boycott and the energy crisis took some wind out of the ecological windmills as Americans remembered that while a clean environment is good, materialism is also good, and sensible environmentalists and sensible materialists tried to figure out ways to have both. Of course, Watergate gave the Movement ideologues a new chance to explain how inherently corrupt is America, but with conservatives like Sam Ervin and John Sirica as the heroes and with traditional-liberal labor chief George Meany leading the fight for impeachment, it was somewhat less than a full measure of political pleasure for the New Pols.

But it was more than changing events that changed American politics. A changing awareness on the part of New Politicians moved them toward sometimes strange, new political turf. Senator Edward Kennedy thought it politically profitable to journey to Decatur, Alabama, on July 4, 1973, to say of formerly segregationist Governor George Wallace:

For if there is one thing George Wallace stands for, it is the right of every American to speak his mind and be heard—fearlessly and in any part of the country.

And Senator Walter F. Mondale, a leading Senate proponent of busing pre-1972, was seen and heard in this dialogue with columnist Robert Novak on "Meet the Press" in 1973:

MR. NOVAK: Let's try the question a different way from the specific.

Senator McGovern was a strong advocate of forced racial busing in
the school system. Are you?

SENATOR MONDALE: I have never been for busing as such. What I have
been opposed to is a stand which would prevent the elimination of
discrimination, which would deny the court the power it must have if
it finds a discriminatory school district from taking steps to end it.

MR. NOVAK: You were known by some of your colleagues as "Mr.
Busing" in the Senate. Do you think that is an unfair appellation;
you are against busing now?

SENATOR MONDALE: I think you didn't hear my answer very well.

MR. NOVAK: I didn't understand it.

* * *

Even more interesting than what was being said about defense, inflation, energy and America's role in the world was what was *not* being
said by those who are often America's most reliable weathervanes, the
practicing pols. Where were the preachments for amnesty? Who went up
front with a new plan for de-criminalizing marijuana? Who reminded his
constituents that he had always believed busing to be one tool to help
desegregate schools? Who was for political quotas? Who announced that
law-and-order was a proto-fascist issue?

A rhetorical era had passed, and it had passed for an elemental reason.
Politicians realized that the much heralded, much touted, much feared
"new class"—the harbinger of New Politics—was a hoax. The idea that
a new army of voters—well educated, well-to-do, white collared, often
suburban, often young—would provide a nouveau-liberal tilt in a new
era of American politics simply did not materialize in the voting booth.
These new voters were indeed younger, more suburban, better educated,
well-to-do and white collared but this Massive Majority Middle Class
was not cast in the image of George McGovern. Nor of John Lindsay.
Nor even of John Gardner. They were demographically new, but politically and attitudinally they were earthy "middle class," which has
never been flamingly liberal in American political history. They were
progressive, they wanted action from government, they accepted many
halfway positions espoused by the New Pols and the Cause People, but
they were not all-the-way or even most-of-the-way left ideological. Like
most middle classniks all over the world, "stability" was high on their
list of priorities. And when runaway inflation and long gas lines threatened that stability—they fumed. Insofar as they represented a "constituency for change," as pollster Louis Harris has called it, they wanted
change *away* from crisscross school busing, *away* from "soft" attitudes
toward criminality, and change *toward* "values and morality." If the new
class is so all-fired, change oriented why, as this book goes to press, are

the polls showing that in the political pairing of Edward Kennedy versus Gerald Ford, the well-educated, well-to-do and white collarites tend toward Ford rather than Kennedy? And Kennedy aside, why are the well-to-do still more likely to vote Republican?

In fact, on most issues in American life today, there is relatively little differentiation of viewpoint when cross tabulations are run by region, occupation, income, age, sex and residence. Some issues, of course, do show important differences, and some patterns of minor gradations show up, but the general impression gained by scanning the standard Gallup list of thirty demographic cross tabulations shows general *similarity,* not wild *differentiation.*[4]

And so, a funny thing happened as the New Politics disintegrated. The oft-mourned, oft-interred, oft-discussed "FDR coalition" showed that its vital signs were still strong.

Who won in the 1973 elections?

Nonpresidential-year elections are always difficult to assess and non-congressional odd-year elections are particularly difficult. A few governorships are up for grabs, a handful of mayoralties, some few state legislatures, and all these races are heavily influenced by local issues.

Still, look at some of the results:

In New York City, Abraham Beame, a sixty-seven-year-old regular Democrat beat off not one but two New Politics challengers (Herman Badillo and Albert Blumenthal) and was elected mayor with 57% of the vote in a *four*-man field, with no other candidate getting more than 16% of the vote. (The New York *Times* endorsed first Badillo, then Blumenthal.)

In New Jersey, a handsome Democratic judge named Brendan Byrne beat a New Politics candidate (Ann Klein) in the gubernatorial primary and won the election with a 68% majority. (The New York *Times* endorsed Ms. Klein.)

In Los Angeles, Tom Bradley, a black former police captain beat Mayor Sam Yorty, who had beaten him in 1969. This time Bradley didn't let anyone talk tougher than he about public safety. (The New York *Times* tut-tutted Bradley for his tough stance.)

In Minneapolis, Al Hofstede, a young man from the Hubert Humphrey wing of the Democratic-Farmer-Labor Party, turned out incumbent law-and-order Mayor Charles Stenvig.

In Virginia, Henry Howell, a self-styled "populist" with a tinge of

---

[4] Here is a typical poll on President Nixon's handling of the war in Vietnam. No group (except non-whites) is more than 47% or less than 27% in the disapproval column—a maximum swing of 20%. Most of the groupings (25 out of 30) are no more than 5% up or down off the base 39% disapproval level. Even the non-white variance on disapproval is only 15% off the national norm.

NIXON'S HANDLING OF VIETNAM

QUESTION: Do you approve or disapprove of the way President Nixon is handling the situation in Vietnam?

February 4-7, 1972

	Approve %	Disapprove %	No opinion %
NATIONAL	51	39	10
SEX			
Male	57	27	6
Female	47	41	11
RACE			
White	53	38	9
Nonwhite	32	54	14
EDUCATION			
College	55	38	7
High School	53	39	8
Grade School	44	41	15
OCCUPATION			
Prof. & bus.	60	35	5
White collar	52	41	7
Farmers	58	33	9
Manual	47	44	9
AGE			
18-20 years	48	40	12
21-29 years	47	47	6
30-49 years	54	40	6
50 and over	52	35	13
REGION			
East	54	38	8
Midwest	50	40	10
South	53	37	10
West	46	44	10
INCOME			
$15,000 and over	60	33	7
$10,000-$14,999	57	38	5
$7,000-$9,999	53	41	6
$5,000-$6,999	47	39	14
$3,000-$4,999	37	44	19
Under $3,000	49	42	9
COMMUNITY SIZE			
1,000,000 and over	49	41	10
500,000-999,999	53	37	10
50,000-499,999	53	35	12
2,500-49,999	57	37	6
Under 2,500, rural	48	44	8

New Politics coloration, dumped his earlier lukewarm pro-busing position and any other semblance of New Politicism—and came within .8% of beating former Governor Mills Godwin, who won by a whisker in a southern state allegedly now solidly Republican.

So who won? Surely, Democrats did well in the year of Watergate. But what kind of Democrats? With what kind of rhetoric? *Non-New Politics Democrats, with non-New Politics rhetoric.*

And there, again, was the FDR coalition, scourge of Republicans for three decades. The poor voted Democratic. The Jews voted Democratic. The ethnics voted Democratic. The big cities voted Democratic. The union members voted Democratic. The "working people," now well into the Massive Majority Middle Class, remembered that they were still working people even if they lived in suburbia, and worked at a desk, not a lathe—and voted Democratic. Of the old FDR coalition, only "the South" may prove to be out of reach for Democrats. But that will only be determined in 1976, and it will depend in large measure on who the Democrats nominate.

Galvanized anew by non-New Politics issues like inflation, recession and energy (as well as Watergate), the party of the little guy was on the march again.

And what of that vaunted great, growing, New Politics-oriented "constituency of change"? What of that "new class"?

The proper analogy comes from the near-final scene of *The Wizard of Oz*. Dorothy and her friends enter the great hall to see the Wizard and hear his powerful and echoing voice speaking mighty platitudes from behind a drape. Awed, the visitors hang on the Wizard's every robust syllable. But Dorothy's dog begins tugging on the drape, and it falls. And there is the "Wizard"—an old faker speaking into an amplifying system. There was no Wizard. And when the drape was pulled aside, there wasn't much New Politics or new class either, just a fine amplification system.

* * *

Here, then, is the political progression:

Through 1972, Americans were by and large anti-anti-Establishment. They resented what they perceived to be the vehement New Politics attacks on America and the American way of life. The election of 1972 sounded the death knell of cultural politics.

But times are changing. Events are changing. People are changing. Politicians are changing. Inflation, recession, energy shortages, a dose of Watergate are turning many Americans into anti-Establishmentarians, or at least into anti-the-current-Administrationites. These switches are, by and large, based on economic judgments. Democrats generally win elections when they are phrased on economic rather than social or cultural grounds. This is generally understood now not only by "old liberals" (who knew it all along) but by most of the smarter "new politics liberals."

There is, then, a sense of coming together within the always-contentious Democratic Party. New politicos have sensed the dead end inherent in cultural politics. And old liberals are sensing that Americans have already made many synthesizing accommodations to the earlier social demands of the left. Cultural change *has* ensued; judgments have been made; and no one is looking to rub salt in any wounds. No one wants to call anyone radical. Within bounds, there is today the bare possibility of that favorite cliché of political writers: "a unified party."

There is only one danger. The new anti-Establishment sentiment should not be confused with the old. If some Democrats, feeling their oats from Watergate, think that Americans are now ready for what they rejected in 1972, that a campaign can be waged on the platform of "America Stinks," there will again be a risk of a sundered party and a Republican victory in 1976.[5]

[5] Democrats may also be legitimately nervous about a May 1974 Gallup poll showing that Americans who regard themselves as "Conservative" are at an all-time high—even though respondents also report all-time low levels of self-identification as "Republican." The mystery and the paradox of the 1974 congressional elections is this: How will voters respond to Conservative Republican candidates?

CHAPTER 22

Today and Tomorrow

And what about now? And what about next year and 1980?

Attitudinally, it is plausible to suggest that the beginning of the 1970s closed out—at least temporarily—a particularly grim era in American attitudinal history. By 1970 and 1971, let us recall, Gallup data (taken for Potomac Associates) showed that Americans felt that the past was better than the terrible present. A Harris survey showed that confidence in leaders had plunged to all-time lows. A Roper survey showed that by 64%–23%, Americans felt America was on the wrong track. The colleges were seething.

And at about that time it began to change. Slowly. Not a sudden elastic hop back to early euphoriant levels. But a bottoming out. And then even a mini-march upward.

By 1972, the Gallup (Potomac Associates) data had shifted somewhat:

NATIONAL LADDER RATINGS

	1959	1964	1971 (Jan.)	1972 (June)
Past	6.5%	6.1%	6.2%	5.6%
Present	6.7%	6.5%	5.4%	5.5%
Future	7.4%	7.7%	6.2%	6.2%

The present was no longer seen as significantly worse than the past as it was in 1971. Neither was it seen as significantly better than the past (as it was in earlier years). At the least, it would seem the slide had ended.

And the Harris data shifted also. Remember the precipitous slide from 1966 to 1971 shown on page 199? It has stopped. *Every field surveyed in September 1973 was higher than 1972 except for the Watergate-ridden*

"Executive branch of government." And most of the fields were up from 1971 to 1972.

TRENDS OF CONFIDENCE IN INSTITUTIONAL LEADERS

	1966	*1971*	*1972*	*1973*	*Change* *1971-73*
GREAT DEAL OF **CONFIDENCE IN:**					
Medicine	72%	61%	48%	57%	−4%
Banks and financial institutions	67%	36%	29%	−	+ 2%
The scientific community	56%	32%	37%	−	+ 5%
The military	62%	27%	35%	40%	+13%
Education	61%	37%	33%	44%[1]	+ 7%
Mental health and psychiatry	51%	35%	31%	−	−4%
Organized religion	55%	27%	30%	36%	+ 9%
Local retail stores	48%	24%	28%	−	+ 4%
U. S. Supreme Court	51%	23%	28%	33%	+10%
Executive branch of federal government	41%	23%	27%	19%	−4%
Major U. S. companies	55%	27%	27%	29%	+ 2%
Congress	42%	19%	21%	29%	+10%
The press	29%	18%	18%	20%	+12%
Television	25%	22%	17%	41%[2]	+19%
Organized labor	22%	14%	15%	20%	+ 6%
Advertising	21%	12%	11%	−	−1%

After a striking plunge from 1966 to 1971, the roller coaster flattened out and began a slow turn up. From 1966 to 1971, the mean change for the combined sixteen categories was *minus twenty points*. From 1971 to the fall of 1973, the mean change was *plus five points*. (Incredibly, when Louis Harris presented this data to the Senate Subcommittee on Intergovernmental Relations, he stressed—and the press echoed—the decline from '66 to '73 taking no real note of the '71 to '73 upturn. Is Mr. Harris a member of the Failure and Guilt Complex?[3])

[1] Called "higher educational institutions" in 1973.
[2] Called "television news" in 1973.
[3] Interestingly, Harris' "confidence" polls ask about a "great deal" of confidence. Gallup allows respondents to choose "a great deal" or "quite a lot" of confidence, and gets substantially higher ratings. Thus, in 1973, Harris showed 36% confidence in organized religion—while Gallup showed 66%. Other variances were about 10%.

In 1974, the University of Michigan's Institute for Social Research released Fall of 1973 data that showed that of fifteen institutions surveyed, the most admired was —*the military*. (Survey directed by Willard Rodgers.)

Roper did not run a comparable "right-track-wrong-track" poll in 1972, but Yankelovich's poll in October of 1972 provided this measure:

Q. How do you feel things are going these days?
Well[4]   57%
Badly[4]   39%

That is quite a difference from the 64% who said, just one year earlier, in the Roper poll, that America was "on the wrong track."

And the war was over. The colleges were quiet.

The pattern in short was that of a fishhook curve:

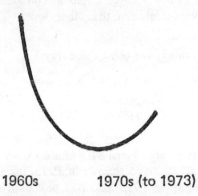

1960s   1970s (to 1973)

Confidence plummeted in the late 1960s and early seventies. Then it leveled out and slowly, but clearly, discernibly, started coming up.

But fishhooks have barbs on their ends and so does this statistical fishhook. In 1973, in rapid succession, Americans were greeted with the following events and conditions:

- Watergate—followed by Agnew, tapes, missing tapes, moves to impeach, etc. In short, high political scandal of first-order magnitude.
- Runaway inflation—for a few of the mid-months of 1973 the cost of living soared faster than at any point in the past twenty years, and the inflation was most acute in the highly visible area of food. From March to September of 1973, meat prices went up by 37%. First quarter of 1974 inflation rates were "double-digit."
- Energy crisis—it was coming anyway but the Middle East war drove it home: allocations, gas station closings, fears of unemployment, talk of rationing, colder homes, etc. As gas lines at service stations stretched as far as the eye could see in early 1974, one predominant, corrosive emotion came to the fore; anger.

[4] Additive percentages of "very well" and "pretty well" on the one hand, and "pretty badly" and "very badly" on the other.

Any one of these three situations might have appropriately thrown Americans into a blue flunk. Public opinion polling is particularly sensitive to yesterday's headlines and when an American sits down to a dinner of soybean hamburgers in a cold house and reads in the newspaper that the Vice-President is a felon and the President is a liar and looks forward to an hour's wait the next day on a gas queue—that's not the ideal time for the polling lady to come by and ask if America's on the right track. It's rather like taking a compass reading while standing on the North Pole.

Still, the Harris survey taken as late as September of 1973 (shown on page 296) continued to show a slight climb in confidence, except in Mr. Nixon's branch of government. On the other hand, Yankelovich's data flip-flopped:

Q. How do you feel things are going these days?

	1972 (Oct.)	1973 (Sept.)
Well	57%	29%
Badly	39%	71%

And Gallup's 1973 data on personal satisfaction dropped a few points, but levels were still massively "satisfied." Gallup data on "the way this nation is being governed" declined sharply in 1973, the year of Watergate. On the other hand, Gallup in 1973 also had poll data showing that 9 of 10 persons rated the United States "favorable" and 3 of 4 thought it "very favorable." In April 1974, Gallup poll essentially re-endorsed these views. And a 1974 poll showed fewer people wanted to emigrate than in 1971 (12% then, 10% now).

Is it fair, then, to say that as this book is being finished (in early 1974) we are in a moment of attitudinal flux? Fair enough. We were down. We leveled off. We started up. New strains have appeared and no one knows what's happening right now or what will happen next.

Still there is room for some speculation, and the author is nothing if not a speculator.

First, we must ask this question: Can we expect the unhappy triumvirate of Watergate, inflation, energy to plunge America back into the attitudinal fever zone?

Maybe. But doubtful. If Watergate, inflation, energy had happened simultaneously in 1970—there would have been a million people in the streets of Washington. In 1973, a few dozen cars drove by the White House and honked their horns. We are out of life in the fever zone.

If we are, what happens next? Americans can be non-feverish but still very unhappy. To try to see what happens next, another question must be asked: Are Watergate, runaway inflation, energy crisis permanent debilitating conditions or essentially transitory?

No one really knows, of course, but the guess here is mostly transitory, with the possible exception of inflation.

Watergate is essentially ephemeral. It is perceived to involve a series of ugly events, not an ugly ongoing condition. Because of these events the President will resign or not resign, be impeached or not impeached. There will be headlines, but everyday life will go on and it will be over one way or the other, and someone will be President, with all the power behind him that that still mighty office holds. Watergate is the least of our problems. It may even turn out that rather than erode "confidence in our institutions," the resolution of such political rip-offs will be seen to show that our institutions can respond even to the most unusual, unexpected and bizarre sorts of wrongdoing in even the highest of places. Americans may indeed be turned off to politicians, but at the end of 1973, the Gallup poll of "most admired man" showed that eight of ten were in political life.[5]

Inflation, surely, will continue. It is at least a three-hundred-year trend, and it is a phenomenon that is indeed erosive of the spirit. "I earn more but it buys less," seems often to be the cruelest of economic fates. Before the full-scale advent and recognition of the energy crisis it seemed safe to say that inflation, while it would continue, was not likely to reach the remarkably high—but short-term—levels reached in mid-1973. Now, because of the energy situation, because of international conditions, no sane economist can make forecasts with surety, although many do. The sharp increases in fuel costs will work their way through the economy and push prices up. Inflation was the "number-one issue" for Americans all through the Watergate year of 1973. It will likely be the number-one issue in 1974 unless the energy crisis itself is perceived to be the prime culprit, responsible for a major recession or even worse.

That too may come about. The only worse plaint than "I earn more but it buys less" is this one: "I lost my job." And there are economists today (early 1974) saying that an energy-induced recession, or even a world-wide energy-induced depression, could send unemployment rates to 6% or 8% or 10% and there has been a 15% figure floated as well. This situation may be compounded by an ever spiraling inflation that just may not go away, further eroding the spirit and confidence of the nation. Inflation, with all its attendant evils—economic and psychological—may just become the Vietnam of the 1970s.

That is speculation. And here is another speculation. Watergate will

[5] The 1973 list: Henry Kissinger, Billy Graham, Richard Nixon, Edward Kennedy, Gerald Ford, George Wallace, Ralph Nader, Henry Jackson, Pope Paul, Barry Goldwater.

pass. There will be inflation, it will be painful but not debilitating—no worse than European rates in recent years, which proved to be manageable, if uncomfortable. There will be fuel hardships. There will be some increased unemployment, at least temporarily. *But the country will cope.*

After all, the energy crisis may well do the following things for America:

Restore a semblance of intellectual balance between materialists and environmentalists, in much the same pattern of synthesis and eclectism that we have observed earlier. The materialists will have to learn what waste is. And waste is surely a 300-horsepower car. And the environmentalists are going to have to learn what utility is. A small car, with low gas consumption, that enables one to get conveniently from point A to point B is utilitarian and not to be condemned. Air conditioning is a waste if a building doesn't have windows to take advantage of a breeze. But air conditioning is a desirable creature comfort when it gets too hot.

Restore to America a view of itself that has become somewhat passé. There used to be a saying that the United States could do anything it set its mind to. Around the time of Vietnam that expression fell into some disrepute.

But this country likely *can do* what it sets its mind to. One of the most dispiriting aspects about the intellectual dialogue in this nation in recent years has been the intense concentration on all things America couldn't do. This nation can build mass transit systems in San Francisco and Washington—and in fifty other cities. We can drill oil offshore without major pollutive effects in the Gulf of Mexico and in the Atlantic. We can turn the incredible technological talent in this country loose to extract oil from shale, to gassify coal, to build twenty and thirty and forty million small cars, to heat our homes with solar power, to build nuclear reactors that are efficient and safe and will one day be a blessing to energy-starved earthlings all over the globe. We can build office buildings out of brick as well as out of glass.

We can, in short, learn what is wasteful materialism and what is humanitarian materialism. And we can provide enough energy to not only meet the requirements of humanitarian materialism for those Americans who can already own a vacation home, but for tens of millions who don't but would like to, Americans who are in the lower reaches of the statistical Massive Majority Middle Class as well as tens of millions who haven't yet made it.

This country will not pursue the economic immorality of turning off the spigot just when blacks and Chicanos and Appalachian whites and urban ethnics and a lot of other people finally are going to get a shot at what the rest of us have—not because of an energy crisis or an environmental crisis. We can—and will—learn to have both: a cleaner environment and the energy to let poor people become middle-class people.

In the course of building those forty million small cars, of building mass transit systems, of building buildings with windows, of building nuclear power and solar power systems, of exporting the most advanced oil-drilling technology in the world, this economy is going to provide the jobs for people who used to make big cars and buildings without windows. And if energy costs more but one learns to use less energy, then the inflationary impact of the crisis may well be somewhat less than one guesses.

Nor will America become the number-two power in the world behind either Saudi Arabia or the Soviet Union. We have, in abundance, the four elements that are critical to deal with the energy crisis: resources, technology, capital and will. This country, recall, happens to sit on the greatest reserve of hydrocarbons in the world. It is the United States that is decades ahead of the world in nuclear and other technological research. America is still by far the wealthiest nation in the world. And it is the United States —having learned the difference between waste and utility—that will stop seriously listening to the chatter about ecologically pure Indian peasants or about the ways to reduce living standards toward "Indian equivalents" and start helping raise levels toward NAE—New American Equivalents. The Massive Majority Middle Class in America has the continuing will to continue to improve their lives. And one day, who knows, there will be a book written about the Massive Majority Middle Class—on the planet. The era of abundance is not ending on this earth. It is just beginning.

And what of matters of the spirit? Will unemployment and inflation and gas lines and rolling brownouts make Americans bitter, angry, resentful, sullen and alienated? Perhaps. No one knows. But there is another way to look at it.

There is a substantial body of psychiatric literature that says the people are happiest when challenged. The lowest rate of mental illness ever recorded in Holland occurred during the years of World War II. The challenge of a cause may have a buoyant effect even if the conditions that generated the cause involved a certain degree of deprivation. "Hardship with honor" is how columnist Mary McGrory has described the beginning of the energy-short years.

This represents a political challenge, in the highest sense of politics. Americans must be shown that the challenge is an important one, that it can be beaten, that the hardship will be distributed equitably—and most critically that the cause is a noble and uplifting one. That is something most Americans already sense.

And so it may be. Americans may just respond nobly in the years to come. The cause, which is *materialism without waste,* is a noble cause. The tools to respond to the challenge are available. The leadership is available —if not in the White House then from other political leaders, and more importantly, it will be found in the folk wisdom of the people.

So—we shall see.

V.

IMPLICATIONS

CHAPTER 23

Guess Who the Hero Is?

It was Daniel Webster who asked the question in the Stephen Vincent Benét story: "Neighbor, how stands the union?"

And now we ask the same question—"How stands the union?"

As this volume is finished in early 1974, the answer is: Not bad. Not bad at all.[1]

The rhetoric of doom, failure, guilt and crisis has been presented—and found wanting in several respects.

It is refuted by *objective data* that reveal a new and Massive Majority Middle Class now enjoying options that never existed before and conditions of life that are better by far than what they replace, even accounting for the problems which may be considered as "side effects of progress."

That rhetoric has been found wanting by attitudinal data that show that Americans think things go well for them personally—and that is an important point, for no amount of hard data of progress would be terribly convincing if people didn't feel that things were better for themselves and their families.

That rhetoric of the Failure and Guilt Complex has, finally, been found wanting by other attitudinal data that show that while Americans think America is in trouble, and that while Americans have accepted a number of specific and generally sensible propositions publicized (but not necessarily originated) by the Failure and Guilt Complex, the public rejects the major premises of failure put forth by the Movement. In fact, the Cause People came to be seen as part of the problem, and Americans have become fed up with those who are fed up with America.

But rebutting the rhetoric of the Failure and Guilt Complex does not solve all the problems this volume set out to deal with. All the round pegs have not yet found round holes.

---

[1] Or maybe, better, as Benét suggested, "You better answer the union stands as she stood, rock bottomed and copper sheathed, one and indivisible."

For even if the Movement's vision of hell in America is neither generally valid nor generally accepted, we must again acknowledge that Americans are a troubled people when they look at their nation and reflect on its well-being. If everything is so good, how come everything is so bad?

And if Americans are still troubled, can our society really have improved to the degree that is suggested here?

Yes. "Troubled" and "improvement" are not mutually exclusive terms; the first is a condition, the second a process. Both the condition and the process can coexist. And, further, the condition of being troubled may not be all bad either, as we may see now.

Let us look again at the kinds of very real and very troubling situations that do exist today and let us consider quickly a number of the general theories of discontent.

There are those who feel that a new quality of urban unease and unrest in modern society is at the root of so much of the modern dilemma. Such a view can be traced back at least to the early years of the twentieth century when Durkheim discussed *anomie,* the haunting aloneness that is allegedly inflicted upon men by urban and industrial society. Surely, there is a sense of that in America today, and the people who point to *Rootlessness* as a major social villain have a point.

There is the related theory of *Size.* Everything has gotten so big and consequently so impersonal that people crave identity and want to destroy depersonalization, smash the computer, to fold, spindle and mutilate the punch cards, and to decentralize decision-making so that people can control their own destiny.

There is the theory of *Lost National Virginity.* America, so the argument goes, is a young nation—but not as young and innocent as it once was. Following World War II, America became the dominant power in the world. With that power, so goes the theory, came the inevitable corruption and arrogance of power. Americans understand that they themselves, as individuals, are far from perfect. They may cheat once in a while on their income tax, maybe they cut a corner or two in business life. But what Americans are prepared to shrug off in their personal lives, they find deeply disquieting in national affairs. Add Vietnam to the Bay of Pigs, add Watergate to My Lai—and mass disillusionment and disenchantment are the result. Virginal no longer, America has lost the special status it once held in the eyes of the rest of the world and, sadly, in its own eyes as well.

There is the *war* theory. It was the war in Vietnam—distressing to hawk and dove alike—that magnified and exacerbated any and all the other symptoms of malaise. Particularly, it turned off young America—unprepared to kill or be killed in a war perceived of as either senseless or immoral. Ultimately, the bitter rejection of the war by the young spread to their parents, and Vietnam poisoned America. If America was evil incarnate abroad, so it must be that America is evil at home as well.

Because young people were in the forefront of so much of the discontent in the last decade, there is also a *demographic* theory of discontent. Because of the Baby Boom in the later Forties and Fifties a huge cohort of Americans became, and are becoming, young adults. Because these young people hold different values from the rest of us, because they are so deeply discontented, and because, ultimately, the young inherit the earth, the greening of America that we are witnessing is far more intense and far more disquieting than might normally be expected.

There is the theory of *the revolution of rising expectations*. People have more but they want even more. Television shows poor people how rich people live and shows it to them with a graphic immediacy that has never before been present in the equation.

There is an *environmental* theory of discontent. The fruits of our labor, once seen as progress, have turned malevolent. Cars pollute the atmosphere, strip mining denudes the countryside, power plants to run air-conditioning units pollute the rivers, noise is pervasive in the metropolis. People have sensed this environmental failure of economic success and they have sensed, then, that America is on the wrong track, which is why when Roper asks if America is on the wrong track, people say, "YES." The argument of this book views this under the rubric, "side effect of progress," but there it is nonetheless.

A concomitant to the environmental theory is that progress has made us discontented for another reason. It was Gertrude Stein who once said of Oakland that "there's no there there." As goes Oakland, so goes America. People earn more money, live in better houses, have more cars, have more vacation time—all the things they once aspired to. Now that they have them, they find out that life is still a hell of a problem: absurd, worrisome, often unfulfilling. There is a phrase from the psychiatric lexicon that surfaced during the reportage of Senator Eagleton's nervous breakdowns, breakdowns that occurred, curiously, when young Eagleton was actively making headway up the greased pole of Missouri politics. The psychiatric phrase was *Success Depression*. Or: There's no there there and you don't find that out until you get there. More Americans are getting there these days, ergo, more depression. Asked if *they* are unhappy, they say no; it's the country that's gone wrong.

An even broader theory of the causes of malaise—which we have discussed—concerns the general *Erosion of Values*. The speed of change in America, the shock of the premature arrival of the future, coupled with so many of the other reasons listed above, have spun the nation around too fast. Accordingly, Americans are seeking a return to traditional values, always a difficult goal, and are discontented with the society that makes it so difficult to go home again.

Finally, there is a *Cyclical* theory. Societies, like men, have bad moods that ultimately pass. We are living through one now and we hope it will go away soon.

These general reasons for the American malaise are listed here because there would seem to be at least a little truth in each of them, and a good deal in some.

Some of these general theories are incredibly broad, are based largely on intuitive judgments and are, accordingly, hardly subject to proof or disproof, for that matter. Some of the theories complement each other—and some contradict each other. Thus, the Environment theory says that people have too much and are disillusioned by it, while the Rising Expectation theory says that people want still more, and fast too.

Some of the theories are at least partially mitigated by events occurring around the world: There is disillusionment and disenchantment reported in Western European nations—nations uninvolved in the Vietnam war, nations indeed vigorously opposing U.S. involvement, nations that happen to be small in size and population.

There is disenchantment in nations with much television and those with little television and there is disenchantment in both centralized and decentralized nations. There is disenchantment in nations where citizens are largely "successful" and in those where "success" is still far, far away, where generations will pass before average citizens ever find out if there is any there there.[2]

Some of the theories don't account for all of the available facts. For example, the feeling of rootlessness is surely with us, but Census data shows that the amount of moving in the United States was roughly constant from 1860 to 1960, and actually *declined* slightly from 1960 to 1970.[3] America has never been a sit-still nation and if we're a nation of strangers, that's nothing new.

The idea of a monolithic Greening of young people doesn't deal with several other facts. Public opinion polls have shown that young people are not that different from their elders. Looking to the future, the salvation-by-

[2] A headline from the July 6, 1973, edition of the New York *Times:* "THE DUTCH ARE SO WELL OFF THEY ARE DISCONTENTED." In that month, too, a report of the Japanese Government received publicity in the United States. A quote: "Japan's young people are becoming more alienated and aimless, more disillusioned and dissatisfied than ever before. A government study recently released in Tokyo, points out that this alienation is reflected in a rising crime rate, increased extremist terrorism and a growing obsession with money and materialism. The report states that young Japanese lack social solidarity and life goals, that they are filled with a nameless discontent."

[3] In 1960–61, the percentage of the population that changed residence was 20.0%. A decade later, 1970–71, the percentage was 17.9%.

youth theory manages not to take account of one of the tragic facts of human existence: that every decade young people get ten years older and that as they get older they face different problems and change their attitudes. For example, since the advent of public opinion polling in America in the mid-1930s, young people have generally voted more liberally than the rest of the population—about 10% more likely to be for FDR than were their elders in 1940. But now that thirty-five years have gone by, it is easily discernible that the once-young don't vote liberally or think liberally in the same proportions as the now-young. It is of course possible that this trend will be broken by the new green generation, but there is no evidence to suggest that it will happen—surely not the 50-50 split of the youth vote between Nixon and McGovern.[4]

Finally, *values*—surely a deep and potent concern in America today. Also a deeply and potent concern for men since times immemorial. The value-busting shock of the speedy arrival of the future has always been with us. And if living through an era that birthed computers, jet planes and television is confusing, compare it to an earlier short moment of history that only saw the advent of the automobile, the electric light, the airplane and the radio.

[4] For a glimpse into the future, consider an American Council of Education survey released in 1974, as this volume was going to press. The "political orientation" of college freshmen looked like this:

Far left	2%
Liberal	33%
Middle of the road	51%
Conservative	14%
Far right	1%

Among freshmen men, four of the top six "objectives considered to be essential or very important" were such material goals as:

"Be an authority in my field"
"Be very well-off financially"
"Raise a family"
"Be successful in my own business"

The other two items in the top six were:

"Develop a philosophy of life"
"Help others in difficulty"

At the *bottom* of the list were such items as:

"Influence social values"
"Influence political structure"
"Become a community leader"
"Achieve in a performing art"

Finally, the survey showed that the two most popular fields of study for freshmen men were "business" and "engineering."

* * *

These are, then, troubled times and the measure of "success" in a troubled world is how a person, or a people or a nation copes with a troubling situation. It is the contention here that the American people have coped well and that, indeed, may be the most valued jewel in the diadem of American success.

Imagine, first, what might so easily have happened during the troubled era we have just lived through.

Given the stresses, for example, it is not farfetched to suggest that a drastic, right-wing, even fascist response might have been elicited. After all, while some American boys were dying in an extremely unpopular war, other American boys were burning the flag and using it for underwear. While some Americans thought drugs were an unmitigated evil, others touted drug use as a higher form of human activity. While some Americans viewed crime as a threat to their wives, daughters and parents, other Americans saw law-and-order as a code word for racism. While some Americans saw abortion as murder, other Americans saw it as an inalienable right. While some Americans thought busing was a solution to segregated schooling, other Americans saw busing as a bad trip, sure to destroy their schools and their children. While some Americans moored their lives to "the traditional morality," other Americans sought to break down and ridicule that morality. While most whites and most blacks felt that burning cities was an obscenity, some blacks and some whites said, "Burn, baby, burn."

Given such polar positions, given the vast publicity tendered to the minority view, given the other generally disquieting factors of life in the second half of the twentieth century, is it not reasonable to suggest that here was an era ripe for witch hunts, scapegoatism, stark rigidity of attitude, violence and counterviolence? Is it unreal to suggest, given the circumstances, that there would have been either a cultural revolution or a countercultural revolution, but in any event a harsh and jolting spasm that could have truly torn the nation asunder?

Given the fiery passions that the war engendered in the peace movement, is it not plausible to think that the move to violence would have proceeded far further than it did? It almost did; there were bombings and some ROTC buildings did go up in flames, but even the radicals ultimately showed moderation.

No, instead of the rigidity—left or right—which could have seared the nation irrevocably, there was a remarkable quality of give-and-take that went on.

Looking back at the data of a turbulent time we can see clearly that what went on was a healthy, spirited *and two-way* change.

Americans faced a changing world, faced the sometimes strident demands for change—and changed. Faced with the centuries-old moral sore of racism—America changed. Faced with a new world reality where enemies were suddenly declared friends—America changed. Faced with a wave of new cultural beliefs—America changed somewhat. Faced with new demands for feminine equality—America changed. Faced with new environmental concerns—America changed. Why, faced with the notion that the population was exploding—Americans even changed their procreative attitudes, reflected now in a sharply declining birth rate! There can be no question but that the Cause People played a critical role in changing America—for the better. In many ways their passion paid off. They deserve the semi-sweet taste of partial victories, and should not be disconsolate.

More important, something else was demonstrated. The massive weight of the public's opinion has changed the thrust of the movement. That is very important. Bowing to the weight—and the wisdom—of the public's opinion, so many ragged edges of the movement's platform have already been smoothed over. Crime is seen now for what it is, blue-collar ethnics are appealed to, elitism shrinks, and on an issue like busing, even the Cause People have learned to identify a non-negotiable demand. This is so important because, for all their excesses and for all their arrogance, Movement cadre are probably vital to guarantee continuing healthy change in America. These young and now not-so-young people are articulate, committed, educated, idealistic and by now experienced. They have on occasion also demonstrated massive stupidity, but ours is a society that believes in redemption, and, besides, no one else recently has been right about everything, not even the author.

* * *

Going somewhat beyond the data-oriented framework of this volume it should also be pointed out that in the course of the last dozen or so years America has also: elected its first Catholic President, elected the first black mayor of a large and largely white city, sent men to the moon, cured diseases that have plagued men for millennia,[5] constructed a world-wide air transportation system that has shrunk the globe, initiated a "green revolution" that feeds billions of earthlings better than they had ever been fed before despite rising populations, fed Russia with subsidized grain, helped Israel fight back when no other nation would, introduced a new computer technology that has and will revolutionize a large part of the labors of mankind, exported to a puzzled world the techniques of management and mass distribution that enabled this society to exercise its own peculiar form

[5] Raising life expectancy in less developed countries from 41.7 years in the 1950–55 era to 52.4 years today.

of genius: the ability to bootstrap so many tens of millions of its citizens into the middle class.

While all *that* was going on, America—for a quarter of a century and more—made and met commitments that kept the world as a whole in a condition of uneasy general peace, even while some hot and ugly but local wars raged. We were indeed "watchmen on the walls of freedom," to use John F. Kennedy's phrase. And if, indeed, to use another JFK phrase, "We paid any price and bore any burden to insure the success of freedom in the world . . ." well, maybe it had to be done, albeit probably differently in some instances. Perhaps the proof of our international success involves an examination today of what are our international problems. American postwar strategy was designed to build a strong, free, prosperous and relatively independent Western world that might even be able one day to look us squarely in the eye as equals. That young Americans in early 1973 drove German cars, played music on Japanese transistor radios, drank French wine, wore Italian shoes—while the American tourists in Europe watched the dollar shrink—gives some validity to the idea that we have succeeded perhaps just a little bit beyond our fondest expectations.

And while all *that* was going on, and while Cause People were preaching that repression was around the corner, this country suddenly saw three hundred "underground" newspapers hawked on public street corners, saw nudity, pornography and "free speech" carried to heretofore incredible distances, saw libel and slander laws all but ruled inoperative, developed a new and impressionistic journalism that allowed opinion to dominate fact and indeed parade as fact. Repression indeed! And if that isn't enough to convince the reader that the Gestapo hasn't quite arrived, consider the idea that Sam Ervin, a septuagenarian southern Senator, anti-civil rights, pro-war and anti-minimum wage in his earlier voting record, has become the folk hero of the left as he battered, badgered and berated the President's men and castigated the President about an ugly sequence of events, grouped around the word "Watergate."

*   *   *

Well, then, are we better off here? Has America been succeeding?

We have. We have succeeded because we've been coping successfully with the problems that we face, even if we're still glum about those problems. Remember, that those two concepts, progress and glumness, are not necessarily contradictory. And consider, in passing, that it may well be that we have come to a point where we are not only glum about our problems but about the fact that no one seems to want to talk up about our successes.

If it is indeed success, it couldn't happen to a better bunch of people. The hero of this volume is the American people. Calumnied, confronted and criticized, they have come through a tough decade in nothing less than heroic fashion. Smarter, wiser, calmer, shrewder, tougher and more forgiving than their critics of the left and of the right, they deserve to have confidence in their ever-changing institutions, their ever-changing nation, and in themselves.

Things may turn out to be tough for a while now. Problems abound. But these folk can cope. No one can be sure, but the guess here is that Americans in the decade to come will keep complaining and keep progressing. Wait for the book about the 1980 Census.

CHAPTER 24

Implications

It has been said, a thousand times, that America and the world are moving into a new era, an era of global conciliation, an era where the United States will no longer dominate the Western world to the same degree as earlier. That is a widely held and broad judgment, and despite our innate suspicions of broad judgments widely held, there is a certain plausibility to it.

If a new era is here it is critical that America and Americans march into it head held high, proud of past accomplishments, confident that it was America that created the conditions that made the new era possible, and confident that we have the ability to do what must be done in the years to come.

This is not important in order to provide a chauvinistic euphoriant to a flagging American spirit. It goes well beyond that. New era or no new era, low profile or lower profile, the cold fact remains that America remains the most powerful, most influential, most prosperous, most imitated nation in the world. That America is still, in Jefferson's words, the last best hope of mankind remains a fact. There are indeed those around the world, friend and foe, who believe, rightly or wrongly, that "America has lost its way"— at least temporarily. But there is a far harsher judgment afloat around the world concerning the Soviet superpower. The Soviet Union, the world knows, is a repressive nation that can neither feed its people well nor manage its economy. And even the most dedicated Sinophiles see no Chinese era for half a century. For all their progress, China is still a rural and essentially underdeveloped nation.

So we're still it, albeit on a different level than before. And if George McGovern believes that no nation can colonize a century, there is respectful disagreement here, and some agreement instead with an unaccustomed ally. Henry Luce, for all his many other excesses, was probably right. This is an American century, like it or not. The world, whether it likes it or not, has been deeply influenced by American ideology, American technology and American outlook—and gives no real sign of stopping as this nation of ours moves into its third century. America has been the real insurgency in the twentieth century.

Without trying to be too portentous, it is probably correct to say that whether America works out or not will dictate the course of civilization in the decades to come. Partly this will come about in the way we conduct ourselves in the world, and partly—as ever—it will come about in the way we conduct our business at home. But in both instances the whole world is watching.

To move into such an era nervously, twitching over imaginary failures, would be doing ourselves and the world a major disservice. Nations, like men, do better when they are confident. The tennis player who dwells on how bad he is at hitting the overhead shot, watches it descend with dread, blows the shot and is to be pitied. The poker player attempting to bluff a hand, and does so nervously and unconvincingly, is a loser and to be pitied. But a poker player *who is nervous and who throws in a winning hand is more than just an object of pity; he is a damn fool.*

As the Red Guards poured across the countryside of mainland China in the mid-1960s, U Thant said that "nations sometimes have nervous breakdowns." But that is not what happened in America. We had a case of the jitters and the remedy for jitters is time, not shock treatment.

America still has a winning hand and only a lack of confidence— confidence we realistically deserve to have in ourselves—can turn this nation into a loser. For a jittery, unconfident America to throw in its hand would be a global tragedy, and if it happens it will be balefully reflected almost immediately in our commerce, art, politics, culture and our spirit. It would induce a global psychological recession that would shake the foundations of modern existence.

So that, then, is one reason why the acknowledgment of success and progress is so important. It should dissuade us from throwing in a winning hand.

* * *

Which leads then to another important question: If the understanding of success or progress in America is so important *who will speak for success?*

That is a doubly important question. For the notion of success and progress does more than effect the nature of international affairs, as outlined above. A case can be made that a good part of our domestic malaise can be laid precisely at the feet of a media system that underreports progress. Consider the two attitudinal bedrocks discussed earlier in this volume. Americans say their own lives are fine. And they say that America is in trouble. There is another way of putting that: What people know of first-hand, they think well of. What people know of secondhand, information gathered through the transmission belt of our system of communications, they think ill of!

After all, this case could be made about American attitudes. If Mr. Smith and Mrs. Jones and Mr. Green and Mrs. Brown all say their lives are pretty good, thank you, and if society, or "America," is only a collection of Smith, Jones, Green, Brown and their friends, then America is not on the wrong track at all, but is in fact a whopping success, and the only reason that Americans think things are lousy is because they are given a bum steer by a media system that lives by one cardinal rule, "Good news is no news."

That is probably too all-inclusive a theory and probably far too harsh on the press. But the fact remains that the press has not learned how to present good news, and this is corrosive.

If the aggregation of the data assembled in this book is anywhere near accurate, then it is fair to say that American progress of varying sorts was surely one of the great, complex and far-reaching stories of the decade, possibly the most important story, but surely no less than second to the Vietnam agony. But who wrote that ongoing story? Who filmed it for television?

There were lots of stories about the corrupt Thieu-Ky clique, about Biafra, about riots, about college disruptions, about never trusting anyone over thirty, about drugs, about black is beautiful and Swahili in the schools, about grapes, about radical chic, about pollution, about Women's Lib, about welfare chiselers, about busing, about law-and-order demagogues, about inflation, recession, devaluation and interest rates, about Bangladesh and tilt, and about Watergate, Watergate and Watergate, chronicled with the detail that might properly be accorded to the discovery of fire.

Now, surely, many of these stories were both interesting and important. But who and what speaks for the broad everyday march of American humanity toward what the public, at least, considers a better way of life, a higher standard of living, and toward—quite simply—an improvement in the human condition that is envied and aped around the world?

The business press deals with it, it's true, but the business press is a special affair. Who tells the American people that headway is being made? Is it so absurd to suggest that if all one reads and all one sees is cast under the rubric of crisis and chaos that Americans will either a) believe the press and think America is on the wrong track or b) believe their own senses and think the press and the crisismongers they headline are elite, arrogant and so far out of touch as to be noncredible and, even worse, irrelevant?

Now, the national press corps, including not only writers and TV newsmen, but their editors, publishers, directors and producers as well, are for the most part honest, intelligent, well-meaning and responsible people. They have perfected beyond imagining the techniques of reporting about trees, bark, blisters on the bark and the molecular structure of the blisters on the bark on the trees. Unfortunately, they haven't yet mastered a way to tell something about the configuration of the forest.

It is an unfortunate situation for which no remedy will be presented here, mostly because none comes immediately to mind. But the problem is quite real, and if the press concerns itself with not only examining the credibility of Presidents and politicians, but with its own credibility canyon —it will be well advised and potentially helpful to the nation's spirit. Americans should be told of their successes with the same vigor and flair that they are told about their failures.

As Douglass Cater has reminded us, "The dinosaur did not go out of business because he was too big or clumsy. What really happened was that the dinosaur's communication system did not create an adequate picture of reality on which he could act."

* * *

Progress is a contagious idea. Once acknowledged it butts in almost everywhere. Consider American domestic politics. If one accepts the notion of American failure, then it is easy to arrive at the Nixon/New Politics position: Things were terrible in the Sixties, liberalism was in the saddle, liberalism didn't work, the "programs" didn't work, let's try something new, either new-fashioned conservatism, new-fashioned elitism or anything.

Such a view is not only subscribed to by Republicans and New Politics types. As sophisticated and intelligent an observer of the American political scene as Theodore H. White buys the same syllogism, but makes an additional mistake—that the New Politics is the logical and inevitable outgrowth of Sixties-style liberalism.

But suppose one invalidates the first step in that syllogism. Suppose one says that, in fact, great progress was made in the Sixties. Suppose, in short, one agrees with the argument of this book. Then what is the judgment on so-called traditional liberalism?

Much better. Much better indeed.

Lest the case for traditional political liberalism be overstated, it should be pointed out that it is the hard work of energetic and highly motivated people—not politicians—that builds the economic strength of a nation. But that is not enough by any means. For politics and political theory play a role in establishing the conditions in which an energetic populace can flourish.

And so, if one traces the course of the so-called old-fashioned liberalism from the moment it assumed political hegemony in 1933, what does one see? First, a nation locked into an economic depression of immense proportions. Then, very slowly, under the impact of the New Deal, the beginnings of a return to economic health and the establishment of some additional equity for the American working class. A World War erupts and America—literally—saves the world. Liberal doctrine after the war is internationalist abroad, progressive at home—and dominant. Eisenhower does not repeal the New Deal and Nixon does not repeal the Great Society.

In the Sixties, two Democratic Presidents pledge to get America moving economically, to give a fair break to the poor and the black, to build the educational system of the nation, to give the elderly health care and dignity in retirement, to preserve the American wilderness and to clean the air and the water. Such was the rhetoric—the alleged rhetoric of "over-promising."

Led by two liberal Presidents, spurred by a genuine liberal impulse in several great Congresses, helped by the political accident of the Goldwater nomination, aided by a liberal infrastructure in the labor movement, in the universities, in women's organizations and down into the PTAs—a cascade of liberal legislation passed the Congress and was signed by the President. Such were the laws in the era of "overpromising."

And as the Seventies opened and one examined the data to see what happened in the Sixties, in that overblown, overpromised decade, what does one see? Massive progress for the poor and the black, a rebuilt educational system, medical care for the aged and greater dignity in retirement, bold steps taken to clean the air and water. Such were the results of a decade of overblown, overpromised traditional liberalism.

Rhetoric. Laws. Results.

Rhetoric leading to laws leading to results. It is possible, of course, that the results came about *in spite* of the rhetoric and the laws and the programs. It is possible that the results came about due solely to nonpolitical American enterprise. But, according to the rules of the road in American political discourse, the burden of proof is on the other side. The rhetoric led to laws. You've seen the results. Liberalism worked.

Traditional liberals look back at the 1960s and say this: We helped America and we elected Democrats. Is there something more that a political party is supposed to do?

Now, the argument is made that the Sixties were the last gasp of traditional liberalism. That the old agenda has been completed. That now we must move on. That we need a new politics to provide mystical cures for depersonalization, rootlessness, and a lack of love, to build a new moral code and a new culture.

A new agenda indeed! Tell it to the blacks—who, for all the progress, are still low men on the economic totem pole. Tell it to the poor in America, still in slums and hollows and shacks. Tell it to the aged. Tell it to the sick, and to the healthy who will live longer if medical research yields up still more fruits. Tell it to city dwellers who can't park downtown but have no mass transit available. Tell it to the migrant farm worker. Tell it to the factory worker in an unsafe factory. Tell them that the old agenda is complete and now we have to concentrate on love and undepersonalization.

Politics is not a substitute for religion. It can't handle the deepest spiritual problems of men. Life is a puzzle and there is no President that can solve it for voters. But politics *can* solve some limited problems. In recent years, it has solved some limited problems and made headway toward solving others. That is the political lesson served up by the progress of recent years.

* * *

And what of the future? Do the lessons of the recent past tell us something about what comes next? Possibly so.

Americans today face major issues: political scandal, international uncertainties, energy shortages and inflation of a greater magnitude than known here for a long time. So it is fair now to ask: *What happens next?*

The author is not a seer. The problems are not trivial ones. Can the political system survive the gross shocks inflicted upon it and remain responsive? Can we, as a people, learn a new energy ethic that minimizes waste without destroying material well-being? Can we play both a prudent and morally decent role of leadership in a still-dangerous world or will we succumb to a new isolationism? And probably most critical for the short term: Can we deal with a high and dispiriting inflation that seems to pick the pockets of every family in America?

No specific answers are offered here; not now, not yet. Only a sense of how things are. What kind of people are these who will be called upon— as people and as a nation—to deal with these difficult problems?

A tale has been told in this volume about an energetic and resourceful folk who have dealt with racial injustice, poverty, unpopular war, automation, riot, massive population shifts, new cultural codes, changing value systems, violence and social turbulence of every size and shape imaginable.

Ingeniously, constructively, flexibly—these folk have coped. They have accommodated and they have held firm; they have listened, they have learned and they have spoken and have taught. One step at a time, sensibly, they have made material and attitudinal progress.

No one knows what outside pressures will be placed upon Americans in the years to come. No one knew that assassinations would come in the 1960s and no one knows if, as some weather forecasters indicate, we are due for a long Midwestern drought that will shoot food prices far higher than they are now! No one knows all the problems and no one knows how Americans will react.

All that is offered here is a sense, a feeling of the American response in the years to come based on their recent past performance: Don't ever sell these folk short. They can cope. They can cope with war and riot—and they can cope with high inflation, with energy shortages and political crises up to and including impeachment of their President. They can cope—and they will cope.

* * *

Finally, reader, a request for a reflective pause and some hard thinking. Stop and consider, honestly now, what has happened in this tumultuous, bubbling, harsh, turbulent and sometimes scary dozen years? Has it really revealed American bankruptcy? Or has it revealed instead just the opposite, the ability of a doughty continental tribe to make headway into head winds?

THE SHORT CENSUS

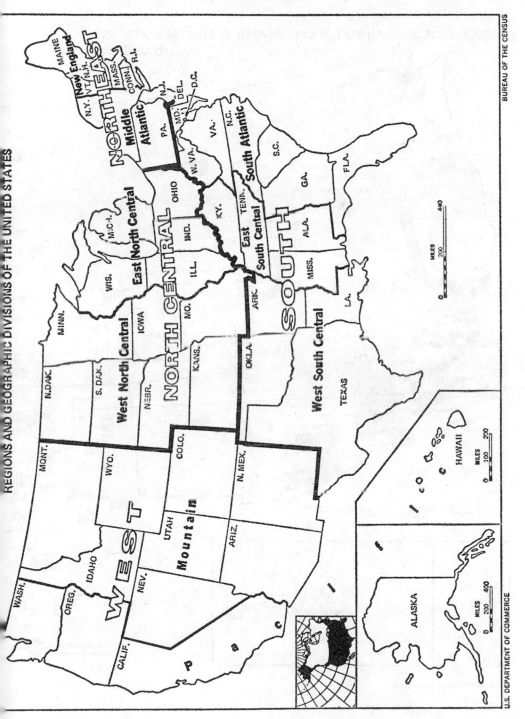

REGIONS AND GEOGRAPHIC DIVISIONS OF THE UNITED STATES

BUREAU OF THE CENSUS

U.S. DEPARTMENT OF COMMERCE

STANDARD METROPOLITAN STATISTICAL AREAS OF THE UNITED STATES AND PUERTO RICO: 1970

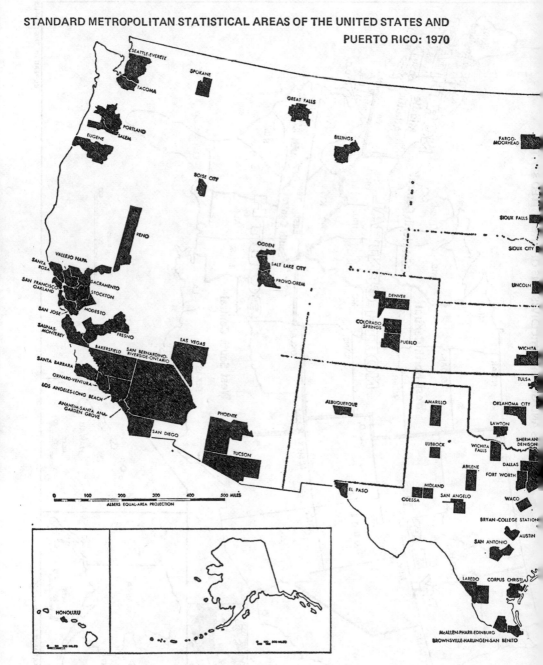

ALBERS EQUAL-AREA PROJECTION

0   100   200   300   400   500 MILES

U.S. DEPARTMENT OF COMMERCE

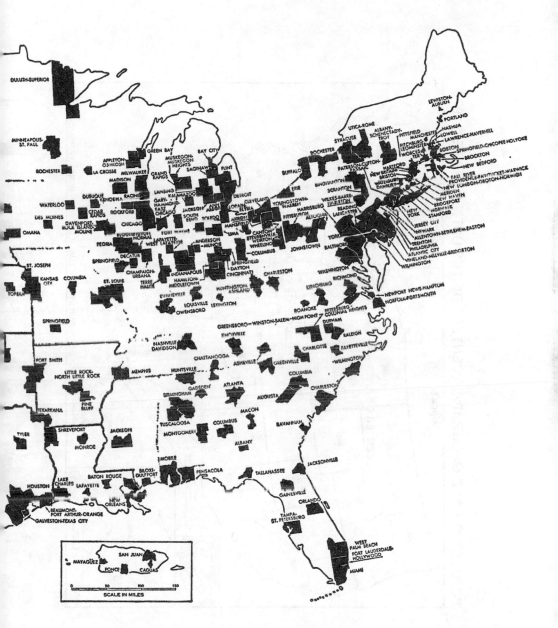

BUREAU OF THE CENSUS

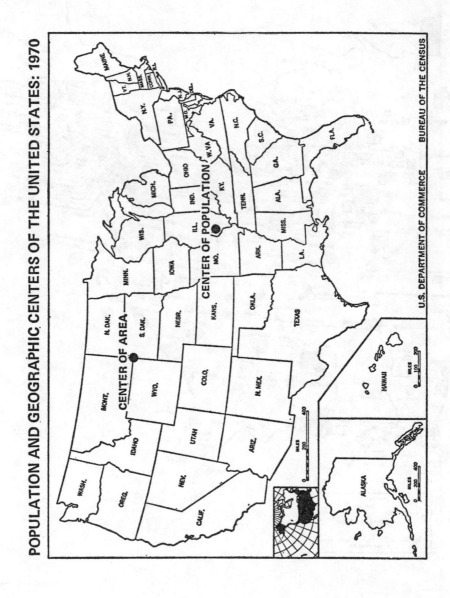

POPULATION AND GEOGRAPHIC CENTERS OF THE UNITED STATES: 1970

U.S. DEPARTMENT OF COMMERCE   BUREAU OF THE CENSUS

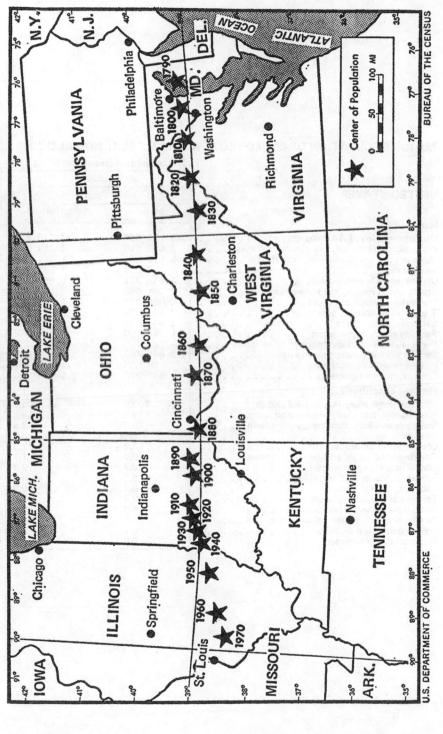

CENTER OF POPULATION FOR THE UNITED STATES: 1790 TO 1970

U.S. DEPARTMENT OF COMMERCE

BUREAU OF THE CENSUS

MAJOR OCCUPATION OF EMPLOYED PERSONS BY SEX: 1970 AND 1960

[Data based on sample, see text.]

UNITED STATES	1970 Total	
	Male	Female
Number		
Total employed, 14 years old and over	48 138 665	29 170 127
Professional, technical, and kindred workers	6 516 610	4 314 083
Managers and administrators, except farm	5 125 534	1 013 843
Sales workers	3 267 653	1 999 794
Clerical and kindred workers	3 452 251	9 582 440
Craftsmen, foremen, and kindred workers	9 501 588	494 871
Operatives, except transport	6 096 313	3 719 842
Transport equipment operatives.	2 644 368	121 819
Laborers, except farm	2 944 649	268 505
Farmers and farm managers	1 281 160	61 934
Farm laborers and farm foremen	783 145	140 721
Service workers, except private household	3 640 487	4 424 030
Private household workers	39 685	1 053 092
Occupation not reported	2 845 222	1 975 153
Percent Distribution		
Total employed, 14 years old and over	100.0	100.0
Professional, technical, and kindred workers	13.5	14.8
Managers and administrators, except farm	10.6	3.5
Sales workers	6.8	6.9
Clerical and kindred workers	7.2	32.9
Craftsmen, foremen, and kindred workers	19.7	1.7
Operatives, except transport	12.7	12.8
Transport equipment operatives	5.5	0.4
Laborers, except farm	6.1	0.9
Farmers and farm managers	2.7	0.2
Farm laborers and farm foremen	1.6	0.5
Service workers, except private household	7.6	15.2
Private household workers	0.1	3.6
Occupation not reported	5.9	6.8

	1960	
UNITED STATES	Total	
	Male	Female
Number		
Total employed, 14 years old and over	43 466 955	21 172 301
Professional, technical, and kindred workers.	4 303 268	2 682 720
Managers and administrators, except farm	4 796 831	828 995
Sales workers	2 985 882	1 651 534
Clerical and kindred workers.	2 921 912	6 203 858
Craftsmen, foremen, and kindred workers	8 667 696	277 140
Operatives, except transport	5 686 805	3 135 449
Transport equipment operatives	2 488 052	37 861
Laborers, except farm.	3 149 108	172 726
Farmers and farm managers	2 389 396	117 918
Farm laborers and farm foremen	1 238 678	247 592
Service workers, except private household	2 791 313	2 962 884
Private household workers	61 063	1 656 856
Occupation not reported	1 986 951	1 196 768
Percent Distribution		
Total employed, 14 years old and over	100.0	100.0
Professional, technical, and kindred workers.	9.9	12.7
Managers and administrators, except farm	11.0	3.9
Sales workers	6.9	7.8
Clerical and kindred workers	6.7	29.3
Craftsmen, foremen, and kindred workers	19.9	1.3
Operatives, except transport	13.1	14.8
Transport equipment operatives	5.7	0.2
Laborers, except farm	7.2	0.8
Farmers and farm managers	5.5	0.6
Farm laborers and farm foremen	2.8	1.2
Service workers, except private household	6.4	14.0
Private household workers	0.1	7.8
Occupation not reported	4.6	5.7

TRENDS IN THE LABOR FORCE: 1960 TO 1973

MILLIONS OF PERSONS

Sources: Chart prepared by U.S. Bureau of the Census. Data from U.S. Bureau of Labor Statistics.

FARM POPULATION, FARMS AND FARM SIZE: 1950 to 1972

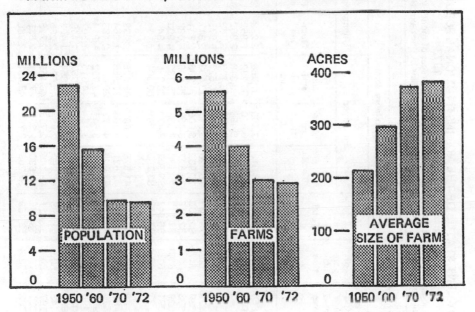

Source: Chart prepared by U.S. Bureau of the Census. Data from U.S. Dept. of Agriculture, Economic Research Service.

EMPLOYMENT STATUS OF THE NONINSTITUTIONAL POPULATION, BY SEX AND RACE: 1950 TO 1973

[In thousands of persons 16 years old and over. Annual figures are averages of monthly figures. See Historical Statistics, Colonial Times to 1957, series D 1-14 and D 20, for similar but not exactly comparable data]

Year or Month, Sex, and Race	Total non institutional population	Labor Force								Not in Labor Force		
		Total including Armed Forces	Per cent of population	Civilian labor force						Total 1	Keeping house	In school
				Total	Employed			Unemployed				
					Total	Agri- cul- tural	Non- agri- cul- tural	Num- ber	Per- cent			
TOTAL												
1950	106,645	63,858	59.9	62,208	58,918	7,160	51,758	3,288	5.3	42,787	32,912	3,542
1955	112,732	68,072	60.4	65,023	62,170	6,450	55,722	2,852	4.4	44,660	33,614	3,517
1960	119,759	72,142	60.2	69,628	65,778	5,458	60,318	3,852	5.5	47,617	35,464	4,489
1965	129,236	77,178	59.7	74,455	71,088	4,361	66,726	3,366	4.5	52,058	35,463	6,399
1967	133,319	80,793	60.6	77,347	74,372	3,844	70,527	2,975	3.8	52,527	34,993	6,657
1968	135,562	82,272	60.7	78,737	75,920	3,817	72,103	2,817	3.6	53,291	35,203	6,900
1969	137,841	84,239	61.1	80,733	77,902	3,606	74,296	2,831	3.5	53,602	34,887	7,013
1970	140,182	85,903	61.3	82,715	78,627	3,462	75,165	4,088	4.9	54,280	35,118	7,033
1971	142,596	86,929	61.0	84,113	79,120	3,387	75,732	4,993	5.9	55,666	35,561	7,524
1972	145,775	88,991	61.0	86,542	81,702	3,472	78,230	4,840	5.6	56,785	35,811	7,422
1973, Apr.	147,729	89,823	60.8	87,473	83,299	3,295	80,004	4,174	4.8	57,906	35,314	9,180
MALE												
1950	52,352	45,446	86.8	43,819	41,578	6,002	35,576	2,239	5.1	6,906	77	1,987
1955	55,122	47,488	86.2	44,475	42,621	5,265	37,356	1,854	4.2	7,634	74	1,834
1960	58,144	48,870	84.0	46,388	43,904	4,472	39,431	2,486	5.4	9,274	84	2,303
1965	62,473	50,946	81.5	48,255	46,340	3,547	42,792	1,914	4.0	11,527	137	3,215
1967	64,316	52,398	81.5	48,987	47,479	3,164	44,315	1,507	3.1	11,919	142	3,326
1968	65,345	53,030	81.2	49,533	48,114	3,157	44,957	1,419	2.9	12,315	180	3,492
1969	66,365	53,688	80.9	50,221	48,818	2,963	45,854	1,403	2.8	12,677	199	3,570
1970	67,409	54,343	80.6	51,195	48,960	2,861	46,099	2,235	4.4	13,066	240	3,591
1971	68,512	54,797	80.0	52,021	49,245	2,790	46,455	2,776	5.3	13,715	272	3,832
1972	69,864	55,671	79.7	53,265	50,630	2,839	47,791	2,635	4.9	14,193	221	3,792
1973, Apr.	70,770	55,792	78.8	53,489	51,203	2,752	48,451	2,286	4.3	14,978	204	4,646

Negro and other:[2]

Year											
1955	3 5,034	(NA)	3 85.0	4,279	3,903	668	3,235	376	8.8	755	(NA)	(NA)
1960	3 5,595	(NA)	3 83.0	4,645	4,148	620	3,529	437	10.7	951	10	246
1965	6,330	5,034	80.3	4,855	4,496	463	4,033	359	7.4	1,246	22	359
1967	6,606	5,253	79.5	4,945	4,646	361	4,285	239	6.0	1,353	19	429
1968	6,755	5,322	78.8	4,979	4,702	353	4,350	277	5.6	1,434	25	453
1969	6,918	5,404	78.1	5,036	4,770	309	4,461	266	5.3	1,513	34	480
1970	7,098	5,507	77.6	5,182	4,803	303	4,500	379	7.3	1,591	39	507
1971	7,286	5,533	75.9	5,220	4,746	271	4,475	474	9.1	1,753	47	597
1972	7,533	5,630	74.7	5,335	4,861	264	4,596	475	8.9	1,902	40	615
1973, Apr.	7,823	5,831	74.1	5,489	5,054	243	4,811	435	7.9	2,023	43	757

FEMALE

Year											
1950	54,293	18,412	33.9	18,389	17,340	1,159	16,181	1,049	5.7	35,881	32,835	1,555
1955	57,610	20,534	35.7	20,548	19,551	1,184	18,366	998	4.9	37,026	33,540	1,683
1960	61,615	23,272	37.8	23,240	21,874	986	20,837	1,366	5.9	38,343	34,381	2,185
1965	66,763	26,232	39.3	26,200	24,748	814	23,934	1,452	5.5	40,531	35,326	3,184
1967	69,003	28,395	41.2	28,360	26,892	680	26,212	1,468	5.2	40,608	34,851	3,331
1968	70,217	29,242	41.6	29,204	27,807	660	27,147	1,397	4.8	40,978	35,023	3,408
1969	71,476	30,551	42.7	30,512	29,084	643	28,441	1,428	4.7	40,924	34,688	3,443
1970	72,774	31,560	43.4	31,520	29,667	601	29,066	1,853	5.9	41,214	34,878	3,442
1971	74,084	32,132	43.4	32,091	29,875	598	29,277	2,217	6.9	41,952	35,289	3,692
1972	75,911	33,320	43.9	33,277	31,072	633	30,439	2,205	6.6	42,591	35,590	3,630
1973, Apr.	76,959	34,051	44.2	33,984	32,096	542	31,553	1,888	5.6	42,928	35,110	4,533

Negro and other:[2]

Year											
1955	3 5,772	(NA)	3 46.1	2,663	2,438	288	2,150	225	8.4	3,109	(NA)	(NA)
1960	3 6,369	(NA)	3 48.2	3,069	2,779	248	2,530	290	9.4	3,300	2,810	274
1965	7,133	3,467	48.6	3,464	3,147	165	2,982	317	9.2	3,666	2,999	415
1967	7,479	3,766	49.5	3,704	3,366	104	3,262	338	9.1	3,773	2,967	456
1968	7,670	3,784	49.3	3,780	3,467	90	3,377	313	8.3	3,886	3,041	467
1969	7,877	3,922	49.8	3,918	3,614	78	3,536	304	7.8	3,955	3,044	511
1970	8,114	4,019	49.5	4,015	3,642	65	3,577	373	9.3	4,095	3,125	543
1971	8,351	4,107	49.2	4,102	3,658	56	3,601	445	10.8	4,243	3,173	618
1972	8,736	4,254	48.7	4,249	3,767	47	3,721	482	11.3	4,481	3,333	642
1973, Apr.	9,078	4,376	48.2	4,369	3,947	43	3,903	423	9.7	4,703	3,404	814

NA Not available. 1 Includes "other", not shown separately 2 Excludes white. 3 Civilian non-institutional population.

Source: U.S. Bureau of Labor Statistics, Employment and Earrings, monthly.

PER CENT OF PERSONS 14 YEARS OLD AND OVER
IN LABOR FORCE
By Age and Sex:

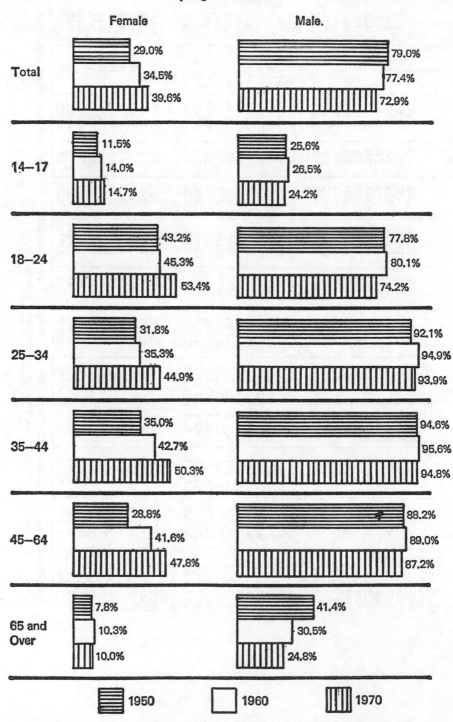

Female

Male.

Total
- 29.0%
- 34.5%
- 39.6%
- 79.0%
- 77.4%
- 72.9%

14—17
- 11.5%
- 14.0%
- 14.7%
- 25.6%
- 26.5%
- 24.2%

18—24
- 43.2%
- 45.3%
- 53.4%
- 77.8%
- 80.1%
- 74.2%

25—34
- 31.8%
- 35.3%
- 44.9%
- 92.1%
- 94.9%
- 93.9%

35—44
- 35.0%
- 42.7%
- 50.3%
- 94.6%
- 95.6%
- 94.8%

45—64
- 28.8%
- 41.6%
- 47.8%
- 88.2%
- 89.0%
- 87.2%

65 and Over
- 7.8%
- 10.3%
- 10.0%
- 41.4%
- 30.5%
- 24.8%

1950   1960   1970

1970 CENSUS OF POPULATION, U.S. Department of Commerce, Social and Economic Statistics Administration, Bureau of the Census

WOMEN IN THE LABOR FORCE, SELECTED YEARS, 1900-72

Year	Women in labor force (thousands)	Women in labor force as percent of	
		Total labor force	All women of working age
1900	5,114	18.1	20.4
1910	7,889	20.9	25.2
1920	8,430	20.4	23.3
1930	10,679	22.0	24.3
1940	12,845	24.3	25.4
1945	19,270	29.6	35.7
1950	18,412	28.8	33.9
1955	20,584	30.2	35.7
1960	23,272	32.3	37.8
1965	26,232	34.0	39.3
1970	31,560	36.7	43.4
1972	33,320	37.4	43.8

Note.—Data for 1900 to 1940 are from decennial censuses and refer to a single date; beginning 1945 data are annual averages.

For 1900 to 1945 data include women 14 years of age and over; beginning 1950 data include women 16 years of age and over.

Labor force data for 1900 to 1930 refer to gainfully employed workers.

Data for 1972 reflect adjustments to 1970 Census benchmarks.

Sources: Department of Commerce, Bureau of the Census, and Department of Labor, Bureau of Labor Statistics.

WOMEN AS A PER CENT OF PERSONS IN SEVERAL PROFESSIONAL AND MANAGERIAL OCCUPATIONS, 1910-70

[Percent]

Occupational group	1910	1920	1930	1940	1950	1960	1970
Clergymen	0.6	1.4	2.2	2.4	4.0	2.3	2.9
College presidents, professors, and instructors[1]	18.9	30.2	31.9	26.5	23.2	24.2	28.2
Dentists	3.1	3.3	1.9	1.5	2.7	2.3	3.5
Editors and reporters	12.2	16.8	24.0	25.0	32.0	36.6	40.6
Engineers	[2]	[2]	[2]	.4	1.2	.8	1.6
Lawyers and judges	.5	1.4	2.1	2.5	3.5	3.5	4.9
Managers, manufacturing industries	1.7	3.1	3.2	4.3	6.4	7.1	6.3
Physicians	6.0	5.0	4.4	4.7	6.1	6.9	9.3

[1] Data for 1920 and 1930 probably include some teachers in schools below collegiate rank. The Office of Education estimates the 1930 figure closer to 28 percent.

[2] Less than one tenth of 1 percent.

Note.—Data are from the decennial censuses. Data for 1910 and 1920 include persons 10 years of age and over; data for 1930 to 1970 include persons 14 years of age and over.

Source: Department of Commerce, Bureau of the Census.

FAMILIES AND UNRELATED INDIVIDUALS BY TOTAL MONEY INCOME IN 1947 TO 1972, IN CONSTANT DOLLARS, BY RACE OF HEAD

(In 1972 dollars. Families and unrelated individuals as of March of the following year)

Race of Head and Year	Number (Thou- sands)	Total	Under $3,000	$3,000 to $4,999	$5,000 to $6,999	$7,000 to $9,999	$10,000 to $11,999	$12,000 to $14,999	$15,000 and Over	Amount (Dollars)	Index (1947= 100)
Families											
Total											
1972	54 373	100.0	7.2	9.4	10.2	16.8	11.5	14.6	30.3	11 116	196
1971	53 296	100.0	7.7	9.8	10.8	17.8	12.5	14.8	26.6	10 578	187
1970	51 948	100.0	7.9	9.4	10.6	18.1	12.7	15.0	26.2	10 617	187
1969	51 237	100.0	7.7	9.1	10.1	18.5	12.5	15.7	26.6	10 766	190
1968	50 510	100.0	7.8	9.5	10.7	19.5	12.6	15.2	24.7	10 381	183
1967	49 834	100.0	9.1	9.7	11.2	20.4	12.6	14.7	22.2	9 940	175
1966	49 065	100.0	9.6	10.2	11.3	21.1	12.7	14.6	20.3	9 667	171
1965	48 279	100.0	10.7	11.3	12.2	21.5	13.0	13.3	18.0	9 221	163
1964	47 835	100.0	11.3	12.3	12.9	21.7	12.2	13.1	16.6	8 861	156
1963	47 436	100.0	12.2	12.1	13.2	22.8	12.3	12.1	15.1	8 543	151
1962	46 998	100.0	13.0	12.5	14.2	23.6	11.4	11.3	13.9	8 247	146
1961	46 341	100.0	14.1	13.0	14.5	23.2	11.6	10.6	13.1	8 019	142
1960	45 456	100.0	14.2	12.8	14.5	24.8	11.3	10.4	12.0	7 941	140
1959	45 111	100.0	14.3	13.5	15.4	25.3	11.1	9.8	10.8	7 769	137
1958	44 232	100.0	15.2	13.9	17.7	25.6	10.8	7.9	9.0	7 353	130
1957	43 696	100.0	15.1	13.7	17.8	25.9	11.3	8.0	8.2	7 365	130
1956	43 497	100.0	15.0	13.8	18.0	24.7	11.1	8.6	8.7	7 357	130
1955	42 889	100.0	16.8	14.7	19.5	24.1	10.0	7.5	7.2	6 898	122
1954	41 951	100.0	19.1	15.9	20.5	22.7	8.9	6.3	6.6	6 482	114
1953	41 202	100.0	17.6	15.5	20.9	24.1	8.8	6.7	6.3	6 630	117
1952	40 832	100.0	18.3	18.5	22.4	22.7	7.7	5.4	5.1	6 138	108
1951	40 578	100.0	18.9	19.1	24.0	21.4	7.1	4.8	4.6	5 975	105
1950	39 929	100.0	20.8	19.4	23.2	19.9		16.4		5 757	102
1949	39 303	100.0	22.5	21.9	23.1	17.8		14.8		5 443	96
1948	38 624	100.0	20.9	22.1	23.6	18.7		14.6		5 527	98
1947	37 237	100.0	20.4	21.9	22.4	18.8		16.7		5 665	100
White											
1972	48 477	100.0	5.9	8.6	9.7	16.7	11.8	15.2	32.2	11 549	195
1971	47 641	100.0	6.6	9.0	10.3	17.8	12.9	15.5	28.1	10 948	185
1970	46 535	100.0	6.7	8.6	10.1	18.2	13.0	15.7	27.7	10 996	186
1969	46 022	100.0	6.6	8.2	9.4	18.4	12.9	16.3	28.2	11 168	189
1968	45 437	100.0	6.8	8.5	10.1	19.5	13.0	15.9	26.2	10·750	182
1967	44 814	100.0	7.8	8.8	10.7	20.5	13.1	15.5	23.5	10 318	175
1966	44 110	100.0	8.3	9.2	10.8	21.3	13.2	15.4	21.8	10 047	170
1965	43 497	100.0	9.1	10.1	11.7	22.0	13.6	14.2	19.4	9 612	163
1964	43 081	100.0	9.6	11.0	12.4	22.3	12.9	13.9	17.8	9 256	157
1963	42 663	100.0	10.3	11.0	12.9	23.5	12.9	13.0	16.3	8 946	151
1962	42 437	100.0	11.0	11.4	13.8	24.5	12.2	12.1	15.0	8 631	146
1961	41 888	100.0	12.1	12.0	14.3	24.2	12.3	11.2	14.1	8 390	142
1960	41 123	100.0	12.0	11.9	14.5	25.7	11.9	11.1	12.9	8 267	140
1959	40 872	100.0	11.8	12.7	15.2	26.4	11.6	10.4	11.7	8 104	137
1958	40 236	100.0	12.9	13.0	17.7	26.9	11.5	8.5	9.6	7 664	130
1957	39 676	100.0	13.0	12.6	17.8	27.1	12.0	8.6	8.9	7 669	130
1956	39 498	100.0	13.0	12.6	18.0	25.9	11.8	9.2	9.5	7 698	130
1955	38 982	100.0	14.7	14.0	19.4	25.3	10.7	8.1	7.9	7 212	122
1954	38 185	100.0	16.8	15.1	20.8	23.9	9.4	6.8	7.1	6 749	114
1953	(NA)	100.0	15.7	14.4	21.3	25.3	9.3	7.2.	6.8	6 877	116
1952	(NA)	100.0	15.7	16.9	23.0	24.4	8.3	6.0	5.5	6 490	110
1951	(NA)	100.0	16.3	18.4	24.9	22.7	7.6	5.2	5.0	6 224	105
1950	(NA)	100.0	18.5	18.7	23.9	21.2		17.6		5 986	101
1949	(NA)	100.0	19.8	21.5	24.0	18.7		15.9		5 662	96
1948	35 345	100.0	18.4	21.6	24.5	19.8		15.7		5 745	97
1947	34 120	100.0	17.4	21.5	23.4	19.7		17.8		5 909	100
Negro and Other Races											
1972	5 896	100.0	17.7	17.5	14.0	17.1	8.6	9.5	15.6	7 106	235
1971	5 655	100.0	18.4	17.0	15.0	17.9	8.9	9.4	13.3	6 936	229
1970	5 413	100.0	18.2	16.1	15.5	18.2	9.4	9.5	13.1	7 018	232
1969	5 215	100.0	17.3	16.8	15.6	19.3	9.8	9.1	12.2	7 062	234
1968	5 074	100.0	17.9	18.7	15.6	18.2	8.7	9.6	11.5	6 718	222
1967	5 020	100.0	20.2	18.6	16.0	19.0	8.3	8.3	9.6	6 380	211
1966	4 954	100.0	21.6	19.9	16.2	18.9	8.2	7.9	7.3	6 008	199
1965	4 782	100.0	24.8	22.2	16.7	17.2	7.3	6.0	5.9	5 349	177
1964	4 754	100.0	25.4	22.8	16.6	16.8	6.5	6.1	5.7	5 183	171
1963	4 773	100.0	29.3	23.1	16.1	16.3	6.6	4.1	4.3	4 751	157
1962	4 561	100.0	31.1	23.3	17.4	15.7	4.7	4.1	3.8	4 608	152
1961	4 453	100.0	33.4	21.6	16.7	14.3	5.2	4.3	4.3	4 461	148
1960	4 333	100.0	33.7	20.8	16.0	16.1	5.3	4.1	3.9	4 564	151
1959	4 239	100.0	37.5	21.6	16.6	13.7	5.0	3.7	2.1	4 178	138
1958	3 996	100.0	37.9	22.4	17.9	13.2	3.9	2.6	2.1	3 938	130
1957	4 020	100.0	36.5	22.6	17.2	15.0	4.5	3.1	1.2	4 106	136
1956	3 999	100.0	36.4	24.2	18.5	13.0	3.9	2.6	1.3	4 052	134
1955	3 907	100.0	38.3	23.1	19.3	12.6	4.0	1.8	0.9	3 977	132
1954	3 766	100.0	41.7	22.9	18.6	11.0	3.1	1.8	1.1	3 759	124
1953	(NA)	100.0	37.5	26.3	17.3	11.7	3.4	2.7	1.1	3 868	128
1952	(NA)	100.0	39.0	31.7	17.0	8.2	2.2	1.2	0.8	3 685	122
1951	(NA)	100.0	45.8	27.0	15.3	9.0	1.9	0.7	0.5	3 279	108
1950	(NA)	100.0	46.2	27.9	16.2	5.7		3.9		3 248	107
1949	(NA)	100.0	51.5	27.3	11.9	6.4		3.0		2 903	96
1948	3 279	100.0	49.0	27.0	13.6	7.3		3.3		3 072	102
1947	3 117	100.0	49.6	25.9	12.4	6.9		5.2		3 023	100

TYPE OF RESIDENCE AND RACE—FAMILIES AND UNRELATED INDIVIDUALS BY TOTAL MONEY INCOME IN 1972

[Families and unrelated individuals as of March 1973. This report excludes inmates of institutions. It includes members of the Armed Forces in the United States living off post or with their families on post but excludes all other members of the Armed Forces; the 1973 survey includes about 979,000 members]

Families — All Races — Total

Total Money Income	United States	Nonfarm	Farm	In Metropolitan Areas Total	1,000,000 or More Total	In Central Cities	Outside Central Cities	Under 1,000,000 Total	In Central Cities	Outside Central Cities	Outside Metropolitan Areas Total	Nonfarm	Farm
Number .... Thousands	54 373	51 860	2 513	36 941	21 127	8 627	12 500	15 814	7 532	8 282	17 433	15 407	2 026
Percent	100.0	100.0	100.0	100.0	100.0	100.0	100.0	100.0	100.0	100.0	100.0	100.0	100.0
Under $1,000	1.3	1.1	3.6	1.0	1.0	1.2	0.9	1.1	1.4	0.7	1.7	1.4	4.0
$1,000 to $1,499	0.9	0.8	1.7	0.7	0.5	0.7	0.4	0.9	1.1	0.7	1.3	1.2	1.9
$1,500 to $1,999	1.3	1.3	2.3	1.0	1.0	1.4	0.7	1.1	1.6	0.7	1.9	1.8	2.6
$2,000 to $2,499	1.7	1.7	2.5	1.4	1.4	2.0	1.0	1.4	1.8	1.1	2.5	2.4	2.7
$2,500 to $2,999	2.0	2.0	2.1	1.7	1.7	2.6	1.1	1.8	2.3	1.3	2.5	2.5	2.4
$3,000 to $3,499	2.3	2.3	3.6	2.0	1.9	2.8	1.3	2.2	2.5	1.8	3.1	3.0	3.6
$3,500 to $3,999	2.2	2.2	2.8	2.0	1.8	2.6	1.3	2.1	2.7	1.6	2.9	2.9	2.8
$4,000 to $4,999	4.9	4.8	7.5	4.4	4.2	5.9	3.0	4.6	5.5	3.8	6.1	5.8	8.4
$5,000 to $5,999	5.0	5.0	6.3	4.5	4.5	6.0	3.5	4.4	4.4	4.4	6.2	6.2	6.9
$6,000 to $6,999	5.2	5.1	6.8	4.7	4.2	5.5	3.3	5.4	5.9	5.0	6.2	6.2	6.7
$7,000 to $7,999	5.6	5.5	6.1	5.1	4.9	5.7	4.3	5.5	5.5	5.6	6.5	6.5	6.4
$8,000 to $8,999	5.4	5.4	5.6	5.0	4.8	5.4	4.3	5.3	5.3	5.3	6.3	6.3	5.6
$9,000 to $9,999	5.8	5.7	6.1	5.5	5.1	5.5	4.8	6.0	5.9	6.0	6.4	6.5	5.6
$10,000 to $11,999...	11.5	11.5	10.9	11.3	10.7	10.5	10.8	12.1	11.8	12.4	11.9	12.1	10.9
$12,000 to $14,999...	14.6	14.8	10.1	15.3	14.8	13.7	15.6	16.0	14.8	17.1	13.1	13.5	9.6
$15,000 to $24,999...	23.0	23.3	16.8	25.6	27.6	21.5	31.8	23.1	20.9	25.1	17.3	17.6	15.2
$25,000 to $49,999...	6.5	6.6	4.9	7.8	8.9	6.3	10.7	6.3	6.0	6.6	3.9	3.8	4.3
$50,000 and Over	0.8	0.8	0.4	0.9	1.1	0.8	1.3	0.7	0.7	0.7	0.5	0.5	0.4
Median Income . Dollars .	11 116	11 225	8 849	11 950	12 489	10 522	13 812	11 360	10 713	11 916	9 477	9 613	8 281
Mean Income .. Dollars .	12 625	12 731	10 431	13 505	14 106	12 234	15 398	12 701	12,180	13 175	10 760	10 865	9 963

NET PER CENT INCREASE, 1959-69 IN MEDIAN INCOME OF FAMILIES
By Race of Head, By Regions: 1960-70

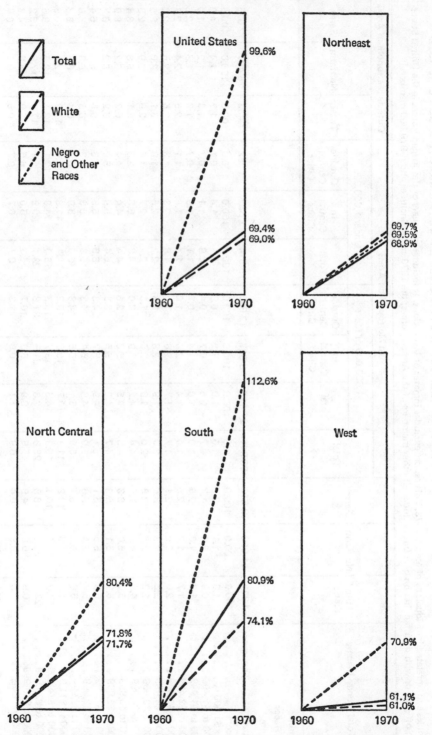

Total

White

Negro
and Other
Races

United States
99.6%
69.4%
69.0%
1960   1970

Northeast
69.7%
69.5%
68.9%
1960   1970

North Central
80.4%
71.8%
71.7%
1960   1970

South
112.6%
80.9%
74.1%
1960   1970

West
70.9%
61.1%
61.0%
1960   1970

1970 CENSUS OF POPULATION, U.S. Department of Commerce, Social and Economic
Statistics Administration, Bureau of the Census

FEDERAL OUTLAYS FOR EDUCATION: 1965 and 1973

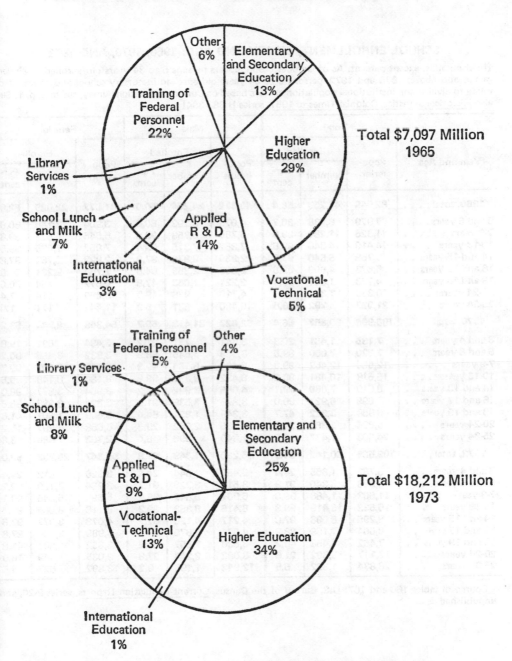

Total $7,097 Million
1965

Total $18,212 Million
1973

Source: Chart prepared by U.S. Bureau of the Census. Data from U.S. Office of Education.

SCHOOL ENROLLMENT, BY SEX AND AGE: 1960, 1970, AND 1972

[In thousands, except percent. As of October, 1960, covers persons 5 to 34 years old enrolled in kindergarten and above; 1970 and 1972, persons 3 to 34 years old enrolled in nursery school and above. Data relate to civilian non-institutional population and are based on Current Population Survey; see text, p. 1. See also Historical Statistics, Colonial Times to 1957, series H 383-394]

Year and Age	Total			Male			Female		
	Popu-lation	Enrolled		Popu-lation	Enrolled		Popu-lation	Enrolled	
		Number	Per-cent		Number	Per-cent		Number	Per-cent
1960, total	82,049	46,259	56.4	40,372	24,234	60.0	41,677	22,025	52.8
5 and 6 years	7,979	6,438	80.7	4,075	3,292	80.8	3,904	3,146	80.6
7-9 years	11,325	11,281	99.6	5,780	5,759	99.6	5,545	5,522	99.6
10-13 years	14,419	14,340	99.5	7,362	7,315	99.4	7,057	7,025	99.5
14 and 15 years . .	5,768	5,640	97.8	2,939	2,878	97.9	2,829	2,762	97.6
16 and 17 years . .	5,573	4,600	82.5	2,805	2,369	84.5	2,768	2,231	80.6
18 and 19 years . .	4,733	1,817	38.4	2,221	1,063	47.8	2,512	754	30.0
20-24 years	10,330	1,350	13.1	4,710	936	19.9	5,620	414	7.4
25-34 years	21,922	792	3.6	10,480	621	5.9	11,442	171	1.5
1970, total	106,996	60,357	56.4	52,627	31,413	59.7	54,369	28,944	53.2
3 and 4 years . . .	7,135	1,461	20.5	3,641	771	21.2	3,494	691	19.8
5 and 6 years . . .	7,820	7,000	89.5	3,988	3,545	88.9	3,832	3,455	90.2
7-9 years	12,550	12,462	99.3	6,400	6,355	99.3	6,149	6,107	99.3
10-13 years	16,618	16,481	99.2	8,432	8,333	98.8	8,186	8,148	99.5
14 and 15 years . .	8,019	7,869	98.1	4,065	3,992	98.2	3,954	3,877	98.0
16 and 17 years . .	7,699	6,927	90.0	3,875	3,539	91.3	3,824	3,388	88.6
18 and 19 years . .	6,958	3,322	47.7	3,349	1,821	54.4	3,609	1,501	41.6
20-24 years	15,594	3,359	21.5	7,036	2,062	29.3	8,558	1,297	15.2
25-34 years	24,603	1,477	6.0	11,840	996	8.4	12,763	480	3.8
1972, total	109,585	60,142	54.9	54,238	31,349	57.8	55,347	28,793	52.0
3 and 4 years	6,782	1,655	24.4	3,457	844	24.4	3,326	812	24.4
5 and 6 years	6,896	6,340	91.9	3,513	3,220	91.7	3,384	3,120	92.2
7-9 years	11,602	11,488	99.0	5,907	5,842	98.9	5,695	5,646	99.1
10-13 years	16,532	16,419	99.3	8,416	8,353	99.3	8,116	8,066	99.4
14 and 15 years . .	8,295	8,098	97.6	4,217	4,120	97.7	4,078	3,977	97.5
16 and 17 years . .	8,064	7,169	88.9	4,075	3,675	90.2	3,989	3,494	87.6
18 and 19 years . .	7,462	3,458	46.3	3,630	1,857	51.2	3,832	1,601	41.8
20-24 years	17,117	3,692	21.6	8,082	2,243	27.8	9,035	1,449	16.0
25-34 years	26,834	1,822	6.8	12,942	1,195	9.2	13,892	627	4.5

Source of tables 166 and 167: U.S. Bureau of the Census, Current Population Reports, series P-20, and unpublished data.

YEARS OF SCHOOL COMPLETED, BY RACE: 1940 TO 1972

[Persons 25 years old and over as of March of year indicated. 1970-1972 based on Current Population Survey; includes inmates of institutions and members of the Armed Forces living off post or with their families on post, but excludes all other members of the Armed Forces; 1972 excludes inmates of institutions. See text, p. 1]

Age and Year	All Races					Negro				
	Years completed—percent				Median school years completed[2]	Years completed—percent				Median school years completed[2]
	Not a high school graduate		High school, 4 years or more			Not a high school graduate		High school, 4 years or more		
	Total	Less than 5 years[1]	Total	College, 4 years or more		Total	Less than 5 years[1]	Total	College, 4 years or more	
25 Years and Over										
1940	75.5	13.7	24.5	4.6	8.6	92.7	42.0	7.3	1.3	5.7
1950	67.5	11.1	34.3	6.2	9.3	88.3	32.9	12.9	2.1	6.8
1960	58.9	8.3	41.1	7.7	10.5	81.8	23.8	20.1	3.1	8.0
1970	44.8	5.3	55.2	11.0	12.2	66.3	15.1	33.7	4.5	9.9
1971	43.6	5.0	56.4	11.4	12.2	65.3	13.5	34.7	4.5	10.1
1972	41.8	4.6	58.2	12.0	12.2	63.5	12.8	36.6	5.1	10.3
25-29 Years										
1940	61.9	5.9	38.1	5.9	10.3	(NA)	27.7	11.6	1.6	7.0
1950	49.5	4.7	52.8	7.7	12.1	80.4	16.8	22.2	2.7	8.6
1960	39.3	2.8	60.7	11.1	12.3	62.3	7.0	37.7	4.8	9.9
1970	24.6	1.1	75.4	16.4	12.6	43.9	2.5	56.2	7.3	12.2
1971	22.8	1.1	77.2	16.9	12.6	42.5	1.8	57.5	6.4	12.2
1972	20.2	0.8	79.8	19.0	12.7	36.0	1.3	64.1	8.3	12.3

NA Not available.
[1] Includes persons reporting no school years completed.   [2] For definition of median, see preface.
Source: U.S. Bureau of the Census, Current Population Reports, series P-20, and unpublished data.

ENROLLMENT IN INSTITUTIONS OF HIGHER EDUCATION COMPARED WITH POPULATION AGED 18-24: UNITED STATES, FALL 1950 TO FALL 1971

Year	Population 18-24 years of age[1]	Enrollment	Number enrolled per 100 persons 18-24 years of age
1	2	3	4
1950	16,076,000	2,286,500	14.2
1951	15,781,000	2,107,109	13.4
1952	15,473,000	2,139,156	13.8
1953	15,356,000	2,235,977	14.7
1954	15,103,000	2,452,466	16.2
1955	14,968,000	2,660,429	17.8
1956	14,980,000	2,927,367	19.5
1957	15,095,000	3,047,373	20.2
1958	15,307,000	3,236,414	21.2
1959	15,677,000	3,377,273	21.5
1960	16,122,000	3,582,726	22.2
1961	16,961,000	3,860,643	22.8
1962	17,608,000	4,174,936	23.7
1963	18,188,000	4,494,626	24.7
1964	18,722,000	4,950,173	26.4
1965	20,202,000	5,526,325	27.4
1966	21,346,000	25,928,000	27.8
1967	22,244,000	26,392,000	28.7
1968	22,787,000	6,928,115	30.4
1969	23,600,000	7,484,073	31.7
1970	24,625,000	7,920,149	32.2
1971	25,701,000	8,116,103	31.6

[1]These Bureau of the Census estimates are as of July 1 preceding the opening of the academic year. They include Armed Forces overseas.

[2]Estimated.

Note.—Data are for 50 States and the District of Columbia. Beginning in 1953, enrollment figures include resident and extension degree-credit students; data for earlier years exclude extension students.

Sources: U.S. Department of Health, Education, and Welfare, Office of Education, circulars on "Opening Fall Enrollment in Higher Education"; U.S. Department of Commerce, Bureau of the Census, Current Population Reports, Series P-25, Nos. 311, 314, 385, 441, and 470.

NUMBER OF 2-YEAR INSTITUTIONS OF HIGHER EDUCATION AND ENROLLMENT, BY CONTROL OF INSTITUTION AND BY SEX: UNITED STATES, FALL 1947 TO FALL 1970

Year	Number of institutions			Total enrollment	Enrollment by control of institution		Enrollment by sex	
	Total	Public	Private		Public	Private	Men	Women
1	2	3	4	5	6	7	8	9
1947	480	250	230	222,045	163,005	59,040	152,003	70,042
1948	492	257	235	210,977	153,970	57,007	139,630	71,347
1949	518	275	243	229,001	170,689	58,312	151,191	77,810
1950	528	299	229	217,403	167,874	49,529	139,868	77,535
1951	511	294	217	199,997	156,239	43,758	120,801	79,196
1952	525	299	226	230,222	191,602	46,620	142,459	95,763
1953	518	293	225	258,241	210,006	48,235	155,806	102,435
1954	474	277	197	282,433	241,145	41,288	171,752	110,681
1955	467	275	192	308,411	265,326	43,085	196,671	111,740
1956	482	278	204	347,345	297,621	49,724	225,635	121,710
1957	490	283	207	368,998	315,990	53,008	237,617	131,381
1958	495	290	205	385,436	330,881	54,555	247,942	137,494
1959	508	310	198	409,195	355,967	53,228	259,504	149,691
1960	521	315	206	451,333	392,310	59,023	282,155	169,178
1961	524	329	195	517,925	456,381	61,544	320,156	197,769
1962	561	349	212	589,529	519,257	70,272	365,624	223,905
1963	573	357	216	624,789	551,308	73,481	386,660	238,129
1964	617	389	228	710,868	620,859	90,009	439,509	271,359
1965	633	399	234	841,437	737,890	103,547	521,846	319,591
1966 [1]	700	450	250	945,000	840,000	105,000	577,000	368,000
1967 [1]	735	495	240	1,075,000	966,000	109,000	653,000	422,000
1968	802	548	254	1,289,993	1,169,635	120,358	782,602	507,391
1969	813	577	236	1,528,429	1,412,610	115,819	910,631	617,798
1970	827	603	224	1,629,982	1,519,762	110,220	953,961	676,021

[1] Estimated. The total number of 2-year institutions, including those offering non-degree-credit programs exclusively, was 752 in 1966 and 786 in 1967.

Note.—Beginning in 1960, data are for 50 States and the District of Columbia; data for earlier years are for 48 States and the District of Columbia. Beginning in 1953, enrollment figures include resident and extension degree-credit students; data for earlier years exclude extension students.

Source: U.S. Department of Health, Education, and Welfare, Office of Education, circulars on "Fall Enrollment in Higher Education."

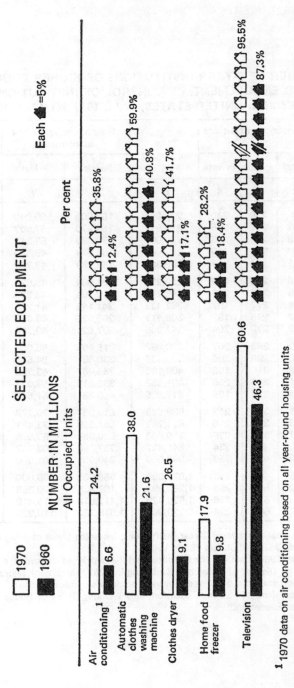

SELECTED EQUIPMENT

NUMBER IN MILLIONS
All Occupied Units

Per cent

Each = 5%

1970
1960

Air conditioning[1]   1970: 24.2   1960: 6.6   35.8%   12.4%

Automatic clothes washing machine   1970: 38.0   1960: 21.6   59.9%   40.8%

Clothes dryer   1970: 26.5   1960: 9.1   41.7%   17.1%

Home food freezer   1970: 17.9   1960: 9.8   28.2%   18.4%

Television   1970: 60.6   1960: 46.3   95.5%   87.3%

[1] 1970 data on air conditioning based on all year-round housing units

1970 U.S. CENSUS OF HOUSING, U.S. Department of Commerce, Social and Economic Statistics Administration, Bureau of the Census.

HOUSEHOLD APPLIANCES: TRENDS AND PROJECTIONS 1967-73

[in millions of dollars, except as noted]

	1967	1968	1969	1970	1971	1972 [1]	1973 [1]	Percent increase 1972-73
Quantity shipped, selected appliances (thousands):								
Refrigerators	4,713	5,150	5,296	5,286	5,691	6,315	6,760	7
Freezers	1,100	1,125	1,195	1,359	1,436	1,576	1,840	17
Dishwashers	1,586	1,960	2,118	2,116	2,477	3,199	3,650	14
Washing machines..	4,323	4,482	4,379	4,094	4,609	5,107	5,400	6
Dryers	2,648	2,862	3,022	2,980	3,377	3,925	4,120	5
Electric ranges....	1,910	2,307	2,343	2,362	2,714	3,232	3,652	13
Gas ranges	2,123	2,286	2,471	2,362	2,549	2,660	2,626	−1
Vacuum cleaners ..	5,677	6,653	7,134	7,392	7,073	8,037	8,587	3

[1] Estimated by Bureau of Competitive Assessment and Business Policy (BCABP).
Source: Association of Home Appliance Manufacturers, Merchandising Week, Bureau of the Census, Bureau of Labor Statistics, and BCABP.

PASSENGERS CARRIED BY PUBLIC TRANSPORTATION: 1950 to 1972

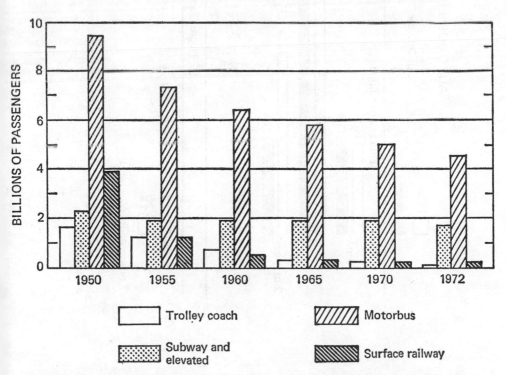

Source: Chart prepared by U.S. Bureau of the Census, Data from American Transit Association, Washington, D.C.

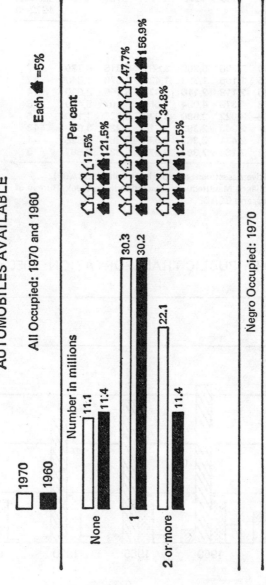

AUTOMOBILES AVAILABLE

1970 ☐
1960 ■

All Occupied: 1970 and 1960

Each 🚗 = 5%

Number in millions

Per cent

None 11.1 / 11.4 — 17.5% / 21.5%

1 30.3 / 30.2 — 47.7% / 56.9%

2 or more 22.1 / 11.4 — 34.8% / 21.5%

Negro Occupied: 1970

None 2.7 — 43.1%

1 2.6 — 41.3%

2 or more 1.0 — 15.6%

1970 U.S. CENSUS OF HOUSING, U.S. Department of Commerce, Social and Economic Statistics Administration, Bureau of the Census.

AVERAGE SIZE OF HOUSEHOLD: 1890-1970

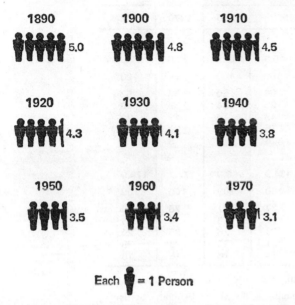

Each 👤 = 1 Person

Source: U.S. Census of Housing, U.S. Department of Commerce, Social and Economics Administration, Bureau of the Census.

PER CENT OWNER-OCCUPIED UNITS BY RACE: 1890-1970

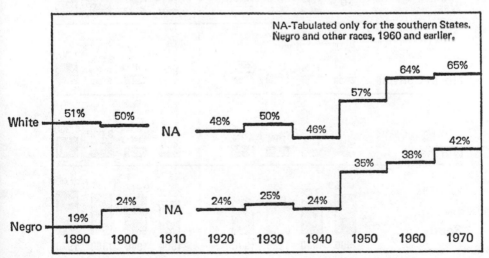

1970 U.S. CENSUS OF HOUSING, U.S. Department of Commerce, Social and Economic Statistics Administration, Bureau of the Census

PERCENT DISTRIBUTION OF THE POPULATION
BY REGION: 1950, 1960, 1970, AND 1972

Subject	1950[1]	1960	1970	1972
Black				
United States . . . millions . .	15.0	18.9	22.6	22.9
Percent, total	100	100	100	100
South	68	60	53	52
North	28	34	39	40
Northeast	13	16	19	20
North Central	15·	18	20	20
West	4	6	8	8
White				
United States . . . millions . .	134.9	158.8	177.7	179.0
Percent, total	100	100	100	100
South	27	27	28	29
North	59	56	54	53
Northeast	28	26	25	24
North Central	31	30	29	29
West	14	16	18	18

[1] Data exclude Alaska and Hawaii.

Source: U.S. Department of Commerce, Social and Economic Statistics Administration, Bureau of the Census.

DISTRIBUTION OF THE BLACK POPULATION

	BY PER CENT	BY THOUSANDS
West	0 1% 6% 8%	30 200 1,000 1,700
North Central	6% 11% 18% 20%	500 1,400 3,500 4,600
Northeast	4% 11% 16% 19%	400 1,400 3,000 4,300
South	90% 77% 60% 53%	7,900 9,900 11,300 12,000
	1900 1940 1960 1970	1900 1940 1960 1970

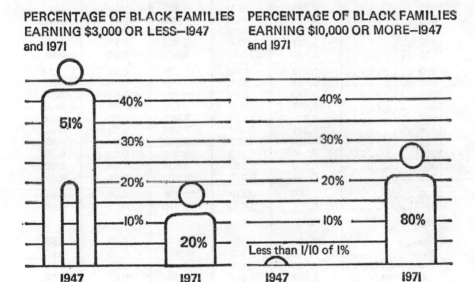

PERCENTAGE OF BLACK FAMILIES
EARNING $3,000 OR LESS—1947
and 1971

51%

40%

30%

20%

10%

20%

1947   1971

PERCENTAGE OF BLACK FAMILIES
EARNING $10,000 OR MORE—1947
and 1971

40%

30%

20%

10%

80%

Less than 1/10 of 1%

1947   1971

MEDIAN INCOME OF FAMILIES: 1950 TO 1972

(In current dollars)

.Year	Race of head			Ratio: . Negro and other races to white	Ratio: Negro to white
	Negro and other races	Negro	White		
1950	$1,869	(NA)	$ 3,445	0.54	(NA)
1951	2,032	(NA)	3,859	0.53	(NA)
1952	2,338	(NA)	4,114	0.57	(NA)
1953	2,461	(NA)	4,392	0.56	(NA)
1954	2,410	(NA)	4,339	0.56	(NA)
1955	2,549	(NA)	4,605	0.55	(NA)
1956	2,628	(NA)	4,993	0.53	(NA)
1957	2,764	(NA)	5,166	0.54	(NA)
1958	2,711	(NA)	5,300	0.51	(NA)
1959	3,161	$3,047	5,893	0.54	0.52
1960	3,233	(NA)	5,835	0.55	(NA)
1961	3,191	(NA)	5,981	0.53	(NA)
1962	3,330	(NA)	6,237	0.53	(NA)
1963	3,465	(NA)	6,548	0.53	(NA)
1964	3,839	3,724	6,858	0.56	0.54
1965	3.994	3,886	7,251	0.55	0.54
1966	4,674	4,507	7,792	0.60	0.58
1967[1]	5,094	4,875	8,234	0.62	0.59
1968	5,590	5,360	8,937	0.63	0.60
1969	6,191	5,999	9,794	0.63	0.61
1970	6,516	6,279	10,236	0.64	0.61
1971[2]	6,714	6,440	10,672	0.63	0.60
1972[2]					
United States	$7,106	$6,864	$11,549	0.62	0.59
South	5,730	5,763	10,465	0.55	0.55
North and West ..	8,604	8,109	12,004	0.72	0.68
Northeast	7,984	7,816	12,307	0.65	0.64
North Central ..	8,574	8,318	11,947	0.72	0.70
West	9,434	8,313	11,724	0.80	0.71

Note: Most of the tables of this section show income data for the year 1971. Income figures for 1972 from the Current Population Survey conducted in March 1973, which recently became available, have been included in tables 7 and 8 of this section. Data for 1959 are from the 1960 census; figures for the remaining years are from Current Population Surveys.

NA Not available. The ratio of Negro to white median family income first became available from this survey in 1964.

[1] Revised, based on processing corrections.

[2] Based on 1970 census population controls; therefore, not strictly comparable to data for earlier years. See Definitions and Explanations section for more details.

Source: U.S. Department of Commerce, Social and Economic Statistics Administration, Bureau of the Census.

PERCENT OF FAMILIES WITH INCOME OF $10,000 OR MORE, BY REGION: 1966 TO 1971

[Adjusted for price changes in 1971 dollars. A $10,000 income in 1971 was equivalent in purchasing power to about $8,000 in 1966]

Area and year	Negro and other races	White
United States		
1966	22	48
1967	25	50
1968	28	53
1969	30	55
1970	30	54
1971	30	54
South		
1966	12	39
1967	14	43
1968	17	45
1969	19	48
1970	20	48
1971	20	48
North and West		
1966	31	51
1967	35	53
1908	38	55
1969	40	58
1970	41	57
1971	40	57

Source: U.S. Department of Commerce, Social and Economic Statistics Administration, Bureau of the Census.

FAMILIES BELOW THE LOW-INCOME LEVEL, BY SEX OF HEAD: 1959 AND 1967 TO 1972

(Families as of the following year)

Subject	All families		Families with male head		Families with female head	
	Negro	White	Negro	White	Negro	White
Number (millions)						
1959 ...	1.9	6.0	1.3	5.0	0.6	1.0
1967 ...	1.6	4.1	0.8	3.0	0.7	1.0
1968 ...	1.4	3.6	0.7	2.6	0.7	1.0
1969[1]...	1.4	3.6	0.6	2.5	0.7	1.1
1970[1]...	1.5	3.7	0.6	2.6	0.8	1.1
1971[1]...	1.5	3.8	0.6	2.6	0.9	1.2
1972[1]...	1.5	3.4	0.6	2.3	1.0	1.1
Percent below the low-income level						
1959 ...	48	15	43	13	65	30
1967 ...	34	9	25	7	56	26
1968 ...	29	8	20	6	53	25
1969[1]...	28	8	18	6	53	26
1970[1]...	29	8	19	6	54	25
1971[1]...	29	8	17	6	54	27
1972[1]...	29	7	16	5	53	24

[1] Based on 1970 census population controls; therefore, not strictly comparable to data for earlier years. See Definitions and Explanations for more details.

Source: U.S. Department of Commerce, Social and Economic Statistics Administration, Bureau of the Census.

PERCENT ENROLLED IN SCHOOL BY AGE:
1967, 1970, AND 1972.

Age	Black			White		
	1967	1970	1972	1967	1970	1972
3 and 4 years.	18	23	28	13	20	24
5 years	67	72	81	80	81	86
6 to 15 years	98	99	99	99	99	99
16 and 17 years . . .	84	86	90	89	91	89
18 and 19 years . . .	41	40	43	48	49	47
20 to 24 years . . .	13	14	17	23	23	22

Source: U.S. Department of Commerce, Social and Economic Statistics Administration, Bureau of the Census.

COLLEGE ENROLLMENT OF PERSONS 18 TO 24 YEARS OLD: 1967 AND 1972
(Numbers in thousands)

Sex and race	1967			1972		
	Total, 18 to 24 years old	Enrolled in college		Total, 18 to 24 years old	Enrolled in college	
		Number	Percent of total		Number	Percent of total
Black·	2,281	297	13	2,986	540	18
Male.	1,032	167	16	1,373	287	21
Female . . .	1,249	130·	10	1,613	253	16
White	17,501	4,710	27	21,315	5,624	26
Male.	7,864	2,761	35	10,212	3,195	31
Female . . .	9,637	1,949	20	11,103	2,428	22

Source: U.S. Department of Commerce, Social and Economic Statistics Administration, Bureau of the Census.

LEVEL OF SCHOOLING COMPLETED BY PERSONS
20 TO 29 YEARS OLD BY SEX: 1960, 1967, 1970 AND 1972

Subject	Male		Female	
	Black	White	Black	White
Percent completed 4 years of high school or more:				
1960	[1]38	64	[1]43	66
1967 . . . . ·.	52	77	56	77
1970 ·. .·.	59	81	63	80
1972	64	84	66	83
Percent completed 1 year of college or more:				
1960	[1]15	28	[1]13	21
1967	14	38	16	29
1970 . . . .·.	19	41	21	32
1972 . . . . .·.	22	45	23	34

[1] Includes persons of "other races."   Source: U.S. Department of Commerce, Social and Economic Statistics Administration, Bureau of the Census.

PERCENT HIGH SCHOOL DROPOUTS AMONG PERSONS 14 TO 24 YEARS OLD, BY SEX AND AGE: 1967 AND 1972

Age and sex	1967		1972	
	Black	White	Black	White
MALE				
Total, 14 to 24 years .	23.9	11.6	17.8	10.7
14 and 15 years old . . .	3.5	1.5	2.4	2.3
16 and 17 years old . . .	11.7	7.0	9.4	7.8
18 and 19 years old . . .	30.6	15.4	27.1	13.5
20 to 24 years old	42.6	18.8	27.2	15.3
FEMALE				
Total, 14 to 24 years .	21.8	13.1	17.2	11.9
14 and 15 years old . . .	4.0	1.4	2.7	2.5
16 and 17 years old . . .	14.6	9.4	7.6	9.6
18 and 19 years old . . .	22.0	16.3	21.0	13.2
20 to 24 years old . . .	36.1	19.0	27.3	16.6

Note: Dropouts are persons who are not enrolled in school and who are not high school graduates.
Source: U.S. Department of Commerce, Social and Economic Statistics Administration, Bureau of the Census.

DEATH RATES FOR THE POPULATION, BY AGE: 1960 AND 1969

(Age-specific death rates per 1,000 population in specified group)

Age	1960		1969	
	Negro and other races	White	Negro and other races	White
Total[1]	10.1	9.5	9.6	9.5
Under 1 year	46.3	23.6	32.0	19.2
1 to 4 years	1.9	1.0	1.3	0.8
5 to 14 years	0.6	0.4	0.6	0.4
15 to 24 years	1.6	1.0	2.1	1.2
25 to 34 years	3.2	1.2	3.7	1.3
35 to 44 years	6.3	2.6	7.1	2.7
45 to 54 years	13.4	6.9	13.2	6.6
55 to 64 years	27.7	16.3	26.2	15.8
65 to 74 years	47.8	37.4	55.6	35.8
75 to 84 years	76.3	88.3	69.3	79.8
85 years and over. . .	139.1	203.5	99.6	202.2

[1]Crude death rate, unadjusted for differences in age structure.
Source: U.S. Department of Health, Education, and Welfare, National Center for Health Statistics.

POPULATION AND AREA: 1790 TO 1970

[Area figures represent area on indicated date. including in some cases considerable areas not then organized or settled, and not covered by the census. Area figures have been adjusted to bring them into agreement with re-measurements made in 1940. For additional area data, see tables 4 and 278. See also Historical Statistics, Colonial Times to 1957, series A 17-21)

Census Date	Resident Population				Area (square miles)		
	Number	Per square mile of area	Increase over preceding census		Gross	Land	Water
			Number	Percent			
Conterminous U.S. [1]							
1790 (Aug. 2)	3,929,214	4.5	(X)	(X)	888,811	864,746	24,065
1800 (Aug. 4)	5,308,483	6.1	1,379,269	35.1	888,811	864,746	24,065
1810 (Aug. 6)	7,239,881	4.3	1,931,398	36.4	1,716,003	1,681,828	34,175
1820 (Aug. 7)	9,638,453	5.5	2,398,572	33.1	1,788,006	1,749,462	38,544
1830 (June 1)	12,866,020	7.4	3,227,567	33.5	1,788,006	1,749,462	38,544
1840 (June 1)	17,069,453	9.8	4,203,433	32.7	1,788,006	1,749,462	38,544
1850 (June 1)	23,191,876	7.9	6,122,423	35.9	2,992,747	2,940,042	52,705
1860 (June 1)	31,443,321	10.6	8,251,445	35.6	3,022,387	2,969,640	52,747
1870 (June 1)	[2] 39,818,449	[2] 13.4	8,375,128	26.6	3,022,387	2,969,640	52,747
1880 (June 1)	50,155,783	16.9	10,337,334	26.0	3,022,387	2,969,640	52,747
1890 (June 1)	62,947,714	21.2	12,791,931	25.5	3,022,387	2,969,640	52,747
1900 (June 1)	75,994,575	25.6	13,046,861	20.7	3,022,387	2,969,834	52,553
1910 (Apr. 15)	91,972,266	31.0	15,977,691	21.0	3,022,387	2,969,565	52,822
1920 (Jan. 1)	105,710,620	35.6	13,738,354	14.9	3,022,387	2,969,451	52,936
1930 (Apr. 1)	122,775,046	41.2	17,064,426	16.1	3,022,387	2,977,128	45,259
1940 (Apr. 1)	131,669,275	44.2	8,894,229	7.2	3,022,387	2,977,128	45,259
1950 (Apr. 1)	150,697,361	50.7	19,028,086	14.5	3,022,387	2,974,726	47,661
1960 (Apr. 1)	178,464,236	60.1	27,766,875	18.4	3,022,261	2,968,054	54,207
United States							
1950 (Apr. 1)	151,325,798	42.6	19,161,229	14.5	3,615,211	3,552,206	63,005
1960 (Apr. 1)	179,823,175	50.5	27,997,377	18.5	3,615,123	3,540,911	74,212
1970 (Apr. 1)	[3] 203,211,926	57.5	23,888,751	13.3	3,615,122	3,536,855	78,267

X Not applicable.   [1] Excludes Alaska and Hawaii.
[2] Revised to include adjustments for underenumeration in Southern States; unrevised number is 38,558,371.
[3] The official 1970 resident population count is 203,235,298; the difference of 23,372 is due to errors found after tabulations were completed.
Source: U.S. Bureau of the Census, U.S. Census of Population: 1920 to 1970, vol. I; and other reports and unpublished data. See also Areas of the United States, 1940, and Area Measurement Reports, series GE-20, No. 1.

POPULATION: 1900 TO 1973

[In thousands. Estimates as of July 1, except as indicated. Prior to 1940, excludes Alaska and Hawaii. Estimates for 1900 to 1909 are sums of State estimates based on local data indicative of population change. See p. 1 for basis of estimates for other years. See also Historical Statistics, Colonial Times to 1957, series A 1-3]

Year	Total resident population[1]
1900	76,094
1901	77,585
1902	79,160
1903	80,632
1904	82,165
1905	83,820
1906	85,437
1907	87,000
1908	88,709
1909	90,492
1910	92,407
1911	93,868
1912	95,331
1913	97,227
1914	99,118
1915	100,549
1916	101,966
1917	103,266
1918	103,203
1919	104,512

Year	Total resident population[1]
1920	106,466
1921	108,541
1922	110,055
1923	111,950
1924	114,113
1925	115,832
1926	117,399
1927	119,038
1928	120,501
1929	121,770
1930	123,077
1931	124,040
1932	124,840
1933	125,579
1934	126,374
1935	127,250
1936	128,053
1937	128,825
1938	129,825
1939	130,880

Year	Total incl. Armed Forces abroad	Total resident population[1]	Civilian resident population
1940	132,594	132,457	132,129
1941	133,894	133,669	132,086
1942	135,361	134,617	131,444
1943	137,250	135,107	128,010
1944	138,916	133,915	127,227
1945	140,468	133,434	128,112
1946	141,936	140,686	138,932
1947	144,698	144,083	143,138
1948	147,208	146,730	145,746
1949	149,767	149,304	148,157
1950	152,271	151,868	150,790
1951	154,878	153,982	151,599
1952	157,553	156,393	153,892
1953	160,184	158,956	156,595
1954	163,026	161,884	159,695
1955	165,931	165,069	162,967
1956	168,903	168,088	166,055
1957	171,984	171,187	169,110
1958	174,882	174,149	172,226
1959	177,830	177,135	175,277

Year and Month	Total incl. Armed Forces abroad	Total resident population[1]	Civilian resident population
1960	180,671	179,979	178,140
1961	183,691	182,992	181,143
1962	186,538	185,771	183,677
1963	189,242	188,483	186,493
1964	191,889	191,141	189,141
1965	194,303	193,526	191,605
1966	196,560	195,576	193,420
1967	198,712	197,457	195,264
1968	200,706	199,399	197,113
1969	202,677	201,385	199,145
1970	204,879	203,810	201,722
1971	207,045	206,212	204,250
1972	208,842	208,230	206,457
1973:			
Jan. 1	209,717	209,123	207,313
Feb. 1	209,826	209,256	207,434
Mar. 1	209,915	209,330	207,555
Apr. 1	210,036	209,470	207,685
May 1	210,157	209,593	207,824
June 1	210,284	209,724	207,971
July 1	210,404	209,851	208,094

[1] Excludes Armed Forces abroad.
Source: U.S. Bureau of the Census, Current Population Reports, series P-25, Nos. 481 and 502.

VITAL STATISTICS RATES: 1925 to 1972

Rate Per 1,000 Population

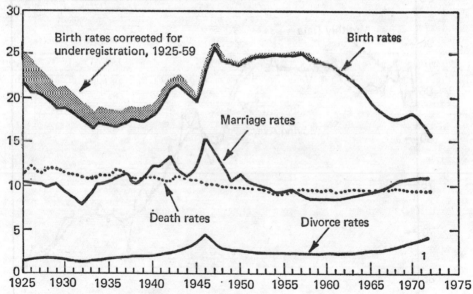

[1] Birth and death rates for 1970, and all data for 1971 and 1972, preliminary.
Source: Chart prepared by U.S. Bureau of the Census. Data from U.S. Public Health Service.

SEASONALLY ADJUSTED FERTILITY RATE

PER 1,000 WOMEN AGED 15-44

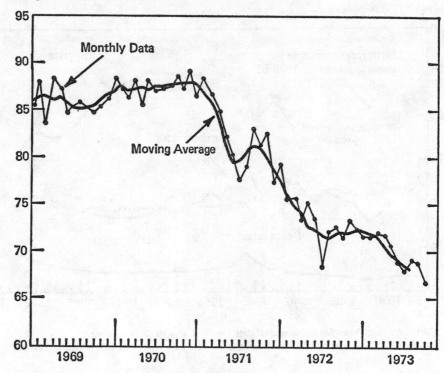

SUMMARY OF PROJECTIONS OF TOTAL POPULATION: 1960 TO 2020

[Population in thousands. Total population including Armed Forces abroad)

Year (July 1)	Series C	Series D	Series E	Series F
Estimates				
1960		180,671		
1965		194,303		
1970		204,879		
1972		208,837		
Projections				
1975	215,872	215,324	213,925	213,378
1980	230,955	228,676	224,132	221,848
1985	248,711	243,935	235,701	230,913
1990	266,238	258,692	246,639	239,084
1995	282,766	272,211	256,015	245,591
2000	300,406	285,969	264,430	250,686
2005	321,025	301,397	273,053	255,209
2010	344,094	318,156	281,968	259,332
2015	367,977	335,028	290,432	262,631
2020	392,030	351,368	297,746	264,564

POPULATION, BY RESIDENCE AND RACE: 1950 TO 1970

[In thousands, **except percent**. As of April. Covers 243 standard metropolitan statistical areas as defined in 1970; see text, section 33. Minus sign (—) denotes decrease]

Residence and Race	Population.				Percent Change		Average Annual Change	
	1950	1960	1970		1950–1960	1960–1970	1950–1960	1960–1970
			Total	Per-cent				
Total	151,326	179,323	[1] 203,212	100.0	18.5	13.3	1.7	1.3
Standard metropolitan statistical areas	94,579	119,595	139,419	68.6	26.4	16.6	2.3	1.5
Central cities	53,696	59,947	63,797	31.4	11.6	6.4	1.1	0.6
Outside central cities	40,883	59,648	75,622	37.2	45.9	26.8	3.8	2.4
Nonmetropolitan areas	56,747	59,728	63,793	31.4	5.3	6.8	0.5	0.7
White	135,150	158,832	177,749	100.0	17.5	11.9	1.6	1.1
Standard metropolitan statistical areas	85,099	105,180	120,579	67.8	23.6	14.6	2.1	1.4
Central cities	46,791	49,440	49,430	27.8	5.7	−0.2	0.6	−0.1
Outside central cities	38,308	55,741	71,148	40.0	45.5	27.6	3.8	2.5
Nonmetropolitan areas	50,051	53,652	57,170	32.2	7.2	6.6	0.7	0.6
Negro	14,972	18,792	22,580	100.0	25.5	20.2	2.3	1.9
Standard metropolitan statistical areas	8,850	12,710	16,771	74.3	43.6	32.0	3.6	2.8
Central cities	6,608	9,950	13,140	58.2	50.6	32.1	4.1	2.8
Outside central cities	2,242	2,760	3,630	16.1	23.1	31.5	2.1	2.8
Nonmetropolitan areas	6,122	6,083	5,810	25.7	−0.6	−4.5	−0.1	−0.5

[1]See footnote 1, table 1.
Source: U.S. Bureau of the Census, U.S. Census of Population: 1960 and 1970. vol. I.

INDEX